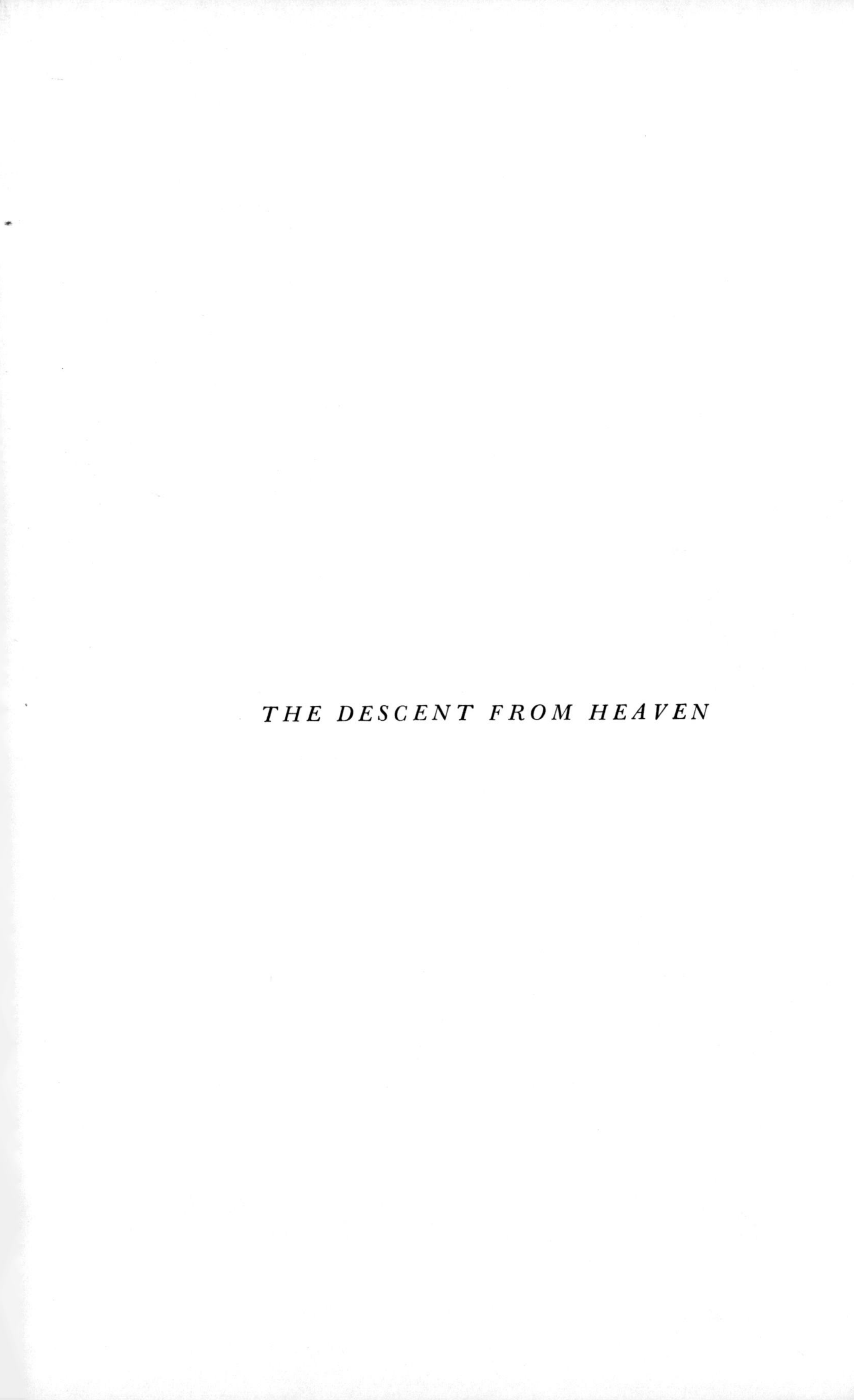

THE DESCENT FROM HEAVEN

THE DESCENT FROM HEAVEN

A STUDY IN EPIC CONTINUITY

BY THOMAS GREENE

NEW HAVEN AND LONDON

YALE UNIVERSITY PRESS, 1963

DESIGNED BY SALLY HARGROVE,
SET IN BASKERVILLE TYPE,
AND PRINTED IN THE UNITED STATES OF AMERICA BY
THE VAIL-BALLOU PRESS, INC., BINGHAMTON, N.Y.

LIBRARY OF CONGRESS CATALOG CARD NUMBER: 63-7934

TO RENÉ WELLEK

The publishers of the following books have kindly granted permission to make quotations: *La Christiada,* by Fray Diego de Hojeda, published by the Catholic University of America Press; *The Iliad of Homer,* translated by Richmond Lattimore and published by the University of Chicago Press; *Elizabethan Critical Essays,* edited by G. G. Smith, and Spenser's *Faerie Queene* and *Minor Poems,* both published by the Clarendon Press, Oxford; Statius' *Thebaid,* translated by J. H. Mozley, and *The Argonautica* by Apollonius Rhodius, translated by R. C. Seaton, both published by the Harvard University Press in the Loeb Classical Library; *The Lusiads* by Luiz de Camoens, translated by Leonard Bacon and published by the Hispanic Society of America; Milton's *Poetical Works,* published by the Oxford University Press, London; Virgil's *Aeneid,* translated by C. Day Lewis, and *The Odyssey of Homer,* translated by T. E. Shaw, both published by the Oxford University Press, New York; Virgil's *Aeneid,* translated by W. F. Jackson Knight, published by Penguin Books, Incorporated. The chapter entitled "The Norms of Epic" was first published, in a slightly different form, by *Comparative Literature.*

PREFACE

A Yale University Morse Fellowship first permitted me the leisure to plan and begin this book. Many people have helped to bring it into being: Frank Warnke, Jeanne Brouwer, and Roger Wiehe gave needed assistance with Vondel's Dutch, and Antonio Regalado with Hojeda's Spanish; Adam Parry cast a professional eye on my translations of Sannazaro's Latin; Donald Holzman, Charles Feidelson, and Geoffrey Hartman read various chapters as kindly critics. Louis Martz and R. W. B. Lewis read the entire manuscript with fitting proportions of generosity and wariness. No one could have more useful and informed assistance, and I am grateful for all of it.

René Wellek, to whom this book is dedicated, has extended his encouragement as the most humane of masters and benefactors. The extent of my debt to my wife, Liliane, can be measured only by the two of us. In her I have found, when I wanted it, counsel, sympathy, criticism, and patience:—these, among other things, but I think that the greatest of them was patience.

New Haven, Connecticut THOMAS GREENE
November 1962

CONTENTS

1. INTRODUCTION

Good Friday, 1338. Petrarch, walking solitary in the Vaucluse, conceived the compelling design of an epic poem upon the life of Scipio. Transported with enthusiasm, he began work upon it only to find, he scarcely knew why, that his imagination was presently caught up with other things. But he did not forget this monument, unwritten but awesome, which would carry his genius to posterity, and presently his friends learned, with high excitement, of his plan to write *Africa.* No work in human history, it has been said, awoke such fervent and impatient hopes. With the passage of years a small fragment was vouchsafed the poet's intimates, and confirmed their assurance that the modern equal of Homer had appeared. Petrarch himself lived for thirty-five years, not without anguish, with the pagan ghost of that Good Friday. One hears of it in the introspective prose works which came so easily to his pen —in the letter to posterity, where he professed himself astonished at the intensity of his enthusiasm for the poem, and in the *Secretum,* where it appears as his principal hope of winning immortality. At the very climax of the *Africa* itself, the hero Scipio is permitted a vision of that future poet—worthy emule of the greatest ancients—who is to glorify him. But despite Petrarch's pride in it and his intermittent labor upon it, the poem was never completed. And when at his death the manuscript was devoured with febrile eagerness, it was found to be something less than Homeric. The literate world of Europe had been deceived by a grandiose myth.

Ronsard, prince of poets, received in 1564 the abbey of Saint-Cosme-les-Tours, the benefice awaited for fourteen years which would afford him the leisure to compose his *Franciade*. It was an event of moment not only to the poet but to his fellows of the Brigade, to the court of Charles IX, and to lovers of poetry throughout France. For the *Franciade* had become the most famous of unwritten poems. First, years earlier, there had been the vaguest of hints at it in Du Bellay's *Deffence et Illustration,* calling for a modern poem to equal the *Iliad* and the *Aeneid*. Then there had been broader hints by Ronsard himself in his odes. Then the title had appeared in a later ode. The subject was known by this time, and the magnificently ambitious length—twenty-four books. The poet had revealed in still another ode to Calliope, the epic muse, his sense of vocation for her service, of even prenatal ordination:

> Dedans le ventre avant que né je fusse,
> Pour t'honorer tu m'avois ordonné . . .[1]

But the *Franciade* had not progressed, although brief fragments were occasionally handed about. It was the king's fault, chiefly, for not providing the security a great poem demands. Two kings would have to die before Ronsard received his abbey. Once installed, he put his secretary to work at once upon a collection of Homeric episodes, similes, and maxims. One does not, he knew, rush precipitately into an epic poem. Two years passed before he began writing, and four years later he had definitively concluded four books, one sixth of the whole. But somehow, he knew not why, the labor was ungrateful to him. And when the four books

1. Pierre Ronsard, *Ode à Calliope, Oeuvres Complètes,* ed. P. Laumonier, *1* (Paris, Hachette, 1914), 174. "You had designated me to honor you before I was born, while still in the womb."

of the *Franciade* were published, his epic vocation was not altogether apparent. A fifth book never appeared. The poet and his public had been the common victims of a myth.

In the Paris of Voiture and Corneille a famous unpublished poem became the subject itself of poems—so many poems that they would fill a solid volume. Although those acquainted with the work were few—chiefly certain initiates of the Hôtel de Rambouillet—it was known to everyone that *La Pucelle,* once it appeared, would establish Jean Chapelain as the Virgil of France, if indeed that title did not underpraise him. But when after twenty years *La Pucelle* did appear, the polemics it attracted would fill much more than a volume. The reborn Virgil was mythical once again.

The myth which deceived all of these victims was the same. For each of these painful comedies was symptomatic of a greater delusion which beclouded the collective mind of literate Europe for more than three centuries. From Petrarch's youth to Milton's age Europe awaited the poet and the poem which would demonstrate the equality of the modern age to antiquity. That hope in itself would not have been delusory had it not involved the corollary of *resemblance:* really to count, the new work would have to look like the *Aeneid.* A great deal was at stake: the respective national pride of each country, the dignity of the vulgar languages, the prestige of various critical theories, but above all, a certain conception of history which denied the necessary decline of man from Augustan Rome. At issue too (although only euphemism could indicate it) was the imaginative richness of the Christian religion. For if on the one hand a poet chose a Christian subject and failed, as Chapelain did, the fault might lie with the unsuitability of Christianity for epic treatment. But if one chose a classical subject and failed, like Petrarch and Ronsard, Christianity might be held accountable for a world which rendered the values of classical epic so remote. Few poets indeed excluded Christianity altogether (as these two did not) from poems about pagan subjects, but the propriety of mingling pagan and sacred elements in whatever proportions was a source of growing uneasiness in many quarters, well before Boileau denounced the *mélange coupable.*

The truly successful epic would presumably settle all these problems at a stroke, and thus the intensity of the expectation. In the confusion over the fate of *Africa* which followed Petrarch's death, Boccaccio wrote a poem addressed to the epic itself, pleading for its conservation and quick circulation. "Consider," he wrote, "how many things will perish wretchedly if you perish unheeded."

> Circumspice, quaeso,
> Quot pereant misere si tu neglecta peribis.[2]

The anguish was not wholly rhetorical. And first in Boccaccio's series of perishable things at stake is "the regenerate honor of Italy and the latin muse." It was the conception implied by "regenerate"—*renovatus*—which required the resemblance to, not only emulation of, the *Aeneid* and the *Iliad.* This was the conception which misled great poets like Petrarch and Ronsard to abuse their natural gifts and which led so many critics to codify pedantically the laws of epic. This conception explains why so frigid a work as Vida's *Christias* was received as a masterpiece, whereas Tasso's less Virgilian poem was bitterly attacked by academic readers and finally deformed by its own author.

The Renaissance failed to produce a Virgil, in the sense of a great poet whose work resembles the *Aeneid.* Perhaps the Renaissance even failed to produce poetry which can properly be described as epic at all in many important senses of the word. But this failure constitutes no real occasion for regret, because in its quest for epic the Renaissance was engaged in the quest for self-definition. It was forced to modify Homer and Virgil, to modify them in those ways characteristically modern, and thus to discover what in the modern age was new and individual. The important poems it did produce in the Virgilian tradition are not at harmony with themselves to the degree of the *Aeneid,* to say nothing of the truly homogeneous Homeric poems. The Renaissance poems to be discussed here are most of them imperfectly coherent, uncertainly unified, divided by powerful forces not altogether controlled and understood. But the finest of them are worthy to descend from Virgil, and they are interesting in their very divisions. To trace the profundity of those recurrent divisions,

2. "Versus Johannis Boccatii de Certaldo pro Africa Petrarchae in vulgus edenda," published as Appendix I in *Africa,* ed. Pingaud (Paris, 1872).

to follow in particular the series of adjustments between a Christian society and antique forms, and to assess each vast effort of the imagination to see steadily and coherently is to understand better the awakening consciousness which would finally turn away from this particular ideal.

We understand today, profiting from the insight which a sustained civilization confers, that the perpetuation of a genre involves a continuity of essence but not of accidents, of spirit rather than convention, that the spirit will develop its forms from the language and traditions and affinities of a given milieu, that no imported forms can mechanically impose themselves without a sense of artificiality; that the norms of a genre like the epic have to be violated if its vitality in a sophisticated society is to remain vigorous. We understand this today, but Ronsard and many like him did not; they thought to capture the spirit by copying the letter. They copied episodes, devices, *topoi,* conventions of all sorts with earnest scrupulosity. Professor Bush has written of them:

> The most Virgilian qualities of Virgil, when appreciated, were not within easy reach, but an unhappily large number of men throughout the neoclassic period thought that a combination of "correctness," funeral games, historical prophecy, and "machines" made an epic poem.[3]

The men who succeeded where Petrarch and Ronsard failed were men who had the impertinence to jolt and damage the public conception of epic, men who often struck the academic critic as *naifs.*

Even these men, however, seldom freed themselves altogether from the window dressing of convention. And so in studying the Renaissance "epic" it is necessary to examine three different kinds of elements which interacted on each other. The first consists of those things, whatever they are, which are truly essential to epic, if the word is to have any meaning—those norms which poems called epic seem repeatedly to approach. These norms in themselves have been variously described by critics through the centuries, and perhaps it is hopeless to look for unanimity about

3. Douglas Bush, *Mythology and the Renaissance Tradition* (Minneapolis, 1932), p. 75.

them. My own thoughts about the essentials of epic are set down in the next chapter, which introduces a few concepts and terms employed through the rest of the book. These are not many, however, and I trust that my general discussion is eclectic enough to find at least tentative acceptance. The second kind of element consists of the accidents, the conventions which the Renaissance arbitrarily imported, but which continued to live their poetic life, not without growth and peripety, under the influence of fresh imaginations. Third, there are the shifting beliefs, ideas, customs, institutions, and languages of Western Europe, which limited and directed each unique poetic imagination as it wrought upon its material. These, including the imagination, are the variables which act upon and change the constants in the first two groups.

The sum of all these elements is so large as to be fully unknowable. The versions of epic produced by the Renaissance are very many and very long. So immense a body of poetry, in several languages, is unmanageable for study, even if it possesses a kind of unity which invites comparative study. The method followed in this book represents an attempt to manage the unmanageable. I have tried to follow a single epic convention through the peripeties of its poetic life from Homer to Milton, hoping that the course of its miniature development might illuminate the greater development as well. Indeed in treating the major poems I have often used the conventional passage as a starting place for discussion of the whole. But my book remains primarily a history of the convention, even though I have not attempted to collect all its extant examples. I have no doubt that some one rummaging about the back attic of literary history could turn up quite as many as I have found. I have not even cited all the examples I am acquainted with, in cases where the citation would serve no useful purpose. But I have attempted to quote generously. In most instances, perhaps all, many more things might be said about the passage than are in fact said, but I found myself early in the writing inevitably resigned to something less than exhaustiveness.

In one or two instances (chiefly that of d'Aubigné), a passage is discussed which does not strictly fall within the convention but which seemed to me fertile for purposes of comparison. In general, though, I have tried to stay within my subject, the history of a minor form within a larger, encompassing form. The convention with so rich a history is one of the noblest that the epic produced: the descent of an emissary god or angel from heaven bearing a message to earth. Literature is full of divine and angelic epiphanies, but to warrant inclusion here a passage must demonstrably derive from a certain passage in the fourth book of the *Aeneid,* or that passage's models in the two Homeric poems. In most respects the celestial descent makes a peculiarly useful point of critical departure. For it does more than describe the swift and dramatic movement of a body through space. It constitutes typically a crucial nexus of the narrative; it represents the intersection of time and the timeless; it points to the human realm of paramount concern to the gods; and it brings divine authority to the unfolding heroic action.

Fully to understand the European epic, every student must begin with the poetry of antiquity. But the focus of this book is intended to fall most sharply upon the Renaissance, and my discussions of the classical texts purport to be no more than they are —the impressions of a nonspecialist. The *Iliad,* the *Odyssey,* and the *Aeneid* are most important here because they evoke, despite their radical differences, a common esthetic experience from which the Renaissance departed even as it thought to ape. Most of this book is devoted to the several departures and mutations from that norm of experience after the revival of learning. The classical norm seems to me closer to the epic norm itself, and the classical poems seem to elicit more directly that experience which I have called "heroic awe." The chapters which follow are concerned first with the description of that norm and others peculiar to epic, then with the classical approximations, finally and most fully with the wider Renaissance variations. Thus, although the subtitle of this book refers to epic continuity, it is equally concerned with transformation. Perhaps it is needless to add that a norm need not be regarded as an ideal, nor a departure as a reprehensible falling away. No one today is likely to share the Humanists' melancholy at the mythicality of their Virgilian dreams.

2. *THE NORMS OF EPIC*

Genre theory since the seventeenth century has gained in subtlety but lost in metaphysical security. As distinctions between genres have grown more gradual and complex, the easy neoclassic sense of the necessity or naturalness of genres has faded. The authority of Croce has denied them any validity. But they continue to be fruitfully discussed—fruitfully if less coherently. In the absence of a general theory which assigns to each its function, the individual genres have to find singly their working principles within themselves. Out of the writer's and critic's effort to redefine we have the opportunity to understand the genres more profoundly.

In the case of epic, one can begin by distinguishing heroic poems, poems produced by barely literate, widely separated societies, whose resemblances confer a unity supported by sociology and history. A second group is comprised of poems written in emulation of or, as it were, out of nostalgia for Homer's two heroic poems (and for the poem of his emulator, Virgil). It is easy enough, in most cases, to show which poems in European literature fall into this second group, simply on the basis of obvious, demonstrable devices and conventions. To isolate that group implies no metaphysical assertion.

The student who wants to pass beyond the historian's rule of thumb and to speak more searchingly of the epic must not seem to assert too much. Aware of literature's natural resistance to tidiness, he yet considers the historian's groups with an intuition of norms less obvious and more essential than the superficial conventions, norms which no single poem fully embodies. He knows that in any exact sense a pure epic has never been written. And yet he intuits an epic mode which Homer's emulators approach along with Homer and with the authors of other heroic poems which attain a certain magnitude and value. To describe the mode as he intuits it is not to insist on its full actualization in any one poem, nor even to ignore this fact: that as the mode crystallized, it tended to choke poetic vitality; that to be perpetuated and renewed, it had to be extended and violated. To describe the mode then is not to prescribe, with the naïveté of some Renaissance critics, nor to deny that each successive great artist who worked in it left it a somewhat different thing. The student should not be disposed to quarrel either over the classification of individual works within or without the genre; he knows that works may *participate* in the mode to varying degrees. But having recognized all this, he will not forget one more historical fact—that the legendary epic ideal was like a spirit that seized and rode great men, haunting and exhausting them, driving them sometimes to misdirect their gifts, but also, in some few cases, to surpass them.

The notes that follow are based on these presuppositions and were written in the hope of isolating some of the epic norms. They are concerned in turn with the imagery, the hero, the structure, and the language of epic.

i.

The first quality of the epic imagination is expansiveness, the impulse to extend its own luminosity in ever widening circles. It contrasts in this respect with both the comic and the tragic imagination. The comic imagination accepts without cramp the fixity of its horizon; it chooses not to press beyond the drawing room or the public place where it is set. It has no ulterior questions to pose.[1] Tragic space, on the other hand, closes in to hedge and confine. It permits at best fragments of knowledge, clearings of light, islands of felicity. The space beyond the clearings remains shadowy and unknowable. But the epic universe is there to be invaded by the human will and imagination. Epic answers to man's need to clear away an area he can apprehend, if not dominate, and commonly this area expands to fill the epic universe, to cover the known world and reach heaven and hell. Epic characteristically refuses to be hemmed in, in time as well as space; it raids the unknown and colonizes it. It is the imagination's manifesto, proclaiming the range of its grasp, or else it is the dream of the will, indulging its fantasies of power. But tragedy dramatizes the isolation of the will, the limits of human apprehension, the inexorability of our hemming in.

This is why tragedy commonly uses partial, fragmentary images. If you think of any familiar Shakespearean metaphor or allusion—the player who struts and frets, Hamlet's unweeded garden, Lear's basest beggar—you see them as *unsituated,* without context and without detail. Each is a brief candle of an impression, which flickers and goes out in the flow of speech.[2] It is compressed, suggestive, unfulfilled; it invites analysis; and it frequently gains resonance from its place in a series of like images scattered through the play. Moreover the speaker and the image are both exterior to each other; we do not think of Hamlet literally moving through the garden, even though it represents metaphorically the world he

1. I am thinking in particular of writers like Terence, Jonson, Molière, Congreve, Shaw, and even Jane Austen, who seem to me to be more or less "pure" comic artists. Some great comic triumphs (as in Cervantes, some of Shakespeare, Kafka, and Joyce) involve an admixture with other genres (tragedy, romance, epic) and do not exemplify my generalizations.

2. It is true that images like these are more natural to speech and so more fitting for the stage, tragic or not. But if the imagery of a Shakespearean comedy which is truly comic and free of tragic mystery—say, *As You Like It*—is compared with the imagery of the tragedies, the comic images are seen to tend toward a relatively greater solidarity and fullness (when at least they are not witticisms). This must remain unproved here. But in any case the fragmentary image is peculiarly effective as a property of tragedy; it is the instrument of an Aeschylus far more than of an Aristophanes.

does move in. All of these qualities of tragic imagery are appropriate to the ultimate unknowability of the tragic universe.

The characteristic imagery of epic is contrary to all this; it expands, exfoliates, fulfills itself in harmony with the expansive, emancipated imagination governing it. The epic simile cannot, by definition, be a brief candle of an impression; it is permitted to fill out space to its natural limits, to include not one but many living things, to detail with leisure the various aspects of its selected scene. It tends to be in itself a miniature, complete action. The scene in the simile need not be described exhaustively or meticulously, but we are told all that we want to know or need to know about it. And this is equally true when the epic poet is at work upon one of the greater images of his poem, upon the landscape of the action. We feel as readers that our eye can move easily over the well-lit space before us, that no occasional shadow will forever baffle our gaze.[3] The darkness of Milton's hell must remain darkness visible.

It would be useful to think of these greater images, with whatever movement or action they contain, as the unit counters of the epic poet's art. The death-agony of Troy as Virgil describes it, with its various episodes, locales, peripeties, its accretion of similes, its moral, historical, symbolic associations—all this intricate but massive bloc exists in our minds as a single, giant image which cannot easily be pulled apart and to which everything in Virgil's second book contributes. That is an example of the epic image in which scenery and symbol merge. Any given detail, any smaller visual unit, has to be related to its place in that larger whole. The whole is what the poet is intent upon and what the reader should be intent upon. Milton's paradise is such a whole; so is the Ogygia or Scheria of the *Odyssey;* so even is Dante's inferno. But of course the greater image need not be so very large as these examples; the African harbor which receives Aeneas' storm-weary ships would be a more modest one. There is no term which designates precisely

3. I take it that this is the distinction Lubbock makes when he speaks of the respective feeling for Russian landscape in Tolstoy and Dostoevsky. Tolstoy's affinities with epic and Dostoevsky's with tragedy are clear. See Percy Lubbock, *The Craft of Fiction* (New York, 1957), pp. 44–47.

this kind of unit; I shall call it an arch-image. It is distinguished from the fragmentary image of tragedy because it invites not exegetical expansion but exploration. And the characters, rather than remaining outside it, are contained by it, help to define it, and indeed to comprise it.

The arch-image becomes inseparable from the action it contains. The experience of whoever moves through it colors the image just as the image controls the experience. The poet may choose to begin an episode by describing an action, and, with the developing narrative and shifting focus, fill in progressively the area about the central figures. That is basically the procedure of Virgil's second book. But more frequently we see the arch-image before we see the experience; this is the case with Milton's paradise. In either case the real movement of the poem is from one arch-image to another, and its vital force depends greatly upon their richness and flow.

Not all epic episodes of course need to be contained within arch-images. There are transitional episodes which take place against sketchy, vague backgrounds. I shall have more to say about this below. Here let it suffice to observe that episodes can be described as "strong image" or "weak image" according to their visual intensity. The poet must decide how much intensity each episode needs, when to strengthen and when to relax the imagistic impression. An excess of either extreme is deadly. But within the broad spectrum of feasible choice, one may study the poet's imagistic style, as it were, through his successive responses to that recurring problem.

ii.

The expansiveness of epic is checked finally by a complementary, containing quality which affects not so much the sense of space as the capacity of the hero. It has to do with a kind of austerity. It has been touched upon in three recent books written from very different orientations. C. M. Bowra, in his *Heroic Poetry,*[4] hypothesizes that the stage of cultural evolution producing such poetry was preceded by a stage producing shamanistic poetry, of which

4. London, 1952.

the Finnish *Kalevala* would be an example. The magician or shaman who is the protagonist succeeds not through physical prowess so much as through hermetic knowledge, magical powers, and initiation into supernatural mysteries. The protagonist of the heroic poem who, according to Bowra, succeeded the shaman, would then have to be seen as an essentially weaker man, gifted at the outset with less formidable capacities, and less likely to control his world, relying as he does chiefly on courage and strength, sometimes intelligence—all merely human qualities. A second scholar, Gertrude R. Levy, working more intensively than Bowra with a smaller number of texts, argues that the action of several ancient epics was based on immeasurably older myths and rituals of the Near and Middle East. In her study, *The Sword from the Rock,*[5] Miss Levy attempts to show that the action of the human hero follows a pattern originally ascribed to divine protagonists, a pattern which descended over a period of centuries and even millennia from the god to the demi-god to the exceptional man. I do not know whether Miss Levy would feel that Bowra's hypothesis conflicts with her own. In any case we find a third writer, interested in laying the basis for a "scientific" criticism, who sees the epic analogously as a postmythical genre. Northrop Frye, in *Anatomy of Criticism,*[6] places the epic in the category of high mimetic which follows, logically and chronologically, the categories of myth and romance. The hero of myth is a god; the hero of romance is superior to other men and to his environment, superior not in kind as a god is but in degree. Romance is the realm of the marvelous, the magical, and the monstrous. The epic would seem to fall just over the line in high mimetic; I imagine Frye would agree that epic commonly treats this line somewhat carelessly. The hero of high mimetic "is superior in degree to other men but not to his natural environment. . . . He has authority, passions, and powers of expression far greater than ours, but what he does is subject both to social criticism and to the order of nature." [7]

All of these writers then view the epic not as an attempt to inflate the hero's naturally meager capacities but as rather the op-

5. New York, 1953.
6. Princeton, 1957.
7. Frye, *Anatomy of Criticism,* pp. 33–34.

posite, in terms of its historical development—as a diminishing of his capacities to approximate more closely those we know. The epic sacrifices the pleasure of pure fantasy in the name of reason or realism or something else. The hero encounters a new sort of resistance and reaches the limitations of his being. He is denied something, particularly those things which would render him a god. He acquires an austerity which is peculiarly human.

This shift from shamanistic or mythical to human, with the concurrent sacrifice it entails, is reflected in perhaps the oldest heroic poem we possess, indeed one of the oldest literary texts we possess—the Babylonian epic of *Gilgamesh*. It survives in several different versions in different languages; the oldest version dates back to at least the third millennium B.C. It concerns a hero who is explicitly and repeatedly compared to a god: "like to a double of Anu's own self"; "two thirds of him are divine, and one third of him human." In the opening episodes Gilgamesh's exploits resemble in valor and magnitude those of many other heroes, although he is aided by his companion Enkidu. Enkidu's death marks the poem's turning point; the remainder is concerned with Gilgamesh's persistent but unsuccessful search for immortality. Confronted for the first time by the truth of death, he is haunted by its anguish, and spurning the *carpe diem* counsel of the beautiful goddess Siduri, is driven upon a futile quest for a means to mitigate his humanity. But he is left at the end with only the anguished despair of that one third in himself not divine. He has discovered the austerity of the mortal. With that discovery the epic becomes possible.

The epic is the poem which replaces divine worship with humanistic awe, awe for the act which is prodigious but yet human. It is the City of man, not of God, which Tasso evokes in the last sentence of his discourse, as the final metaphoric evocation of the genre he loved most; he saw the epic as

> alcuna nobilissima città piena di magnifiche, e di reali abitazioni, ed ornata di templi, e di palazzi, e d'altre fabbriche reali, e maravigliose.[8]

8. Torquato Tasso, *Discorsi del Poema Eroico* in *Prose*, ed. E. Mazzali (Naples, 1959), p. 729. "Some very noble city full of magnificent and royal dwellings, adorned with temples and palaces, and with other royal and marvelous buildings."

The last word of the quotation, which is the last word of the discourse, deliberately placed there, lays stress upon that quality of *maraviglia,* awe, which Tasso with so many other critics postulated as the essential response to epic poetry. Epic awe, as distinguished from religious or mythic awe, springs from the realization that a man can commit an extraordinary act while still remaining limited. It does not matter that, in practice, the poet occasionally describes heroic action which is beyond human powers, if the hero is understood to be subject to ignorance or foolhardiness and above all to death. The most important recognition scenes in epic are not between two people but between the hero and his mortality.

The act which induces heroic awe must be performed by a single individual or at most by a very small group of individuals. The hero must be acting for the community, the City; he may incarnate the City, but he must be nonetheless an individual with a name. What he does must be dangerous, not only for other people but for him. It must involve a test. Moreover it must make a difference; it must change in some manner the hero's situation or the community's. Games and contests find their way into epic poetry, but they do not in themselves induce heroic awe. Arbitrary feats are admirable but not awesome. The situation which tests not only strength but courage and will is by definition serious and must be taken seriously by the characters in the poem, by the poet, and by his audience. Such a situation occurs in the closing cantos of Pulci's *Morgante,* where the poet's accustomed buffoonery fails to reduce the great tragic action of Roncesvalles. Above all the heroic act must be visible, external, objective. However profound its moral implications, however complemented or imitated by internal action, it must certify itself in the world of space and time, the world which the eye can see or the inner eye imagine. Cassirer's remarks on myth are apposite:

> In mythic conception . . . things are not taken for what they mean indirectly, but for their immediate appearance; they are taken as pure presentations, and embodied in the imagination . . . In the myth nothing has any significance or being save what is given in tangible reality.[9]

9. Ernst Cassirer, *Language and Myth,* trans. S. Langer (New York, 1946), pp. 56–57.

At the heart of the epic is tangible reality, swiftly apprehended, simple with the simplicity of violence and of wonder. The complexity which many poems attain must organize itself around that stabilizing concreteness. It was in this respect (among others) that the later Renaissance was to depart from the epic norm.

Why is it necessary that the hero bear a name? The right to a name means that a man can commit acts which vary qualitatively from another man's acts. Man in his middle state shares with the animals his mortality, and with the gods his right to bear an individual name. A man's name is very important in heroic poetry; it becomes equal to the sum of his accomplishments. It is always assumed that a man's action is knowable and is known, and is known to be *his.* (Hence the importance of the heroic poet within his own world.) It is important that every combatant who is killed in the *Iliad* have a name, for the name is an index to the victor's accomplishment. A hero wears his victims' names like scalps, and his own name is aggrandized by theirs. The epic tries to define the relation between the hero's name and his death.

Epic narrative in other terms is a series of adjustments between the hero's capacities and his limitations. His life as a hero is devoted to informing his name with meaning. Because, unlike an animal, he can accomplish a distinctive, personal thing, and unlike a god, he has no past accomplishments, the hero must discover and demonstrate at the outset what meaning his name may have. He is impelled to act, and, as action among men is agonistic, he is plunged into a contest of *areté, virtus,* capacity—a struggle to impose his being on his world. He can do this by demonstrating his control over a piece of his world: by subduing another man or men or a monster, or by pitting himself victoriously against some natural hazard of his environment. To remain a hero he must continue to demonstrate control, and so his career imitates the expansiveness of the epic imagination. But at the end of that movement, implicitly or explicitly, his inescapable limitations await him.

It follows from this that tragedy is not incompatible with epic; that, on the contrary, tragic elements complement and fulfill it. They become explicit when the sense of limit yields to a tragic contraction of capacity and control. In those epics (such as the *Iliad* and *Beowulf*) where the arch-images are few and the amplitude in time and space is restricted, one finds the statement of epic accomplishment to be most heavily qualified by tragic limitations. But these poems simply weight more heavily one member of the dialectical struggle which is always involved in epic narrative. Comedy, with its classical acquiescence to limits, is much less compatible with epic because it evades that struggle.

The conclusion imposes some stable equilibrium, some final adjustment or definition. In *Beowulf* the hero's control reaches its widest point about two-thirds through the poem, and then, with the supravention of his death and his people's probable military collapse, his control is reduced to nothing. But his name will remain, perpetuated by the barrow raised in his honor. These three conceptions, of Beowulf's honor, power, and death, related to each other ironically as they are, constitute the elements of which the deeply tragic conclusion is made. This represents one extreme kind of equilibrium; at the other extreme might be placed the equilibrium of the *Odyssey,* which anticipates a remote and easy death balanced against a glorious name and a degree of control—certainly not total control—over the known world. The hero learns—and the reader with him—wherein lies his power and to what degree, and wherein lie his limitations and to what degree. The conclusion formalizes these discoveries.

If Dante's *Commedia* does not altogether satisfy one's sense of what an epic is, the reason may lie in the protagonist's failure to acquire or lose power over his world; he acquires it only over himself. Subjective conquest may complement the objective in epic, but cannot replace it. In a sense Dante's universe does not permit an individual to acquire power because for him all power belongs to God.

In certain Renaissance epics, like Spenser's, the landscape which is contested can be taken to represent the hero's own soul. It might be argued that Spenser's story is essentially Dante's story. This could truly be argued of Spenser's follower, Phineas Fletcher, whose *Purple Island* is based on nothing more than a very simple psychomachia. To the degree that Spenser frees himself from the simplifications of the crudest allegory, to the degree that he evokes a world exterior to the hero whose existence is imaginatively compelling, he participates in the epic.

The subject of all epic poetry might thus be said to be politics, but a politics not limited to society, a politics embracing the natural and the fabulous worlds, embracing even the moral or spiritual words they sometimes shadow forth, and involving ultimately the divine. The implications expand to suggest, if not frankly to assert, a cosmic power struggle. The heroic act assumes its highest prestige by its divine authorization, the authorization which became symbolized with increasing frequency in the Renaissance by the literal descent of the angelic messenger to the hero.

Heretofore I have seemed to suppose that a given poem contained a single hero, but of course the epic is not always so simple. One may set against a poem like *Beowulf,* whose hero we scarcely lose sight of once he is introduced, the more complex *Chanson de Roland,* wherein two complementary heroes are brilliantly balanced. It could be said that the whole poem belongs essentially to Roland, even though a considerable part of the action occurs after his death; Charlemagne's victory would thus be read as a response to Roland's defeat. This is a defensible reading but so is the contrary one—that the poem belongs essentially to Charlemagne, with whom it begins and ends, and that Roland's defeat should be seen as a peripety in his liege's larger, circumscribing career. Both readings are legitimate; to the degree that they conflict, the poem could be called complex. But the complexity is still limited because the power of the two heroes is directed toward controlling the same world under the same authority. Epic becomes truly complex when, as in the *Iliad,* the political goals of the multiple heroes are opposed. Here the City becomes divided against itself and some tragic outcome is much more likely.

Not many poems resemble the *Iliad* in this respect. The *Gerusalemme Liberata* resembles the *Song of Roland,* assigning the Charlemagne role to Goffredo and the Roland role to Rinaldo, Tancredi, and others. In many poems the older, wiser, less active figure is withdrawn to a second plane, leaving the foreground to the younger Roland figure or figures: thus it is in Ariosto, and thus in *Beowulf,* where two men, Hrothgar and Hygelac, divide the Charlemagne role. Beowulf's tragedy is explicable in a sense by his attempt at the conclusion to play both roles. So also is explicable Aeneas' tragedy, if that term is the right one to represent the sense of loss, privation, and denial which underlies his ostensible accomplishments. I think one might even consider the characters of *Paradise Lost* in terms of this duality: Adam's action as protagonist is circumscribed by the wisdom and criticism of God and His angels, to whom Adam must render an account just as Beowulf does to Hygelac. Charlemagne in the *Song of Roland* is in fact a kind of surrogate for God and so to a degree is Tasso's Goffredo. Another reason for the *Iliad's* structural complexity lies in the hostility between *its* Roland and Charlemagne figures.

This distinction, where it exists, between the director and executor of action reflects the two-fold concern of politics—the establishment of control through violence and the right use of control in government. The focus in epic is upon violence rather than administration, but violence needs some frame of ulterior meaning. The Charlemagne figure is there to ensure, among other things, that the violence not be betrayed by its consequences. Action is most fully realized through changes of institutions or regimes, changes which extend its consequences throughout society and throughout time. Thus the epic is the great poem of beginnings and endings. The *Aeneid* is typical, beginning with an ending and ending with a beginning.

iii.

The distinction between violence and its consequences, execution and direction, subduing and administering, is made in another fashion also—by the structure of epic. The distinction can best be understood perhaps through a comparison with novelistic structure. Lubbock recognizes two kinds of narration in the novel: the *panoramic,* which surveys plot development from above, as it were, over a length of time, and the *scenic,* which descends to a given incident at a given hour and place. Of these two procedures, epic depends very little upon the panoramic. It hurries through whatever transitional material is necessary with some embarrassment and evident eagerness to be done with it. What it wants to give us is a series of specific scenes. But the scenes themselves tend to fall generally into two kinds, one of which assumes some of the functions of panoramic narration in the novel.

The first kind of scene or episode lays stress upon activity and movement; it contains the *agon*, the struggle between capacity and limitation, the vital cruxes of the narrative. It is not only high keyed emotively, but since imagistic intensity in the epic tends to accompany emotive intensity, it is the more brilliant and showy; it is always a strong-image episode. It contains the crises in which violence occurs, *virtus* is tested, the deed is accomplished, the terror confronted, the name enhanced. It tends to focus upon the Roland figure. The second kind of episode depends primarily on dialogue, although "dialogue" is a misleading term, since epic avoids the abruptness of stichomythia just as it avoids all other abruptness. Speech in the epic is ampler and more formal than common speech; it is the vehicle by which the political and moral associations of an action or image are commonly revealed, and by which they are situated in an historical context. The second kind of episode then is concerned with the significance and consequences of the violence. It is commonly a weak-image episode although it need not be. It tends to focus upon the Charlemagne figure. I shall refer to the first kind of episode as "executive" and to the second as "deliberative."

The deliberative episode takes to itself most of the functions of panoramic narration in the novel. Through the speech of the well-informed character (well-informed through accident, wisdom, or divinity) we are given that sense of the passage of greater time which action needs to assume its full resonance; we are moved backward and forward in history, through reminiscence and prophecy, with the same free expansiveness that we are moved in space. It does not matter if the visual background of the dialogue remain sketchy and vague; what we learn from such a scene is useful only for the fuller apprehension of the major action of the executive scenes. It is a necessary link; because of it, the great scenes will be more dramatic, profounder, richer in symbolic suggestiveness. The striking thing is that the deliberative episode is used so consistently in preference to simple exposition. It would appear that the poet insists on some sort of scene capable of visualization, however vague—a scene which will remain before the reader's eyes. But when historical perspective needs particular emphasis, then the deliberative presentation is dropped and some other means of heightened visualization is found. This may be a pageant-vision of the future, such as Anchises shows Aeneas, Michael shows Adam, and Melissa shows Bradamante. Or it may be a work of art representing remote events—conventional bas-reliefs, woven hangings, or decorated shields.

Some balance between action as spectacle, as *geste,* as object of awe, and action as political event seems necessary to epic. When the balance tips too far either way, the poem participates so much the less in the epic mode. If you read Lucan you are struck immediately by his overriding interest in the historical and moral meanings of the action he narrates—narrates rather than describes. He is neglectful of spectacle, of visual immediacy; he tells you very little about the landscape around Pharsalus. His central characters are directors, not executors of violence. He is fond of speeches which concern military or diplomatic issues, and he narrates frequently in a panoramic, novelistic fashion. He must have felt himself to be doing something halfway between what Virgil had done and what versifiers of history like Ennius had done. To compensate for his imaginative aridity he had to fall back on sensationalism. We may contrast with him a writer of romance like Boiardo, bent on charming an audience into hearing his tale—a tale which depends on atmosphere, gesture, the marvelous, and narrative entanglement. Between these two extremes lies the epic, opposing the melodrama to which both tend with its own dramatic firmness.

Both extremes are represented in epic by the alternation of executive and deliberative episodes. Perhaps more examples would clarify the distinction. Books II and III of *Paradise Lost* are both based on a balance of executive and deliberative. The demonic council in pandemonium is deliberative; Satan's flight through chaos is executive. The exchange of speeches in heaven is deliberative, preceded as it is by only a brief evocation of setting. But when the exchange has concluded, the great arch-image of heaven is more fully evoked; with the angelic adoration and hymn Milton passes to the executive, which will govern the rest of the book, including Satan's descent through the planetary spheres to earth. The speeches in the opening episodes of both books contain perspectives of the future: in Book II, the demonic, tentative, illusory perspectives; in Book III, the true perspective. But both serve to provide moral and historical frames for the action of the latter part of each book as well as for the rest of the poem. Similarly, the executive episode opening the second book of Tasso's poem—the episode of Sophronia and Olindo—balances the deliberative second half which brings together the Egyptian ambassadors with Goffredo. In the first book of the *Aeneid,* we are given two major arch-images at the opening and the close: the tempest and the banquet at Dido's palace, images which mark the general movement of the book from exposure to security or pseudo-security. The tempest is followed by the paler image of landing; the banquet is preceded by the paler image of Dido dispensing laws at the temple. Connecting and interpreting these four major images is a wealth of deliberative episode: once the panoramic introduction has been gotten through (not even here, however, without the accent of a human voice, the poet's voice, speaking in the first person) we are given Juno's speech, which looks backward and forward, and the ensuing scene with Aeolus, which helps to inform the tempest to follow with moral meanings. Later the great central scene between Venus and Jupiter will provide much broader historical, almost eschatological perspective, Jupiter's famous prophecy answering and balancing Venus' review of the past. The subsequent meeting of Venus and Aeneas provides another perspective into the past, now into Dido's past; Ilioneus' account of his men's fortunes serves the same purpose, whereas Venus' exchange with Eros turns us about to the future again, facing us toward the fourth book. That book will move from deliberative to executive, from dialogue to spectacle and agony.

iv.

One can observe the care with which the great epic poets fitted together their pieces of narrative, following laws which have more to do with tonality and feeling than with causation or chronology. But the ultimate epic quality is less susceptible of analysis—the quality of heroic energy, the superabundant vitality which charges character and image and action alike. Without it the most carefully plotted work is as dust and ashes. It is a quality of the imagination which imparts life to men and things through words, the quality possessed pre-eminently by the poet of the *Iliad*. You sense in Achilles his measureless reserves of living power, his inexhaustible capacity for fury; you sense them equally whether he is active or at rest. To create that sense is the work of the epic imagination, and it must be done without effort; it must be done with language which is unstrained. To achieve it, to create a character possessed of heroic energy, is to obviate "personality" as an artistic goal—as it is more or less obviated in Virgil's Turnus, in Ariosto's Orlando and Rodomonte, in Tasso's Argante. But you feel that energy equally, if more subtly, in landscape; it is in this:

> As when Heaven's Fire
> Hath scath'd the Forest Oaks, or Mountain Pines,
> With singed top thir stately growth though bare
> Stands on the blasted Heath.[10]

But it is not in this :

> Even the wild heath displays her purple dyes,
> And 'midst the desert fruitful fields arise,
> That crowned with tufted trees and springing corn,
> Like verdant isles the sable waste adorn.[11]

The energy of epic breathes a kind of excitement which is like the basic human excitement of living bodily in a physical world. It draws upon sexual springs to invigorate the imagination. It animates the City with that electric dynamism the ancients thought was divine or demonic and which the Renaissance thought was ancient. It dramatizes the fact of death. Upon it depends, really, the humanistic awe, the *maraviglia,* for that which quickens the self but surpasses the self. This energy is not much admired today. But without a proper sense of it, the epic will always seem a little puffy, flatulent, overblown, and dull.

The language which imparts epic energy must be itself in some sense *alive*. The living impulse of heroic verse stems from a discovery about language which must have been made very early in human history, perhaps as early as language was used, which is to say as early as man existed at all. This was the discovery that

10. *Paradise Lost,* I.612–15.
11. *Windsor Forest,* 25–28.

language can do more than denote, that it can possess, exorcise, invoke, bind with a spell, that it has magical, demonic properties transcending its concern with statement. The fearful, demonic god in words must have been discovered early, and one wonders whether he was discovered with joy or terror. In any case, the demon is there in all the primitive compositions we know. The heroic poet made use of him, and with time he learned to restrain the demon; he set him customary limits of meter and syntax and formula. But happily he never tamed the demon altogether, as rhetoricians of later ages wanted to do. The creature who possesses and binds is at work still within the poet's marvelous chant. That for the poet is the fundamental task—to tether the creature but not to hobble him.

Heroic verse lives with the life of that demon. But as heroic becomes epic, as the demon is caught upon the written page, his wildness is threatened; he must have recourse to a new cunning. The formula is liable to lose its energy. So there occurs a shift from the poetry of the expected to the poetry of the unexpected. Now the demonic life is more frequently smothered, but when it is quickened again, its life is more various, though scarcely more free, than before.

This is the first quality of epic language—the living impulse which imparts energy to men and things. But of course that impulse is not limited to the epic. There is a second quality, inherent in the feeling proper to epic: its language must become, in whatever way the poet finds, the language of awe; it must itself register awe, and it must invite the audience to awe. It must remind the audience that the story told is no ordinary story, concerning no ordinary men; it must withdraw into its heroic remoteness, with its own uncommon rhythms and diction and tropes. It cannot permit itself the abandon of lyric poetry or its slender grace or its coloring of personality. It must remain the expression of the ritual community, the collective City of man. The language must emulate the weight of the story with its own austere solemnity. This is the quality of language which rhetoricians came to call or assimilate with the "high style" and which, like so much in epic, lent itself to imitative debasement. But of course it is really very difficult to imitate. Once the epic has passed out of the pre-literate, formulaic stage of the heroic poem, the poetry of the expected, every new work poses afresh the problem of a fitting heroic language.

In his language as in other things, the poet stands implicitly midway between the hero and his audience. He is the amphibian, the mediator, the messenger, the guide, who is inspired and inspires in turn. He is the Knower of the Names, the speaker to those who cannot speak of high things. But he is not the actor; he, like the audience, has only heard of those things. He can say "we" to embrace himself and the audience, but never himself and the hero.

> Hwaet! we Gar-Dena in geardagum
> þeodcyninga þrym gefrunon . . .
>
> Lo! we have heard of the past glory of Danish kings . . .

And in the old poems he joins his audience in a common anonymity.

The foregoing remarks attempt to reformulate some norms of the epic mode, but they pretend neither to completeness, nor, for the most part, originality; in such a discussion there can be no real pretension to either. Rather, in the case of the epic, reformulation must partly involve rediscovery. For when a genre falls into relative neglect, as the epic has fallen, its potential audience begins to forget how to read it. And that forgetfulness leads to more neglect. Today there are ten readers of Sophocles for one of Virgil or ten of Molière for one of Ariosto. The charm of lyric poetry, above all, has dimmed the appeal of bulkier, imperfect work. Marvell, with his fine aristocratic precision, has become more attractive than Milton. This is perhaps as it had to be. But one must deplore such exclusive preferences if they lead us to forget the very experience which Ariosto and Virgil and Milton afford, so that we no longer know what to expect of them or what questions to ask about them. In these remarks I have tried to recall what questions about epic poems there are to be posed.

3. *THE ILIAD*

i.

It happens a score of times in the *Iliad* that an immortal has occasion to leave Olympus for the theatre of human action. Iris most frequently, but also Athene, Apollo, Thetis, Zeus himself, among others, descend to intervene in the theatre which seems to afford so large a part of the gods' amusement. There are indeed few theatres which permit the fortunate spectators to alter the drama's peripeties. But this is a right vouchsafed, within limits, to the Homeric gods, and so the line between Olympus and Troy becomes a kind of divine highway.

In Book Fourteen Hera leaves Olympus to seek, not the armies of Troy but the personified figure of Sleep, whom she needs for a trick designed to gull Zeus and help the Achaians. This episode inspired a long series of imitations by Ovid, Statius, Chaucer, and Spenser, to name only the best known. Or rather it initiated a convention which presently ceased to be associated very closely with Homer. *This* convention is to be distinguished from a second which is also traceable to the *Iliad,* in this case to a passage in Book

Twenty-four which involves a descent from Olympus to Troy by Hermes. On the whole, poets for two millennia after Homer were quite clear about the distinction between these two conventions, and only a few (like Ariosto) attempted to combine them. The knowledge of such things constituted, during later antiquity and the Renaissance, an important part of a poet's professional equipment. The second convention, deriving from Hermes' descent, is the immediate subject of this study.

Its source in the *Iliad* appears almost at the end of the poem, in that superb coda which exalts and illumines in retrospect all the bloody turbulence of the preceding action. Out of respect for the dead Hektor and compassion for his doomed people, Zeus arranges for the hero's body to be returned to Troy. At his bidding, Thetis persuades her son Achilleus to surrender the body, and Iris descends to inform Priam of the plan. Priam, guided by Hermes, is to cross the Achaian lines, accompanied only by a single herald, and is to throw himself as a suppliant upon Achilleus' mercy. When Iris has delivered this shattering message, there follows a poignant, tenderly comic scene between the old man and Hekabe who would dissuade him from going but fails, and then between him and his surviving sons, whom he rails at—chiefly, it seems, because they are not Hektor. We have a sense of his senile petulance, his willfulness, his courage, and his grief. He prays to Zeus to confirm his message by an omen, and Zeus responds by sending an eagle on the right. Then Priam sets out in the dusk with his herald Idaios for the tent of Achilleus, the killer of his dearest son. His venture seems very quixotic. But Zeus sends Hermes to guide him. This is the first account of a descent of Hermes, who has not heretofore played a very large role in the poem.[1] Although he is regarded as a messenger god in other poems, it is clear that Iris is the ordinary messenger in the *Iliad* and Hermes here is important as a guide. This is Homer's account of the encounter:

> And Zeus of the wide brows failed not to notice
> the two as they showed in the plain. He saw the old man
> and took pity

1. In Book Twenty, Hermes is mentioned briefly as fighting with other gods on the side of the Achaians. But the descent itself is not narrated and Hermes' role is small.

upon him, and spoke directly to his beloved son, Hermes:
"Hermes, for to you beyond all other gods it is dearest
to be man's companion, and you listen to whom you will, go now
on your way, and so guide Priam inside the hollow ships
of the Achaians, that no man shall see him, none be aware of him,
of the other Danaans, till he has come to the son of Peleus."
He spoke, nor disobeyed him the courier, Argeïphontes.
Immediately he bound upon his feet the fair sandals
golden and immortal, that carried him over the water
as over the dry land of the main abreast of the wind's blast.
He caught up the staff, with which he mazes the eyes of those mortals
whose eyes he would maze, or wakes again the sleepers. Holding
this in his hands, strong Argeïphontes winged his way onward
until he came suddenly to Troy and the Hellespont, and there
walked on, and there took the likeness of a young man, a noble,
with beard new grown, which is the most graceful time of young manhood.
Now when the two had driven past the great tomb of Ilos
they stayed their mules and horses to water them in the river,
for by this time darkness had descended on the land; and the herald
made out Hermes, who was coming toward them at a short distance.
He lifted his voice and spoke aloud to Priam: "Take thought,
son of Dardanos. Here is work for a mind that is careful.
I see a man; I think he will presently tear us to pieces.

Come then, let us run away with our horses, or if not, then
clasp his knees and entreat him to have mercy upon us."
So he spoke, and the old man's mind was confused, he was badly
frightened, and the hairs stood up all over his gnarled body
and he stood staring, but the kindly god himself coming closer
took the old man's hand, and spoke to him and asked him a question:
"Where, my father, are you thus guiding your mules and horses
through the immortal night while other mortals are sleeping
Have you no fear of the Achaians whose wind is fury,
who hate you, who are your enemies, and are near? For if one
of these were to see you, how you are conveying so many
treasures through the swift black night, what then could you think of?
You are not young yourself, and he who attends you is aged
for beating off any man who might pick a quarrel with you.
But I will do you no harm myself, I will even keep off
another who would. You seem to me like a beloved father."
[24.331–71] [2]

Priam answers the god with poise and warmth, and the exchange of speeches continues for another seventy lines. Then Hermes leads the two old men past the Achaian sentries, whom he puts to sleep, and through the formidable gate leading to Achilleus' shelter. Before leaving, Hermes reveals his identity (having earlier

2. *The Iliad of Homer,* translated with an introduction by Richmond Lattimore (Chicago, 1954), pp. 484–85. All of my quotations are drawn from Lattimore's translation. The references to book and line are to his translation, where the numbering of lines follows the original very closely. I have also adopted his spelling of proper nouns for the sake of consistency.

posed as a henchman of Achilleus), but Priam makes no comment upon the revelation and enters forthwith the terrible house where he must play the suppliant. The scene which follows is so fine that it renders praise impertinent. Priam will return to Troy the following day with the body of his son, and even in this return the humane greatness of the poet's art is sustained. Priam is vindicated now for the recklessness of his foray, and purged a little of his sorrow. He says nothing at first as the Trojan women obstruct his little procession, tearing their hair, and as the city crowd all about raises the death wail. One sees him as a bit tight-lipped and alien from that show of grief he himself had indulged a day earlier. About him now is a quiet pride. He is impatient with hysterics:

> And now and there in front of the gates they would have lamented
> all day till the sun went down and let fall their tears for Hektor,
> except that the old man spoke from the chariot to his people:
> "Give me way to get through with my mules; then afterwards
> you may sate yourselves with mourning, when I have him inside the palace." [24.713–17]

Priam is allowed to pass, and the poem concludes with the stark and noble description of Hektor's funeral. With that final exception, the tragedy of the last book is suffused with the tenderest comedy, so mature and delicate that heroic poetry contains almost nothing to compare with it. Throughout his adventure Priam remains marvelously tangible, pathetic, and grand.

Although the encounter of the king and the god upon the plain is lower keyed than the rest of the book, it is still full of dramatic life. The reader must see, first of all, how on the face of it, Priam's expedition truly is absurd. The kinsmen who lament his departure "as if he went to his death" are certainly justified, given their ignorance of divine purposes. No clownish wild goose chase could be more grotesque than this preposterous odyssey of dotards and mules. So inept are these old men that the first unarmed stranger transfixes them with terror. As Hermes approaches, the king's resolution falters; the hair stands erect "all over his gnarled body" and he remains staring, impotent with fear. But the beautiful moment which follows transmutes the comedy. Hermes advances, takes the king's hand in his own, and speaks soothingly, concluding with a tender compliment: "You seem to me like a beloved father." It is impossible to say whether or not Priam recognizes the god. Iris has informed Priam that Hermes would appear to guide him, and Priam replies to the god's first speech as though he guessed his divinity:

> Yes, in truth, dear child, all this is much as you tell me;
> yet there is some god who has held his hand above me,
> who sent such a wayfarer as you to meet me . . .
> [24.373–75]

Hermes seems half to assent to Priam's guess by replying:

> Yes, old sir, all this that you said is fair and orderly. [379]

But he goes on to ask deliberately naïve questions as though he knew nothing of Priam's goal. And Priam counters with a comparable show of ignorance:

> But who are you, o best of men, and who are your parents?
> Since you spoke of my ill-starred son's death, and with honour. [387–88]

Hermes will have his fabricated answers ready. Is this on both sides a ritual of subtle courtesy, a knowing comedy of ignorance? There is no way to be sure. But Priam's later remarks will seem still more pointed hints:

> My child, surely it is good to give the immortals
> their due gifts; because my own son, if ever I had one,
> never forgot in his halls the gods who live on Olympos.
> Therefore they remembered him even in death's stage. Come, then,
> accept at my hands this beautiful drinking-cup, and give me
> protection for my body, and with the god's grace be my escort . . . [24.425–30]

These remarks accompanying the offer of the cup strongly suggest Priam's awareness of his guide's identity, and thus explain the absence of surprise when the guide reveals himself. If we accept this suggestion, then we must alter our view of Priam's comic pathos to admit a quite sophisticated discretion, a discretion which anticipates his poise and eloquence during the interview with Achilleus. It is characteristic of Homer that he too remains discreet, allowing Priam's recognition of the god to be half-divined rather than known. This encounter, like all the divine interventions in the poem, stays a little shadowy in its implications.

The dramatic richness, however shadowed, is increased by the preliminary scene on Olympos. Hermes' preparations for his flight are not gratuitous. They remind you that he is awesome. The ten lines devoted to him alone stress in particular three attributes. His sandals symbolize his divinely rapid ease of movement. The staff symbolizes his power over the eyes and minds of men:

> the staff, with which he mazes the eyes of those mortals
> whose eyes he would maze, or wakes again the sleepers.

A hundred lines below the staff will be used to put the Achaian sentries to sleep. The third attribute—the youthful gracefulness of his assumed form—serves of course to set off Priam's senility. In many subsequent poems these same elements (particularly the first two), rigidly conventionalized, enhance the god's prestige in order to dignify the hero he honors by his attention. In these poems divine awe contributes to heroic awe. But in the *Iliad* the relation is reversed; divine awe leads to human irony. The king to whom the god descends is not a king in the high style. He has no metaphysical prestige. The cinematic shifts of the action from Olympos to Troy and back serve to contrast divine omnipotence with human frailty, divine omniscience with human ignorance. The contrast might have generated either irony or tragedy. Here, though, in the encounter of Priam and Hermes a kind of comedy instinct with compassion is created which only a few great writers have ever achieved. It is a quality which is, in the best sense, modern—a quality one associates with Cervantes, Dostoevsky, and Kafka but with scarcely any other writer of antiquity. Part of the *Iliad*'s uniqueness lies in this anticipation of our latter-day wry humanity.

ii.

The episode of Hermes' flight to Troy falls naturally into two sections, the brief scene on Olympos and the longer scene with Priam which I have truncated in my quotation above on page 29. As the convention crystallized in later poems, a middle section was commonly introduced which is missing here. This section describes the physical movement of the flight itself, generally evoking its speed and sometimes indicating geographical landmarks along the way. The passage in the *Odyssey* which imitates this one already contains such a section. But here there is the barest account of the flight—"Argeïphontes winged his way onward until he came suddenly to Troy." Some other accounts in the *Iliad* of divine descents from Olympos are slightly more circumstantial. This is typical of several:

> So she spoke, nor did the goddess grey-eyed Athene
> disobey her, but went in speed down the peaks of Olympos,
> and lightly she arrived beside the fast ships of the Achaians. [2.166–68]

In three places the god in flight is compared to a hawk:

> She in the likeness of a wide-winged, thin-crying
> hawk plummeted from the sky through the bright air. [19.350–51] [3]

and elsewhere (4.75–79) to a shooting star. In Hera's descent to Sleep, some place names are given (14.224–30). Once the speed of Iris' flight is awarded a slightly fuller simile (15.170–73). Such impressionistic evocations however tend to be exceptional. In many passages the fact of the flight is simply stated without elaboration.

3. See also 15.237–38, and 18.615. It is not altogether clear in these passages whether the god takes the form of the bird or is said to resemble the bird.

I shall show below why I think this is worth noting. But first another feature of the Hermes passage's very simple structure should be noted. The first section, the scene on Olympus, can be subdivided into two parts: one which focuses on Zeus and contains his speech, and a second which describes Hermes' preparations—the donning of sandals and the taking of his staff. Counterparts to this preparation can be found in two other accounts of a divine descent; one involving Zeus himself:

> He spoke, and under the chariot harnessed his bronze-shod horses,
> flying-footed, with long manes streaming of gold; and he put on
> clothing of gold about his own body, and took up the golden
> lash, carefully compacted, and climbed up into his chariot . . . [8.41–44]

and another longer description of Book Five (720–47). There Hebe harnesses the horses of Hera to her chariot, which is described in detail; Athene, who is to accompany Hera, puts off her dress to don Zeus' war tunic, throws her aegis about her shoulders, dons her golden helmet, takes up a huge spear, and steps into the chariot. Hermes' preparation is clearly comparable to these others.

I cite so many accounts of divine descents to show that they constitute what has been called a *theme*.[4] This category of oral poetry contains those recurrent situations or actions, too elaborate for a single formula, which nevertheless appear frequently enough to require some stock treatment from the bard—some stock terms, phrases, and images. Greetings and partings, the arming and the death of a warrior, the taking of a bath, the sacrificial killing of an animal, embarcation—situations as different as these lend themselves to repetitive treatment and become themes. A well-trained bard is able to expand at will a given theme, adding more and more details which are themselves traditional, and indeed he must decide at each recurrence how fully the theme ought to be expanded. Thus many scenes in oral poetry are by nature *elastic*.

It looks as though the divine descent were another such theme

4. A. B. Lord, *The Singer of Tales* (Cambridge, 1960), pp. 68–98.

which Homer inherited along with hundreds of other particular solutions to common poetic problems. If we take the case which is to be our chief concern—the dispatching of a messenger by Zeus—how may we suppose this theme could be most fully expanded according to the conventions of Homer's oral tradition? The best basis for an answer to this is supplied by the *Odyssey,* but the several descents in the *Iliad* taken compositely would point to a similar answer. First Zeus is shown in deliberation on Olympus and his motivations for sending a message are explained. Then he summons the messenger, usually Iris or Hermes, and his message is quoted in direct discourse. The speech is commonly followed by the formula: "He spoke, nor did [Hermes—Iris] disobey him . . ." Thereupon the messenger prepares for the descent. The account of the descent itself may contain an indication of the messenger's lightness and speed, illustrated by a simile; it may also indicate what specific places or what sort of landscape he passes by. Once he has reached his destination, there may be a description of the immediate occupation of the message's recipient. Thus when Iris commands Priam to ransom his son's body, she finds him seated mourning in the palace courtyard, covered with the dung which in his grief he has smeared upon his head. The message is commonly repeated verbatim, with only the syntactic changes necessary for the changed situation and perhaps a few introductory lines. Finally the divine messenger leaves with little further description devoted to him or her, and the narrative goes on to follow the subsequent action of the auditor-hero. If such a sequence is natural, it is not necessarily inevitable. But such was the authority of Homer (and of his imitator, Virgil) in the Renaissance that this precise sequence was followed in dozens of poems.

If you compare the hypothetical expansion of the descent theme to any single descent in the *Iliad,* you see that the poet must have chosen deliberately not to employ the fullest possible version of the theme on any single occasion. On the whole, as I have already remarked, it is the middle section, descriptive of the flight itself, which is omitted, although there is some evidence in the *Iliad,* more evidence in the *Odyssey,* that traditional poetic means were available to the poet, had he chosen to evoke that flight more frequently and fully. He chose rather to suppress the showiest part of the theme, the most brilliant, the most seductive, the most lovingly developed by his imitators. He retained the opening and closing deliberative scenes but suppressed the executive middle. Hermes' descent here remains unique among the long series it opens by the dimness of its visual appeal.

But the art of the entire *Iliad* is an art of visual dimness and imagistic reticence. In the last chapter I drew a distinction between the strong-image and weak-image scenes of epic poetry. The *Iliad* tends as a whole to weaken slightly the image of even its most powerful scenes. It may well be true, as Arnold wrote, that "Homer invariably composed with his eye on the object." [5] But if so, the Homer of the *Iliad* chose only rarely to register in language the object in his eye. There are, certainly, detailed descriptions of things, chiefly implements and accoutrements of war, among which Achilleus' shield is pre-eminent but not unique. But there is little attempt to render in detail the appearance of the things we care most about—the city of Troy, the Greek encampment, a god, or a hero.[6] Occasionally we are given a striking impression of a multitude struggling together in a dusty mass. Occasionally the death of a single warrior is narrated with painfully exact detail. But the poet is clearly not intent on the pictorial entity but the dramatic entity. He gives us the pictorial only when he judges the dramatic to require it, and he so judges more austerely than most poets, including the poet of the *Odyssey*.[7] One prizes for their rareness such fine pictorial strokes as the glimpse of Priam at Hermes' approach:

> . . . the old man's mind was confused, he was badly frightened,

5. Matthew Arnold, *On Translating Homer* (London, Routledge, n.d.), pp. 22–23.

6. "Homer almost never describes anyone's actual appearance. His method is strictly dramatic, emphasizing always deed, motive, and consequence." Cedric Whitman, *Homer and the Heroic Tradition* (Cambridge, 1958), pp. 89–90.

7. I shall not pretend to argue here the question whether a single poet wrote both Homeric poems. I used the name "Homer" for convenience as others have done. My remarks would seem to point to a theory of double authorship, but they are scarcely decisive, and I am not competent to press the argument further.

> and the hairs stood up all over his gnarled body and he
> stood staring . . .

or the beautiful, melancholy sketch of Achilleus' idle encampment which follows the catalogue of ships (2.771–79). These lovely things are rare, but I do not mean to say that Homer's austerity weakens his poem. Rather that austerity contributes to the peculiar sense of space and light which distinguishes the *Iliad.* The flat, even, "vertical" light, void of brilliance or color, tends to mute the exact outlines of things upon that dusty plain. It contrasts with the pure, precise light of the *Odyssey* and its brilliant Mediterranean fullness, light which sharpens outlines, clarifies contours, and which vision penetrates effortlessly. In the encounter of Priam and Hermes there is a universal and deepening twilight through which Hermes advances darkly.

One's sense of the light's evenness is enhanced by the flatness of the Troad, which interposes so few obstacles to one's imaginative vision. There are to be sure the Achaian wall and the bastions of the city, with Mount Ida in the distance, but by far the greater part of the action takes place on the plain between the two, against a low horizon. And so in the battle scenes on that plain, as one follows each individual fighter and each combat, one has a sense of all the other combats round about it, out of focus as it were. Rarely in the *Iliad* does one feel a scene to be contained or *framed,* perhaps because so much of it takes place out-of-doors. The land stretches always about one. How easily the space of the Troad is traversed; how many times the respective armies advance and retreat across it! Its traversibility too stems from its flatness. But this sense of the Troad's openness is always qualified by its opposite, by one's knowledge of the Troad's limits, the confining sea, and of this mortal arena's terrible inescapability. The epic expansiveness is checked by that intense, monotonous confinement. As Hermes appears out of the dark, you feel on the one hand the three figures' isolation in the expanse of the broad plain, but you also feel, more faintly, that to Hermes it is a little place, Hermes whose sandals carry him "over the water as over the dry land of the main abreast of the wind's blast."

We are relieved from the confinement of the Troad, the one

arch-image, by the welcome alternative world of the similes. They permit the imagination refuge on a plane of lower tension and prove, had we no other proof, that Homer was quite capable of masterful description. The finest similes are minor but complete works of art, touching the soil of the narrative by a single slender stem, to exfoliate and blossom in their own air, according to their own laws.[8] The audience's response to the familiar world evoked by the similes contrasts with its awe before the world of the narrative. The poet says implicitly: "You all have seen a man hunting a boar . . ." The similes refer to a plane of repeated, generalized action; the boar is any boar; he requires in translation the indefinite article. (Greek has none.) The similes describe vividly a series of unspecified figures; whereas the narrative proper, which takes care to be specific and commonly accords each warrior as he dies his name, his place of origin, his own individual wound, dims the impressions of these specified individuals. There is much violence in the similes but it is violence-as-usual, the routine violence of herd and farm and sky and sea. And there are many genre scenes of a pastoral serenity. Significantly the Mycenean elements of the narrative tend to disappear in the similes, which seem rather to reflect the culture of Homer's own period.[9]

Is there a functional reason why the familiar plane should be seen distinctly and the heroic more dimly? We cannot suppose any uncertainty in Homer's imagination. Rather we should submit ourselves to that faint mistiness which heightens the extraordinary plane of the heroes, the plane of marvelous history, of the unique event, of the definite article. In part this dimness corresponds to the distance of time across which Homer saw the heroic age. In part it suggests the heroic awe with which he saw it. But it seems to me that were we able to articulate the subtlest elements of our response to this quality, itself so indefinable, we should have to say more than this. We should have to associate

8. Such attempts as those by T. B. L. Webster to rationalize the similes, to demonstrate a "technique of cross-reference," and to multiply correspondences with the main narrative seem to me misguided. This approach ignores not only the technique of oral composition but the effects of contrast within similitude mentioned above. See *From Mycenae to Homer* (London, 1958), pp. 223–39.

9. C. M. Bowra, *Tradition and Design in the Iliad* (Oxford, 1930), p. 221.

this quality of dimness with the very moral and metaphysical perplexities of the poem.

That such perplexities are there no one will argue. The starting point of any moral system—the willed act—is itself a mystery. Priam's decision to visit Achilleus' tent is prompted by the descent of Iris. But Priam at the same time wants to go. No one in the *Iliad* is ever prompted by the gods to do something that repels him or something of which he would otherwise be incapable. Homer permits you to read the divine prompting allegorically, as an inspired idea. But he will not leave you with that reading either; he wants you to imagine Iris literally descending. He leaves you with the mystery of behavior, with a modern sense that a decision, like an emotion, is something that *happens to you.* You are responsible but then again you are not. Agamemnon and Achilleus both agree that the former's folly in angering Chryses and taking Briseis stems from *até,* from irrationality induced by Zeus. Agamemnon pleads this as an excuse in Book Nineteen (85–94), as though it would render him less responsible. But Achilleus speaks of the same *até* to the envoys in Book Nine to justify his continued anger against Agamemnon as though it did *not* render him less responsible. So both the origin and the blame of a decision may be ambiguous. This is why the characters are so dense, so impenetrable, and unpredictable. Even a man's prowess is not constant. The *aristeia* of a Diomedes or an Agamemnon is also something that happens to him, caused in part perhaps by a beneficent god, but not unrelated either to his natural capacity.

The perplexities do not end here. The gods themselves experience emotions, make decisions, which are not clearly functions of their character, which rather are also things which happen to them. As Zeus observes Priam setting out from Troy, he takes pity upon him. Pity is neither typical nor atypical of Zeus. It is simply an event to be accepted, as elsewhere his capricious cruelty must be accepted. Zeus is impenetrable too. One's sense of his unpredictability corresponds to one's sense of insecurity in a world he rules. This insecurity is heightened by the occasional lapses of Zeus' power and knowledge. Hera can gull him. Poseidon might choose to disobey him. Thetis can persuade him because he owes her a debt of gratitude. He is not altogether omnipotent. And besides these complications there is the mysterious force of an individual's *moira,* his fate, which seems stronger than the will of Zeus on those occasions when they are not identified.

All these tangled perplexities, complications, ambiguities, delicate balances of power, combine to unsettle the Homeric universe. Fate and the gods are objective correlatives of the profound Greek sense of metaphysical vagueness. The final consequences of an act cannot be foreseen any more than its ultimate cause can be understood. How hazy is the causation underlying the sequence of events which culminate in Priam's expedition! Hektor's body must be ransomed because Hektor (with help) has killed Patroklos. Why is Patroklos killed? First and simplest, because Apollo is on the scene and sympathetic to Hektor; second, because Patroklos has chosen rashly to disregard Achilleus' advice and to pursue the Trojans beyond the encampment wall. But third, it is rather Zeus who is to blame because he has deluded Patroklos' mind:

> Besotted: had he only kept the command of Peleiades
> he might have got clear away from the evil spirit of black death.
> But always the mind of Zeus is a stronger thing than a man's mind. [16.686–88]

Zeus however has previously indicated that he has no choice in the matter; he predicts the death of Patroklos as early as the eighth book and adds: "This is the way it is fated to be." Patroklos himself, at the moment of his death, affirms that he has been killed by fate, *moira,* and predicts that Hektor will soon die by the same agency.

There is no use in asking what the precise relationships are between chance, human responsibility, fate, and divine will. The poet does not know—or rather he would never formulate such a question. He is discreet; he is even reticent. He does not penetrate too far the ultimate phenomenology of his story any more than he penetrates officiously the mind of Priam as Priam speaks to Hermes. He knows too well the uncertainty of things, and represents it in the very atmosphere of his poem.

Through the mist of confusions there remains however a single unmistakable certainty—the fact of death, the fact which prompts Priam's mission. For the reader as for the hero, the experience of the *Iliad* involves an almost intolerable exposure to death. The *Iliad* indeed is our greatest poem of mortality. It might be possible to read most of Dante's *Commedia* without thinking much about the upsetting *physical* event. But the first image of the *Iliad,* placed in the very invocation, pictures dogs and birds feeding on the corpses of Achaians. And thereafter the poet is pitiless of his audience's sensibility as he details the violent end of each victim, unhurriedly, through book after book. At the conclusion Priam will sit with Achilleus, both soon to die, with the corpse of a third man outside, in an atmosphere heavy with mortality. When you finish the *Iliad,* you know what it is to die. The twin funerals in the closing books serve to release the accumulated grief and shock, not only for Patroklos and Hektor but for the manifold dead of all the poem.

The Achaian warrior's antagonist is not so much the Trojan as it is death itself, and time, flux, oblivion, mutability, operating within the grey ironic perplexities of that dim world. There seems to be little enough hostility between the two camps—little personal animus or what Yeats called "intellectual hatred." One fights because *noblesse oblige,* or more truly, as a critic has remarked, because *la mort oblige,*[10] because death and oblivion can be overcome only through glory. Both motives appear in Sarpedon's famous exhortation to Glaukos, but the second is the more compelling:

> . . . seeing that the spirits of death stand close about us
> in their thousands, no man can turn aside nor escape them,
> let us go on and win glory for ourselves, or yield it to others. [12.326–28]

Combat is less a vendetta than a performance.

Glory is the conventional meed of heroism in the *Iliad* as in most heroic poems; it is valuable because it represents a form of continuity. Glory is a figurative extension of life beyond the pyre,

10. S. E. Bassett, *The Poetry of Homer* (Berkeley, 1938), p. 223.

an extension so prized that one willingly shortens the physical life to lengthen the invisible one. One bargains life for fame, without in the least depreciating the precious value of life. Most of the heroes in the poem are prepared to make that bargain unquestioningly, and doubtless it went altogether unquestioned during earlier stages of oral poetic development. But the bargain *is* questioned explicitly at one point in the poem, and elsewhere by implication. The issue emerges during Achilleus' interview with the envoys, where it appears that Agamemnon's affront has led Achilleus to doubt the very basis of heroic enterprise. The issue is pointed for him by the exclusive alternatives of glory or longevity his fate has posed. Achilleus for one is no longer prepared to make the bargain:

> . . . a man's life cannot come back again, it cannot be lifted
> nor captured again by force, once it has crossed the teeth's barrier . . .
>
> And this would be my counsel to others also, to sail back
> home again, since no longer shall you find any term set on the sheer city of Ilion . . .
>
> [9.408–09, 417–19]

It is true that Achilleus will fight again, but then no longer for glory. That combat *will* be a vendetta. And as we see him at the last, in the somber loneliness of his resignation, the pursuit of glory can only seem a puerile game. He will certainly fight still again, but without purpose or hope, in a ritual suicide. The continuity of glory must appear a pseudo-continuity in the desolation of grief and death. For one hero who has achieved it, it does not suffice. The one supreme value endowed with social authority and poetic prestige is itself beclouded in the poem's swirl of ambivalence.

iii.

The willed acts of men in the *Iliad* are not peculiarly mysterious: the acts and impulses of the gods are equally unpredictable. Most of the divine interventions into human affairs have about them a spontaneity and sometimes even a capriciousness. Although most of the gods harbor fixed sympathies for one or the other camp, only Zeus seems capable of carrying out a sustained plan, and even Zeus, within the limits of his plan, allows himself plenty of eccentric variation. It is important to remember that Hermes, whose affectionate solicitude for Priam seems so genuine at their encounter, has fought with the assailants of Priam's city barely three books earlier. Hermes is sent to Priam as a kind of gift by Zeus, after prodding by Apollo. Little in the nature of the gods would have allowed the reader to foresee such a gift, but this is not to say that it is inconsistent with the gods' behavior through the poem. The gods play many roles, but one of the foremost is their role as givers, as undependable and inexplicable sources of blessings. It is they who give strength and courage and happiness, they who infuse a fighter for an hour or a day with extraordinary prowess; it is they frequently who save a man's life by stopping a spear in his shield, and they who counsel or inspire with exceptional wisdom.

The *Iliad* has often been misapprehended partly because it is so easy to impose upon it the familiar moral and religious categories that come to hand—and so difficult to intuit with sympathetic precision the implicit attitudes which are there. Such has been the case with the Achilleus drama (which critics simplify by introducing tragic flaws and other red herrings) and such is the case if one considers the gods as givers of gifts. For if, in their irregular fashion, they are benefactors, the gods represent no tidy principle of justice as naïve neoclassic readers once supposed. It is true that Priam's expedition results from an appeal to Zeus by Apollo which makes essentially a moral protest: Hektor's body rightfully belongs to his family; Achilleus is without justice or pity; and the wanton humiliation of his enemy serves no honorable purpose. But the absolute justice of the gift to Priam weighs less in Zeus' mind than the sacrifices with which the dead man has gratified him. The gods as givers are less than justicers, nor are they either more or less charitable than men. They give out of whim or favoritism or gratitude for worship but seldom out of anything like pure generosity. And their gifts, such as they are, must never be counted on too much. "The gods," says Nestor with prudent understatement, "give to mortals not everything at the same time" (4.320). Priam is vouchsafed his son's body only as a small mercy between the greater disasters of his son's death and his city's fall. Achilleus is granted his wish to win honor, but only with an added circumstance—Patroklos' death—which renders the wish's fulfillment as dust and ashes. Agamemnon is given an *aristeia* only as a prelude to his humiliation and near-defeat, and Hektor's finest hours anticipate his tragedy. Achilleus' very prowess is given him at the price of an early death. And when he prays that Patroklos beat off the Trojans from the ships and return to him safely, Zeus chooses to grant the first prayer but not the second. The gods do not indeed give everything at the same time, and even when a gift is truly gratuitous, when it involves no price for the receiver, it may well involve the pain of another. For this is an agonistic world where one hero's fulfillment requires the death of his antagonists.

In view of these partial and costly blessings from the gods, one might consider them as sardonic and malicious givers, granting only the letter but not the spirit of the wish, granting too little or too late or the less important half, or granting it all with the one corollary which cancels the benefaction out. There are grounds in the *Iliad* for a conception of the gods as ironists, but this conception too is ultimately fallacious. For the deepest wisdom of the poem lies in a noble and paradoxical reverence for the gods and in gratitude even for their ambivalent gifts. This gratitude is really the burden of Achilleus' consolation of Priam, a consolation which is not vacuous because its achievement for Achilleus has been so recent and so agonized.

The first discovery Priam and Achilleus make about each other is their alikeness in grief. They have neither of them succeeded in receiving the gift of bereavement without protest, and each has befouled himself—Achilleus with dust and Priam with dung—to symbolize the degradation of his wretchedness. But a man's role is to accept the god's gift with grace—whatever it be—and remain open to receive more. Such at least seems to be the purport of Achilleus' speech, after they have both wept, the suppliant and the supplicated, in shared bereavement, and Achilleus has felt his passionate agony purged from him, and has raised Priam to his feet. "Come then," he says, "and sit down upon this chair . . .

> and you and I will even let
> our sorrows lie still in the heart for all our grieving. There is not
> any advantage to be won from grim lamentation.
> Such is the way the gods spun life for unfortunate mortals,
> that we live in unhappiness, but the gods themselves have no sorrows. [24.522–26]

Achilleus mentions the absence of divine suffering without acrimony, and in the myth of Zeus' two urns with which he continues one feels a tempering of that natural self-pity both men have been driven to. In this beautiful speech all human joy and sorrow are considered as the gift of Zeus, distributed unequally among individuals and so mysteriously that Achilleus does not pretend to explain the inequalities. "There are two urns," he says, "that stand on the door-sill of Zeus."

> They are unlike
> for the gifts they bestow: an urn of evils, an urn of blessings.
> If Zeus who delights in thunder mingles these and bestows them
> on man, he shifts, and moves now in evil, again in good fortune.
> But when Zeus bestows from the urn of sorrows, he makes a failure
> of man, and the evil hunger drives him over the shining
> earth, and he wanders respected neither of gods nor mortals.
> Such were the shining gifts given by the gods to Peleus . . .
> But even on him the god piled evil also. There was not
> any generation of strong sons born to him in his great house

but a single all-untimely child he had, and I give him
no care as he grows old, since far from the land of my
fathers
I sit here in Troy, and bring nothing but sorrow to you
and your children.
And you, old sir, we are told you prospered once . . .
But now the Uranian gods brought us, an affliction upon
you,
forever there is fighting about your city, and men killed.
But bear up, nor mourn endlessly in your heart, for there
is not
anything to be gained from grief for your son; you will
never
bring him back; sooner you must go through yet another
sorrow. [24.527–34, 538–43, 547–51]

The myth of the urns and the foreboding conclusion might have justified a response contrary to the one Achilleus enjoins; they might have been expected to justify an utter yielding to despair. From his present vantage, Priam's former felicity is slight enough consolation to him. But Achilleus' simple observation that many men are given good with evil invokes implicitly the radical Greek sense of the value of life, an instinct and a faith which not even tragedy suppresses altogether. On the contrary, that instinct renders conceivable the tragic resignation into which both men are growing. For Achilleus is speaking to himself as well as to Priam, and when a few lines below, he reasserts the claims of life by urging his guest to eat, we recall his own earlier refusal to eat in the face of Odysseus' remonstrances (19.145–237).

By coming to accept the gods' gifts, which is to say the painful partiality of life, Achilleus achieves an understanding which is fundamental to epic poetry.[11] In Auden's phrase he "finds the mortal world enough." Like Gilgamesh, Achilleus has been forced to discover death through the loss of a comrade, and the grief of both heroes involves anguish for their own mortality. Gilgamesh never overcomes that anguish but Achilleus, in his strange communion with Priam, does find himself suddenly and inexplicably

11. See above, Chapter 2, pp. 12–14.

liberated. Just as the gods' gifts sometimes prove treacherous, so this deprivation by the gods becomes a blessing. Achilleus recognizes without protest the limits of human life and heroic capacity. The first and greatest of Western epics ends with the kind of recognition scene which is peculiar to epic.

iv.

The slender and paradoxical affirmation which makes the *Iliad's* ending bearable is strengthened by the emergence of two particular values, two forms of continuity set over against the flux. The first of these is fatherhood, the continuity of genealogy. The last book reveals the *Iliad* as a great poem of fatherhood. When Hermes, taking Priam's hand, says "You seem to me like a beloved father," the words and the gesture sound a note already familiar in the poem, but now at its close to be echoed more persistently and beautifully. The story is full of fathers—Zeus, to begin with, whose title, "Father of the gods," is not the least of his epithets, and Nestor, and Menoitios (whom we never see but whose name weighs heavily when invoked at a critical moment—11.764–90), and Phoinix, Achilleus' touchingly paternal foster father, and Achilleus himself, and Hektor, whose celebrated encounter with wife and child colors with its humanity all of the later action in which he figures. Not much is made of Achilleus' son, Neoptolemus, but his quasi-paternal relation to Patroklos is underscored by a significant simile. Achilleus mourns at Patroklos' funeral as "a father mourns as he burns the bones of a son" (23.222). He mourns as the bereaved Zeus has wept for Sarpedon

> . . . whom now Patroklos was presently
> to kill, by generous Troy and far from the land of his
> fathers. [16.460–61]

Even the last phrase, formulaic as it is, is rich with tragic meaning. Priam's own paternity is insisted upon at the outset of his mission, as he chides his surviving sons (24.247–64). He is comically petulant and choleric here, as perhaps he needs to be if his later greatness is to be credible. Hermes in his turn will speak of a fictive father—"Polyktor, a man of substance, but aged as you are" (24.398)—and we are reminded that a man's very identity is involved with his father's. But the motif of fatherhood reaches its highest dramatic resonance only when Priam enters his enemy's shelter and begins to speak:

> Achilleus like the gods, remember your father, one who
> is of years like mine . . .

This proves miraculously the right thing to have said. Achilleus weeps, now for Peleus and now for Patroklos, and after the tears relieve his long bitterness, he himself alludes, in his reply, to a likeness between Peleus and Priam. It is possible doubtless to make too much of the communion between king and hero; they both understand its necessary limitations. Yet, for a moment, there is a quasi-paternal gentleness between them, and an overwhelming recognition of the dignity of fatherhood. Now, during this pause in the violence, the prestige of heroism counts for much less.

The second form of continuity to emerge at the poem's close is represented by the funeral. I spoke above of the funerals' purgative effect upon the reader, but one may still ask why within the fictive world a funeral is of such transcendent importance as to justify a divine intervention. Why are the bodies of Patroklos and other fallen warriors fought over so bitterly at the risk of more lives? Because a funeral is an answer to death, a partial, inadequate answer, certainly, but an assertion nonetheless that man can contain death within his scheme of things.[12] It incorporates death within the other events, foreseen and unforeseen, of a man's life; and it demonstrates, however great the honor due his valor, that his loss is not unique, that his is the last in a series of losses which the community has always known how to deal with. This sense of continuity doubtless remains unformulated in the archaic mind. But one intuits it even when it is mingled with the contrary sentiment: that the loss of a hero is irreparable. Even as the women lament Hektor's uniqueness in the poem's closing lines, they lament within a containing social context that is like other contexts for other laments. Tradition stylizes their grief, as it

12. The belief that the soul of an unburied man cannot enter Hades is alluded to in the *Iliad* (23.69 ff.), but is not stressed in the case of Hektor.

could not before the body was recovered and a ritual made possible. And even as the burning and the burial dramatize the loss of a great man, they begin to heal the wound of his passing and to absorb disaster into continuing history.

Neither gods nor men formulate this conception but they all understand it at some unspoken level. Thus the gift to Priam of his son's body involves a tacit gesture to the continuity of social tradition. It honors the decencies of the ordered community, even though this particular community is doomed. This continuity is not necessarily more enduring than heroic glory, but in the desolation of lost hope its consolation is noble and peaceful.

The style and meter of the *Iliad* are particularly well suited to these themes. Not only is the language formulaic, and thus in a sense ritualistic, but the long, swift-flowing lines seem to accentuate in a subtle way their own unhesitating continuity. The Homeric hexameter contrasts both with the short, heavily punctuated line of *Beowulf,* which requires frequent pauses, and with the quicker but end-stopped and caesural line of the *chansons de geste.* In Homer there are few pauses of any kind. The division into twenty four books was made not long after the poems' composition but not by the poet himself, and although the breaks are convenient and well-chosen, they alter faintly one's impression of the poems as they were originally composed. To have the truer impression one must imagine the *Iliad* without any breaks at all, for even though no bard could chant so long a poem without interrupting himself, he would have considered the interruptions fortuitous. The poem as its creator conceived it ran from its first line to the last with only the natural divisions of line and episode. To hear that poem one has to imagine a voice which is forever onflowing, forever renewing itself, reiterating the cadence of the hexameter over and over, serene and even and equal to itself, measuring the variety of feeling with its steady and tolerant rhythm. Part of the poet's manner of detached, Olympian control stems from the evenness of his tone despite the variations of pathos and violence in the successive scenes he describes. And this evenness, in turn, must partly stem from the exigencies of oral composition. A modern performer who wanted to imitate the chant of a Homeric rhapsode would surely be misguided to suit his voice's intensity to the episode he describes; he ought rather to present the story as Homer does, with reverent imperturbability.

It is dangerous to dogmatize about the artistic effect of Homeric formulas, but I am inclined to feel that they too acquire an extraordinary charm because their regularity is so welcome, that they soften by repetition the harsh abruptnesses of death and oblivion, that they pierce the perplexing dimness with assertions of identity. Were you to remove them all; were you to introduce each divine descent with a different phrase, rather than the recurrent:

> He spoke, nor disobeyed him . . .

were each victim's death described in different terms without any familiar repetition:

> He fell, thunderously, and his armour clattered upon him . . .

were the Achaians not repeatedly "strong-greaved" nor Athene "grey-eyed" nor Hermes "Argeïphontes"—the Argus-slayer—then, I submit, the terror of the *Iliad* would be even more intolerable. The fixed epithets tend significantly to become honorific. It is reassuring, in a world of so little assurance, to know that Zeus, whatever his caprices, will remain a cloud-gatherer, and that the Dawn, whatever it brings, will appear with rosy fingers. Whatever happens to men or nations, their attributes remain harmoniously predictable.

The language of the *Iliad* is not the language of enthusiastic wonder; it is not demonstrative or exclamatory. But it communicates heroic awe nonetheless, while abstaining from vulgar praise. Some modern critics, missing the humility which underlies heroic awe, have reached misguided moralistic interpretations of Homer. But the poet is not quick to officious moral judgment. The imperturbability of his tone is more than a stylistic accident. He is truly tolerant; he accepts men as he accepts the gods; the existence of suffering does not lead him to look for a culprit. He is aware, to be sure, of degrees of heroism; his awe is proportioned to its object, and for those who merit no awe at all—such as Paris and Thersites—he registers awe's opposite, scorn. But he is not presumptuous enough to make flat moral judgments. If Achilleus rejects the offers of Agamemnon's envoys, the poet wonders at the intensity of Achilleus' continuing anger, but it never occurs to him to condemn it. Condemnation for such conduct would only spring from habits of thoughts that developed in later centuries, in periods less sensitive to the world's ambiguous uncertainties.

The awe which produced the *Iliad* is an awe for physical strength and endurance, for valor, for the transcendent, inscrutable, imperfectly generous gods, for the intensity of men's passions —love and anger and grief, for the magnitude of their suffering, and for the religious wisdom that grows out of the worst suffering. There is awe for the fullness, the pitch of human life in a universe governed by death. It is not a sentiment which concerns itself with juridical pedantries. But it is concerned with the mind and spirit as well as the body. The *Iliad* was to be so healthy an influence on later poetry because it maintained so finely divided an interest between the outer and inner worlds. This is a balance not quite maintained in the *Odyssey,* whose hero changes far less than Achilleus, but recaptured, more self-consciously, by Virgil, a balance which the Renaissance appreciated even while failing to emulate it. Perhaps so discreet a balance between the two worlds can only be struck by a society which does not fully distinguish them.

4. FORM AND CRAFT IN THE ODYSSEY

i.

The *Odyssey* contains only two episodes which derive from the theme of the divine descent. The first and shorter of these appears early in Book One, where it forms a transition from the opening dialogue on Olympus to the subsequent scene at Ithaca. Athene first announces her intention of sending Telemachus upon a journey and then goes on to make the necessary preparations. She takes her great spear and dons sandals, whose properties are described in precisely the same formulaic language as are Hermes' sandals. The account of her descent is brief: [1]

> Downward she now glided from the summit of Olympus, to alight on Ithaca before Odysseus' house, by the sill of the main gate. With that war spear in her fist she seemed some

1. *The Odyssey of Homer,* trans. T. E. Shaw (New York, 1951), p. 3. All quotations are given in Shaw's translation. References hereafter will be made first to this edition and then to the book and line of the Greek text.

> traveller seeking hospitality: she had a look of Mentes, a chief in Taphos. [1.102–05]

Athene intervenes in many other earthly situations throughout the poem but she is never represented elsewhere as descending to do so.

The second divine descent in the *Odyssey* constitutes the fullest development of the theme in either Homeric poem. It appears in Book Five and serves again as a transition from Olympus to earth. At this second, briefer Olympian council Zeus executes a suggestion Athene had made at the first one: he dispatches Hermes to order Calypso's release of Odysseus.

> He turned to Hermes, the son he loved, and said, "Hermes, hear your commission as our particular messenger. Inform this nymph of the love-locks of my fixed decision that long-suffering Odysseus shall return home as best he can, without furtherance from gods or mortal men. Therefore he is to lash together a raft as firm as may be, on which after twenty days of hazard and disaster he will make rich-glebed Scheria, the Phaeacian land." [pp. 69–70; 5.28–35]

Zeus goes on to foretell the Phaeacians' generous reception of Odysseus and the hero's subsequent homecoming, although these have little to do with Hermes' immediate mission to Ogygia. (Hermes, as it happens, will not even mention the raft to Calypso, although she will suggest it to Odysseus.) When Zeus concludes, Hermes' donning of sandals and taking of staff are narrated in seven lines identical with their counterparts in the *Iliad*. But once these formulaic gestures have been made, the account of Hermes' descent is amplified by a brief geographical indication and by a striking simile, and these are followed in turn by a very full and beautiful description of his destination.

> . . . with [the staff] in hand the Argus-slayer leaped out upon the air and flew strongly. Over mount Pierus he dived down from the firmament to sea level: and then along the waves he sped like a cormorant which down the dread troughs of the wild sea chases its fish and drenches its close plumage in

> the salt spume. Just so did Hermes skim the recurring wave-crests.
>
> But when at last he attained that remote island, he quitted the purple sea and went inland as far as the great cave in which lived the nymph of the well-braided hair. He chanced to find her within where a great fire burned on its appointed hearth, perfuming the island far across with the fragrance of flaming cedar-wood logs and straight-grained incense trees. Inside the cavern the nymph's sweet voice could be heard singing as she went to and fro before her loom, weaving with a golden shuttle. All round the cave-mouth there flourished a luxuriant copse of alder trees and black poplars and rich-scented cypresses: therein roosted birds of long wing, owls and hawks and chattering hook-billed crows—birds of the sea whose livelihood was from the waters. A young strong vine loaded with bunches of grapes wreathed the opening of the cave. Four springs quite near together jetted out translucent water in separate rills ingeniously contrived, each to water its own garden-plot. The soft lawns were starred with parsley and violets. Even an immortal coming upon the nook would pause before its beauty and feel his heart made glad: the messenger, Argus' bane, halted in amazement.
>
> When his heart had taken its fill of wondering, he entered the great cave: nor was his figure strange to Calypso, the very goddess, when she saw him come into her presence. (It is a gift to the gods, to know one another when they meet, however distant the home of one of them may chance to lie.) In the cavern he did not find great-hearted Odysseus, who sat weeping on the shore as was his wont, crying out his soul with groaning and griefs and letting flow his tears while he eyed the fruitless sea. [pp. 70–71; 5.49–84]

This expansion of the descent theme may serve to measure the distance between the two poems. It is not enough to say that the *Odyssey* contains more description, or that its narrative image, episode by episode, tends to be stronger. The tautness of the *Iliad* is here relaxed to permit a certain urbane leisure, and its austerity gives way to an indulgence of the senses: four are invoked in this description. Dramatic intensity is sacrificed, a little, for imagistic pleasure. You feel that the poet is a man who can afford to take his time, to linger, even, over the scenes he most enjoys. He is in no haste to open the dialogue which is about to take place. But he is, at the same time, quite firmly in control; he knows, usually, what is relevant to the story, and he is seldom garrulous in the bad sense. He has the wisdom not to amplify Athene's earlier descent when it is Hermes' he wants to make the most of.

I have already spoken of the precise, Mediterranean clarity of things in the *Odyssey* and of the pure light which leaves contours sharp. The space of this world can be penetrated effortlessly by our vision, so that the luminosity and elegance of the several arch-images are apprehended undimmed. So it is with the lovely garden in Ogygia. This visual property of the *Odyssey's* space has a corollary in the properties of movement within it, for movement too is easy here. The splendid dynamic simile of the cormorant renders expressively the verve of Hermes' flight. The first half of the *Odyssey* is a great poem of voyage because it creates a world which is penetrable as well as alluring: like most remote worlds, this one contains the disagreeable along with the romantic, but more than most it gives you a sense of freedom as you explore it. You must suffer, doubtless, if you voyage, and few men would face the hazards, but should you choose to face them, why then the marvelous world is there, after all, for the seeing. This sense of amplitude and liberty is a hallmark of epic space. In the *Odyssey* the heroic will is situated proudly against a landscape less confined than the Troad of the *Iliad.*

There are perhaps not one tenth as many similes in the *Odyssey* as in the *Iliad.* This may be because the *Odyssey* does not require the particular relief which they afford the circumscribed space in Troy. The *Odyssey* does not need the contrast of another plane, because it juxtaposes within the narrative so many planes, locales, arch-images. It does not need the reassurance of familiar crises because its fictive crises are not so intolerable. It does not need so frequently the elaborated image of the simile, because its narrative image is generally strong. If the *Odyssey* contained as many similes as the *Iliad,* page by page, it would seem glutted. The cormorant one is effective despite its proximity to the following description, because it remains discreetly brief. The circumstantiality reserved for similes in the *Iliad* is here transferred—not consistently, to be sure, but frequently—to the theatres of the epic action.

The clarity of things and places in the *Odyssey* implies a world which can be known and reckoned with and coped with. The true greatness of Odysseus can only be understood to contrast to the other Homeric heroes: Achilles, Menelaus, Ajax, and above all Agamemnon, whose fate is knelled from the first book to the last. All these others, in various ways, are unable to control the consequences of their acts, through ignorance or miscalculation or naïveté. Odysseus is great because in the long run he copes with his destiny, he calculates accurately the consequences of his behavior. He copes indeed with a much more diverse and bewildering destiny than anyone else's. He is fallible, to be sure, and he is baffled occasionally by ironies and perverse enigmas reminiscent of the *Iliad*. His universe is not unfamiliar. But it is not, ultimately, tragic, because it reveals itself to the shrewd eye. It is often deceptive but not unknowable. So as Hermes approaches this beautiful grotto on Ogygia (and it is our first approach, too, as readers) we may intuit a subtle perversity underlying the loveliness (as on Circe's island) but the secret in the goddess' heart is made manifest quite soon. And so the tears of Odysseus might be deceptive, might lead us to mis-estimate him and his destiny, but his opening words, skeptical and wary, will give us immediately the key to his nature. Although like the heroes of the *Iliad* he suffers from things which happen to him, he is much more responsible than they for the sum of his behavior. This responsibility is both the prize of his own astuteness and the condition of a less muddled universe.

The sense of fate, *moira,* is weaker here, and the gods who matter are fewer and more comprehensible. They even seem, at moments, to be struggling toward a rough justice. Hermes' descent results from an appeal by Athene to Zeus based on the injustice of Odysseus' plight, and this appeal is heard. We must not exaggerate, however, the clarity and benevolence of Zeus' motives. He decrees that long-suffering Odysseus is to reach Phaeacia unaided by man or god, and only after "twenty days of hazard and disaster." But this latter condition, which seems to be a decree, may simply be a prophecy. Zeus appears to speak as absolute arbiter of the gods although in fact he seems usually to act as arbitrator. The name of Poseidon, away among the Ethiopians, is not pronounced at this second council, but the thought of him is clearly not absent from Zeus' mind. In comparison with his counterpart in the *Iliad,* the Zeus of this poem is something of a figurehead. His first words express vexation at the unfounded (as he says) grievances of mortals against Olympus. The earlier Zeus would never have stooped to such petulance.

The gods who really count in the *Odyssey* are Athene and Poseidon. This simplifies the story enormously, because human destiny is not the resultant of a half-dozen wills working confusedly at cross-purposes (and themselves overshadowed by fate), but rather the creation of a human will, however crippled by misfortune, a will alternately abetted and frustrated by two divinities whose motives can be relied upon. Neither is inscrutable, and that circumstance permits the human intelligence to come into its own.

We feel impressionistically that Hermes does not have far to descend from Olympus to the sea. In the Renaissance, the movement of the celestial messenger is generally vertical, emphasizing the *aboveness* of heaven. But here it is mostly horizontal, emphasizing the distance of Ogygia. The gods are above, but they are not so very awesomely, mysteriously, remotely above. We may divine a certain domestication of the gods, a certain dwindling of their grandeur, behind the religion of the *Odyssey.* The poem does not altogether confirm the relation implied by Odysseus' generalization: "Of all that creep and breathe upon her, Earth breeds no feebler thing than man" (p. 250; 18.130–31). A man's ultimate destiny remains, as Odysseus says, in the hands of the gods, but a man is not by nature so contemptible that the gods will necessarily disregard his will. They may even be—as Athene is, in the case of Odysseus—passionately concerned about its fulfillment.

It is important, however, that Hermes does not descend to prod Odysseus into anything, as Iris prods Priam in the *Iliad,* as Athene prods Telemachus, as Mercury prods Aeneas, and as the celestial messenger commonly does in Renaissance epic. There is not any moral pressure from the gods upon the hero. The will of Odysseus is a constant which is known, unwavering, not to be tampered with. The tears he sheds bear witness, not to his weakness but to the firmness of his will. Hermes needs simply to remove a barrier to its fulfillment.

This simplicity of Odysseus' values is another factor which clears the air of the *Odyssey*. He never doubts them, as Achilles does after the quarrel with Agamemnon. He may be tempted momentarily to despair—as when his sailors open Aeolus' sack of winds—but his resolution to endure always triumphs. He may have to choose between two forms of good—as when he chooses to remain with Circe for a year before attempting to go home. In the same way he has chosen to remain voluntarily with Calypso during his first years with her. Now his desire to return outweighs her attractiveness. It is an elementary decision. After his feelings change, he is untroubled by remorse for his undomestic backwardness. He is incapable of any deep-seated doubt, any division within himself.

This is why the action of the *Odyssey* is mostly external, visible, objective. Even though it depends upon the courage of its protagonist, it is not the story of that courage. It is the story of events which occur in space and which we apprehend primarily with our senses. In this regard the *Odyssey* resembles many other heroic poems, but it does not resemble many of the poems considered in this study. The Renaissance epic, under the influence of Virgil and of Christianity, was generally to weight moral achievement as heavily as physical achievement. But Odysseus is purged of nothing; he learns nothing and improves little; he acts and endures. So the luminosity which plays over the surface of things in the poem is a true luminosity; it rightly leads us to expect a drama we can follow with our eyes. The other faculties are most certainly called into play, but they must bend themselves more intently to the discipline of the objective thing.

ii

The important question about Calypso's garden is whether it is artificial. The opening lines of its description seem to imply that the "copse" is wild. But allusion is later made to the four springs "ingeniously contrived" to water their respective plots, and the parsley and violets studding the lawn seem to be there by design. This may lead us to wonder about the transitional detail: the grapevine which enwreathes the cave's entrance. May not this also represent deliberate training? Doubtless one is not meant to wonder too precisely, but rather to enjoy. This, indeed, is the real point: the garden is as artificial as it needs to be to afford the fullest appreciation. The god himself is bewitched by the beauty, and so might well be the human audience. For the garden is an object of contemplation; it is an esthetic object from which one stands aside and admires. As such it again measures the distance between this poem and the *Iliad,* where (as we see it chiefly through the similes) nature is destructive, familiar, awesome, wearying, joyful, but seldom to be admired dispassionately, never felt as over against the observing self. Here, however, as Hermes pauses to enjoy, the garden *is* outside of him, as it would remain equally outside a human observer. It is an object of admiration as it has been, partly, an object of cultivation and "training." It is half-way toward being an artifact.

Wholly finished artifacts abound in the *Odyssey.* The poet's characteristic way of evoking an arch-image is to begin with representative objects, and when the arch-image is a well-appointed house—like the home of Odysseus and the palaces of Menelaus and Alcinous—its artifacts serve to demonstrate its wealth. The socio-economic arrangement of gift-friendship affords the poet occasion to dwell upon particularly precious things—like the gifts Menelaus and Helen make Telemachus. On Ogygia the poet chooses to enhance most the garden, but he mentions also Calypso's golden shuttle and the "splendid polished throne" whereon Hermes seats himself. The opening scene at Ithaca is richest of all in artifacts, suitable for the entertainment of a goddess:

> Telemachus led the way into the noble house. Pallas followed until he set her spear in *the polished spear rack* beside a *high pillar,* amongst *weapons* once used by the long-suffering Odysseus. Then he spread *smooth draperies* over *a throne of cunning workmanship* and seated her upon it. For her feet

> there was *a foot-stool,* while for himself he drew up *a painted lounge-chair* . . .
>
> A maid came with *a precious golden ewer* and poured water for them above *its silver basin,* rinsing their hands. She drew to their side *a gleaming table* and on it . . . arranged her store of bread and many prepared dishes . . . A carver filled and passed them *trenchers of meat* in great variety, and set out on their table *two golden beakers* which the steward, as often as he walked up and down the hall, refilled for them with wine. [p. 4; 1.125–43]

Later, when Telemachus retires, Eurycleia hangs his "long clinging tunic" on a peg by the "fretted, inlaid bedstead" and goes out drawing the door by "the silver beak which served as handle," sliding the bolt by its leather thong, leaving her young master covered by "a choice fleece."

What is the effect of this Balzacian plenitude? It demonstrates wealth, to be sure, but it demonstrates slightly more—something I have adumbrated by the adjective "well-appointed." It suggests that the masters of the home are people of taste and decorum, refined enough to live in the high style, knowledgeable enough to value precious things. It creates a reassuring ambience of amplitude and ritual, courtesy and grace, like the "house where all's accustomed, ceremonious" which Yeats wished for his daughter. The reception of Athene is an aristocratic ritual which is the polar opposite of that other aristocratic ritual—heroic combat. The weapons of Odysseus in their rack do not fit ill into the scene of Athene's reception, but the activity they symbolize is now in abeyance. Hospitality has its own rules, its own form, which Telemachus demonstrably knows.

This feeling for decorum is very highly developed in the *Odyssey.* It informs the otherwise meaningless statement that a fire burns in Calypso's cave *on its appointed hearth;* it informs the epithet "the nymph of the well-braided hair." It informs very strongly the dialogue between the goddess and the god who knows he is bringing her unwelcome news. Her good form as hostess is impeccable and his, in the role requiring diplomacy and tact, is equally fine.

> Calypso, the fair goddess, made Hermes seat himself on a

splendid polished throne, and asked him, "Hermes of the gold rod, ever honoured and welcome, from of old you have had no habit of visiting me: why do you come here to-day? Tell me your mind. My spirit is eager to second your desire if its fulfillment be in my gift and such a thing as may lawfully be fulfilled. Yet first enter further into the cave that I may put before you the meed of guests." With such words did the goddess bring forward a table bounteously set with ambrosia. She blended him ruddy nectar. Then did the messenger, Argus' bane, drink and eat: but when he had dined and made happy his spirit with the food, he opened his mouth and said:—

"As goddess to god you ask me, you order me, to tell why I have come. Hear the truth of it! Zeus commanded my journey: by no choice of my own did I fare to you across so unspeakable a waste of salt water. Who would willingly come where there is no near city of men to offer sacrifice to the gods and burn us tasty hundreds of oxen? Listen: in no way can another god add or subtract any title from the will of Zeus, the aegis-bearer. He declares that you have with you the unhappiest man of men—less happy than all those who fought for nine years round the citadel of Priam and in the tenth year sacked the city and went homeward . . . The wind blew him and the sea washed him to this spot. Wherefore now the Father commands that you send him hence with speed: for it is decreed that he is not to die far from his friends . . ."

[pp. 71–72; 5.85–113]

Both gods manifest their refinement by their restraint. Calypso is curious but insists that her guest refresh himself before he speaks. Hermes leads up gradually to his painful message, avoiding any breath of accusation in his résumé of the past. ("The sea washed him to this spot. Wherefore now the Father commands . . .") He suppresses the harsh things said of Calypso at the divine council, and he is at pains to dissociate himself from its outcome. At the same time he reminds her that Zeus' will is inalterable. Discreetly he says nothing of what he knows regarding Odysseus' future. His accomplishments as a courier are distinguished. Calypso's anguish is dramatized by the breakdown of *her* manners when she turns upon Hermes to reply: "Cruel are you gods and immoderately jealous of all others . . ."

The value placed on social form by this poet aligns him, *mutatis mutandis,* with other students of aristocratic manners—Castiglione, Lady Murasaki, Saint Simon, James, and Proust. The comparison is not grotesque, but it leads one to consider how many, so to speak, are the *mutandis.* I think the greatest difference lies in the *insecurity* of form within Homeric society. In the books of these other writers, form is taken for granted and serves simply as a basis for some ulterior comedy or wisdom. But in the *Odyssey* it is much more precious because it coexists with vulgarity, brutality, and monstrosity. It is still something hard-won. So Menelaus' anger is all the more heavy in Book Four when his gatekeeper asks what to do with the unidentified guests.

I have used the word *form* deliberately because it can be applied to the gifts of Menelaus, the bedstead of Telemachus, the garden of Calypso, as well as the diplomacy of Hermes. All these things depend upon knowledge of techniques, upon civilized arts which distinguish cultured men from human or animal brutes. Just as Hephaestus works silver and Demodocus composes lays, just as the natural beauty of the garden has been wrought to a higher loveliness, so the capacity to order and manipulate a social situation is a technique to be learned, a *techné*—and it is the highest of all techniques. Those who are most proficient not only follow the rules but use them to gain prestige, influence, and gifts. Odysseus is the greatest artist or technician of the poem because in addition to his good manners he has the poise, shrewdness, perception, and wit to impose the form of his own will upon a community like the Phaeacian. He is able to be as cruel as, but no more cruel than, he needs to be to Nausicaa. He is a virtuoso and his conduct at Scheria from beginning to end is a little masterpiece of his craft. When he opens his long narrative with a tribute to his auditors:

> Lord Alcinous, most eminent, we are in very deed privileged to have within our hearing a singer whose voice is so divinely pure. I tell you, to my mind the acme of intelligent delight is

> reached when a company sits feasting in some hall, by tables garnished with bread and meat, the while a musician charms their ears and a cup-bearer draws them wine and carries it round served ready for their drinking. Surely this, as I say, is the best thing in the world. [p. 120; 9.2–11]

when Odysseus says this he is at once praising the poetic art of Demodocus and the Phaeacian art of living, and demonstrating his own elegant artistry. The two meanings of *craft* touch; cunning and technique blend into a supreme *savoir faire*. After he leaves Ogygia, the form of the narrative becomes increasingly the product of the hero's contrivance.

Because these ostensibly unheroic qualities count for so much in the poem, the distinction between executive and deliberative episodes tends to blur. Strictly speaking there are only one or two executive episodes (as I have used the term) in the first eight books: the encounter with Proteus (4.431–586) and the voyage by raft (Book Five). And although Books Nine to Twelve are consistently executive, the second half of the poem is deliberative with the exception of Book Twenty-Two and the closing lines of the last. This predominance explains how Aristotle could have called the *Odyssey* as a whole an ethical epic. But in fact the two types tend to move toward each other. The episode in Polyphemus' cave, which reminds one of folk tale and might have been written as pure narrative, acquires a deliberative tinge through its emphasis on trickery and comedy. And on the other hand, the episodes at Menelaus' and Alcinous' palaces, like the briefer one in Calypso's cave, differ from most deliberative episodes by the strength of their visual image and the dramatic weight they must bear. If social accomplishment can influence one's destiny, then a banqueting hall can test a man's capacity, contain a sort of *agon*. *Ethos* and *mythos*, manners and action, begin to fuse.

iii

In his embassy to Calypso Hermes suppresses his sympathies for Odysseus, just as in the *Iliad* he has concealed his Achaian sympathies from Priam. But his gift of moly on Aeaea indicates that

Odysseus is in his favor. I have remarked that epic poems tend to be about politics. The politics of this Olympus are not complex, but the issue of Odysseus' fate does lead to a rudimentary alignment against Poseidon. Athene agitates actively on the hero's behalf, Hermes less consistently; Zeus is hostile after the Thrinacian disaster, but later throws his weight with them at the diplomatic moment. This incipient power struggle works itself out in the human action of the poem, and we might, if we chose, extend the conflict of the Athene-principle and Poseidon-principle even to those episodes where neither god appears. Doubtless such a reading would exceed the cognitive experience of Homer's audience, but it would not violate the poem at its most suggestive and profound.

We might trace then a politics pitting the forces of the land and of civilization against the forces of the sea and brute mindlessness. It is the struggle, in essence, of intelligence against force, order against incoherence, the urban against the rustic, aristocracy against democracy, historical achievement against flux, form against matter. One might sum up the values of the land, the values of Athene and Odysseus, by playing as I have played on the double meanings of the word *form* and the related word *craft.*

The sea is by its nature the element which cannot be controlled; it can at best be put to use through the uncertain art of navigation. When the sea is unruly, Odysseus is most nearly helpless. He has no opposing mind to work upon, nothing to manipulate with his art. He is pitted against pure force. The figure in the poem closest to the sea is Polyphemus, whose brute stupidity is almost as destructive. It is no coincidence that he is Poseidon's son. There are other embodiments of the same unruly force—the Lestrygonians, Scylla and Charybdis, and even those sailors under Odysseus' loose command who open Aeolus' sack of winds, refuse to retire after the victory at Ismarus, and kill the oxen of Helios. Calypso (like Circe) is an ambiguous figure. The remoteness and littleness of her isle in the vast sea, the very water birds roosting at her door, suggest a connection with the sea, which has washed Odysseus to her. But she at least is beautiful and gracious, if subtly dangerous. The one fully realized incarnation of sea-monstrosity is Polyphemus.

The important things about the Cyclops are related before the episode proper begins—in the quasi-sociological remarks Odysseus makes about them at the outset. They are people who cultivate not even the basic arts:

> We came to the land of the arrogant iniquitous Cyclopes who so leave all things to the Gods that they neither plant nor till: yet does plenty spring up unsown and unploughed, of corn and barley and even vines with heavy clusters: which the rains of Zeus fatten for them. They have no government nor councils nor courts of justice: but live in caves on mountain tops, each ruling his wives and children and a law unto himself, regardless . . . The Cyclopes have no ruddle-cheeked ships, nor shipwrights to make them such seaworthy vessels for pleasuring among the cities of mankind, like those ordinary men who tempt the seas to know others and to be known.
>
> [p. 123; 9.105–15, 125–30]

Odysseus goes on to make clear how rich the soil is, how fine the port, how easy the pursuit of the civilized arts might have been, had the Cyclops chosen to pursue them. Polyphemus' lack of breeding is manifest the moment he opens his mouth: he asks the one question never to be asked a guest before he refreshes himself: "Why strangers, who are you and where have you come from?" This lapse of *savoir faire* is seconded by his boast that he is too big to fear the gods. With this he brands himself a hopeless barbarian and his subsequent violations of the hospitality code come naturally in the course of things.

For religion too is partly a matter of knowledge in the *Odyssey*, of training, culture, rules, and form. The early Greeks never conceived of a human love for the gods (with the possible exception of Athene).[2] But the civilized man was wise enough to know that Zeus must be propitiated. Nestor is the outstanding figure of the devout man in the *Odyssey*, and as I have suggested, it is fitting that his sacrifice of a heifer should be the sacrifice most fully detailed in the poem. The details assure you that it is performed according to the rules, punctiliously, *religiously*. And just as Nestor's

2. See E. R. Dodds, *The Greeks and the Irrational* (Berkeley and Los Angeles, 1956), p. 35.

piety is a form of his wisdom, so the impiety of the suitors is a token of their stupidity.

The suitors have no ostensible link with the sea, as Polyphemus has, but they represent in the Ithacan episodes the same principles of ignorance, disorder, barbarousness, and religious irreverence. These drunken unruly louts never sacrifice a bull and never recognize a divine omen. Antinous reveals his ignorance when he laughs at Telemachus' new assurance after the visit of Athene:

> Why, Telemachus, those very gods must have been giving you lessons in freedom of speech . . . [p. 12; 1.384–85]

Antinous is precisely the man never to imagine that a visitor might be a god. He is too provincial. The real crime of the suitors, their unpardonable crime, is their lack of breeding. They have no form and no *savoir faire*. They are condemned not only by the poet but by Zeus himself. Hermes descends in part to free Odysseus to kill the suitors.

The suitors are an offense to economy, to morality, and to esthetic decorum, and their liquidation, however unesthetic it looks, justifies itself in all these realms. It is the poem's major imposition of form on disorder, the major victory for the forces of civilization, and it is proper that the definition of this victory require nine or ten books. The form it imposes is a living form, a situation in history, a set of domestic, social, and political relations which are felicitous and proper. It restores that aristocratic elegance, ritual of custom, and appreciation of fine objects, which render living in the high style a form of art.

Odysseus however does not remain long to enjoy these pleasures; he will leave, not altogether reluctantly, to wander until he discovers the symbolic people who know nothing of the sea, who cannot recognize an oar. He must wander to the ends of the world, to encounter more hardships and marvels. Should we regard this fate as a turning away from civilization, from form? It might appear so, but I think the question is not so simple. There has always been in Odysseus, side by side with his nostalgia for civilization, a taste for the exotic and the hostile, a taste for braving the sea to reach the far shore—not touristic curiosity, but an exhilaration in the encounter between Odysseus the man and the marvelous or monstrous, the more or less than human. It affords the pleasure of measuring the self against the non-self, the pleasure of perceiving, apprehending, knowing that other opposing thing, of encountering it without defeat and of possibly overcoming it, through understanding. This virile pleasure, which Odysseus never confesses but readers have always sensed in him, infuses physical strength with intellectual power and renders his craft more robust. It is a craft of body and mind together, and if the form it imposes is intangible, dissipated in a sequence of acts on a picaresque voyage, the form is nonetheless real. All the world becomes the matter of the hero's manipulative skill.

We should not therefore accept too naïvely his polite estimate at Scheria of "the best thing in the world." The forms of Phaeacian culture are graceful, but they are a little pallid seen through his veteran eyes. "I confess" says Alcinous, "that we are not polished fighters with our fists, nor wrestlers: but we can run swiftly on our feet and are experts on shipboard: we love eating and harp-playing and dancing and changes of clothes: and hot baths and beds" (p. 110; 8.246–49). These are arts and customs to be admired, as the Phaeacians as a race are admirable. Zeus, in dispatching Hermes, alludes to them as "godlike in race and habit." But these exemplars of refinement seem almost shallow set against the more robust artist Odysseus. The Phaeacians are indisposed to effort; they avoid contact with other peoples; they shun war; they know of Troy only by hearsay; their ships sail without human work or hazard. Although like the Cyclops they are descended from Poseidon, they are really the opposites of the Cyclops. They have had to flee their original homes for fear of the Cyclops' plundering. In their culture and their treatment of Odysseus they are unlike the Cyclops, unlike Poseidon, and it is not surprising that their divine patron turns against them. Through their culture and destiny, the poem seems to warn against the excessive refinement of arts which in themselves are good. Perhaps a similar mistrust underlies Odysseus' second departure from Ithaca.

Thus you find a certain formalism emergent in the *Odyssey,* a peculiarly dynamic, vital formalism compatible with heroism. There is a conflict between form and its opposite, and there is also a tension between different kinds of form—the Phaeacian and the Ithacan. It is like the tension you find in the language of the poem itself, which is both elegant and powerful; the tension in the landscape by Calypso's cavern, where the artificial garden is roughened by the alders and poplars growing wild, the sea birds perching undisturbed. It is like the tension in the hero, who resembles both the decorous accomplished god and the cormorant which "down the dread troughs of the wild sea chases its fish and drenches its close plumage in the salt spume." Odysseus too drenches his figurative plumage but his will retains something of the predatory bird's firmness. The finest art just skims the element it cannot control, and strengthens itself by the contact. Odysseus will die at an advanced age "far from the sea." The tension is essentially healthy.

The price of formalism, even *this* sort, is emotional hardness; the *Odyssey* is a very hard poem. Odysseus throughout is cold, in spite of his tears; in the recognition scene with Eurycleia and the reunion with Laertes, he is offensively cold. The *Iliad* is a far more tender work in spite of its bloodier action. The *Odyssey* has been sentimentalized by readers who think Odysseus yearns for his wife and son. But Zeus' words to Hermes formulate his goal better:

> The decree is, that so furnished he shall once again behold his friends and enter his stately house in the country of his fathers. [p. 70; 5.41–42]

The poem is not very concerned with personal sentiment, beyond what use can be made of it. It has rather a cool lucid beauty which anticipates the later Attic love of rational form. It announces astonishingly early those themes which were to possess the Greek mind. But its charm lies in its freshness, the luminous objectivity, the narrative verve, the youthful worldliness, the disingenuous faith in life, and the actual flecks of foam on the rapid cormorant's wings.

iv.

The next complete extant epic is the *Argonautica* of Apollonius Rhodius, which dates probably from the latter 3rd century B.C.—that is to say, roughly five centuries after Homer. We know that other epics were composed during the interim—in particular the six poems of the so-called epic cycle—but only summaries and fragments of them have come down. There is little doubt that the poems of the cycle postdate the Homeric poems, but the gap between Homer and the oldest is probably not very large. On the whole, the summaries give the impression that these poems contained relatively few divine interventions, with the exception of the longest poem, the *Cypria.* In this there seem to have been several interventions, including at least one by Iris (to inform Menelaus of Helen's adultery) which probably followed the Homeric theme of the celestial messenger's descent. Hermes appears only as the guide of the three rival goddesses to Mount Ida for the judgment of Paris.

The *Cypria,* if it did contain a conventional descent, would have contributed to rigidifying the convention inherited by later poets like Apollonius. But the *Argonautica* is very different from the Homeric poems and doubtless from the cycle also. It is a product of Alexandria, where Apollonius probably was born and certainly was trained. The literary climate of third century Alexandria must have resembled in certain respects the climate of contemporary Anglo-American poetry on its closer afternoons. Alexandria was self-conscious, cultish, absorbed by criticism; it preferred highly-wrought small forms to the looser large ones; it made a good deal of erudition and literary allusion; it welcomed originality within decorous limits; it despised crudity. It led the poet to show off his learning and skill without appearing to make much effort, without accepting joyfully the theatricality of his performance. He became a sort of virtuoso. Such a climate is not necessarily stifling to poetry, but it is unpropitious to the very finest poetry, and above all to epic. The *Argonautica* is an anomaly, and it does not entirely succeed either as an Alexandrian poem or as an imitation of Homer.[3]

It is important to consider, though, because it is the oldest extant European epic produced by a literate sophisticated society, the

3. The *Argonautica,* however, is not the only epic produced by the Hellenistic age. There are traces of other poems, presumably not very distinguished. Little is known of these beyond a few titles and authors. They seem to have been based on mythological subjects (e.g. the labors of Hercules) and to have displayed a certain antiquarian erudition.

oldest written out of nostalgia for the heroic poem, as were written all the remaining poems to be studied. It is interesting because it already suffers from some of the diseases congenital to the literary epic—from a certain antiquarianism, artificiality, sensationalism, pedantry, and worst, dullness.

It consists of four longish books narrating the voyage of the Argonauts to Colchis, their capture of the golden fleece, and return. The first two books, which deal with the voyage, are episodic; the dramatic center of gravity lies in the events at Colchis, which occupy the third book and part of the fourth. The third book opens with a dialogue between Hera and Athene. Both are concerned with the fate of the Argonauts. They appeal to Aphrodite, who agrees to send her son Eros to enamor Medea of Jason, thus ensuring the success of Jason's quest. Medea is an enchantress whose charms will render the hero virtually invincible. Aphrodite then proceeds to seek out her son.

> . . . And she found him apart, in the blooming orchard of Zeus, not alone, but with him Ganymede, whom once Zeus had set to dwell among the immortal gods, being enamored of his beauty. And they were playing for golden dice, as boys in one house are wont to do. And already greedy Eros was holding the palm of his left hand quite full of them under his breast, standing upright; and on the bloom of his cheeks a sweet blush was glowing. But the other sat crouching nearby, silent and downcast, and he had two dice left which he threw one after the other, and was angered by the loud laughter of Eros. And when he had lost these with the others, he went off empty-handed, helpless, and did not notice the approach of Cypris.[4]

Aphrodite playfully chides her son for cheating, but promises him a marvelous ball if he will pierce Medea's heart with an arrow.

> . . . Thus she spoke, and her words were welcome to the listening boy. He threw down all his toys, and eagerly seizing her robe on this side and on that, clung to the goddess. And

4. I quote with slight alterations the translation of R. C. Seaton in the Loeb Library edition (London, 1930), pp. 201–03. In the Greek text the passage runs from 3.114–27.

he implored her to bestow the gift at once; but she, facing him with kindly words, touched his cheeks, kissed him and drew him to her, and replied with a smile:

"Be witness now your dear head and mine, that surely I will give you the gift and will not deceive you, if you will strike Aeetes' daughter with your shaft."

She spoke, and he gathered up his dice, and having well counted them all threw them into his mother's gleaming lap. Straightway with golden baldric he slung round him his quiver from where it leant against a tree trunk, and took up his curved bow. And he fared forth through the fruitful orchard of the palace of Zeus. Then he passed through the gates of Olympus high in air; hence is a downward path from heaven; and the twin poles rear aloft steep mountain tops—the highest crests of earth, where the risen sun grows ruddy with his first beams. And beneath him there appeared now the life-giving earth and cities of men and sacred streams of rivers, and now in turn mountain peaks and the ocean all around, as he swept through the vast expanse of air. [p. 205; 3.145–66]

There is an interlude recounting the arrival of Jason and others at the Colchian court before Eros reappears to fulfill his mission:

Meanwhile Eros passed unseen through the grey mist, causing confusion, as when against grazing heifers rises the gadfly, which oxherds call the breese. Quickly beneath the lintel in the porch he strung his bow and took from the quiver an arrow unshot before, messenger of pain. And with swift feet unmarked he passed the threshold and keenly glanced around; and gliding close by Aeson's son he laid the arrow-notch on the cord in the centre . . . and shot at Medea . . . and the bolt burnt deep down in the maiden's heart, like a flame. [p. 213; 3.275–87]

The rest of the passage continues to dwell upon the girl's anguish and distraction.

The convention has altered a good deal but the main outlines of the Homeric theme show through: deliberation and decision on Olympus; the speech of the superior divinity indicating the errand (and followed by the conventional "Thus she spoke . . . "); the preparations for the flight; the flight itself (here expanded to evoke a panoramic vision of the earth); the conclusion of the flight and its immediate consequences. All of this remains, and yet you feel immediately the great distance of the episode from its models. This is not surprising of course, since his models lay almost as far from Apollonius as Malory lies from us.

We might begin to analyze the alteration by remarking that the little incident stands by itself more easily than the Homeric descents manage to do. It is no more interesting than they but it tends to have a greater independence, a kind of qualified completeness which they do not. The scene between mother and son is a pretty genre scene, fit to be represented by a Hellenistic painter or sculptor. The boys playing dice are sensuously, almost seductively, portrayed; Ganymede's sexual attractiveness is mentioned explicitly. They are charming children who are quite amoral; indeed, Eros' precocious cleverness, his naughty proclivity for cheating, seem to enhance his charm. The gestures of Aphrodite—the finger on his lips, the caress of his cheek, the kiss, the full embrace—suggest progressively his plump desirability. But the whole scene has little to do with the rest of the poem; it is to be enjoyed for its own overripe tenderness. It is an anthology piece. And so is Eros' subsequent flight, which leads him through so towering and vast and beautiful a sky. The space described is grandiose and impressive, but it lacks a correspondingly solemn action: it contains only a small, mischievous, audacious boy-god faring blithely through the great expanse. It is not relevant that the earth over which he flies is life-giving or that its streams are sacred. There is nothing serious about the image despite its elegance; there is something titillating. It does not matter if the descent is only concluded a hundred lines later; the image qua image is here complete, even if the dramatic continuity is broken.

The great epics are marked by a firmness of tone, a virile economy of sentiment, and these are the first qualities to go when a poet unequipped for epic attempts it. Apollonius, whose gifts were far from negligible, was not equipped for the genre and so a certain showiness insinuates itself into his poem. In the affair between Jason and Medea, which does not lack psychological penetration, this showiness turns naturally into melodrama. This engrafting of romantic passion upon the epic, as it happened, was to have a profound effect upon its future. For Virgil was to follow Apollonius closely in writing the fourth book of the *Aeneid,* and the Renaissance in turn was to regard Virgil's example as absolutely authoritative. So this uneasy and difficult hybrid was to be considered natural. One is led to wonder how much soberer Tasso's poem would have been, for better or worse, had Apollonius not written and led Virgil to write as he did.

The gods of the *Argonautica* are devoid of mystery or sublimity, but they inherit from the gods of the *Iliad* a certain officious pleasure in tampering with human affairs. The mission of Eros is concerted by the three goddesses even though its consequences will be disastrous and sinful. (Apollonius stresses the confusion and pain caused immediately by Eros' presence among men.) Indeed the poem does not even offer a cogent reason why the golden fleece should be captured at all. Jason seems to have set out on a challenge or capricious command from King Pelias. The gratuitous perversity of the adventure is like a parody of the gratuitous element in true heroic poems. It is true that this was a part of the myth Apollonius inherited. But he seems to have exercised some freedom of selection and invention, and of course he need not have chosen this myth in the first place.

The real change in the epic attitude lies with the decadent loss of faith in the human will. Eros must enamor Medea of Jason because unaided he is incapable of success. He is not great enough to yoke Aeetes' fire-breathing bulls or to overcome the armed men born of dragon's teeth. So Medea's charms must aid him. There can be no equal struggle between Jason and the antagonistic powers; without magic he is much weaker and with it much stronger. If, as Bowra hypothesizes, a stage of shamanistic poetry tends to precede heroic poetry, then the *Argonautica* partly reverts to the easier achievement of that primitive imagination. The dialectic of the *Iliad* between glorious achievement and mortal limitation would now be unthinkable. Perhaps only the poet assured of heroic capacity (and assured of his own poetic capacity to render it) can risk a tragic qualification.

5. VIRGIL

i

The loss of Virgil to the modern world is an immeasurable cultural tragedy. For we have lost in him not only one of the greatest of world poets but also the master of European poetry. Ignorant of him, we are ignorant of aspects of other poets we think we know better. Virgil's earlier poetry was taught in Roman schools even before his death, and from then on, from the first century to the nineteenth, he was generally at the core of European education. More than the Bible (so little read in so many places at so many times), far more than Homer, Virgil has been *the* classic of Western civilization. This has been true partly because he is more fitly a poet of maturity than of youth, because his work continues to educate as the understanding ripens. Fully to know him, one must know him long. If he teaches the schoolboy style, to the man he imparts nobility.

The very word *nobility* is suspect in an age which has seen the decline of Virgil's influence. The word has overtones of snobbery and social privilege, and its moral associations suggest today an offensive pretentiousness, a shallow posturing, a cardboard dignity, qualities wholly un-Virgilian which he would have considered vulgar. Nobility in Virgil is concerned with authenticity, labor, and humility; it involves above all a spiritual generosity and an incapacity for triviality. Second-rate imitators of Virgil (we shall encounter some later) have tried to achieve nobility by the artificial exclusion of commonplace things, but he himself wrote cheerfully about fertilizers. Our own century, reacting against that artificial exclusion, has embraced the commonplace and the trivial, so that a whole generation of poets has felt obliged to strew their work with the bric-a-brac of recent civilization. The same misplaced conscientiousness leads Day Lewis doggedly to measure out his clichés for each line of the *Aeneid:*

> To speak with brutal frankness
> And lay all my cards on the table—please take to heart
> what I'm saying—
> I never had the right to promise my daughter . . .[1]

The high style of the original Latin is earned by the high style of its author's feeling—style which cannot easily be imitated but to which one rises slowly, out of respect and emulation. In those rare places where the *Aeneid* courts the danger of flatulence, where the trumpets begin to sound a little too sonorously, Virgil's native magnanimity almost always saves him. Thus when, in the eighth book, Venus anticipates her gift of arms by a series of thunder crashes and a celestial vision of the gift, the potential emptiness of this grandiloquence is filled by the subsequent speech of Aeneas:

> heu quantae miseris caedes Laurentibus instant!
> quas poenas mihi, Turne, dabis! quam multa sub undas
> scuta virum galeasque et fortia corpora volves,
> Thybri pater! poscant acies et foedera rumpant.
> [8.537–40][2]

1. C. Day Lewis, *The Aeneid of Virgil* (London, 1952), p. 262.

2. All the Latin quotations from Virgil in this chapter are taken from Virgil, *Opera,* ed. F. A. Hirtzel (Oxford, 1959). All the translations of Virgil are taken from *The Aeneid,* trans. W. F. Jackson Knight (Baltimore, Penguin Classics, 1962). "Oh, piteous, that such fearful massacre hangs over the poor Laurentine people! Terrible, Turnus, is the penalty which you shall pay to me! And, Father Tiber, how many the valiant men, how many their

Aeneas' joy at this encouraging omen is tempered by pain for his enemies' future suffering. That pain is the token of his authentic generosity, not the hollow goodness of a wooden paragon. The pain is *in character;* it is related to other things in Aeneas which hurt him and his mission and which might be regarded as faults. Virgil's nobility lies in his capacity for writing at a high moral level without losing verisimilitude or dramatic intensity. His generosity is spontaneous and human, and so it never dishonestly ignores the cost or the regrets that generosity may involve.

Why has Virgil become so inaccessible? It would appear that the decline of classical education cannot wholly be blamed for his remoteness, since Homer is still read and appreciated in translation. But Virgil in our time has not found his Lattimore, and there is a question whether his poems will ever yield themselves to translation as gracefully as the *Iliad.* It is very hard to understand anything important about Virgil without his language.[3] Perhaps he is also neglected because the *Aeneid,* as a whole, is not so supremely great as the *Iliad,* and thus Virgil seems to run a negligible second best. The comparison with Homer is regrettably unavoidable, because Virgil invited it and built it into his poem, but in fact the *Aeneid* is so different from the Homeric poems that comparisons are often unfruitful. Despite appearances, and despite the author's own conscious intent, the *Aeneid* is unique among epics.

Perhaps the taste for Virgil is unfashionable because he has been identified with the literary Establishment against which the Romantics reacted—as a later generation of rebels reacted in our

---

shields and helms, which shall be swept rolling down beneath your waves! Now, let them break our compact! Now let them insist on battle!"

3. The truth of this generalization may be illustrated by the unfortunate case of Mark Van Doren. Van Doren opens his book, *The Noble Voice* (New York, 1946), by stipulating that the greatest poetry is susceptible of translation, without troubling to see if this is so. He then upbraids Virgil for all those shortcomings which a translation imposes. It is as though he had arbitrarily disqualified all music composed in B Minor, and then criticized a transposition of Bach's Mass into C Major. Such a circle of reasoning is itself protected from all attack, but it leads Van Doren into still odder and less guarded operations. He devotes many pages to the earnest analysis of the style of Jackson's prose translation, with the notion that he is contributing to Virgilian criticism. "The style of the *Aeneid,*" he writes, fresh from Jackson, "is the most palpable thing about it."

century. The individual admiration of a Chateaubriand or a Wordsworth—or an Eliot or a Valéry—has not sufficed to obliterate the stigma of neoclassic associations, a stigma intensified by Tennyson's homage. But these historical circumstances would not have sufficed to discredit Virgil did he not fail to supply what we habitually demand from poetry. He is never, for instance, a comic poet; there is a little horse play in the fifth Aeneid, but not much, and not very funny. He is generally serious, but he is not tragic in any very recognizable fashion—not tragic like Sophocles or Shakespeare. I shall have to speak below of his oblique relation to tragedy. But these wants might be excused if at least the texture of his verse were roughened with irony. Yet here too, alas, he fails. Homer seems closer to the modern world because his ironies are so terrible. When Achilleus taunts the tears of Patroklos who is weeping for his beleaguered comrades, when Achilleus compares him to a little girl, there is a bitter irony for the reader who anticipates Achilleus' own flood of tears for his friend's approaching death. And when, just before his fatal wounding Patroklos taunts his victim Kebriones for the gracefulness of his plunge to death, there is a tragic irony in the fine, gay sarcasm of the doomed victor. Virgil was not given to this Sophoclean cruelty, not, however, because he was ignorant of that complexity in life which irony commonly underscores. Virgil was aware of it, perhaps too aware for the gentleness of his temperament. He was not as *hard* as Homer, and he would have found the Homeric form of tragic irony intolerable. His only form was the straightforward, more bearable sarcasm of Roman oratory, the sarcasm to which Mercury has recourse in his most important epiphany to Aeneas. Before any more generalizations, we ought now to consider that passage.

The gods have frequent occasion to intervene in the action of the *Aeneid;* the superior gods both appear in person (in particular, Venus, Juno, and Apollo) and dispatch emissaries or agents like Iris, Juturna, Opis, and so on. Mercury is dispatched three times by Jupiter—first in Book One (297 ff.), to render Dido hospitable to the storm-weary Trojans, and twice in Book Four (222 ff. and 556 ff.) to command Aeneas' immediate departure from Carthage. Of all these interventions, only one is described very circumstantially, and only one follows closely the Homeric theme.

This is Mercury's second flight. This account is ample; all the others are bare. Virgil may well have chosen to imitate once only this particular convention, and then selected this crux of the narrative in which to do it.

Jupiter's attention is called to Aeneas by his son Iarbas, a Libyan king who has sued unsuccessfully for Dido's hand. Iarbas has heard gossip of Dido's pseudo-"marriage" with Aeneas, an arrangement contrived by Juno with Venus' approbation. Iarbas complains to his father that Dido has yielded to "this second Paris, wearing a Phrygian bonnet to tie up his chin and cover his oily hair, and attended by a train of she-men." [4] This complaint succeeds in turning Jupiter's eyes upon Carthage:

> Talibus orantem dictis arasque tenentem [5]
> audiit Omnipotens, oculosque ad moenia torsit
> regia et oblitos famae melioris amantis.
> tum sic Mercurium adloquitur ac talia mandat:
> "vade age, nate, voca Zephyros et labere pennis
> Dardaniumque ducem, Tyria Karthagine qui nunc
> exspectat fatisque datas non respicit urbes,
> adloquere et celeris defer mea dicta per auras.
> non illum nobis genetrix pulcherrima talem
> promisit Graiumque ideo bis vindicat armis;
> sed fore qui gravidam imperiis belloque frementem
> Italiam regeret, genus alto a sanguine Teucri
> proderet, ac totum sub leges mitteret orbem.
> si nulla accendit tantarum gloria rerum
> nec super ipse sua molitur laude laborem,
> Ascanione pater Romanas invidet arces?
> quid struit? aut qua spe inimica in gente moratur
> nec prolem Ausoniam et Lavinia respicit arva?
> naviget! haec summa est, hic nostri nuntius esto."
>
> Dixerat, ille patris magni parere parabat
> imperio: et primum pedibus talaria nectit
> aurea, quae sublimem alis sive aequora supra

4. 4.215–17. "ille Paris cum semiviro comitatu,/Maeonia mentum mitra crinemque madentem/subnexus . . ."

5. "Such were the words of his prayer, and as he prayed he touched the altar. The Almighty heard, and turned his eyes on the queen's city and on

seu terram rapido pariter cum flamine portant.
tum virgam capit: hac animas ille evocat Orco
pallentis, alias sub Tartara tristia mittit,
dat somnos adimitque, et lumina morte resignat.
illa fretus agit ventos et turbida tranat
nubila. iamque volans apicem et latera ardua cernit
Atlantis duri caelum qui vertice fulcit,
Atlantis, cintum adsidue cui nubibus atris
piniferum caput et vento pulsatur et imbri,
nix umeros infusa tegit, tum flumina mento
praecipitant senis, et glacie riget horrida barba.
hic primum paribus nitens Cyllenius alis
constitit: hinc toto praeceps se corpore ad undas
misit avi similis, quae circum litora, circum
piscosos scopulos humilis volat aequora iuxta.
haud aliter terras inter caelumque volabat
litus harenosum ad Libyae, ventosque secabat
materno veniens ab avo Cyllenia proles.
ut primum alatis tetigit magalia plantis,
Aenean fundantem arces ac tecta novantem
conspicit. atque illi stellatus iaspide fulva

---

these lovers who had forgotten their nobler fame. He then spoke to Mercury, and entrusted him with this commission: 'Up, son of mine, go on your way. Call to you the western winds. Glide on your wings! Speak to the Dardan prince who is now lingering in Tyrian Carthage with never a thought for those other cities which are his by destiny. Go swiftly through the air and take my words to him. It was never for this that the most beautiful goddess, his mother, twice rescued him from his Greek foes. This is not the man she led us to think that he would prove to be. No, he was to guide an Italy which is to be a breeding-ground of leadership and clamorous with noise of war, transmit a lineage from proud Teucer's blood, and subject the whole earth to the rule of law. And even if the glory of this great destiny is powerless to kindle his ardour, and if he will exert no effort to win fame for himself, will he withhold from his son Ascanius the Fortress of Rome? What does he mean to do? What can he gain by lingering among a people who are his foes, without a care for his own descendants, the Italians of the future, and for the lands destined to bear Lavinia's name? He must set sail. That is what I have to say, and that is to be my message to him.'

He finished, and Mercury prepared to obey his exalted Father's command. First he laced on his feet those golden sandals with wings to carry him high at the speed of the winds' swift blast over ocean and over land alike. Then he took his wand; the wand with which he calls the pale souls forth from the Nether World and sends others down to grim Tartarus, gives sleep, and

ensis erat Tyrioque ardebat murice laena
demissa ex umeris, dives quae munera Dido
fecerat, et tenui telas discreverat auro.
continuo invadit: "tu nunc Karthaginis altae
fundamenta locas pulchramque uxorius urbem
exstruis? heu, regni rerumque oblite tuarum!
ipse deum tibi me claro demittit Olympo
regnator, caelum ac terras qui numine torquet:
ipse haec ferre iubet celeris mandata per auras:
quid struis? aut qua spe Libycis teris otia terris?
si te nulla movet tantarum gloria rerum
nec super ipse tua moliris laude laborem,
Ascanium surgentem et spes heredis Iuli
respice, cui regnum Italiae Romanaque tellus
debetur." tali Cyllenius ore locutus
mortalis visus medio sermone reliquit
et procul in tenuem ex oculis evanuit auram.

[4.219–78]

Virgil's copy of Homer was open as he wrote this passage, but the innovations he has made in the theme are considerable. Both his indebtedness and his originality are most easily studied in the middle section beginning "Dixerat," a word which is itself a rendering of the Greek "Ἦ ῥα." The line that follows—"Ille . . . imperio" echoes but does not follow precisely Homer's formulaic statement of Hermes' obedience. The next three lines, however, ("et primum . . . portant") do follow word for word Homer's praise of the marvelous sandals. Virgil's treatment of the staff, in

---

takes sleep away, and unseals eyes at death. So shepherding the winds before him with his wand, he swam through the murk of the clouds. And now as he flew he discerned the crest and steep flanks of Atlas the enduring, who supports the sky upon his head. His pine-clad crown is perpetually girt by blackest mist and beaten by wind and rain, his shoulders swathed in a mantle of snow, his aged chin a cascade of torrents, and his wild and shaggy beard frozen stiff with ice. Here Cyllenian Mercury first stopped, poised on balancing wings. And from here he plunged with all his weight to the waves; like a sea-bird flying low close to the sea's surface round shores and rocks where fish are found. So did the Cyllenian fly beneath earth and sky to the sandy shore of Africa, cutting through the winds from the Mountain Atlas, his mother's sire.

As soon as his winged feet had carried him as far as the hut-villages of

turn, is a significant expansion of Homer's two lines. Homer had alluded only to the staff's power of inducing and waking from sleep. Virgil repeats this idea in three words ("dat somnos adimitque") but chooses to emphasize rather Mercury's role as *psychopompus,* guide to the Lower World—guide both for the newly dead into that world and for ghosts who are summoned from it. The key phrase in this sentence is the last—"lumina morte resignat" ("unseals eyes from death")—which might be applied to either of these duties. We shall want to consider below the effect of this expansion. Let us note here that the following line, which ostensibly continues to describe the staff, forms in fact a transition to the act of flight:

> Illa fretus agit ventos, et turbida tranat
> nubila.

This fine image owes its felicity largely to the juxtaposition of *turbida* and the verb *tranat* which contains a suggestion of swimming and thus of effortless, unbroken movement through the swirling clouds.

From this point the passage becomes increasingly Virgilian. The powerful image of Atlas is original and so is the description of the overdressed hero, although the simile which separates these two constitutes a modification of Homer's corresponding cormorant

---

Africa, he saw Aeneas engaged on the foundations of the citadel and the construction of new dwellings. He had a sword starred with golden-brown jasper, and wore a cloak of bright Tyrian purple draped from his shoulders, a present from a wealthy giver, Dido herself, who had made it, picking out the warp-thread with a line of gold. Mercury immediately delivered his message: 'What, are you siting foundations for proud Carthage and building here a noble city? A model husband! For shame! You forget your destiny and that other kingdom which is to be yours. He who reigns over all the gods, he who sways all the earth and the sky by the power of his will, has himself sent me down to you from glittering Olympus. It is he who commanded me to carry this message to you swiftly through the air. What do you mean to do? What can you gain by living at wasteful leisure in African lands? If the glory of your great destiny is powerless to kindle your ardour, and if you will exert no effort to win fame for yourself, at least think of Ascanius, now growing up, and all that you hope from him as your heir, destined to rule in an Italy which shall become the Italy of Rome.' With this stern rebuke, and even while he was still speaking, Mercury vanished from mortal vision and melted from sight into thin air."

simile. Mercury speaks with curt sarcasm and disappears as he concludes, with a virile abruptness much more Roman than Greek, an abruptness which will typify the very close of the poem. Mercury's speech is more or less his own, but it does contain many phrases used by Jupiter ("tantarum gloria rerum"; "celeris . . . per auras"; "Quid struis, aut qua spe . . . ?") and one line of his speech (273) is quoted verbatim from Jupiter's except for the shift to the second person.[6] Virgil remembers but does not imitate Homer's word-for-word repetitions of entire speeches.

All of Virgil's innovations in this passage are made in the same spirit: they introduce a moral dimension into the action while maintaining, or heightening, the grandeur of the god's movement. Virgil is concerned with conferring a certain metaphysical prestige upon right conduct. Aeneas' conduct as the god finds him appears exemplary but is in fact misguided. It represents an evasion, a futile rehearsal of his duty to found the Roman state which was destined to impose order upon the world. Aeneas' evasion stems not so much from any love for Dido as from a dreamy willingness to indulge himself under her opulent, oriental hospitality. Mercury's role as *psychopompus* is relevant because through his descent he is symbolically unsealing the eyes of a man asleep or dead. The instantaneous effect of his epiphany upon Aeneas resembles an awakening or an unsealing of eyes:

> At vero Aeneas aspectu obmutuit amens,
> arrectaeque horrore comae et vox faucibus haesit.
>
> [4.279–80][7]

The chthonic associations of Mercury's staff anticipate as well the literal death of Dido, a death which his descent is to bring about. Mercury's mission is actually to send a soul to the Lower World, the "Tartara tristia," even though the allusion in its context seems irrelevant. Aeneas is to encounter Dido as one of the pale shades, the "animas pallentis," when he visits the underworld. Thus the lines devoted to the staff have a two-fold reference—to Aeneas and

6. This particular line is not found in all the manuscripts and has less authority.

7. "Aeneas was struck dumb by the vision. He was out of his wits, his hair bristled with a shiver of fear, and his voice was checked in his throat."

to Dido—even though Virgil leaves their ulterior meaning unstressed.[8]

This transformation of Homeric elements is characteristic of Virgil's procedure throughout. He imitated the episodes and characters and speeches and similes of Greek epic—in particular of Homer—to a point which scandalized some of his early readers. But precisely at those points where he appears most derivative, he is most Virgilian. The broad context of the *Aeneid* metamorphoses the derivative passages and acculturates them to the world of a distinctive, Roman, far more self-conscious imagination. Similes which in the *Iliad* retain a kind of independence from their context, find themselves grafted more firmly and dependently upon the new poem, acquiring now a new moral and symbolic richness. It is a pity that so many of Virgil's imitators during later antiquity and the Renaissance followed his practice but missed the dimension of originality which justified it.

The Virgilian stamp is set upon Mercury's descent partly through the vigorous description of Atlas on which it hinges. The Atlas image is one of those which allows itself most easily to be translated into moral equivalents. There is, to be sure, a slender mythological pretext to justify its appearance, since Atlas was said to be the father of Maia and grandfather of Mercury ("materno veniens ab avo Cyllenia proles"). But the important justification for the image lies in the contrast between Atlas and Aeneas. The great shaggy ice-bound figure sustaining the sky is an *exemplum* of heroic self-denial, of austere exposure to the elements for the sake of the world community. Atlas embodies the qualities which Aeneas has temporarily forgotten. As we first encounter him, Aeneas is exposed to the violence of the elements, enduring as Atlas endures and as Romans would learn to endure. In the *Aeneid* as in the *Georgics,* the human lot depends upon weather. Only a god like Mercury is master of the elements; as he descends the poet remembers that mastery which is symbolized by the sandals and staff ("quae . . . pariter cum flamine portant"; "illa fretus agit ventos"). But Aeneas, who can only be the victim of

8. I am indebted for several comments in this chapter to the brilliant study by the German critic Viktor Pöschl, *Die Dichtkunst Virgils* (Wiesbaden, 1950).

the elements, now takes cover from them in Dido's splendid palace. His reprehensible instinct of self-indulgence is visible in the cloak she has given him, the cloak made of Tyrian purple interlaced with golden threads. This cloak and the idle sword, studded ostentatiously with jasper, point the contrast with Atlas' huge battered head. They represent as well Dido's unnatural and possessive hold upon him. Aeneas appears the dandy which Iarbas has scornfully pictured him to be, and this evasive rehearsal at Carthage is an act of cowardice. Thus Mercury's sarcasm:

> Tu nunc Karthaginis altae
> fundamenta locas pulchramque uxorius urbem
> exstruis?

Because of Aeneas' unrelenting servitude to fate, *pulcher* is a word to be used with stinging reproach.

The value placed by the *Odyssey* on beautiful artifacts and on the cultural refinement they manifest is here suspect. There are historical and sociological reasons (as well as reasons private to the poet) why such a shift in values should have occurred. Virgil was writing, not for an audience whose achievement of culture was precarious and thus uncritical, but for an audience whose traditions of austerity were threatened by power, luxury, and corruption. As a result the questions to be posed about Virgil's places are not those viable for his predecessors. In the *Odyssey* one asks "How barbarous or how refined?" In the *Aeneid* one asks "How austere or how decadent?" The beautiful thing was too familiar to be marvelous, as it once had been. The romance of culture had been lost, as Roman eyes were opened to its supposedly insidious seductiveness. The characteristic ritual of the *Odyssey* is the ceremony of hospitality—a ritual of courteous indulgence. But the rituals Virgil admires are the communal habits of work and piety. Dido's brilliant reception of the weary Trojans—with its swirl of ornate gold and silver and fine cloths and music and hecatombs to be feasted on beneath the glowing candelabra and the inlaid ceiling—is a dangerous ritual. It contrasts unfavorably with the simpler hospitality of Pallanteum, where Aeneas spends the night on a pallet of bearskin and leaves.

But if Virgil admired primitive plainness, he did not really admire archaic unrestraint. His primitivism is the backward-looking idealism of a Roman, nothing like the naïve serenity in nature of a Homeric Greek. The bird to which Mercury is compared in the *Aeneid:*

> . . . avi similis, quae circum litora, circum
> piscosos scopulos humilis volat aequora iuxta.

is less vivid than the cormorant, its Homeric equivalent, because it has less wild freedom, less rapacity; its genus is not specified—it is simply "a bird," *avis;* moreover it is a timider bird, haunting the shore rather than crossing seas like the cormorant—and like Mercury. Thus Virgil's bird is less natural and less "real." It is given life by no detail comparable to the salt upon the cormorant's wings. Virgil was not truly at home in the world of untamed nature; he did not feel that fellowship with wild animals which one divines even in those Homeric similes that pit men against animals. He came to the *Aeneid* from writing a great handbook for domesticating natural unruliness.

His largest poem is a handbook for political domesticating—"sub leges mittere orbem." It is a guide as well for the domestication of the self, which also knows its wild beasts. *Empire* is the key idea—empire over the world, over nature and peoples, over language, and over the heart. The respective struggles for command over these various realms imitate and illustrate each other. In the end it is hard to say which *imperium* shows the strictest control—the government of Caesar Augustus, or the hexameters which celebrate it, or the terrible moral discipline which Caesar's ancestor is brought to obey.

ii.

The character of Aeneas has frequently been criticized, and perhaps most frequently for his conduct after Mercury's descent. The fourth book of the *Aeneid* being its best known (although the second, third, sixth, and eighth are at least as fine), Aeneas is remembered as a paragon of deserters, a "master-leaver," to use Enobarbus' phrase. Aeneas is supposed to be unfeeling, wooden, ungrateful, and worse—a cad. The alleged betrayal—the act of a rotter—stands out, and the presentation of his character through the rest of the book, more subtle and understated, counts for less.

Nobody today, I imagine, is going to try to *clear* Aeneas, if only because such an attempt would falsely imply that Aeneas is everywhere admirable. Virgil of course is forever judging his hero, indeed holding up such high standards to judge him by that one is inclined to protest their inhuman strictness. No one will want to absolve Aeneas, but the cliché criticisms, to mean anything, need a context of understanding they do not always receive. First of all, Aeneas' character in Book Four never gets out of hand; it cannot be blamed on the poet's narrative clumsiness or gross moral insensitivity. For better or worse Virgil wants Aeneas to appear as he does. The rest of the poem is there to attest to the powerfully controlling imagination and the almost painfully rigorous moral sense. Virgil has chosen to assign his hero the role of the cad, a little upstage, colorless, and apparently composed, while downstage the heroine tears her passion to magnificent tatters. The Dido drama demonstrates Jackson Knight's remark that "Virgil always sees two sides of everything." He does see them and feel them; that is the reason one can speak of the "painfulness" of his morality. In Book Four he allows one side alone its full pathos, knowing that the weight of the remaining eleven books suffices to right the balance. But such nice artistic calculations are wasted upon the hasty or sentimental reader.

A second qualification to the cliché attacks concerns Aeneas' emotional depth. Whether or not he is in love with Dido—probably he is not—Aeneas is not cold. He would suffer less if he were. The depth of his feelings constitutes the most important thing about him, the thing to start with in speaking of him; it is what makes him interesting and complicated, what leads him to err and disobey, what underlies his nobility. For just as Virgil's nobility is genuine because his generosity is native and human, so the nobility of his hero escapes appearing factitious because it has real emotional substance. Aeneas has dramatic life because his feelings are lifelike; they are impure and fragmentary, confused and intermittent; some of his motives ripen and others wither in the course of the poem. Thus when Mercury leaves him, a malicious reader might find his first response too conventional, too rehearsed:

At vero Aeneas aspectu obmutuit amens,
arrectaeque horrore comae et vox faucibus haesit.

but the succeeding line introduces that division of impulses which is the mark of human feeling and above all the mark of Aeneas' feeling:

ardet abire fuga *dulcisque* relinquere terras . . .
[4.281] [9]

Already in the very phrasing of Mercury's disappearance:

mortalis visus medio sermone reliquit
et procul in tenuem ex oculis evanuit auram.

there is a flicker of Virgilian melancholy, of loneliness and regret at the brevity of the gods' apparitions which recalls the more accentuated pathos when Venus leaves Aeneas in Book One. Here in the later scene we know the hero well enough to impute that fleeting regret to his own sensibility although the poet does not explicitly lead us to do so.

Aeneas' emotional intensity is particularly striking in the quality of his religious feeling, that feeling which leads him against his will away from Carthage. His critics tend to discount this strain in him, and yet it is powerfully realized in the poem. Aeneas is not only stolidly pious, in the English sense, or *pius* in the much richer, humane, Latin sense, but he is religious in a more inward way. He is not only punctilious in his duties to the gods and in the divinely-sanctioned duties to those about him. That is his *pietas,* his conscientiousness, but the more remarkable thing about him is the fervor which informs his conscientiousness, a fervor which has no counterpart in the Homeric poems. Aeneas is forever open to a capacity in earthly things for assuming divinity, and he comes to have an intuition of a transcendence in human history. He has occasion in the poem to make several prayers, and in these, curiously, he emerges almost more convincingly and dramatically than anywhere else, as his language becomes most charged and eloquent. Thus the opening of his beautiful prayer to Apollo in the Cumean cave:

9. "Already he was ardently wishing to flee from the land of his love and be gone."

Phoebe, gravis Troiae semper miserate labores,
Dardana qui Paridis derexti tela manusque
corpus in Aeacidae, magnas obeuntia terras
tot maria intravi duce te penitusque repostas
Massylum gentis praetentaque Syrtibus arva:
iam tandem Italiae fugientis prendimus oras,
hac Troiana tenus fuerit fortuna secuta.

[6.56–62] [10]

Weariness, gratitude, pride, melancholy, faith are mingled here, although translation strains out the poignance of their merging. The prayer exemplifies too that association of Virgilian religion with geography which makes part of its charm, as well as those associations with tradition and festival which the unquoted remainder will introduce.

The charm and beauty of Virgil's religion are actually far more winning in his accounts of human worship, where he is most himself and most spontaneous, than in the heavier, more perfunctory scenes on Olympus, the councils and disputes, where the derivations from Homer are least successful. Virgil's gods, tending as they do to embody abstract principles or forces, court the risk of transparency, and Homeric mystery starts to fade into Virgilian machinery. The descent of Mercury, which lies open to the charge of perfunctory imitation, is saved by those accretions of dramatic meaning we have already noticed. In general, Virgil is at his weakest with his gods, particularly while they remain on Olympus, and this weakness can be attributed to his lack of belief in them as they are thus represented. Virgil's faith must have been like his hero's: inward and intuitive, taking sustenance from places known, from ritual and tradition, from tree and bush and earth. His faith must have been vague in some respects, blurred around the edges, shot with doubts, but his fervor, his openness to some transcendence, were very vital and enriched the dramatic substance of his hero.

10. "Phoebus, you have always pitied Troy in her grievous suffering. It was you who guided the hands of Paris when he aimed his Dardan arrow to strike Achilles the Aeacid. It was you who led me forth to sail over all those seas which thrust against the vast continents and to force a way even to nations of the remote Massylians and lands screened by the Syrtes. Now at the last we have gained a foothold on Italy's elusive shores. From now on, let Troy's old ill-fortune pursue us no farther."

It can be granted that Aeneas remains a little muted as a character; he is deep but he is not brilliant. Virgil may well have been incapable of creating a figure as brilliant as the Achilleus of the *Iliad* or the Odysseus of the *Odyssey*. He had no supreme talent for the color and variety of personality. His genius was not quite of that temper, and this is one of the main reasons why he is not to be ranked with Homer, Dante and Shakespeare. Having granted that, one has then to recognize that Virgil does turn Aeneas' greyness to artistic advantage in the *Aeneid*. For there is an artistic wisdom, as many great writers have discovered, in subordinating the dramatic interest of a protagonist to the interest of those lesser characters he meets and of those events through which he passes. Thus in the *Divine Comedy* the characters of Dante and Virgil acquire their dramatic life much more gradually and subtly than the vivid, spontaneous souls they encounter, and this graduation of revealed drama ultimately lends a firmer, deeper, soberer power to their respective lives within the poem. Thus Mann introduces the protagonist of *The Magic Mountain* by emphasizing his mediocrity, and we come to appreciate the intelligence of his choice of heroes as the macabre story develops. Thus Joyce dismayed Pound by displacing Stephen Dedalus from the center of his novel for a nonentity. Aeneas is not mediocre or simple, but there are places where he is flat, and needs to be flat, if Virgil's emphases are to fall as they should. The *Aeneid* does not hinge so much on personality as upon experience, events, and history. Aeneas' occasional flatness actually helps the reader to lose himself within the hero, to experience what the hero experiences; it is easier to imagine one's self into a neutral character than an eccentric one.

The poem is partly about the moral ambivalences which personality entails. The strongest, most vital personalities in the poem —Dido and Turnus—are defeated and humiliated, while Aeneas comes to succeed only as he gives up his selfhood. He has to surrender the pride and willfulness and energy which his two great victims refuse to surrender and so pay for with their lives. But Aeneas has to surrender still more than that; the deeper selfhood which situates one in a historical and social context, that which gives one a role and makes *pietas* possible. About this deeper kind of identity there are no ambivalences in Virgil's mind: it is the good that makes life possible. When Troy falls, Aeneas loses that identity, that situation in a context, and when he loses it, he tries to die. He is preserved to create another context, another social fabric elsewhere—which he individually is never to enjoy, having created it. He will scarcely have time to descend from his Mount Pisgah. That is his real loss. Troy falls to rise elsewhere, but in him, in his life, it remains fallen. That is why he is so weary, so reluctant, hesitant, and erring, why he lacks the marvelous, Homeric vital energy. He has no place.

It is touching to watch his attempts to reduplicate the fallen city—building his futile Aeneados and Pergamea, envying the miniature Troy of Helenus and the illusory Troy of Dido. Fortunately, perhaps, he does not learn the fullness of his loss all at once, as he gropes through this third book which is so moving and so underestimated. But when after the severest stroke—Anchises' death, Aeneas is swept off-course by the tempest, his *cri de coeur* vents the whole bitterness of his desolation. It is significantly his first speech in the poem, and one of the most brilliant of the Homeric adaptations.

> o terque quaterque beati,
> quis ante ora patrum Troiae sub moenibus altis
> contigit oppetere! o Danaum fortissime gentis
> Tydide! mene Iliacis occumbere campis
> non potuisse tuaque animam hanc effundere dextra,
> saevus ubi Aeacidae telo iacet Hector, ubi ingens
> Sarpedon, ubi tot Simois correpta sub undis
> scuta virum galeasque et fortia corpora volvit!"
>
> [1.94–101][11]

The general sense of the first sentence recalls the words of Odysseus in another storm, but the most interesting phrase—*ante ora patrum*—is new. The nostalgia for Troy embraces a nostalgia for

11. "How fortunate were you, thrice fortunate and more, whose luck it was to die under the high walls of Troy before your parents' eyes! Ah, Diomede, most valiant of Greeks, why did your arm not strike me down and give my spirit freedom in death on the battlefields of Ilium, where lie the mighty Sarpedon, and Hector the Manslayer, pierced by Achilles' lance, and where Simois rolls down submerged beneath his stream those countless shields and helms and all those valiant dead!"

the heroic comradeship of Hector and Sarpedon, for such beloved landmarks as the Simois, but most of all for the city of fathers, the city of beloved customs and familial bonds, with a living history of generations and a past flowing into the present. In such a city it is easy to know one's role, and if one's role is to die, even that is relatively easy. One remembers the pathos of Sarpedon's death in the *Iliad,* "far from the land of his fathers"; Aeneas' pathos is to have no land and no father, nor the death which those twin losses bring him to desire.

The nostalgia Aeneas vents at our first sight of him is like a burden of which he has to free himself. He has to stop looking over his shoulder. He is still doing it as Book Five opens: holding his fleet for Italy but looking back at Carthage and the pyre of Dido:

> . . . iam classe tenebat
> certus iter . . .
> moenia respiciens, quae iam infelicis Elissae
> conlucent flammis.
> [5.1–4][12]

In the next book, at the Cumaean temple, he pauses to admire the reliefs in which Daedalus has depicted the old stories of Crete, only to earn the sybil's reprimand:

> non hoc ista sibi tempus spectacula poscit . . .
> [6.37]

Not *these* sights do the times demand, but rather such visions of the future as Anchises himself will show his son at the end of the same book. From that experience, Aeneas learns to put his burden down. He has borne it heretofore as he once bore Anchises from the rubble of Troy. He has another burden, the burden of the future, which he now more knowingly shoulders in the latter half of the poem. It is all on the shield which his mother gives him; as he takes it up, pleased though uncomprehending, he bears the glory and destiny of his race.

> attollens umero famamque et fata nepotum. [8.731]

12. "Aeneas and his fleet . . . set course resolutely. . . . As he sailed he looked back to walled Carthage, now aglow with tragic Dido's flames."

Aeneas' identity no longer derives from tradition—Yeats' "spreading laurel tree"—but from the chilly glory of the nation he may not see. He is no longer a son; he must remember he is a father, as Jupiter and Mercury have urged ("Ascanium surgentem et spes heredis Iuli respice."). The beloved, defeated, human past is exchanged for the bright, metallic future. By the close of the poem, Aeneas is becoming the faceless, official person his new identity requires him to be, the complete and finished *imperium*. His former personality is fast waning, and if in the final brutality, the knifing of Turnus, he reveals a flash of his older impulsiveness, his personal loyalty to Pallas and Evander, he also reveals—the impassivity of the public executioner. The marriage with Lavinia will be the one ritual of his life conducted without feeling. If Aeneas' name is related to the Greek *aineo* (as has been suggested), he becomes at last fully the character his name suggests—"the consenting." Beneath his increasingly effectual activity lies the passivity of acceptance.

No one could possibly be more sensitive to the cost of Aeneas' sacrifice than the poet himself, who hated the violence he felt it necessary to commemorate. It is worth repeating: "He always sees two sides of everything." Just as he allows his hero no moment of indulgence without reproof, so he never allows himself the luxury of the ambivalent. Apparent loss always turns out to be real gain, but so apparent gain turns out—perhaps in spite of him—as profound loss. That is why this poem of celebration and hope reads so often like an elegy. The trees which Virgil praised and loved and imbued with sacred symbolism, the trees which, "rooted in one dear perpetual place," represented that living and growing stability he needed, these—the ashes, oaks, pines, and cedars of the poem—are repeatedly being felled for the pyres of soldiers. Nothing in the *Aeneid* is more elegiac than these litanies of falling timber: for Misenus—

> itur in antiquam silvam, stabula alta ferarum,
> procumbunt piceae, sonat icta securibus ilex
> fraxineaeque trabes cuneis et fissile robur
> scinditur, advolvunt ingentis montibus ornos.
>
> [6.179–82] [13]

13. "They penetrated into an ancient forest of tall trees where only wild animals lived, and soon spruce-trees were falling, the holm-oak rang under

and later for the dead of the first battle in Italy:

> . . . pace sequestra
> per silvas Teucri mixtique impune Latini
> erravere iugis. ferro sonat alta bipenni
> fraxinus, evertunt actas ad sidera pinus,
> robora nec cuneis et olentem scindere cedrum
> nec plaustris cessant vectare gementibus ornos.
> [11.133–38] [14]

When Troy falls like an ash tree in the great central simile of Book Two (2.624–31), the resonance of its crash never ceases to echo in heartbreaking rhythm. The perpetual elegiac note of the *Aeneid* never turns to tragic, because tragedy involves the confrontation of loss and the purgation that follows acceptance. Virgil wants always to exalt the loss even as he winces at it. He denied himself even the luxury of tragedy.

iii.

In my second chapter I made a distinction between the poetry of the expected and of the unexpected, a distinction more or less equivalent to the one between formulaic and nonformulaic poetry. Now that we are dealing with work of the far larger second category, it is time to recognize that it spreads itself out over a broad spectrum. That is to say that all the verse of literate poets since Homer is not equally unlike his verse in its degree of what might be called predictability. Accustomed as we are today to the fireworks of words and images in contemporary poetry, Virgil and poets like him look almost as far from us as Homer does. But if we allow for the foreshortening of historical bias, the work of Virgil and most literate poets writing between about 600 B.C. and 1800 A.D. (to choose a conservative terminal date) falls into a

---

the strokes of the axes, ashen beams and the hard oaks good for splitting were rent apart by wedges, and they rolled down giant rowan-trees from the hills."

14. "Peace held the pledges; and Trojans and Latins mingled without hurt as they wandered through woods or on mountain-slopes. Strokes of the two-edged axe of iron rang on tall ash-trees. They overthrew pines which towered towards the sky. Unwearyingly they wedged and split tough oak and scented cedar; and on groaning wagons they transported rowan-trees."

middle class flanked on the one hand by formulaic poetry and on the other by such a figure as Hart Crane. In the poetry of this huge class, you cannot divine precisely what phrase or image is to follow but the possibilities are limited; the transitions are not jarring; the images are compliant with their contexts. A poet like Shakespeare would have to be placed very close to the moderns upon such a spectrum; a second rate Petrarchan poet, with his sharply restricted stock of conventional conceits, would belong near the opposite end. Virgil belongs near the center.

At first reading one notices those features of his style which are most conventional and even unpleasantly artificial. Thus, although Virgil's Mercury has no fixed epithet like the Homeric "Argeïphontes"—Argus-Slayer—applied to Hermes, he is called *Cyllenia proles*—Cyllenian scion—with a certain preciosity very far from modern taste. There is a comparable artificiality in Jupiter's allusion to Aeneas as "Dardanium ducem" or to Latium as "Lavinia . . . arva," the Lavinian fields. These circumlocutions are used chiefly in place of proper nouns, but not always; to indicate that Misenus played the trumpet spiritedly, Virgil writes:

> . . . Misenum Aeoliden, quo non praestantior alter
> aere ciere viros Martemque accendere cantu.
>
> [6.164–65] [15]

Aside from this kind of diction, Virgilian language in general looks conservative; for example, he rarely pairs an unexpected adjective with a noun. He makes frequent use of rhetorical tropes like the chiasmus in line 229:

> . . . gravidam imperiis belloque frementem

tropes which permit the demonic magic in words only a minimum of freedom. Despite this conservatism and these conventional mannerisms, however, Virgil's verbal originality is considerable and appears increasingly greater as one knows him better and knows Latin better. I am not equipped to analyze adequately the subtle mastery of Virgil's style; fortunately Knight's extended treatment

15. "The Aeolid Misenus, who had been excellent beyond all others in stirring hearts with his trumpet of bronze and kindling the blaze of battle with his music."

is available to obviate an amateur's fumbling.[16] But even the reader unable to register with assurance Virgil's artful liberties with syntax and rhythm is likely to feel the warmth and resonance of his poetry, Sainte-Beuve's "calme et puissante douceur," the proud, solemn cadences, the suggestivity, the interpenetration of sound and sense, the powerful organization of large grammatical groups. This impression of broad organization, inevitable to Latin poetry, was heightened by Virgil who gradually abandoned Catullus' "golden line" for a larger, more complex rhythmic unit—the "verse-group." [17]

The poetic effect of Latin verse is necessarily conditioned by its intricate word order, which differs not only from modern syntax but also from the looser-jointed Homeric syntax. A Latin sentence is so dense that it seems not to move in a given linear direction but rather to fill out and form a hypotactic block. A good example is the sentence beginning "Haud aliter . . ." at line 256, where the grammatical subject is delayed till the end, and the place to which ("litus harenosum ad Libyae") precedes the place from which ("materno veniens ab avo"). Reading such a sentence is like watching a photograph come into focus. One gets the impression of weighty materials obedient to their manipulator's will but little impression of movement. Each sentence is a unique little realm governed strictly and not quite effortlessly according to the laws of grammar.

Because its syntax is intricate and hypotactic and its meter so heavily punctuated, Latin poetry tends to render physical movement less well than it renders static situations. I remarked above on the force of the phrase "turbida tranat nubila" (which appears significantly in a short grammatical unit) but I did not add that this is almost the only effective evocation of Mercury's movement. It is followed immediately by the static image of Atlas, and that is followed in turn by the bird simile which does not really succeed in capturing the god's flight. It fails perhaps because the repeated preposition *circum* ("circum litora, circum piscosos scopulos") interferes with the flight's linear direction. This failure to represent movement is typical of Virgil and is compensated for

16. W. F. Jackson Knight, *Roman Vergil* (London, 1956), pp. 180–281.
17. Ibid., pp. 181–85.

by an ability to render great areas within a single perspective. The poetry of the *Odyssey* is the poetry of a maritime people accustomed to voyage a great deal for military or commercial purposes but without any unifying sense of a single political authority. The poetry of the *Aeneid* is the product of a people who voyage incidentally for administrative purposes and who see any given place as part of a vast whole.

Virgil indeed is a great poet of geography. No epic poet conveys a firmer sense of space, of geographical relationships, and no poet is more sensitive to the coloring with which a man's country imbues him. Consider how many names of peoples and places appear in the episode of Mercury's descent: *Dardanium, Tyria Karthagine, Graium, Italiam, Romanas, Ausoniam, Lavinia*—all these proper nouns in Jupiter's speech alone. Among the finest passages in the great third book are the resonant roll calls of place names. The poet did not in fact travel a very great deal, but he wrote as an imperial Roman, aware of distances and habituated to command vastness. The number of Latin verbs with which spatial prepositions are compounded demonstrates the firm and continuous conception of space in the Roman mind.

Virgil is supreme in his ability to suggest the amplitude of spaces. The concept that the world can be controlled is a powerful motive in the *Aeneid,* as it could not have been before this time and would seldom be again after the fall of the empire. To think that one really controlled the whole vast globe! Jupiter speaks to Mercury of the Roman mission to render all the world subject to law—"totum sub leges mitteret orbem." Virgil's grandeur is manifest in the ease with which his imagination accepted this idea. He does not invade the remote; he contains it. The *Aeneid* is rich in passages which embrace immense space in a phrase or a line of regal simplicity: Dido's allusion to Atlas, for example (enriched as it is by the earlier description we already know):

> ultimus Aethiopum locus est, ubi maximus Atlas
> axem umero torquet stellis ardentibus aptum.
>
> [4.481–82] [18]

or Creusa's prediction to Aeneas:

18. "The land of Aethiopia lies on the edge of the world, where giant Atlas holds, turning, on his shoulders the pole of the heavens, inset with blazing stars."

longa tibi exsilia et vastum maris aequor arandum . . .
[2.780] [19]

or the beautiful epitaph for Priam, in which the final proper noun creates a magnificent sense of immensity:

haec finis Priami fatorum, hic exitus illum
sorte tulit Troiam incensam et prolapsa videntem
Pergama, tot quondam populis terrisque superbum
regnatorem Asiae.
[2.554–57] [20]

One kind of image characteristic of Virgil is the broad crowded scene viewed from above. The *Aeneid* contains several of these: Aeneas' view of Troy in flames from his rooftop (2.302–13); the vision of the Elysian souls waiting in their valley to be reborn (6.703 ff.); Dido's view of the departing Trojans from her high tower (4.397–411).[21] The fullest of all these images is the first panorama of Carthage as Aeneas sees it from an overlooking hill:

iamque ascendebant collem, qui plurimus urbi
imminet adversasque aspectat desuper arces.
miratur molem Aeneas, magalia quondam,
miratur portas strepitumque et strata viarum.
instant ardentes Tyrii: pars ducere muros
molirique arcem et manibus subvolvere saxa,
pars optare locum tecto et concludere sulco;
iura magistratusque legunt sanctumque senatum.
hic portus alii effodiunt; hic alta theatris
fundamenta locant alii, immanisque columnas
rupibus excidunt, scaenis decora alta futuris.
[1.419–29] [22]

19. "You have to plough through a great waste of ocean to distant exile."

20. "Priam's destiny ended here, after seeing Troy fired and Troy's walls down; such was the end fated to him who had augustly ruled a great empire of Asian lands and peoples."

21. Many of the battle scenes in the closing books are also described in broad, panoramic compositions, as though the poet were observing them from some elevated place. Such compositions are much rarer in the *Iliad,* which usually places the reader on the ground amidst the combatants.

22. "They were now climbing a massive hill which overhung the city and commanded a view of the citadel. Aeneas looked wonderingly at the solid structures springing up where there had once been only African huts, and at the gates, the turmoil, and the paved streets. The Tyrians were hurrying

There follows the well-known comparison with a hive of bees, just as the view from Dido's tower leads into a comparison with ants. Passages like these are keys to Virgil's conception of history. He tended habitually to discern patterns where other men would see only excrescences, digressions, and eccentricities. There is order in the Carthaginian activity, but no easily grasped order, any more than the pattern of Roman history is easily grasped. The stylistic equivalent of this habit is Virgil's tendency to group in a series elements of various orders of being, as he groups *molem, portas, strepitum,* and *strata* in the passage above. This procedure, resembling as it does the trope of zeugma, gives the effect of reducing diverse things to unity, eliminating particulars for generalities, just as the final two feet of the hexameter, the dactyl and the final firm spondee, cut across the grammatical and word divisions to punctuate the shifting cadences of the first four feet. If such a view of history is taken seriously, then it is easy to see how human beings can be compared to bees or ants.

In many episodes, the *Aeneid* takes this long view of history and the reader too looks down as though from above, almost as though from the throne of Jupiter, to follow the struggling course of progress, with its rhythm of anticipations, correspondences, and recurrences organizing all the variety. The Trojan war itself is incorporated in the synthesis, so that the war in Latium emerges as a re-enactment of that earlier war, replacing Hector with Aeneas, Helen with Lavinia, Priam with Evander, and both Achilles and Pyrrhus with Turnus, himself of Greek descent. When Turnus makes his fateful joke:

> Hic etiam inventum Priamo narrabis Achillem.
> [9.742] [23]

---

about busily, some tracing a line for the walls and manhandling stones up the slopes as they strained to build their citadel, and others siting some building and marking its outline by ploughing a furrow. And they were making choice of laws, of officers of state, and of councillors to command their respect. At one spot they were excavating the harbour, and at another a party was laying out an area for the deep foundations of a theatre; they were also hewing from quarries mighty pillars to stand tall and handsome beside the stage which was still to be built."

23. "You will soon be telling Priam how you have found here a second Achilles."

he is unwittingly echoing the mysterious utterances of the sybil (6.88 ff.). Virgil rewrites the *Iliad* to bestow victory on a regenerate Troy, with an implication that the earlier defeat was providential and temporary. By comparable parallels, a vast amount of history and legend is brilliantly made to fit into a network of intermeshed threads.[24]

The difficulty with such Olympian perspectives is that poems cannot be limited to them, and so Virgil has constantly to shift from the grand view to the intimate, from Jupiter making his high prophecies to Aeneas' worries and nostalgias, all the particular roughnesses that destiny ignores. Neither we nor Virgil can help viewing the action from on earth, from the perspective of destiny's victims who cannot take the long view. The sorrow running through the poem has as its source this duality of perspective, which asks us both to pity and accept the suffering which destiny entails.

Few poets have asked so much of their heroes. Of all the celestial descents in the classical epic, none symbolizes so strong a pressure on the human will as Mercury's descent to Aeneas at Carthage. In the *Iliad* the celestial messengers commonly intervene to prompt or suggest, and seldom represent a categorical imperative. Priam can debate with Hekabe whether to follow Iris' admonition; Hermes as a guide is gentleness itself. His descent in the *Odyssey* simply removes an obstacle from the path of the free human will. Apollonius' Eros descends to inflame, actually to weaken the will. But Virgil's Mercury asks that the self be made an *imperium.* Mortality, the great Enemy of the *Iliad,* is very little at issue here, and time is no longer enemy at all, but friend. The true enemy is the unguided human spirit, and the deepest awe is for *its* overcoming.

The corpus of Virgil's poetry possesses a unity which few poets' work attains. In a sense the *Aeneid* requires the *Eclogues* and even more the *Georgics* because it presupposes a quiet reverence for Roman life that modern readers lack. It only gives us glimpses of the felicity which justifies Aeneas' effort. Virgil seems to have taken for granted that his audience would respond to the names of Roman families and ceremonies and places. He assumes that

24. See Robert W. Cruttwell, *Virgil's Mind at Work* (Oxford, 1946).

we too love the rivers and trees and farms of Italy, whose serenity justifies centuries of violence. If one does not share that love, even in one's imagination, then one ought to read the earlier poems before returning to the epic. The piety toward family and community, whose *exemplum* is Aeneas, is complemented in the *Georgics* by the pious but pragmatic and unsentimental bond to the soil. One returns to the *Aeneid* grateful for the simpler, sturdier, more cheerful poet, enlivened by a kindliness that tempers duty. That poet has not vanished from his greatest work, but one could wish its bleak nobility to be graced by a mellower, unpremeditated joy. For without that, all empire is as sounding brass.

iv.

The Roman epic after Virgil declined rapidly. Just as Roman sculptors of the empire copied Greek statues, so epic poets imitated second-rate Greek originals. Valerius Flaccus wrote an *Argonautica* heavily indebted to Apollonius Rhodius, and Statius modelled his *Thebaid* on a huge poem of Antimachus, a forerunner of the Alexandrian school. It is true that the *Punica* of Silius Italicus is not based on any single model, but its general indebtedness to epic traditions is only too clear. The finest and most original Roman epic written after Virgil's is Lucan's *Pharsalia.* This is an episodic, confused, and incoherent poem containing, nonetheless, a few powerful and well-written scenes. It virtually dispenses with the Olympic pantheon in favor of gods of greater moment to its audience—the goddess Fortuna and the chthonic divinities of the Lower World.

For examples of a celestial descent during the silver age one must turn to Statius' poem (80–90? A.D.) which contains several. The first, shortest, and most conventional sends Mercury to Tartarus, there to guide the shade of Laius back to the living world. Laius must instruct his grandson Eteocles to deny lawful return to Thebes to Eteocles' brother Polyneices. Jupiter wants to foment war between the brothers in retribution for their impiety toward Oedipus and for the long-standing wickedness of Argos and Thebes. Mercury's descent is thus described:

Paret Atlantiades dictis genitoris et inde
summa pedum propere plantaribus inligat alis,
obnubitque comas et temperat astra galero.
tum dextrae virgam inseruit, qua pellere dulces
aut suadere iterum somnos, qua nigra subire
Tartara et exsanguis animare adsueverat umbras.
desiluit, tenuique exceptus inhorruit aura.
nec mora, sublimis raptim per inane volatus
carpit et ingenti designat nubila gyro.

[1.303–11] [25]

This description is typical of Statius in several ways: in its general indebtedness to Virgil; in the unfortunate attempt to add a non-Virgilian detail—the hat which shades Mercury's eyes from star-light; in the effect of the verb inhorruit—"shuddered" or "trembled"—which diminishes the god's dignity and renders his flight slightly painful; and in the felicity of the concluding phrase, which demonstrates that Statius did not lack talent. Mercury's errand is equally typical of the *Thebaid,* because it is intended to foment violence through broken faith. Jupiter hypocritically professes anger at human wickedness but incites to further wickedness. The poem is in fact a series of violent episodes, empty of moral or historical meaning, alternating with deliberative episodes which themselves tend to hysteria. The whole lurid, frenzied, blood-sodden poem, attempting pitch past pitch of melodrama, exemplifies that sickly and hectic strain of Roman culture which developed rather suddenly during the first century of the empire. The sensationalism of Lucan has a kind of justification in its protest against Caesarism; but Statius' sensationalism, heightened by

25. Statius, trans. J. H. Mozley, Loeb Classical Library (London-New York, 1928). I have altered slightly the Loeb versions of this passage and the other quoted below. "Obedient to his father's word the grandson of Atlas straightway fastens on his ankles the winged sandals, and with wide hat veils his locks and tempers the brilliance of the stars. Then he took in his right hand the wand wherewith he was wont to dispel or call again sweet slumber, wherewith to enter the gates of gloomy Tartarus or summon back dead souls to life. Then down he leapt, and shuddered as the frail air received him; with no delay, he wings his speedy flight through the void on high, and draws a mighty curve upon the clouds."

the artificial style and the disconnected, turgid structure, has no justification, no point of reference beyond itself. It chronicles no significant moral or symbolic victory; both sides are evil and both sides suffer, and at the end there is scarcely any important shift in political power. Statius' chief theme, indeed his only true theme, is violence.

He is not very interested in his arch-images, and so the landscape of his poem remains relatively thin. Nor is he really interested, despite the machinery, in the relations of a divine principle with the human. The will of Jupiter, which appears so authoritative in the descent episode, seems to be bound by fate, itself an empty abstraction. It is significant that Mercury descends, like Apollonius' Eros, to weaken the will and cut familial bonds. The divinities closest to the spirit of the poem are the Furies, who appear frequently, and Mars, who becomes in Statius' imagination a fearful incarnation of destructiveness. The other principal descents (3.227 ff.; 7.1 ff.) both involve Mars, and perhaps we may read in this circumstance the reduction by antique epic of heroic awe to the obsessive cult of violence for itself. Jupiter's commands to Mars as he dispatches him in the third book, in their attempt to evoke the ultimate frenzy of anarchy, represent well the hectic stage of Latin epic:

> talis mihi, nate, per Argos,
> talis abi, sic ense madens, hac nubilus ira.
> exturbent resides frenos et cuncta perosi
> te cupiant, tibi praecipites animasque manusque
> devoveant, rape cunctantes et foedera turba,
> cui dedimus, tibi fas ipsos incendere bello
> caelicolas pacemque meam . . .
>
> [3.229–35] [26]

This passage might well constitute for our purposes an endpoint to the classical epic, did not variations of the descent con-

26. "Even as you are, my son, even so hurry through Argos, with your sword dripping as it is, in this cloud of wrath. Let them cast off the sloth that curbs them, let them hate all and desire only you, let them in frenzy vow to you their lives and hands; sweep away the doubting, confound all treaties; you may consume in war—to you I have granted it—even gods themselves, yes, and the peace of Jove."

vention appear in the work of Claudian, chiefly in his best-known work, the unfinished *De Raptu Proserpinae*. Claudian was a gifted young Egyptian writing in Italy, inventive, ambitious, unscrupulous enough to flatter in verse for advancement, who reached a pinnacle of brief celebrity before dying abruptly and mysteriously, early in the fifth century. He was a kind of Marino of antiquity—clever, decadent, bombastic, imitative, conceited, servile, and successful. In the *De Raptu* it is Pluto, the god of the underworld, who dispatches Mercury with a message to Jove, a message that is really a threat of the same universal chaos evoked by Statius. The threat is made in a purely and artificially literary context: Pluto desires to marry and is prepared to wage war with heaven should he be restrained. Eventually he will be permitted to abduct Proserpina. The context was absurd but the threat corresponded to something real—the imminent fall of the Roman Empire. "The framework of the world," cries Pluto, "shall be loosened and the shining heavens mingle with Avernus' shades."

compage soluta
lucidus umbroso miscebitur axis Averno. [1.115–16]

The coherence of the world—the *compages*—was indeed loosening, and it seems now in retrospect as though the violence in later Latin poetry almost represented a secret, unconscious premonition of the cataclysm to come. In any case, the cataclysm occurred and put an end for about a thousand years to most of the polite literary conventions nourished in antiquity.

6. ARIOSTO AND THE EARLIER ITALIAN RENAISSANCE

i.

The convention of the celestial messenger's descent disappears from classical literature after Claudian to reappear only in the wave of post-Petrarchan Humanism which swept Italy in the fifteenth century. It would of course be incorrect to assume from this disappearance that the influence of Virgil ceased to be felt during the intervening centuries. It remains a point of scholarly dispute whether even the poet of *Beowulf* was not familiar with the *Aeneid* and did not reflect his familiarity in his poem. But if Virgil operated as an influence, he did not figure as a model for the sort of imitation to which the Renaissance subjected him—the sort which involved the adaptation of just such conventions as the celestial messenger.[1] It was Virgil himself, of course (and

1. It is curious that even in the *Roman d'Eneas,* the twelfth century poem based (with many accretions and changes) on the *Aeneid* story, this particular episode is virtually omitted, as are most of the supernatural interventions. The whole scene is drastically abridged and the focus kept unswervingly upon Aeneas:

to a degree the other epic poets of literate antiquity), who first demonstrated the feasibility of such imitation. If you want to measure the force and popularity of that literary habit in Europe after the fourth century, then the convention which has concerned us here will serve as a convenient indicator. It seems to have remained neglected for a millenium.

One would not expect to find the convention in Dante, nor does one, although Virgil refers to Beatrice's descent to limbo (*Inferno,* II), and although an angel must descend to open the gates of Dis (*Inferno,* IX). Doubtless Dante's first person narrative precluded his use of the convention; doubtless the three realms of the afterworld were intended to retain a discreteness which the convention would have destroyed. But the basic reason for its absence from the *Commedia* is that Dante never thought of imitating Virgil in so precise a way, even though he was bent on emulating him. Despite his reverence for Virgil, despite the debt implied by his first words to Virgil:

> . . . Tu se' lo mio maestro, e il mio autore;
> tu se' solo colui, da cui io tolsi
> lo bello stile, che m' ha fatto onore.

Dante maintained an independence of his master which contrasts with the indebtedness of epic poets after Petrarch.

> Un jor estoit dedanz Cartage,
> de par les deus vint uns mesage,
> que li comande de lor part
> qu'il laist ester icel esgart
> et qu'il s'en alt an Lonbardie,
> aprester face sa navie,
> deguerpisse la Tiriane,
> tote la terre Libicane:
> ce n'est sa terre ne ses feus,
> altre est la providence as deus.
> Eneas fu molt esmaié
> de ce que cil li a noncié,
> set qu'il ne puet mes remanoir,
> qu'il ne s'en alt par estovoir.
> Molt li est grief a departir
> et la dame a deguerpir . . .

Eneas, Roman du XIIe Siècle, ed. J. J. Salverda de Grave, Classiques français du Moyen Age (Paris, 1925), pp. 1615–30.

It was Petrarch indeed who invented the archaizing Humanist epic, the genre which is chiefly to occupy us through the remainder of this study. His importance as an innovator is hard to exaggerate, and so his *Africa* has an importance out of all proportion to its poetic value. As a poem it is not contemptible, but it is at best uneven. As a historical event, it is crucial.

Petrarch imitated several conventions of the classical epic—among others the invocation of the muse, the descent to hell, the description of bas reliefs depicting mythological subjects. But although his fable might well have accommodated a celestial messenger, his poem does not contain one, and for good reason. He could not afford to deal very extensively with divine machinery because he wanted to make his deity ambiguous. He wanted to identify the Jove of Virgil (and of his hero Scipio) with the Christian God. He did not in fact succeed in doing this effectively, and the one scene in his poem which presents divine personages is among its most clumsy. This scene occurs in the seventh book, on the eve of the battle of Zama, and its main action consists of alternate supplications before the throne of Jove and Juno by the personified figures of Rome and Carthage. A certain balance between pagan and Christian details is scrupulously kept throughout the scene. It is set not on Olympus but in heaven, and it involves beings whom Petrarch calls *caelicolae*—literally, heaven dwellers, by which term we are free to imagine either angels or Olympian gods. Carthage, who speaks first, addresses her supplication for divine aid in the battle to Juno and thus implicitly recalls the action of the *Aeneid*. But Rome addresses Jove, and it is he who answers. He does not name the victor of the morrow but he predicts that it will be the juster of the adversaries. He goes on to lament the decline of virtue on earth; discloses that he himself will presently descend to suffer as a mortal and to restore virtue; and announces finally that his own seat and empire will remain eternally with the victor, once his sacrificial mission has been concluded. When his speech is ended the *caelicolae* spread their wings and dance for joy. Now it is clear that they are angels. Petrarch has audaciously modulated out of a pagan heaven into a Christian one. But the audacity of the whole scene is *too* great and the anachronism is too glaring. The poem remains neither a skillful antiquarian reconstruction nor a celebration of Christian Providence. It hangs in its own limbo of metaphysical unreality.

This unreality blighted Petrarch's life. You meet it in the very invocation of the *Africa,* where, after calling upon the pagan Muse, he turns to Christ to make apology for his poetic neglect:

> Tuque, o certissima mundi
> Spes superumque decus, quem secula nostra deorum
> Victorem atque Herebi memorant, quem quina videmus
> Larga per innocuum retegentem vulnera corpus,
> Auxilium fer, summe parens. Tibi multa revertens
> Vertice Parnasi regeram pia carmina, si te
> Carmina delectant; vel si minus illa placebunt,
> Forte etiam lacrimas, quas (sic mens fallitur) olim
> Fundendas longo demens tibi tempore servo.
>
> [1.10–18] [2]

Petrarch went to his grave with the bad conscience he betrays in this passage. Carducci alluded to "Petrarch's innocent betrayal of the Middle Ages" [3] and another critic has suggested that the tension in his mind between pagan and Christian, faith and art, "weighed heavily upon the poem and explains in great part the vicissitudes of its composition and the many uncertainties and the interminable vacillations of the author regarding the value and the destiny of his work." [4] Petrarch's problem, solved so lamely in the *Africa,* was approached with greater sophistication by later Christian epic poets, but it remained tenaciously to try them all, to sap the elaborate synthetic structures which they successively contrived.

The earliest example I have discovered of a celestial messenger's descent in Renaissance poetry appears in a little Latin epic en-

2. "And Thou, O surest hope of the world and glory of heaven, whom the ages remember for Thy victory over the gods of Erebus, whom we have beheld laying bare the five great wounds of Thy innocent body, be of aid to me, supreme Father. When I redescend from the peak of Parnassus, I shall bring Thee many sacred songs, if songs delight Thee; or if songs are less pleasing, then perhaps tears as well, tears long due Thee, which I in my folly—so senseless is the mind—have long withheld."

3. Giosue Carducci, *Prose* (Bologna, 1933), p. 721.

4. Nicola Festa, *Saggio sull' "Africa" del Petrarca* (Palermo and Rome, 1926), pp. 6–7.

titled *Antoniados,* written by the Humanist Maffeo Vegio in 1437.[5] Vegio's story is simple and devout; it concerns a journey made by Saint Anthony to meet another hermit, Saint Paul (not of course Saint Paul of Tarsus). Anthony is impelled to go by the angel Gabriel, who descends to communicate God's will that the meeting take place. The first of Vegio's four books consists largely of the preceding scene in heaven, wherein God recalls the revolt of Satan, the fall of man, and Christ's redemption, predicts the future power of his saints on earth, and dispatches Gabriel. I quote the passage which immediately follows his speech and concludes the first book.

> . . . Haec Divum Pater, & toti mira addita caelo est
> Laetitia haud aliter, quam Graiûm si quis amicas
> Vel Danaûm ductor placida dum voce catervas
> Hortatur, magno innumeram cum robore gentem
> Venturum auxilio, multa ardua corpora narret,
> Laetantur: speque ingenti complentur ovantes.
> Tum vocat, & caelo Gabrielem mittit ab alto,
> Utque ferat sancto, quae sint facienda, parenti:
> Nuntiet & quaenam sua sit sententia, mandat.
> Ille volat, tacitaque virum sub nocte quieti
> Dum servit, verbis invadit talibus ultro.
> "Haec tibi de summa caeli fero nuntius arce
> Antoni: mandat Divumque, hominumque Creator,
> Ut quae sacra colit Paulus, locaque abdita poscas
> Accelerans, hominem nulli iam nomine notum,
> Praestantemque incredibili virtute videbis.
> Non tu, ut rere, prior deserti occulta subisti.
> Desertum prior ille, annis & grandior ille.
> I, certum Pater almus iter tibi pandet eunti."
> Sic ait, in tenueis fugiensque relabitur auras.
> At sacer atherei volvens ingentia secum
> Iussa Patris, noctem quam primum Antonius atram
> Dispelli, nitidum viditque rubescere caelum,

5. Vegio (1407–1458) is better known as the author of a thirteenth book of the *Aeneid* and an influential work on education, *De Educatione Liberorum*. He also wrote satiric, encomiastic, and other short epic verse in Latin, as well as distinguished archeological and other philological studies.

Haud mora, carpit iter iussum, baculoque senileis
Sustentans artus graditur, per quae horrida nescit,
Deserta: & quorum fidens sub Numine tendit,
Caelicolae mitis, coeli Regemque precatur.[6]

Vegio's poem stands somewhat in the same relation to later epics as the work of a minor contemporary painter would stand to a masterpiece of the high Renaissance. It lacks suavity and it lacks scope, but in its sobriety and fervor it breathes a certain charm. It recalls Sassetta's painting of Saint Anthony's journey hanging in the National Gallery at Washington, although it is not nearly so fine. The warmest touches in the passage quoted appear in the closing image of the old man, staff in hand, setting off into the unknown wilderness with prayers upon his lips to God and the angels. The Christian sense of creaturely frailty is genuine and moving. The classical touches are not quite so well assimilated. There is a perfunctory bow to the Virgilian model in the line

Sic ait, in tenueis fugiensque relabitur auras.

which echoes

6. *Maxima Bibliotheca Veterum Patrum et Antiquorum Scriptorum Ecclesiasticorum, 26* (Lyon, 1677), 774. ". . . Thus spoke the Father of the gods, and such pure delight was felt throughout heaven as when some leader of the Greeks or Argives encourages his loyal troops with a quiet voice, informing them that a vast force of allies, very powerful and robust, is coming in relief, and they are all overcome with joy; so these are filled with great hope and rejoice. Then He calls Gabriel and dispatches him from heaven, to carry instructions from the holy Parent; He sends him to announce his Will. He (Gabriel) sets off on his flight, and when he discerns the man in the silent, still night, he accosts him with these words: 'I bear these commands as a messenger to you, Anthony, from the topmost height of heaven; the Creator of gods and men bids you to seek out speedily the holy place inhabited in seclusion by Paul; he is a man known by name to none, but you will see in him one who is pre-eminent in unbelievable goodness. You have not been the first to expose yourself to the solitude of the desert; he preceded you, although he is older than you. Be on your way, and your gracious Father will open a safe route for you as you go.' Thus he speaks, and fades into thin air as he leaves. But the holy Anthony, meditating the great commands of the heavenly Father, as soon as he sees the dark night to be past and the bright sky redden, sets out on the journey commanded him with no delay; the old man makes his way through the wilderness, ignorant of whatever dangers await him, supporting his old body with a staff. As he journeys, trusting in the God of deserts, he prays to the gentle dwellers in heaven and to heaven's King."

Et procul in tenuem ex oculis evanuit auram.

The simile of the Greek general with its self-conscious classicizing is rather stiffly "noble," but it is interesting because it draws attention to the divine pronouncement rather than to the visual action of Gabriel's flight. The flight indeed is bare of any kind of imagery, as is a good deal of the poem. I think that this bareness is typical of early Christian Humanism because each tradition tended to cancel out, for poetic purposes, the abundant iconography of the other. Christian imagery must have seemed indecorously unbecoming to the high style, and classical pagan imagery must have seemed in great part impious. The sensibilities of later Christian Humanists were to be less fastidious. Here the "noble" but imagistically weak and dramatically thin simile that we have must suffice.

Vegio opens his poem by rejecting the false muses and swollen pomp of earlier epics for a Christian subject and Christian inspiration. And yet his sacred muse is not altogether unrecognizable. When he follows his invocation by announcing the matter of his poem, he comments in a line which deliberately echoes a famous Virgilian tag:

Haec operis tantum nostri est, haec summa laboris.[7]

Moreover Vegio's tone and manner and vocabulary are strongly Virgilian. Note his use of the word *divus* for *angel* (in the quotation God is "divum Pater"; "divum . . . Creator"), a word calculated to offend Christian sensibilities even more than Petrarch's *caelicola*. It would be foolish to deny that the Virgilian coloring affects the spirit of the hagiology. We have only to reflect how near to earth heaven seems in the poem, how few pains are taken to project heaven higher than the conventional Olympus.[8]

We need not wonder at the naturalness with which Gabriel is made to play the role of Mercury. This substitution, which was to become common in Christian epics, was made easy by the doc-

7. "So great is our task, so great our labor."

8. Vegio is important as one of the first Christian poets to adapt for Christian purposes the episode of the demonic council, an episode he would have found in Claudian's *De Raptu Proserpinae*. See the opening of Book Two of the *Antoniados*.

trines of Christian angelology. The Greek word *angelos* itself meant *messenger.* And at least as early as Paul's epistles the angel is represented as a benevolent intermediary between God and man:

> Are they not all ministering spirits, sent forth to minister for them who shall be heirs of salvation? [9]

This role, and particularly the role of transmitting divine revelation, was emphasized by the pseudo-Dionysius, whose *Celestial Hierarchy* was probably the most influential of all works on angelology.[10] The same emphasis is found in the *City of God,* where Saint Augustine provides a kind of theological rationale for poetic accounts of angelic descents:

> And so it has pleased Divine Providence . . . that the law enjoining the worship of one God should be given by the disposition of angels. But among them the person of God Himself visibly appeared, not, indeed, in His proper substance, which ever remains invisible to mortal eyes, but by the infallible signs furnished by creation in obedience to its Creator. He made use, too, of the words of human speech, uttering them syllable by syllable successively, though in His own nature He speaks not in a bodily but in a spiritual way . . . And what he says is accurately heard, not by the bodily but by the mental ear of His ministers and messengers, who are immortally blessed in the enjoyment of His unchangeable truth; and the directions which they in some ineffable way receive, they execute without delay or difficulty in the sensible and visible world. [10.15] [11]

Vegio and later poets would have felt themselves authorized by such a passage as this, as well as by scriptural example, to transmute the classical convention into a sacred one.

Vegio's poem is important because it exemplifies the mixture

9. Hebrews 1:14. Paul would have found abundant examples of angelic messengers in pre-Christian Hebrew literature.

10. See particularly chapter 4, sections 2 and 3.

11. *The City of God,* trans. M. Dods (New York, 1950), pp. 319–20. Compare Tasso, *Il Messaggiero,* speaking of angels: "L'ufficio loro altro non è che congiungere per via di messaggio la natura umana con la divina." Torquato Tasso, *Prose,* ed. E. Mazzali (Milan and Naples, 1959), p. 57.

of traditions with particular clarity and with the significance of its historical primacy. I shall not quote a second celestial descent from the *quattrocento,* although a pedestrian example appears in the *Hesperidos* of Basino Basini. Basini's poem belongs to a group of encomiastic epics written to celebrate a given patron's military achievements (in this case, Sigismondo Malatesta's). This was a genre which happily died, for all important purposes, with its century. Vegio's *Antoniados* had many successors for more than two hundred years, of which Sannazaro's *De Partu Virginis* was the next major instance. But the next important celestial descent, and the next major poem which achieves epic amplitude, is Ariosto's.

The *Orlando Furioso* is descended, of course, neither from Basini nor Vegio but from the romances of Pulci and Boiardo. In these latter poems, as in most true romances, an episode like a conventional celestial descent is anachronistic. Needless to say, this is not because romance excludes supernatural intervention. But romance characteristically presents only the conclusion of the intervention. One may hear a disembodied voice; one may witness a miracle; one may even encounter some marvelous unearthly creature; but one never glimpses their origin or starting-place.[12] This explains the mystery and melancholy of romance, which always accepts less than total knowledge. Ariosto chose romance as an artistic point of departure, but he did not altogether lack aspirations to a "higher" genre. In the *Furioso* he gives us the extraterrestrial origin of the epiphany, the court of heaven, but, with the irreverence learned from Pulci, tinges it with burlesque.

ii.

The reader of Ariosto will remember the unexpected episode which opens the battle of Paris, that long and turbulent day of fighting, rich with incident, which bridges the fourteenth and the eighteenth cantos of the *Orlando Furioso.* On the eve of the battle a solemn mass is held for the Christian armies, at which they confess and communicate. The Emperor himself attends, and sets an example by praying humbly to God for victory. His prayer is

12. See Pulci, *Il Morgante,* 27. 132 ff.

heard on high by his guardian angel, who brings it to the throne of Christ, where the other prayers of the Christian armies are being received. The saints encircling the throne indicate their common approbation of the Emperor's cause. Whereupon Ariosto writes:

> E la Bontà ineffabile, ch'invano [13]
> Non fu pregata mai da cor fedele,
> Leva gli occhi pietosi, e fa con mano
> Cenno che venga a sé l'Angel Michele:
> "Va (gli disse) all'esercito Cristiano
> Che dianzi in Picardia calò le vele,
> E al muro di Parigi l'appresenta
> Sí che 'l campo nimico non la senta.
>
> Truova prima il Silenzio, e da mia parte
> Gli di' che teco a questa impresa venga;
> Ch'egli ben proveder con ottima arte
> Saprà di quanto proveder convenga:
> Fornito questo, subito va in parte
> Dove il suo seggio la Discordia tenga;
> Dille che l'esca e il fucil seco prenda,
> E nel campo de Mori il fuoco accenda.
>
> E tra quei che vi son detti piú forti
> Sparga tante zizanie e tante liti,
> Che combattano insieme; et altri morti,
> Altri ne sieno presi, altri feriti;

13. All Italian quotations from Ariosto's poetry are taken from Ariosto, *Orlando Furioso,* ed. N. Zingarelli (Milan, 1954). All translations are taken from *Orlando Furioso,* trans. A. Gilbert (New York, 1954). "And the ineffable Goodness, who by a faithful heart was never prayed to in vain, raises his pitying eyes and makes a sign with his hand that the angel Michael should come to him. 'Go (he said to him) to the Christian army that just lowered its sails in Picardy, and so lead it to the wall of Paris that the hostile force may not be aware of it.

'First find Silence, and say to him for me that he is to come with you for this undertaking, for he will know well how with the utmost art to furnish all that needs to be furnished. When this is done, go at once to the place where Discord has her dwelling; tell her to take her tinder and firelock and kindle a flame in the camp of the Moors,

'and scatter so many discords and so many quarrels among those who are reported strongest there that they may fight among themselves, and some may be dead, some taken captive, some wounded, and that anger may carry

E fuor del campo altri lo sdegno porti,
Sí che il lor Re poco di lor s'aiti."
Non replica a tal detto altra parola
Il benedetto augel, ma dal ciel vola.

Dovunque drizza Michel Angel l'ale,
Fuggon le nubi, e torna il ciel sereno;
Gli gira intorno un aureo cerchio, quale
Veggian di notte lampeggiar baleno:
Seco pensa tra via, dove si cale
Il celeste corrier per fallir meno,
A trovar quel nimico di parole
A cui la prima commission far vuole.

Vien scorrendo ov'egli abiti, ov'egli usi,
E se accordaro infin tutti i pensieri,
Che de frati e de monachi rinchiusi
Lo può trovare in chiese e in monasteri;
Dove sono i parlari in modo esclusi,
Che 'l Silenzio, ove cantano i salteri,
Ove dormeno, ove hanno la piatanza,
E finalmente è scritto in ogni stanza.

Credendo quivi ritrovarlo, mosse
Con maggior fretta le dorate penne;

---

some out of the camp, so their king will get little aid from them.' The holy angel does not reply a word to such a speech, but flies from heaven.

Wherever the angel Michael turns his wings, the clouds depart and the sky becomes clear. A golden circle extends all about him, as we see lightning flaming at night. The celestial messenger considers on the road where to descend that he may least probably fail to find that enemy of words with whom he intends to carry out his first commission.

He keeps running over where Silence lives, where he usually is; and finally all his thoughts agreed that he can find him in the churches and the monasteries of the cloistered friars and monks, where talk is in such a way shut out that *Silence* is written where they sing their psalters, where they sleep, where they take their food, and in short in every room.

Believing he would find him there, he moved his golden feathers with greater haste, and felt himself sure to see that Peace would also be there, Quiet, and Charity. But when he came into the cloister, he quickly found

E di veder ch'ancor Pace vi fosse,
Quiete e Carità, sicuro tenne:
Ma da la opinion sua ritrovosse
Tosto ingannato, che nel chiostro venne;
Non è Silenzio quivi; e gli fu ditto
Che non v' abita piú, fuor che in iscritto.

Né Pietà, né Quiete, né Umiltade,
Né quivi Amor, né quivi Pace mira;
Ben vi fu già, ma ne l'antiqua etade,
Che le cacciar Gola, Avarizia et Ira,
Superbia, Invidia, Inerzia e Crudeltade.
Di tanta novità l'Angel si ammira:
Andò guardando quella brutta schiera,
E vide ch'anco la Discordia v'era;

Quella che gli avea detto il Padre eterno,
Dopo il Silenzio, che trovar dovesse.
Pensato avea di far la via d'Averno,
Che si credea che tra' dannati stesse;
E ritrovolla in questo nuovo inferno
(Ch'il crederia?) tra santi ufficii e messe:
Par di strano a Michel ch'ella vi sia,
Che per trovar credea di far gran via.
[14.75–82]

The angel Michele recognizes Discord by the hundred clashing stripes of his clothing, by his tousled, varicolored hair, by the

---

he had been deceived in his opinion. Silence is not there, and he was told he dwells there no more, except in writing.

He sees there neither Piety nor Quiet nor Humility nor Love nor Peace. Once they had really been there, but in early days, before Gluttony, Avarice, and Wrath, Pride, Envy, Sloth, and Cruelty drove them out. The angel wonders at such news; he kept gazing at that ugly throng and saw that Discord was also there,

she whom after Silence the Father Eternal had told him he must find. He had expected to take the road to Avernus because he thought she lived among the damned, and he found her in this new inferno (who can believe it?) among holy offices and masses. It seems strange to Michael that she is there, for he had thought he would go a long way to find her."

bundles of legal papers in his arms, and the swarm of notaries and advocates about him. The angel announces God's orders to him and asks where he might find Silence. Discord himself cannot say but indicates Fraud, one of his associates, who is sure to know. Fraud explains that Silence has changed his habits since the times of Pythagoras and Benedict.

> Mancati quei filosofi e quei santi
> Che lo solean tener pel camin ritto,
> Degli onesti costumi ch'avea inanti,
> Fece alle sceleraggini tragitto:
> Comminciò andar la notte con gli amanti,
> Indi coi ladri, e fare ogni delitto;
> Molto col Tradimento egli dimora,
> Veduto l'ho con l'Omicidio ancora.
>
> [14.89] [14]

Fraud suggests that Michele seek Silence at midnight at the house of Sleep, where in fact the angel does find him and informs him of his divinely appointed task. Silence sets off obediently to fulfill it, and Ariosto returns us to the human preparations for the battle proper.

This little anecdote is not, in many respects, representative of the poem as a whole. For although there is a certain amount of allegorical personification scattered throughout, although Discord and Michele themselves reappear at later stages of the narrative, and although some other famous episodes share the same sort of whimsical fantasy, such passages make up only a small fraction of the total work. Nevertheless the reader who knew no Ariosto could draw some useful conclusions from what has been quoted above.

The restricted vocabulary, the limpidity of the language, its subdued musicality, and unobtrusive shifts of tone, as well as the neatness with which it fits into the little eight-sided boxes, are all typical. The two persistent qualities of Ariosto's language are first, serenity—the evenness and self-contented assurance with which it

14. "When those philosophers and saints that kept him in the straight way were gone, he changed from his early good habits to wicked ones. He began to go about at night with lovers, then with thieves, and to do all sorts of evil deeds. He passes much time with Treachery; I have also seen him with Homicide."

urbanely flows, and second, brilliance—the Mediterranean glitter and sheen which neither dazzle nor obscure but confer on every object its precise outline and glinting surface. Only occasionally can Ariosto's language truly be said to be witty, but its lightness and agility create a surface which conveys a witty effect. Too much wit could destroy even the finest poem, but Ariosto's graceful *brio* is at least as difficult and for narrative purposes more satisfying.

> Vien scorrendo ov'egli abiti, ov'egli usi,
> E se accordaro infin tutti i pensieri,
> Che de frati e de monachi rinchiusi
> Lo può trovare in chiese e in monasteri;
> Dove sono i parlari in modo esclusi . . .

It is a middle style which denies itself the highest effects, the broadest gestures. There is almost nothing of the ritualistic in it, beside an occasional formal simile. It is completely subservient and faithful to the demands of the narrative whole, and even where these demands are heavy—as for example at the court of Alcina—the language never dramatizes itself, never calls attention to its own compelling force. There is a reticence in Ariosto's manner which gives the hint how to take him; he is not ostensibly imitating the great epic poets. If the poet is to be concerned in any sense with heroism, his language will not be an instrument to create heroic awe; it will not seek to create a heroic distance, and it will not appear to imitate, so to speak, heroic effort through its own density or labored stylization. In this respect Ariosto is at the other extreme from Statius, from Ronsard, from Milton, who formalize their language in order to insist upon the rigid genre distinctions. Here the less pretentious style is open to the magic, the demonic potentialities of language, but they insinuate themselves silently and unobtrusively into the neat octaves in rows. The octaves themselves Ariosto inherited from Boiardo, whose poem he was supposed to be completing; the *Furioso* is perhaps the first poem in octaves to contain a conventional divine descent. By enforcing a close rhyme scheme and a break at every eighth line, they prevent too sustained or majestic a description and thus impose the more modest account which Ariosto would doubtless have preferred in any case.

We know that Ariosto's mature life was given over to his work almost with the singlemindedness of a Saint Simon or a Proust, allowing for the fact that Ariosto, with no private income, was necessarily distracted by the service of his patrons. But despite the long nightly vigils he complained of, his pages never suggest the blear-eyed wisdom born of midnight oil, and here the facility of Michele's descent is exemplary. The effect which other poets strove for in longer descriptions is achieved here in four lines, at a single stroke:

> Dovunque drizza Michel Angel l'ale,
> Fuggon le nubi, e torna il ciel sereno;
> Gli gira intorno un aureo cerchio, quale
> Veggian di notte lampeggiar baleno . . .

The supernatural power, brilliance, and speed are felt; we apprehend them; it is enough. Structurally, there is a comparable concealment of the artistic manipulation behind the scenes. The episodes which follow each other with inexhaustible profusion and apparent aimlessness, the world of errant characters whose encounters seem so random and so remote from others, are in fact bound together in their creator's mind; by the end of the poem the mutual relations are manifest. Even in the ordering and placing of the episodes one finds a secret artfulness. So, for example, the episode which precedes the battle of Paris is devoted to Mandricardo's seduction of Doralice. The juxtaposition may look fortuitous until we remember that Doralice is the betrothed of Rodomonte, who is to emerge as the one towering champion of the battle. The knowledge of his mistress' infidelity colors our impression of his titanic arrogance and rage. The two stories are linked, but Ariosto chooses rather to emphasize their remoteness in his transition:

> Or l'alta fantasia, *ch'un sentier solo*
> *Non vuol ch'i' segua ognor,* quindi mi guida,
> E mi ritorna ove il Moresco stuolo
> Assorda di rumor Francia e di grida . . .
> [14.65] [15]

15. "Now my lofty phantasy, *that does not permit me always to follow one path only,* guides me thence and makes me return where the Moorish army deafens France with its noises and outcry . . . "

There follows immediately Charlemagne's mass and prayer, the descent of Michele, and then the battle. The esemplastic control of Ariosto's imagination is firm, but it is too courtly, too finely tempered, to proclaim itself. One thinks of Castiglione's courtier, who must practice fencing apart so that his proficiency appear effortless. The pressure of the will must be concealed and the myth of life's easefulness be preserved.

Thus one of the delights of reading Ariosto lies in sounding his subterranean devices and catching the marvelous shifts of his subtle Italian hand. We have seen above his fine evocation of Michele's movement downwards through space. But already, before the stanza is finished, an alchemy characteristic of his tone is at work. Michele has the irresistible magnificence of a lightning flash, but he has equally an almost human uncertainty, perhaps even a fallibility.

Seco pensa tra via, dove si cale
Il celeste corrier per fallir meno,
A trovar quel nimico di parole
A cui la prima commission far vuole.

In itself the modulation is slight, but the anecdote will be capable now of entertaining the irreverent accents which conclude it. Rereading the whole passage, one is unable to say where the irony first makes itself felt, so fine is the poet's urbanity. Perhaps it begins in this first shift from Michele's brilliant passage across the sky to our glimpse of his internal hesitation. The key phrase—*per fallir meno*—humanizes the figure of the angel and reduces the epic vastness of his descent even as the effect is created. With each succeeding stanza, the irony reveals itself more broadly, until the parenthesis of the last stanza quoted ("Ch'il crederia?") shows us the straight face of a comedian. Not only here but throughout the poem the tone is elusive and slippery. That Protean elusiveness is responsible, in great part, for the poem's charm and also for most of the problems it poses its interpreters.

iii.

The comic manner of the Michele episode implies a clear independence of both Humanist and Christian traditions. To speak first of the Christian elements, it is remarkable that not only the priests and monks are implicated in the satire but, more obliquely, Michele himself. As we follow his flight, we are made to feel the possibility that he may bungle it. And once he has arrived at a monastery, we discover not only the clergy's viciousness and vulgarity, but also Michele's naïve astonishment. He has been foolishly mistaken:

Ma da la opinion sua ritrovosse
Tosto ingannato, che nel chiostro venne . . .

he is badly behind the times:

Ben vi fu già, ma ne l'antique etade . . .

and can only wonder at so many novelties:

Di tanta novità l'Angel si ammira . . .
Par di strano a Michel ch'ella vi sia . . .

The authorized version of society, the heavenly version, is hopelessly outdated, and Michele can only stare in bemusement, before accepting aid from the unsavory figures he finds about him. It is even hinted gently that Michele, like any pedestrian messenger, is grateful to find his mission cut short:

Pensato avea di far la via d'Averno . . .
. . . per trovar credea di far gran via.

If there were still any doubts about his comic dimensions, his second appearance in the poem would suffice to dispel them. As it turns out, he has made rather a mess of his mission: Discord has returned to his monastery after only a brief sojourn with the pagans; the Christians are losing badly; orphans and widows are suffering, and Michele must return to straighten it all out. But his first concern is that his Lord hear nothing about the slip-up.

Nel viso s'arrossí l'Angel beato,
Parendogli che mal fosse ubidito
Al Creatore, e si chiamò ingannato
Da la Discordia perfida, e tradito:
D'accender liti tra i Pagani dato
Le avea l'assunto, e mal era esequito;

Anzi tutto il contrario al suo disegno
Parea aver fatto, a chi guardava al segno.

Come servo fedel, che piú d'amore
Che di memoria abondi, e che s'aveggia
Aver messo in oblio cosa ch'a core
Quanto la vita e l'anima aver deggia,
Studia con fretta d'emendar l'errore,
Né vuol che prima il suo signor lo veggia;
Cosí l'Angelo a Dio salir non volse,
Se de l'obligo prima non si sciolse.

[27.35–36] [16]

The low-comedy scene which follows gives us Michele belaboring Discord over the head and back with a cross, while behind them the lusty monks, unable to agree on their elected officials, pitch breviaries at each other. It is a fine Rabelaisian moment. Michele, with his blushing cheeks, his bad memory, his lackey's concern for the master's anger, is more intimately human than most of the truly human figures in the poem. The suspicions we had of him at his first appearance were only too justified.

But if in fact he is a bungler, what are we to think of the Master who employs him, the Ineffable Goodness who is never prayed to in vain? It would be dangerous to give a name to the poet's treatment of the godhead, dangerous above all to call it blasphemy, because this would render precise what is made deliberately fluid. But we can scarcely take the edicts of Providence quite so simply on faith again. Even the solemn mass of Charlemagne, which seemed so purely devout when we first read it, is now subject to our doubt; how solemn is it?

16. "The blessed angel grew red in the face, for it seemed to him he had not obeyed the Creator, and he confessed himself deceived and betrayed by treacherous Discord. He had given her the duty of kindling strife among the pagans, and it was not carried out; on the contrary she seemed, to one who looked at the signs, to have done everything opposed to his plan.

As a faithful servant who abounds more in love than in memory, and who realizes he has forgotten something he ought to have as much at heart as life and soul, endeavors to correct his error with haste and hopes his lord will not see it first, so the angel did not wish to mount up to God without first acquitting himself of his duty."

L'Imperatore il dí che 'l dí precesse
De la battaglia, fe' dentro a Parigi
Per tutto celebrare uffici e messe
A preti, a frati bianchi, neri e bigi:
E le gente che dianzi eran confesse,
E di man tolte agl'inimici Stigi,
Tutti communicar, non altramente
Ch'avessino a morire il dí seguente.
[14.68] [17]

The phrasing of the sixth line, with its bland allusion to the "inimici Stigi," is clearly tongue in cheek. The presence of the priests and monks is scarcely reassuring, and in the line which names them—

A preti, a frati bianchi, neri e bigi

we may hear a faint anticipation of the colors of Discord's hair:

I crini avea qual d'oro e qual d'argento,
E neri e bigi . . . [14.83] [18]

Ariosto's detachment is clear: the Christian cause for which the grandiose and bloody battle is fought, for which the very war is fought that constitutes the spine of the plot, that cause is not at every moment to be revered or even to be taken seriously. Inevitably these ironic reservations will qualify whatever conception of heroism the poem contains.

One might say that the Christianity of the *Furioso* is not so much disbelieved as made insubstantial just as the figures of God and Michele are insubstantial. They are unlikely to remind anyone of Michelangelo. They are first presented to us without any painterly detail or descriptive trait; one encounters rather a poverty of that imagination which everywhere else is like a horn of

17. "On the day that came before the day of the battle, the Emperor had offices and masses celebrated everywhere in Paris by priests and friars, white, black, and gray; and had the people, who before had been confessed and taken from the hands of their Stygian foes, all receive the sacrament not otherwise than if they were going to die on the following day."

18. "Some of her hairs were of gold and some of silver and black and gray . . . "

plenty. We sense Michele's movement but we do not sense his presence—not at least until his representation becomes openly farcical. Perhaps one can justifiably find in the bareness of Ariosto's heaven a symbol of the religious bareness of his poem. Although the war being fought is a holy war, the devotion of the great knights to their respective faiths is clearly tepid. The laws of the chivalric code which transcend religious distinctions are far more compelling, and when a knight has to choose between them, he always chooses the former. Honor supersedes salvation. Thus Ruggiero follows his chivalric duty to his pagan king, despite his vows to be baptized. Only near-death at sea can shake his loyalty and lead to an unconvincing conversion. Imaginatively Ariosto was untouched by religious feeling as he was incapable of philosophical curiosity.[19] In the moments of the *Furioso* when Christian elements are not openly smiled at, when the reader is asked to care, for example, that Christendom defeat paganism, then this underlying indifference is a dramatic weakness.

Ariosto's relation to the epic tradition is at least as difficult to define as his religiosity. The corruption of the clergy was of course one of the tritest of Renaissance themes, and its appearance here might not seem to be cause for surprise. Trite it was, but its appearance in a poem of heroic pretensions was not quite so common, and still less common in a passage that deliberately echoed Virgil. The descent of the divine messenger was already a convention of the Renaissance Latin epic by the time Ariosto came to it. Already in Ariosto's time it smacked of the sublime, the

19. "His was . . . a distinctly jesting outlook upon religious beliefs, God, Christ, Paradise, angels and saints; and Charlemagne's prayer to God, the vision of the angel Michael upon earth and the voyage of Astolfo to the world of the Moon, his conversations with John the Evangelist, the deeds and words of the hermit with whom Angelica and Isabella find themselves, and finally those of the saintly hermit who baptises Ruggiero, accord with this laughing and almost mocking spirit. Here we do not find even the seriousness of the game and in the game, with which he treats of knightly doings; nor could there be, because relation towards religion admits only of complete reverence or complete irreverence. And Ariosto was irreverent, or what comes to the same thing, indifferent; his spirit was as areligious as it was aphilosophical, untormented with doubts, not concerned with human destiny, incurious as to the meaning and value of this world, which he saw and touched, and in which he loved and suffered." Benedetto Croce, *Ariosto, Shakespeare and Corneille,* trans. D. Ainslie (New York, 1920), pp. 64–65.

high style, and the humorless. Perhaps even more significant than the irreverent play with angelic machinery in the *Furioso* is the irreverent handling of the classical heroic ideal.

One must remember that Ariosto in his youth was primarily a neo-Latin poet and a good one; he was counselled by the authoritative voice of Bembo to forsake the vulgar tongue for Latin, and Carducci comments that, given the quality of the youthful Ariosto's Latin verse, the advice was intelligent. The evidence of Ariosto's familiarity with classical poetry, and above all with Virgil, is scattered throughout the *Furioso,* up to its closing lines, and where they appear the echoes are often far from parodistic. Ariosto was not of course learned in the sense that Tasso or Milton were —poets who might have ranked in Humanistic erudition with the greatest contemporaneous scholars. Ariosto's bourgeois background and worldly tastes precluded any education like theirs, and he regretted the loss publicly in his satires. But the culture he did possess was solidly assimilated, and in his great poem he makes deft use of it. Take as an example the dramatic moment at which Orlando regains his sanity, a moment dignified with what piercing reverberations by the fugitive allusion to Virgil's sixth eclogue!

> Girava gli occhi in questa parte e in quella,
> Né sapea imaginar dove si fusse;
> Si maraviglia che nudo si vede,
> E tante funi ha da le spalle al piede.
>
> Poi disse, come già disse Sileno
> A quei che lo legar nel cavo speco:
> "Solvite me," con viso sí sereno,
> Con guardo sí men de l'usato bieco,
> Che fu slegato . . .
>
> [39.59–60] [20]

For the very reason that Ariosto's Humanistic feeling was deep, the irreverent treatment of Michele's descent bears significance for

20. "He turned his eyes in this direction and in that and could not imagine where he was. He is astonished that he sees himself naked and has so many ropes from his shoulders to his feet.

Then he said, as once Silenus said to those who bound him in the hollow cave: 'Solvite me,' with so calm a face and with a look so much less distorted than his former one that he was loosed."

the *Furioso* and in fact for literary history. The liberties taken with an enshrined epic convention anticipate the mock-heroic or burlesque modes of the seventeenth and eighteenth centuries. Ariosto is less obvious than Scarron or Boileau, and Pope himself is no defter. But the liberty is particularly momentous in reference to the date; it is astonishing to find in the morning glow of Humanism a literary independence which was to emerge as a logical, historically explicable, widely shared spirit only in an age when the most enlightened moderns could quarrel with the ancients. There had been anti-Humanistic movements in Italy well before Ariosto, but not this Olympian toying with a beloved thing.

The most sustained imitation of Virgil constitutes the most persuasive testimony of Ariosto's independence. The Cloridano and Medoro episode of the eighteenth and nineteenth cantos derives from the Nisus and Euryalus episode in the *Aeneid* as well as from Statius' own imitation in the tenth book of the *Thebaid*. The older Moorish soldier, Cloridano, and the younger, Medoro, are on guard during the night which follows the repulse of the pagan attack on Paris. Their leader, Dardinello, has been killed by Rinaldo during the day's fighting; Medoro, youthful and impetuous, resolves to seek the body still lying on the battlefield in order to bury it decently, and Cloridano, unable to dissuade, agrees to join him. After putting to death several of the slumbering Christian soldiers, they are able to find Dardinello's body and make off with it, only to be interrupted by sunrise and a troop of mounted Scots. The two pagans take refuge in a dense wood, Medoro quixotically refusing to put down his beloved burden in order to save himself. There follows a series of peripeties in which Cloridano is killed and Medoro left for dead; he will be discovered by Angelica, smitten with his innocent beauty, and will be restored to health by her and later married to her. But that is another story.

The reader of Virgil will recognize the several elements which Ariosto has borrowed in his account of the nocturnal expedition: the two comrades, differentiated by age; the slaughter of the sleeping enemy; the troop of horsemen; the refuge in the wood; the bloody ending, mitigated only in part by Ariosto. Several minor details strengthen the parallel. But the originality of the imitation is equally striking. Virgil's story is of a piece throughout; the tone is defined by a noble pathos which varies little, despite a certain ambivalence in the poet's attitude toward his heroes. He clearly regrets Euryalus' childish eagerness for trophies and both men's imprudence as soldiers even as he praises their courage. Ariosto's fondness for his heroes is troubled by no ethical strictness of this kind. To render their virtue unambiguous he adds the motivation of loyalty to a leader which is more acceptable to modern taste than Nisus' pederastic affection. Virgil's veiled symbolism of the tangled wood, which suggests the emotional confusion of his heroes, confers a moral and artistic dimension which Ariosto could not have understood. *His* wood is tangled too, but the intricacy is simply a narrative detail.

The characterization of Cloridano is more realistic and successful than either figure in Virgil; toughened, pragmatic, and sardonic, he is yet capable of heroic generosity. This new element is important because Cloridano's wit sets the tone for the middle phase of Ariosto's story. The opening has been quiet, dominated by the earnest ardor of the handsome younger man to earn glory while paying homage to his dead king. But once they have reached the Christian camp, it is Cloridano who takes the initiative:

> Fermossi alquanto Cloridano, e disse:
> "Non son mai da lasciar l'occasioni;
> Di questo stuol che 'l mio Signor trafisse,
> Non debbo far, Medoro, occisioni?
> Tu, perché sopra alcun non ci venisse,
> Gli occhi e l'orecchi in ogni parte poni;
> Ch'io m'offerisco farti con la spada
> Tra gli nimici spaziosa strada."
>
> [18.173] [21]

"Non son mai da lasciar l'occasioni"—it is the earthy, soldierly proverb, the grim joke of the veteran who has learned to kill.

21. "Cloridano paused a little and said: 'I am never for letting chances go. Ought I not, Medoro, to do some slaughter among this troop that pierced my lord? You turn your eyes and ears in every direction that no one may come upon us, while I devote myself to making you with my sword a wide road among our enemies.' "

Ariosto will have another joke like it for each of the victims. For an astrologer:

> Ma poco a questa volta gli sovenne,
> Anzi gli disse in tutto la bugia;
> Predetto egli s'avea, che d'anni pieno
> Dovea morire alla sua moglie in seno:
>
> Et or gli ha messo il cauto Saracino
> La punta de la spada ne la gola . . .
> [18.174–75] [22]

for a drunkard:

> Troncogli il capo il Saracino audace,
> Esce col sangue il vin per uno spillo,
> Di che n'ha in corpo piú d'una bigoncia;
> E di ber sogna, e Cloridan lo sconcia.
> [18.176] [23]

for a pair of lovers:

> Medoro ad ambi taglia il capo netto;
> Oh felice morire, oh dolce fato,
> Che come erano i corpi, ho cosí fede
> Ch'andar l'alme abbracciate alla lor sede!
> [18.179] [24]

We are very far from Virgil, from his noble pathos and his sense of decorum, his sharp moral distinctions between Trojan and enemy. Ariosto allows us to forget that the victims are Christian. But when he chooses he will be able within a few octaves to leave his uncomfortable humor behind. In the darkness of the corpse-

22. "But it availed him little at this time, rather it told him a lie in everything. He had predicted for himself that he was going to die full of years, in the arms of his wife, and now the stealthy Saracen has put the point of a sword in his throat."

23. "The audacious Saracen cut off his head; with his blood the wine comes out at a single hole, for he has more than a tub of it in his body; and he dreams he is drinking, and Cloridano disturbs him."

24. "Medoro cuts off clean the heads of both. O happy death! O sweet fate! for I believe that like their bodies their souls went embracing to their abode."

strewn field, Medoro prays reverently to Diana to reveal his lord's body.

> "O santa Dea, che dagli antiqui nostri
> Debitamente sei detta triforme;
> Ch'in cielo, in terra, e ne l'inferno mostri
> L'alta bellezza tua sotto piú forme,
> E ne le selve, di fere e di mostri
> Vai cacciatrice seguitando l'orme;
> Mostrami ove 'l mio Re giaccia fra tanti,
> Che vivendo imitò tuoi studi santi."
>
> [18.184] [25]

The classical references sound oddly in the mouth of the humble foot soldier. But no matter; Ariosto is interested in the imaginative effect of the stillness, the dark cloud overhead, the blood-soaked earth, the two stealthy figures, the sound of the earnest voice rising in a prayer which will of course be granted. Virgil is seldom so picturesque.

There follows presently another modulation, now to a pathetic theatricality which is virtually operatic. Surrounded by the enemy cavalry, their leader's sword at his throat, Medoro begs permission to bury his king before dying, begs so eloquently that his fervor and beauty soften the Scot's heart. Only a villainous and insubordinate underling is cruel enough to stab him. But soon the lovely head of Angelica, dressed in pastoral garb, will bend over his unconscious face.

The incident does not represent the highest level of Ariosto's art. But there is no need, I suppose, to put a comparative value upon the two poets. It is helpful rather to see in what deep ways Ariosto shows his modernity. He follows the classical texts with enough fidelity to invite comparison. But once compared, the originals are striking for their simplicity. Ariosto's mercurial artistic sense is alive to all of the possible vantage points upon a single scene, and he proffers in turn the heroic, the mordant, the

25. " 'O holy goddess, who by our aged men art fitly called triform, for in heaven, on earth and in hell thou showest thy noble beauty under many forms, and in the forests thou dost follow as huntress the tracks of wild beasts and monsters, show me where among so many my king lies, who while alive imitated thy holy pursuits.' "

melodramatic, the idyllic. He has the alert Italian pragmatism, quick to sense what can be made of a situation and quick to sense when the possibilities are exhausted. Even in Dante, where the tone shifts quickly enough, the harmony is rarely based on modulations so abrupt. Ariosto's pragmatism stems from a profoundly modern sensibility, a sensibility incompatible with the classical spirit, above all with the classical conception of epic. In his critical sense, his artistic independence, his freedom from any tradition, Ariosto stands as a more modern figure than any of the men who attempted after him to write epic poetry. He depended neither on Virgil nor on the Bible; he used medieval materials while rejecting medieval authority. Comparing his work to the ancients', we remark the comparative clutter of modern literature, its impurity, its resistance to classification. And in his sensibility we encounter, astonishingly early, the blurred edge of consciousness, the reflexive irony, the unwillingness to see quite whole and quite clear, the capacity to entertain simultaneously more than one thought—those brilliant susceptibilities which have enriched and devastated the literature of the nineteenth and twentieth centuries. But unlike most post-Romantic writers, Ariosto chose not to extend his self-consciousness to his characters. In his artistic methods and goals he remains very far from us.

iv.

Ariosto's first and supreme purpose in the *Furioso* was to tell his story, and nobody has ever denied that he told it well. But his position vis-a-vis his audience was a little uncertain. Although he wanted to please primarily the aristocratic class upon which his living depended, the argument of his poem was drawn from popular sources and had only begun to catch the aristocratic imagination a generation or two before him, with the advent first of Pulci and then Boiardo. To complicate his position more, Ariosto himself was a bourgeois who never entirely lost a certain bourgeois outlook, despite his long service for the d'Este family. Many of the real or imagined problems posed by the *Furioso* can be explained away in historical terms if one takes into account the poem's hybrid social genesis. An Italian critic has suggested that it explains, for example, the famous irony which every critic has enlarged upon, that divinely enigmatic smile which seems to permit everything and believe in nothing.[26] At the elegant and mannerly court of Ferrara, Ariosto had to take upon him the role of the *cantastorie,* the vulgar story-teller. He loved the story and the audience loved it, but they all understood that their love involved a certain lowering, a humbling, and they could not enjoy without betraying their consciousness of the descent. Ariosto's smile reveals the self-consciousness of an adult who gladly stoops to play with a child's toy.

The paradox is simple enough but it embraces a great deal of the poem; it shows how the poet can be, on the first page of his poem, the creator of

Cosa non detta in prosa mai né in rima

and yet can remain in the next stanza "l'umil servo vostro" of his master, the cardinal Ippolito d'Este. The poet must play at once Virgil to Ippolito's Augustus and the mountebank who dazzles a gaping crowd with marvelous absurdities. The *Furioso* is as rich as it is partly because its creator tapped each class of his society for the elements which could give it strength: the elegance of the nobility, the moral shrewdness of the bourgeois, the narrative flair of the common people. But out of this cross-breeding there also appear strains which the poet's artifice does not quite conceal.

The implications of the Michele episode have already confronted us with some of these strains. By ridiculing the church, Ariosto ridiculed one of the theoretical props of the social order. By doubting the efficiency of the divine messenger, he doubted the foundations of the universe. Skepticism in one form or another pervades most of the poem—skepticism of Angelica's chastity (and of all women's), of Ruggiero's constancy, of Astolfo's prowess, skepticism of the very chivalric code which was the fabric of his art, skepticism of the new, less attractive code which had replaced it. All of this is insinuated in the poem by a certain wispy playfulness in the tone which hovers and dissolves without troubling the clear air. Only once, perhaps, does the poet choose to spell out its mean-

26. Giuseppe Toffanin, *Il Cinquecento,* Storia Letteraria d'Italia (Milan, 1954), p. 186.

ing—during the voyage of Astolfo to the realm of vanity on the moon. Guided by St. John the Evangelist, that gifted visionary, Astolfo discovers the storage house for all vain things lost on earth: the crowns of ancient kingdoms, metamorphosed into noisy inflated bladders; verses in praise of lords, now crickets which have burst open; the favors of princes to their Ganymedes, now changed to bellows; treaties and plots, now ruined castles; the beauty of handsome women, now snares set with birdlime. The witty and melancholy list is too long to copy out in full. The wits of many living men are here (including Astolfo's own) and only madness is absent, for it remains eternally on earth below. The scene is imitated in two celebrated English poems. But neither *Paradise Lost* nor *The Rape of the Lock* reach, nor are intended to reach, into the limbo of futility which the *Furioso* here explores. In this cool tranquillity of meaninglessness, the world of action is folly and the world of poetry appealing only if it admits to being an unreal game. For many readers this mock-heroic, mock-Dantesque voyage into disillusion is the quintessence of the whole work.

The terrible sadness of the voyage stems from the serene knowledge that nothing on earth truly is as it is supposed to be. The authorized version seems to touch the truth at no point at all. And hence derives a skepticism directed at language itself, for language is the instrument of the authorized version. It is precisely Michele's experience:

> Non è Silenzio quivi; e gli fu ditto
> Che non v'abita piú, *fuor che in iscritto.*

But that which drove Lear mad restores sense to Astolfo. In place of the destructive rage of Lear and Timon, Ariosto preserves the unruffled appearance of *tolerance.* There is no religious hatred as there will be in later epics, no anger, no disgust. The mellowness is Horatian. No pressure of personal passion, of ambition, retribution, zeal, or scorn from the poet's historical world obtrudes to shatter the crystalline purity of the fictive world.

So at least runs a traditional reading of the poem and so it is on most of its pages. But there are moments when the moral concerns of the bourgeois converge upon the aristocratic skepticism, and strains of tension begin to show. For all its urbanity, the

Michele episode quite obviously *has* a moral theme, the more effective for its urbanity. "The satire is all the more effective," wrote De Sanctis, "from seeming to be utterly unintentional; indeed, it has the simplicity and want of malice that make the irony of Ariosto the delicate thing it is." [27] Satire implies an ethical sense, and if this is what the tolerant manner conceals, then the traditional faith in Ariosto's detachment (which De Sanctis himself helped to foster) has to be qualified.

The truth is that Ariosto took his role of Ferrarese Virgil seriously, although this role was not altogether compatible with his irony. He wanted to write not only a delightful story but a heroic poem, a poem whose literary pretensions and intellectual horizons would extend far beyond those of the humbler Boiardo. The proof is everywhere in the book—in the stylistic finish and formal elegance, in the moralistic comments which introduces each canto, in the several allegorizations of moral qualities, and in the various historical digressions. You feel the poet's ambition in his very opening lines. Boiardo had begun in a manner characteristic of his unassuming pose:

> Signori e cavallier che ve adunati
> Per odir cose dilettose e nove,
> Stati attenti e quieti, ed ascoltati
> La bella istoria che 'l mio canto muove;
> E vedereti i gesti smisurati,
> L'alta fatica e le mirabil prove
> Che fece il franco Orlando per amore
> Nel tempo del re Carlo imperatore.
>
> [1.1] [28]

And Ariosto thus:

> Le donne, i cavallier, l'arme, gli amori,
> Le cortesie, l'audaci imprese io canto,

27. Francesco De Sanctis, *History of Italian Literature,* trans. J. Redfern, 2 (New York, 1931), 512–13.

28. "Lords and knights gathered to hear of delightful and novel things, be attentive and silent, and listen to the fine story that enlivens my song; and you shall see the extraordinary deeds, the great labor and marvelous exploits performed for love by the valorous Orlando, in the time of the Emperor Charles."

Che furo al tempo che passaro i Mori
D'Africa il mare, e in Francia nocquer tanto,
Seguendo l'ire, e i giovenil furori
D'Agramante lor re, che si diè vanto
Di vendicar la morte di Troiano
Sopra re Carlo Imperator Romano. [1.1] [29]

The Boiardo has the virtues of its precious and enduring charm. But Ariosto reveals not only the richer poetic gift, but the greater elevation of manner which befits a more grandiose flight of the fancy. You sense that elevation as his voice first bursts upon you, in the proud, chiasmatic appositives chanted in the grand style; you sense it in the bold use of the personal pronoun:

. . . l'audaci imprese *io canto* . . .

which Boiardo avoids in order to stress the second person, the audience; you sense it in the intricate syntax which telescopes so much and relies on a more Latinate hypotaxis.

For a contemporary reader this elevation would encounter no bathetic drop in the ensuing dedication to Ippolito; it would have been understood rather as another gesture of epic formality. Epic poems written to glorify a contemporaneous prince or noble family were common in Italy in the fifteenth century; they were serious poems, because nothing could be more serious than patronly approval. Ariosto too was serious about the d'Estes, and it matters little if he complained of them in his satires. Aside from whatever hopes of personal advancement he had, he cared deeply about the future of Ferrara and the future of Italy. To understand the meaning of courtly praise in the Renaissance, I think that we have to read a hortatory pressure into the declarative statements. "You are clement and just" means partly "May you be clement and just"; so the Renaissance epithalamist would address the bridegroom: "How devoted and considerate you are!" with the same tacit understanding.

Through the d'Este family Ariosto put his poem into connec-

29. "The ladies, the knights, the arms, the loves, the courtesies, the bold exploits I sing, of the time when the Moors came over the sea from Africa and did so much harm in France, following the angers and the youthful frenzies of Agramant their king, who boasted he would revenge Troyan's death on King Charlemagne the Roman emperor."

tion with history, and his pages are crowded with historical people, movements, and events. Artistically sometimes, his hand was less sure in dealing with actuality than with romance, and the historical passages have always been those most neglected. This is how the myth of his detachment has had currency. But for better or worse, history is in the poem to modify inevitably the rest of it, and from history, moreover, Ariosto is never detached. We have seen how cavalierly the fictive sufferings of those widows and children oppressed by the pagan armies are taken, and how their plight leads only to Michele's farcical tussle with Discord. But compare this eloquent and bitter denunciation six cantos later of the foreign invaders who caused in actuality the Italian innocent to suffer through their perverse greed:

Oh famelice, inique e fiere Arpie
Ch'all'accecata Italia e d'error piena,
Per punir forse antique colpe rie,
In ogni mensa alto giudicio mena:
Innocenti fanciulli e madri pie
Cascan di fame, e veggon ch'una cena
Di questi mostri rei tutto divora
Ciò che del viver lor sostegna fora.

[34.1] [30]

This is the opening of the thirty-fourth canto which contains, as it happens, Astolfo's voyage to the moon. The contrast between fantasy and history is clear. Fantasy offers a realm in which moral judgments can be smiled away if one chooses; history is the realm where judgments have to be made and defended.

But analogies exist between the world of fantasy and the cutthroat Italy confronting the d'Estes, analogies which the poet is ever at pains to point out. To the degree that violent action, real or fictive, always involves given moral qualities and certain recurrent situations, then the two worlds overlap and the chivalric universe is relevant to the court of Ferrara. So, for example, the Pyr-

30. "O famished, wicked and fierce harpies whom in blinded Italy full of error, perhaps to punish old and heavy faults, High Judgment leads to every table! Innocent children and pitying mothers are perishing from hunger and see that one banquet of these wicked monsters devours all that might be the support of their lives."

rhic victory of the Saracens which opens the poem recalls the battle of Ravenna, won by the French and Alfonso d'Este at a great cost (14.1 ff.). So Ippolito, unlike the Saracen leader Rodomonte, is victorious without shedding the blood of his own troops (15.1 ff.). So the magnanimity of Ippolito during the siege of Padua resembles the courteous generosity of Bradamante, a virtue rarely found in modern times although common among ancient warriors. Scores of Ariosto's contemporaries make brief appearances in the poem—generals, nobles, members of the clergy, painters—

> Leonardo, Andrea Mantegna, Gian Bellino,
> Due Dossi, e quel ch'a par sculpe e colora,
> Michel piú che mortale Angel divino;
> Bastiano, Rafael, Tizian, ch'onora
> Non men Cador che quei Venezia e Urbino . . .
> [33.2] [31]

and finally, at the opening of the last canto, a troop of the poet's well-wishers, each named individually in a litany of friendship, who figuratively wave welcoming greetings from the port as his poetic bark concludes its voyage. These manifold allusions which have seemed dry to many readers need not prove so if they are read with a sense of history; they bring to the poem an amplitude and a sonority; they provide a heroic dimension which history, even contemporaneous history, had not yet lost. They constitute a robust and stiffening element of fact or quasi-fact in the fluid element of poetic fancy. Above all, the historical allusions recall situations which the poet could not consider simply with an easy skepticism, and so they force us to qualify our impression of his moral sensibility. One ought to add moreover that in his dramatic grasp of politics and his interweaving of fact and fable, his transitions, his comparisons, his didactic comments, Ariosto was much more skilful than most Renaissance poets.

It may be worth a digression to note that history was bound up with the conception of epic throughout its long development. It

31. . . . Leonardo, Andrea Mantegna, Gian Bellino, the two Dossi, and that one who carves and paints equally well, Michel, more than mortal, angel divine; Bastiano, Raphael, Titian, who gives Cadoro no less honor than they do Venice and Urbino . . . "

was natural that early epic, the traditional vehicle of myth, should find itself the vehicle of history also, for myth flourishes only when it is scarcely distinguishable from history. This relation was recognized by Virgil and perpetuated through his example into the Renaissance. As a result very few Renaissance epics of the conventional length are without a vision of the hero's historical past or future, or without a verbal recapitulation by a given character for the instruction of another. The Virgilian passage which served as principal model was of course the passage in Book Six evoking the heroes who dominated Virgil's Roman past and Aeneas' future. Petrarch in his Humanist zeal gave over the first three books of his *Africa* to a more detailed review of Roman history. Doubtless Ariosto could have found other precedents in the panegyrical Latin epics of the *quattrocento.* After Ariosto, the historical summary became one of the most stereotyped elements of the epic, alternating with genealogical catalogues like that in Book Four of the *Furioso.* Such summaries occupy the greater part of three books of *Os Lusíadas,* three books of d'Aubigné's *Les Tragiques,* Vida's *Christias,* and Voltaire's *Henriade,* and there are other long summaries in Sannazaro's *De Partu Virginis,* Ronsard's *Franciade,* in Du Bartas' *Judit,* in the *Gerusalemme Liberata* and *The Faerie Queene,* in Saint-Amant's *Moyse Sauvé,* Cowley's *Davideis,* and in *Paradise Lost.* The list could be lengthened indefinitely. In almost every poem—*Les Tragiques* is only a partial exception—the epic context "poeticizes"—confers luster and dignity, suppresses and distorts facts, leaps great stretches of time to dwell minutely on moments of glory. One may well ask why these accounts, so many of them tedious today, were cherished by their authors. Although some were written to please a patron, many more were quite gratuitous. Historically they might be explained as vestiges of a medieval conception of art as pedagogy, late successors in a tradition of encyclopedic literature. In some poems—*Os Lusíadas,* perhaps *Le Franciade*—they reflect genuine nationalistic fervor. But there were probably deeper motives for including these accounts. To attach epic action to history is to attach it, at however great a remove, to the reader's world and thus to render it more imminent, more relevant, and more credible. The poet is enabled to cast a brighter halo of majesty upon his hero, borrowed from the royal line he has fathered, enabled too to suggest that heroism is not only a fictive phenomenon, that life has truly been lived in the grand style. In a poem like *Paradise Lost,* the concluding review of history, with its open end on the present, is meant to impinge acutely on the reader's own moral life.

Ariosto's personal concern with history was nourished by his nostalgia for a golden past, that quixotic image of felicity which obsessed so happily for literature so many poets of the Renaissance. In several passages of the *Furioso,* the chivalric myth is represented as exemplary, as a finer age from which the present has fallen, containing

> Di cortesia, di gentilezza esempii

which

> Fra gli antique guerrier si vider molti,
> E pochi fra i moderni . . .
>
> [36.2] [32]

Passages like these are difficult to read because they may or may not conceal the sarcasm of disenchantment. It is clear enough sometimes that one's leg is being pulled:

> Ben furo aventurosi i cavallieri
> Ch'erano a quella età, che nei valloni,
> Ne le scure spelonche e boschi fieri,
> Tane di serpi, d'orsi e di leoni,
> Trovavan quel che nei palazzi altieri
> A pena or trovar puon giudici buoni:
> Donne che ne la lor piú fresca etade
> Sien degne d'aver titol di beltade.
>
> [13.1] [33]

but I think not always, not for example in the famous apostrophe to gunpowder:

32. "Of courtesy and of nobility many instances were to be seen among the ancient warriors and few among the moderns."

33. "The knights who lived in that age were surely fortunate, for in valleys, in dark caverns and wild groves, dens of serpents, of bears and of lions, they found what now good judges can hardly find in proud palaces: Ladies who in their fresh youth deserve to get title from beauty."

Per te la militar gloria è distrutta,
Per te il mestier de l'arme è senza onore;
Per te è il valore e la virtù ridutta,
Che spesso par del buono il rio migliore:
Non piú la gagliardia, non piú l'ardire
Per te può in campo al paragon venire . . .

E crederò che Dio, perché vendetta
Ne sia in eterno, nel profondo chiuda
Del cieco abisso, quella maladetta
Anima appresso al maladetto Giuda.
[11.26, 28] [34]

There is an echo of the same nostalgia when Michele, arrived at the monastery, learns that Silence has been there *once:*

Ben vi fu già, ma ne l'antique etade.

Whether or not Ariosto gave wholehearted credence to the *antique etade,* he gave weight to the values which he associated with it. So one must not be misled by his irony, however exquisitely it makes itself felt; the *Furioso* is only intermittently amoral. It wavers rather between a bourgeois impulse to moral judgment and a wearier, more refined inclination to shrug the shoulders. The risk run by such a wavering lies with the poem's heroic ambitions; in the moral ebb and flow, they are likely to get lost.

v.

It is plain that the heroic dimensions of the action in the *Furioso* are reduced by the moral ambiguity. We have no reason certainly to cavil at the superb work Ariosto left us, or to ask it to be other than its brilliant self. But we have the right to distinguish the frontiers of the world Ariosto created, beyond which we may see him only venturing ineffectually. The frontiers stop somewhere

34. "Through you the soldier's glory is destroyed, through you the business of arms is without honor, through you valor and courage are brought low, for often the bad man seems better than the good; through you valor no more, daring no more can come to a test in the field . . .

And I believe that God, to take eternal vengeance for it, will imprison that accursed spirit in the bottom of the dark abyss, next to the accursed Judas."

short of the realm of the epic. In this limited respect, in this respect which has troubled few readers but which forms our special concern in this study, his poem fails to fulfill itself.

His limitations are basically those of his material, which for all its appeal represents a shrunken form of the great medieval stories. Vulgarized as well as embellished by popular storytellers, Orlando and the other peers no longer could compare in stature with their counterparts in the *Chanson de Roland.* Ariosto received a lesser tradition, accepted it lovingly, and made of it everything that could be made. He understood instinctively the rules of his art. If he erred, it was in supposing that his art was truly capable of epic resonance.

Why in fact is the poem not an epic? To answer we may well return to our original text. Michele alights on earth with a message which places no real pressure on man to act; he leaves behind an insubstantial deity and he seeks an abstract figure. Any pressing moral imperative would destroy the charm of the passage and we should be foolish to ask for any. Ariosto as poet may apply satiric pressure upon the clergy, but that is another matter. Within the fictive universe the godhead makes no absolute demands upon human beings and they, as we have seen, do not feel any very strongly. Whatever supernatural machinery the *Furioso* contains is lighter, more ineffectual than air. So the knight is essentially on his own; he is motivated by a sense of honor, loyalty to himself rather than anyone else, and he wins his battles by his own strength, or by his enchanted weapons, rather than through external help. So far so good; of such stuff are heroes made. But in Ariosto the code of honor, so rich a dramatic conception in the *Chanson de Roland* or the *Battle of Maldon,* loses its vitality because nobody ever suffers from it; it never involves true sacrifice. And in the strength of the knight himself there is something arbitrary, something almost as automatic as the enchanted lance which cannot fail to bring down the adversary. We are almost never made to feel any austerity in the hero, any effort, any limitation. De Sanctis says this very well:

> The heroic side of chivalry is individuality, that force of initiative which makes a free man of every knight, and which finds its limits only in itself, or to put it differently, which

> finds its limits in the laws of love and honor, which the knight obeys of his own free will. But once we remove these limits, then individual initiative turns to confusion and anarchy: the heroic becomes comic.[35]

Heroism becomes an external thing, something visible in the bearing and countenance and manners. There is a near-infallible correspondence between appearance and essence. Astolfo says to Ruggiero when he first sees him:

> Se tu sei cortese e pio
> Come dimostri alla presenza bella . . .
> [6.28] [36]

It would be unlikely that Ruggiero be courteous and not handsome.

Courage like beauty is a quality which one is given in the chivalric world; it results from chance or fortune or birth but not from an effort of the will. Rather the will is slack, impulse is strong, and so the knight is *errant,* not impelled by rational determination but drawn by accident or passion to wander. If one looks for moral zeal, for true courage and self-mastery, one has to turn to Don Quixote, who has not been given anything and is ridiculous. In Ariosto one always senses the aimlessness of the individual, as it is evoked for instance in the following beautiful octave. It concerns the beginning of Orlando's ill-starred search for Angelica:

> Tra il fin d'ottobre e il capo di novembre,
> Ne la stagion che la frondosa vesta
> Vede levarsi e discoprir le membre
> Trepida pianta, fin che nuda resta,
> E van gli augelli a strette schiere insembre,
> Orlando entrò ne l'amorosa inchiesta;
> Nè tutto il verno appresso lasciò quella,
> Nè la lasciò ne la stagion novella. [9.7] [37]

35. *Italian Literature,* p. 512.

36. "If you are courteous and merciful, as you seem by your handsome appearance."

37. "About the end of October and the beginning of November, in the season when the quivering tree is seen to take off its leafy clothing and

The poetic density here seems to depend partly on the very fine rhythmic control, reinforced by the subtle repetitions through which the melancholy lingers ("Ne la stagion . . . ne la stagion"; "Nè lasciò quella, nè la lasciò . . ."); perhaps it depends also on the use of a single vowel for all the rhymes (echoed frequently—as in the fifth line—by the nonrhyming words). But the poetry also depends on the implied comparisons. Orlando gives himself up to his odyssey as the tree gives itself up to winter, in passivity and loneliness. The birds which pass in clustered flights contrast with his solitude. But they are also like him, in their dumb instinct; for he is in some sort a natural thing, incapable of self-conflict and almost of self-consciousness. He will continue to wander until something happens to him, until he is distracted by chance into another adventure, or until by chance he finds traces of Angelica. Chance is the mainspring of the plot, controlled by Ariosto's mind but almost never by the individual character; thus Orlando in spite of his prowess has less control of his destiny than Homer's Odysseus or Tasso's Goffredo.

Chance and love are the greatest adversaries of the knight; able to vanquish everything else, he is powerless before them. In this also he is not heroic. Ariosto is interested—and interests the reader—in the contrast between physical strength and emotional weakness in a character like Orlando. But heroism is of all things the last to emerge from this combination. There is no contest between the will and the limits of the will; for the will is almost instantaneously crushed. And elsewhere, in battle, the will is instantaneously successful, the knight is victorious, and he is no more heroic than a god.

The facility of Astolfo's exploits—the deafening power of his horn, the flights of the hippogriff—is only a few degrees more striking than the facility of the other knights. But these few degrees make the difference between romance and buffoonery. The horn is a hilarious caricature of the enchanted lance, the spell-bound armor, the supernatural strength of others. Early in the poem the hippogriff is an inspired creature of Ariosto's fancy—

uncover its limbs until it is naked, and the birds go away in close-packed companies, Orlando began this lover's search; neither did he leave it all winter following nor did he leave it in the spring."

delightful, fantastic, marvelous but not funny. When Astolfo is on its back, it becomes absurd, an animated toy. Through him the poet winks at his readers and hints his own amusement at the improbability of his story.

At the other extreme is Rodomonte, whose very animal savagery lends him a corporeality which the other knights lack. It is Rodomonte, more than Ruggiero or Rinaldo, who recalls the great primitive champions such as Roland and Achilles. It might be said that he submits to no more austerity than these others and makes no more sacrifices. But this is not quite true; he is capable of death. And he moves, as the others do not, in an atmosphere where death has meaning, pain has meaning, where the sword cuts actual flesh. The *terribilitas* of the awesome mass cremation suffered by the Saracens beneath the walls of Paris gains part of its intensity from his gigantic and furious figure dominating the agony. What an intruder he is when he makes his brusque entry in the last canto, in the midst of courtly revelry! What unwelcome associations hang about him! He is capable of dying. He will prove it shortly. Ruggiero has tried to die and has failed; there are supernatural powers to prevent it. Melissa is somewhere about at the worst crises; she has brought him food and drink and Leone to make him well. (There is a prophecy that Ruggiero will die in seven years, but Ariosto is unwilling or unable to make it dramatically real.) Rodomonte has no Melissa; he has only his own titanic body, which will be humbled in the grim and dirty blood-letting which ends the poem. He is one of the few mortals it contains. The thousands of anonymous victims who fall in battle beneath the swords of the great champions do not count; they expire but they do not die. Rodomonte dies, after a year of asceticism, penance for a loss of honor. And he resents dying; he rebels against death instinctively like the magnificent living creature he is. His soul flees to hell with curses; he is furious at his fate. He is human. Now the inhuman and delightful happiness of the wedded couple will be undisturbed by mortality.

In certain passages portraying Rodomonte, Ariosto most nearly approaches epic intensity and heroic awe. Closest to him in stature is Orlando, whose grotesque suffering for Angelica is moving beyond the usual serene limits of Ariosto's art. But Ruggiero, who is meant to embody the most serious heroic ideals of the poem, is lamentably a failure, neither noble nor believable nor finally very interesting. One has the impression that many of the knights —Ruggiero among them—all have the same face.

Considerations such as these help to mark the limits of Ariosto's imagination, the frontiers of his fictive country. But once we re-enter his country they fall away as pedantic foolishness. Ample, bright, labyrinthine, and seductive, that country's peculiar gift is that its visitor wants it to be nothing more than itself. Ariosto's richest achievement was the creation of that fine insidious world where heroism is not necessary.

7. *SANNAZARO: FEIGNING WITHOUT SCANDAL*

i.

In the litany of his friends and well-wishers with which Ariosto opens his last canto, he names one man whom he has never met and knows only by reputation:

> Veggo sublimi e soprumani ingegni
> Di sangue e d'amor giunti, il Pico e il Pio;
> Colui che con lor viene e da piú degni
> Ha tanto onor, mai piú non conobbi io:
> Ma se me ne fur dati veri segni,
> E l'uom che di veder tanto desio,
> Iacobo Sanazar, ch'alle Camene
> Lasciar fa i monti et abitar l'arene.
>
> [46.17] [1]

Gianfrancesco Pico and Alberto Pio were two old friends of the poet; it is surprising—and a token of his esteem for Jacopo Sannazaro—that the latter is named with them. (Ariosto's wish to meet

1. "I see lofty and superhuman abilities joined in blood and in love, Pico and Pio. He who comes with them and has so much honor from the

him, expressed here, was never realized.) But Sannazaro's name was in fact much better known and respected in that era of genius than it is in ours. He was a Neapolitan Humanist, the author, among other things, of Latin eclogues which substituted fishermen for shepherds and of the romance entitled *Arcadia* which was to influence Sidney. We shall be chiefly concerned here, however, with his Latin rendering of the nativity story which appeared in 1527, five years before the revised and enlarged version of Ariosto's poem. Coming from Ariosto to the *De Partu Virginis,* one can measure the spiritual distance which separated in those years Italian from Italian, city from city, north Italy from south, anti-ecclesiastical from pro-ecclesiastical. Confronted with the *Orlando Furioso,* Sannazaro's work seems to issue from a very different climate. But it is a jocund and serene little poem; its hexameters, meditated and reworked for over twenty years, are firm and controlled; it is not altogether unworthy of the confrontation.

Although the poem is centered upon the nativity, Sannazaro encircles it with a cluster of other Gospel stories: the annunciation, the visitation of Elizabeth, the adoration of the shepherds, briefer glimpses of the presentation in the temple, the massacre of the innocents, the crucifixion, the harrowing of hell, and more. With this there are ulterior scenes of the poet's invention: evocations of the gleaming halls of heaven, thronged with decorative angels; a descent to limbo where King David prophesies the advent of the Messiah; a pastoral scene dominated by the Jordan, a hoary personification of the river. All of this various material is fitted neatly, even precisely, into the three books which comprise the poem. The architecture indeed is carefully calculated; each of the books is in turn divided roughly into three sections, and the sections tend to counterpoise one another symmetrically. So the descent of Gabriel to the Virgin in Book One, for example, is balanced by the descent of the allegorized Laetitia in Book Three. The workmanship which Ariosto strove to conceal is not paraded here but it is plain enough, less intricate but equally assured.

Of the two descents, Gabriel's is closer to the Virgilian model

---

greatest, I have never known, but, if true indications of him have been given to me, he is the man I so much desire to see, Jacopo Sannazaro, who makes the Muses leave the mountains and live on the sands."

and perhaps the more interesting for our purposes. The sovereign Ruler of heaven has pondered his design to redeem man from the ancient blot:

> Tum pectus Pater aeterno succensus amore
> Sic secum: Ecquis erit finis? tantisne parentum
> Prisca luent poenis seri commissa nepotes?
> Ut quos victuros semper, superisque crearam
> Pene pares, tristi patiar succumbere letho
> Informesque domos, obscuraque regna subire?
> Non ita, sed Divum potius revocentur ad oras,
> Ut decet, et manuum poscant opera alta mearum:
> Desertosque foros vacuique sedilia coeli
> Actutum complere parent . . . [1.40–49] [2]

has summoned the angel, explained his design, and designated the woman worthy to bear his son. Whereupon the angel takes his leave and makes his shattering annunciation:

> Dixerat: Ille altum Zephyris per inane vocatis [3]
> Carpit iter, scindit nebulas, atque aera tranat
> Ima petens, pronusque leves vix commovet alas.
> Qualis, ubi ex alto notis Maeandria ripis
> Prospexit vada seu placidi stagna ampla Caystri
> Praecipitem sese candenti corpore cycnus
> Mittit agens, iamque implumis segnisque videtur
> Ipse sibi, donec tandem potiatur amatis

2. All Latin quotations from Sannazaro are taken from the critical edition by Antonio Altamura (Naples, 1948). There is a convenient Italian translation with facing texts by Alessandro Guidi (Rome, 1877). "Then the Father, spurred by eternal love, communed thus with himself: 'What will be the end of it? Must posterity pay so heavily for the primeval sins of its parents? Shall I allow those born for victory, almost equal to the angels themselves, to perish by a miserable death and descend to those shapeless mansions, those gloomy realms below? Assuredly not. Rather let them be recalled to the shores of the gods, their rightful place, and let them seek out the great works made by my hands; let them prepare now to occupy the deserted courts, the thrones heretofore empty.' "

3. "Thus he spoke, and the other, having called the Zephyrs to help him, begins his journey into the empty void, cuts through the clouds, swims down through the air, seeking the lower regions, and scarcely moves his light wings as he sinks. As a white swan which descries from on high the famous shores of the Meander, or the broad pools of the placid Caystros, dives downward, and seems to itself featherless and sluggish, until at last

Victor acquis, sic ille auras nubesque secabat.
Ast ubi palmiferae tractu stetit altus Idumes,
Reginam haud humiles volventem pectore curas
Aspicit; atque illi veteres de more Sybillae
In manibus, tum si qua aevo reseranda nepotum
Fatidici casto cecinerunt pectore vates.
Ipsam autem securam animi laetamque videres
Auctorem sperare suum: namque adfore tempus,
Quo sacer aethereis delapsus Spiritus astris
Incorrupta piae compleret viscera matris,
Audierat. Proh quanta alti reverentia Coeli
Virgineo in vultu est! oculos deiecta modestos
Suspirat Matremque Dei venientis adorat:
Felicemque illam humana nec lege creatam
Saepe vocat: nec dum ipsa suos iam sentit honores.
Cum subito ex alto Iuvenis demissus Olympo
Purpureos retegit vultus: Numenque professus
Incessuque habituque, ingentes explicat alas:
Ac tectis late insuetum diffundi odorem.
Mox prior haec: "Oculis salve lux debita nostris,
Iam pridem notum coelo iubar, optima Virgo,
Cui sese tot dona, tot explicuere merenti
Divitiae superum, quidquid rectique, probique

---

it takes possession victoriously of the beloved waters: so he cleaved the winds and the clouds. But when he reached the palm-bearing country of Idumaea, he discovered the queen turning over no mean concerns in her heart. She holds in her hands the books of the ancient sybils, her accustomed reading, or whatever other secrets have been disclosed by holy, prophetic bards for posterity. You would have seen her awaiting her Creator confidently and joyfully, for she had heard that at some future time the Holy Spirit would descend from the starry sky and fill the unviolated womb of a virtuous mother. Oh how much reverence for heaven is there in her virgin features! She sighs and casts down her modest eyes, adoring the mother of the god to come, again and again calling her happy, created by no human law. She has no presentiment yet of her own high honor.

Then abruptly the radiant faced youth sent from high Olympus appears; his divinity is evident in his aspect and bearing, as he opens his great wings; the house is filled with an exotic odor. He addresses her thus:

'Hail, O light long due to our eyes, splendor long known in heaven, best of women, in whom so many gifts and treasures of the gods are worthily displayed, and whatever proceeds from the divine mind which is upright

Aeterna de mente fluit: purissima quidquid
Ad terras summo veniens Sapientia coelo
Fert secum et plenis exundans Gratia rivis.
Te Genitor stabili firmam sibi lege sacravit,
Perpetuos Genitor cursus qui dirigit astris:
Mansuramque tuo fixit sub pectore sedem.
Idcirco coetus inter veneranda pudicos
Una es, quam latis coeli in regionibus olim
Tot Divum celebrent voces: proh gaudia terris
Quanta dabis! quantis hominum succurrere votis
Incipies!" Stupuit confestim exterrita Virgo:
Dimisitque oculos totosque expalluit artus.
Non secus ac conchis si quando intenta legendis
Seu Micone parva scopulis seu forte Seriphi
Nuda pedem virgo, laetae nova gloria matris,
Veliferam advertit vicina ad litora puppim
Adventare, timet, nec iam subducere vestem
Audet, nec tuto ad socias se reddere cursu:
Sed trepidans silet obtutuque immobilis haeret.
Illa Arabum merces et fortunata Canopi
Dona ferens, nullis bellum mortalibus infert,
Sed pelago innocuis circumnitet armamentis.
Tum rutilus coeli Alipotens, cui lactea fandi
Copia, divinique fluunt e pectore rores

---

and spotless; and whatever indeed is conferred by the purest Wisdom, when it descends to earth from the Empyrean, and by Grace overflowing from its swelling shores. The Father who controls the ceaseless wheeling of the stars has consecrated you by an unshakeable decree, and has fixed His unmoving seat within your heart. For this you are honored among all the company of the chaste, and one day holy voices may sing your praise through the wide reaches of heaven. Oh how much joy will you bring to earth! what great human prayers will you begin to answer!'

Now the astonished virgin took fright, lowered her eyes and paled in all her limbs. She was like a barefoot maiden, the young pride of a happy mother, bent upon gathering shells on the Myconus or perhaps among the rocks of Seriphus, who sees the prow of the sailing ship near shore and is frightened, and hesitates both to raise her skirt and to run back to her comrades, but remains trembling where she is and stares with a fixed look. The ship of course has no hostile intentions toward anyone; its harmless armaments gleam upon the sea, and it moves on bearing its Arabian merchandise and lavish gifts from Canopus.

Then the strongwinged spoke again, the brilliant one from heaven, from

Ambrosiae, quibus ille acres mulcere procellas
Possit et iratos pelago depellere ventos:
"Exue, Dia, metus animo, paritura verendum
Coelitibus Numen sperataque gaudia terris
Aeternamque datura venis per saecula pacem.
Haec ego siderea missus tibi Nuntius arce,
Sublimis celeres vexit quem penna per auras,
Vaticinor, non insidias, non nectere fraudes
Edoctus: longe a nostris fraus exsulat oris.
Quippe tui magnum magna incrementa per orbem
Ipsa olim Partus, Virgo, Sobolisque beatae
Adspicies: vincet proavos proavitque longo
Extendet iura imperio populisque vocatis
Ad solium late ingentes moderabitur urbes,
Nec sceptri iam finis erit nec terminus aevi.
Quin iustis paulatim animis pulcherrima surget
Religio: non monstra, piis sed Numina templis
Placabunt castae diris sine caedibus arae."

[1.82–154]

I have not quoted the entire scene, which continues for another seventy lines, and concludes with the mystical conception of the divine child. Had I quoted the whole, it would have been clearer that its unfolding follows with fidelity, however great the stylistic distance, the much briefer scene in Luke 1:26–38. The angel's first

---

whose heart flow streams of eloquence like milk or ambrosia, by which he can calm rough storms and drive the furious winds from the sea:

'Have no fear, Goddess; you come as the long awaited blessing for the world, to give birth to the adorable God of heaven and to bring eternal peace through the ages. I, the messenger dispatched to carry you this word from the starry citadel above, borne by my lofty wing through the strong winds, I make this prophecy, unskilled in weaving plots and frauds together. Fraud has long been exiled from our shores. You yourself, Lady, will really see the great works of your blessed child, the fruit of your womb, throughout the wide world. He shall surpass his forebears, promulgating their law by means of an enduring empire, and from his throne surrounded by all the nations, shall govern the great cities of the earth. There shall be no limit to his power in space or time. Rather a new religion of the highest beauty shall arise among the upright. Pure altars free from any revolting bloodshed and set in holy temples shall honor, not the monsters worshipped heretofore, but true gods.' "

speech (109–23) is an expansion of the famous greeting: "Hail, thou that art highly favored, the Lord is with thee; blessed art thou among women" (28). The Virgin's uncertainty (described in 123–34) follows from this verse: "And when she saw him, she was troubled at his saying, and cast in her mind what manner of salutation this should be" (29). The angel's second speech in Sannazaro (139–54) expands and transmutes a somewhat longer passage:

> And the angel said unto her, Fear not, Mary: for thou hast found favor with God. And behold, thou shalt conceive in thy womb, and bring forth a son, and shalt call his name *Jesus.* He shall be great, and shall be called the Son of the Highest: and the Lord God shall give unto him the throne of his father David: And he shall reign over the house of Jacob for ever; and of his kingdom there shall be no end. [30–33]

In the remainder of the scene, the angel resolves the Virgin's doubts regarding the manner of the child's conception, and refers to the miraculous conception in the womb of her cousin Elizabeth. Whereupon Mary accepts with humility her appointed role. Sannazaro's only true structural departure is his concluding attempt to describe the conception itself, which the original account leaves discreetly in the shadow.

Thus we have, on the one hand, a scrupulous respect for the Gospel narrative, so far as it goes, and on the other hand, the greatest liberty taken with style, with background, with details from the poet's own imagination. This is the paradox of the scene as it is indeed the paradox of the poem. The angel, who lacks a single distinguishing trait, a single adjective, in the Gospel, acquires a *presence* in the poem, deriving not only from his fuller speeches but from the precise and beautiful description of his descent, the long swan simile, the epithets accorded him ("rutilus coeli Alipotens"), the few strokes suggesting his physical appearance ("Iuvenis," "purpureos vultus"), the scent which he emits, his eloquence ("lactea fandi copia"), his power over natural forces ("acres mulcere procellas possit"). The Virgin is not so fully developed, but she too acquires traits not found in Luke: a certain regal majesty (she is called "Regina" and "Diva") and an intellectual curiosity (she is discovered reading, according to an old tradition, prophecies of the Incarnation). The girlish hesitation which the Gospel records is evoked here with more sophisticated art by means of the shell-gatherer simile.

The material which has been added is drawn clearly enough from two principal sources: from Italian painting and from classical poetry. Had the poet never seen a fresco of the Annunciation, one imagines, the episode would lack a part of its freshness, its delicacy, its coolness; the angel might have been made less youthful, less graceful, rather weightier, and more mature. But so deep is the influence of antique Latin poetry that it is impossible to say what the scene would have been without it. One feels it in the language which seeks always control, nobility, clarity, and restraint, and in the imagery, in the reminiscences of Virgil and Ovid and the formality of the similes. Scholars have been able to point to specific passages of the *Aeneid* or Virgil's *Eclogues* which might have inspired a given detail: the swans haunting the Caystros or the scent which accompanies Gabriel.[4] It is obvious that the descent as a whole, in its conception, stems from Mercury's descent to Aeneas. The only other indisputable derivation from a specific passage occurs at the end of the angel's second speech; in the evocation of the child's future power, Sannazaro alludes directly, for reasons discussed below, to Jupiter's panegyric of Roman power in Book One of the *Aeneid*. The line

> Nec sceptri iam finis erit nec terminus aevi

corresponds to the Biblical expression

> Et regni eius non erit finis. [Luke 1:33] [5]

but is also meant to recall Virgil's

> His ego nec metas rerum nec tempore pono,
> Imperium sine fine dedi.
> [*Aeneid* 1.278–79] [6]

4. The most exhaustive, perhaps too exhaustive, collection of classical "imitations" in the poem appears in Vittorio Borghini, *Il più nobile umanista del Rinascimento* (Turin and Milan, 1943). Sig. Borghini counts exactly 127 imitations of Virgil alone.

5. "Of his kingdom there shall be no end."

6. "I set no limits, material or temporal; I have given them empire without end."

This however is surely the single deliberate *allusion* to a classical text. So steeped in classical imagery was the poet's imagination that he least of all, doubtless, could have specified the provenance of a given detail. Sannazaro was attempting to write a poem which, despite its subject, might have been read without confusion by a patrician of the first century. Thus the omission of the Virgin's name—Mary, and the angel's name—Gabriel, although both are named of course in the Gospel; thus the reference in line 153 to "Numina"—the gods—in the plural; thus the references to the Zephyrs and to Mount Olympus; thus the vague circumlocution in lines 94–95 for the Hebrew prophets. The poem is written according to a strict and hampering sense of decorum, a decorum scarcely compatible at first view with any Biblical story whatever.

As a result of its rigid decorum, the style is slightly flattened out by a kind of academicism. Like the bulk of neo-Latin poetry, it has a tendency to stiffen; it becomes less open to the demonic properties of language at the same time that it conserves, mummified as it were, the devices by which classical poets had introduced the demonic. Thus the similes, lovely as they are in themselves, tend to function more as decorations, less as narrative devices which impose subtle colorings of feeling upon their contexts. This is particularly true of the swan simile. The development is important because it helps to explain why neo-Latin poetry was abandoned by major continental poets as abruptly as it was, on the whole, towards the middle of the sixteenth century. The cruder vulgar languages, lacking a vocabulary and a syntax to accommodate the high style, still came to be preferred for poetry at every stylistic level because they possessed a plasticity which Latin was seen to lack. Too much had been done with Latin that was of a piece, monumental, invariable; it could no longer be manipulated to create fresh and dynamic poetry. But the sacrifice of Latin was not made without a cost—the cost precisely of the formal elegance which Sannazaro's style exemplifies.

The *De Partu Virginis* is the product of an age not yet ready to make the sacrifice, an age on the contrary obsessed with classical culture. *Obsession* is not too strong a word. It is difficult to exaggerate the magnetism of antiquity during a few decades upon the educated Italian mind. Certainly no other country experienced any comparable Humanistic awakening and in no other country is neo-Latin literature so integral and so sizable a part of the national literature. In France, in England, in Germany, the discovery of the classical world was an important intellectual experience, but that world was almost always seen from without, as though through a pane of glass. For only a very few men, in these countries, did the experience concern immediately the senses and the nerve ends. In Italy one had the sensation of moving and breathing *within* the classical world, and thinking and writing within it too. The sensation doubtless was illusory. But nonetheless it was felt; it is a fact of cultural history. And whereas at its worst Italian Humanism (particularly at Rome) was a ridiculous, pedantic fad (with its absurd refusal, for example, to use words not found in Cicero), at its finest it enriched immeasurably the mind of Europe.

Although Sannazaro was a Neapolitan, his ties with Rome were close. The *De Partu Virginis* was to have been dedicated to Leo X, godfather of Roman Humanism, and was finally dedicated to Clement VII after Leo's death. It was motivated by the same eclecticism which brought, through Raphael's brush, Plato, Aristotle, Pythagoras, and the other pagan philosophers face to face with St. Thomas, St. Bonaventura, and the theologians, in a single chamber of the Vatican. The classical mannerisms we have observed in Sannazaro's Annunciation are less striking than several subsequent anomalies—for example the imitation of Virgil's messianic fourth eclogue placed in the mouths of the Hebrew shepherds at the nativity. The shepherds' names are Lycidas, Tityrus, and Menalca. There is, in fact, scarcely a Biblical proper noun in the whole work; neither Gabriel, nor Mary, nor Joseph, nor Jesus, nor David, nor Elizabeth is named directly once, although all figure in the action. The proper nouns which do appear belong to the incidental figures drawn from mythology: Tethys and Amphitrite, Cerberus and Pluto, the Muses, Apollo and Proteus. The mythological machinery reaches its most bathetic point when the feet of Christ, walking upon the waves and surrounded by Nereids, are kissed by a reverent Neptune!

The classical coloring "dignifies" the Gospel stories, substituting for their bareness and simplicity a more ornate and aristocratic tonality. The epic manner, as understood by the Renaissance, required a certain grandiosity which might have reduced the original stories to absurdity. So Sannazaro's most formidable artistic problem was to raise the level of the material without destroying its essential dramatic qualities. He could not, for example, "dignify" the Virgin so greatly at the outset as to permit our wonder at the angelic visit to fade. She had to remain, to a degree, virginally delicate and girlishly uncertain. But in the Annunciation scene, this problem is complicated by the particular paradox of the situation: the Virgin is apparently inferior to the angel in the scale of being, but as mother of the godhead is worthy of his reverence. The paradox has already been made explicit before the angel's entrance; God the Father has described her as worthy of reigning gloriously in heaven:

> Digna polo regnare altoque effulgere Divum
> Concilio, et nostros aeternum habitare penates.
> [1.71–72] [7]

whereas in fact she dwells under a humble roof (*paupere tecto*). The problem for the poet was to make the most of the paradox dramatically without violating either of its aspects. Against all probability Sannazaro brings off the scene masterfully.

It was necessary first to establish the dignity of the two figures. The angel's speed, power, and grace, emerging first from the account, are turned in a sense to the honor of the girl for whom he descends and whom he compliments so graciously. But despite that honor, and despite her deep religious feeling which we perceive immediately, her dignity is qualified by a human ignorance: filled with awe for the future mother of God, she cannot know that she is herself that mother. Her humanity shows itself more fully in her confusion and fear after the angel's greeting and is intensified by the shell-gatherer simile. At this point the apparent distance between angel and girl is widest, and widened more by the greater powers now attributed to the angel: if she is like a poor frightened girl by the sea's edge, he is like a god who can still the raging sea with a word. Here Sannazaro's perilous balance

7. "Worthy of reigning in heaven, of shining in the high council of the gods, and of dwelling in our habitations forever."

might have been irretrievably lost. But in fact the simile is brilliantly conceived, with the cool distinctiveness of its language, with the natural grace one intuits in the girl, with the tranquillizing reassurance following the illusory alarm. The Virgin loses no true dignity but gains a gentle delicacy. And the angel's second speech, evoking the vastness of her son's future empire, makes a contrast with her gentleness and rights the balance of greatness in her favor. So it will remain through the rest of the scene.

Thus, in the moments when it touches us, the poem's success involves discreet solutions of very nice artistic problems. The wonder is that the Gospel story is not crushed by the elevated tone and the extrinsic pagan apparatus. Transmuted it certainly is, but not unrecognizably. In his personal life, it appears that Sannazaro retained a devout orthodox faith (despite the superstition and hypocritical skepticism of his contemporaneous Naples) to balance his Humanistic enthusiasm; so analogously his poem communicates a Christian fervor through the welter of classical divinities. It is a *tour de force* which no other age could have produced, depending as it does on both the supplest religiosity and on a Humanistic sense of great spontaneous vitality. Sannazaro brought his Humanistic art, the only art he knew, as an offering to the church and to the Virgin. He could scarcely have modified the nature of his art, and had he tried could only have made an inferior thing. In a curious way he was an erudite *jongleur de Notre Dame.*

ii.

Sannazaro's transmutation of the Gospel story is representative in several ways of Italian religious feeling in the early sixteenth century. I have said above that his faith was orthodox, but orthodoxy under Leo X was not the orthodoxy of St. Augustine or St. Francis. And one may speak in this regard not only of orthodoxy in doctrine but in sensibility also. The sensuousness of Renaissance religiosity, its emotional facility, its easy optimism, its ostentation, its pagan eccentricities, its need for pictorial imagery—all find their reflection in the *De Partu Virginis.* With what half-pagan pleasure in sound and color, what faith in the externals of religious ceremony, is the Virgin's aid invoked at the opening of the poem!

> Tuque adeo, spes fida hominum, spes fida Deorum,
> Alma Parens, quam mille acies quaeque aetheris alti
> Militia est, totidem currus, tot signa tubaeque,
> Tot litui comitantur ovantique agmina gyro
> Adglomerant; niveis tibi si solemnia templis
> Serta damus, si mansuras tibi ponimus aras
> Exciso in scopulo, fluctus unde aurea canos
> Despiciens celso se culmine Mergilline [8]
> Adtollit, nautisque procul venientibus offert:
> Si laudes de more tuas, si sacra diemque
> Ac coetus late insignes ritusque dicamus,
> Annua felicis colimus dum gaudia partus:
> Tu vatem ignarumque viae insuetumque labori,
> Diva, mone, et pavidis iam laeta adlabere coeptis.
>
> [1.19–32] [9]

The poetic élan swells unbroken throughout the single long sentence, with its opening clarion summons of chariots and trumpets, its suspenseful repetition of "si" clauses, and its ultimate resolution delayed until the last line and sprung climactically by the twin imperatives. It is a poetry of gleaming surfaces, reflecting the radiance of the central feminine figure, smiling and gracious, wreathed with the pomp of heaven. Something of the concreteness, splendor, joy, and music in Milton's heaven may derive from this brilliant Italian vision.

8. The Mergellina was Sannazaro's home near Naples.

9. "And you, Who embody the hope and faith of men and of the Gods, glorious mother, surrounded by a thousand squadrons and all the armies of high heaven, with their chariots, their banners, their horns and trumpets, wheeling about you in a circle of hosannas: if in our gleaming temples we bring you ceremonious garlands; if we erect enduring altars to you set upon hollowed rock, where the golden Mergellina, looking down upon the silver waves, towers high on its peak and reveals itself to distant seamen; if we chant your praise in the traditional way, celebrating annually in great assemblies your holiday, your holy service, the happy commemoration of your motherhood: then instruct your poet, unfamiliar with his journey, unaccustomed to his task, and approach his uncertain enterprise joyfully."

But the world which this poetry evokes emerges nonetheless as a little emasculated, lacking the vital energy of the finest epics. Thus the swan to which Gabriel is compared does not truly communicate the sensation of quickness, although it is apparently supposed to. You need only think of Homer's cormorant to feel the difference; this bird is comparatively leisurely in its descent to the quiet Caystros—"placidi stagna ampla Caystri." Nature is tamed as man and the world are tamed. The poet conveys an imperial view of things, the view of ecclesiastical imperialism, which softens the violence it would like to subdue. The imperial principle extends even to Sannazaro's heaven, where the Deity appears as a kind of Renaissance prince with angels for courtiers, each angel assigned to his own palace, each palazzo bearing its owner's name and heraldic arms.

> Namque ferunt olim leges cum conderet aequas
> Rex Superûm et valido mundum suspenderet axe,
> Diversas statuisse domos diversaque Divis
> Hospitia et dignos meritis tribuisse penates
> Ordine cuique suos. Illi data tecta frequentant
> Armaque et aeratis adfigunt nomina valvis.
>
> [3.8–13] [10]

It is impossible to be offended by this but it is difficult not to be amused. Clearly the Christian tradition has undergone a radical shift of emphasis.

The shift is made explicit in the Pelagian interpretation which Sannazaro placed upon the redemption. In dispatching Gabriel to earth, God has chosen to wipe away all vestiges of original sin and to raise man to the status of the angels. Once the Son's sacrifice has been made, man will regain his rightful place in paradise and the infernal powers will be forever thwarted.

> . . . Divum potius revocentur ad oras,
> Ut decet . . .

10. "For it is said that when the King of Heaven first ordained just laws and balanced the world firmly on its axis, he assigned various mansions and chambers to the gods, and specified in due order a fit dwelling for each according to his rank. They dwell under the roofs given them and fix their names and arms upon their bronze doors."

The contrast with Milton imposes itself. Nothing is said by the Father of those who will not be saved after the Redemption, although these for Milton will be in a heavy majority. Sannazaro scarcely glances at the harsh theology which requires human sacrifice for Adam's sin, the theology which Milton's God will be at such pains to explain. It is characteristic of Catholicism before the Council of Trent that it place emphasis on the Redemption (not only in Sannazaro but in Mantuan's *Parthenicae,* Vida's *Christias,* and other poems) just as it is characteristic of Puritanism that its greatest, most representative poem dramatize the Fall. Buoyed up by Renaissance individualism, intoxicated by an oversimplified perspective upon antiquity, the church's conception of man never placed him closer to the angels than during these decades. In this it followed the philosophy of the fifteenth century. As unlike as the aging Sannazaro was from Pico della Mirandola, one senses in the former's untroubled optimism a pale afterglow of the latter's youthful and magnificent manifesto—the *De Hominis Dignitate.*

A corollary of the Pelagianism is the absence in the poem of a diabolic principle. There are, to be sure, picturesque allusions to Gorgons and Hydras and Chimeras dire in Hades, but the Incarnation represents their total and irrevocable defeat. As a result the poem is ultimately passionless, a pageant rather than a drama. The note of joy, struck first by Gabriel ("pro gaudia terris quanta dabis!") and sustained almost uninterruptedly through the three books, permits no dramatic tension. The poised and regal figure of the Virgin lacks a heroic dimension because her moral distinctiveness is asserted but never dramatized; no moral austerity is demanded of her. Here, I think, the point of contact becomes clear between the two extremes which Sannazaro and Ariosto seem to represent. For Sannazaro's descent of Gabriel breaks with Virgil, if less ostentatiously, in the same basic sense that Ariosto's descent does: it has nothing to do with divine pressure upon human will. Gabriel descends to announce, not to command, and later the personified Laetitia will descend only as a source of refulgent joy. No effort is asked of anyone, and given the exaggerated view of the human condition which animates the poem, no effort has to be asked.

The force which one does feel operating in the poem is the poet's creative, esemplastic will, moving with precision and grace human beings whose personal wills are slight. The harmony between the creative and personal will which Virgil achieved, was to take the Renaissance a long time to discover. In the panegyrical epic of the *quattrocento,* the personal will had been dominant and the creative will less inclined to impose order. A typical example, Basini's *Hesperidos* (1455), shows the angel descending to command Sigismondo Malatesta to fight a battle which, historically, Malatesta needed no divine sanction to fight. In and out of the poem his will was so strong that no pressure from heaven was really needed. A century later the late Renaissance slackening of the will makes itself felt to the point of comedy in Trissino's *L'Italia Liberata dai Goti* (1547). The angel Onorio descends to command Justinian in a dream to drive the barbarians out of Italy. But the emperor's awakening is something less than heroic: it involves chiefly making his fastidious toilet. I have space only to quote the beginning of this lengthy procedure:

> Svegliossi il gran Signore, e ben conobbe,
> Ch'era l'Angel di Dio quel, che gli apparve;
> E disse al fido Pilade, che sempre
> Stava al governo della sua persona:
> Pilade, non dormir, ma sorgi, e tosto
> Porgimi i panni miei, ch'io vo' levarmi . . .
> Levossi il Cameriero, e tolse prima
> La camiscia di lin sottile, e bianca,
> E la vesti sull' onorate membra;
> Poi sopra quella ancor vestì il giuppone,
> Ch'era di drappo d'oro; indi calzogli
> Le calze di rosato, e poi le scarpe
> Di velluto rosin gli cinse ai piedi . . .[11]

11. Giangiorgio Trissino, *L'Italia Liberata dai Goti* (London, 1779), pp. 4–5. "The great lord awoke and recognized that it was indeed the angel of God who had appeared to him; and he spoke to his faithful Pilade, who always took care of his personal wants: 'Pilade, don't sleep, but get up and bring me quickly my clothes, because I want to rise . . ." The valet rose and took first the shirt of white, fine linen, and arrayed the honored limbs in it; then over this he placed the coat, made of gold cloth; after this he put rose-colored stockings on his feet, and then shoes of rose velvet."

In contrast, d'Aubigné's poem, a product of the north European Protestant reaction to southern Pelagianism, will apply the intensest kind of moral pressure on the individual but will represent a weakening of the esemplastic pressure. Tasso will dramatize the Counter-Reformation demands upon a moral will not quite able to bear them, and fifty years later Marino will demonstrate something near to the collapse of Renaissance moral idealism in Italy. Only in Milton, perhaps, will an alert artistic will be balanced by a firm moral sense, and not even there without strains.

In Sannazaro this kind of harmony between esthetic and ethical is scarcely attempted. The Crucifixion itself, which in the Gospel account requires a profound effort of courage, appears here only as the last in a series of scenes evoked prophetically by David in limbo. The center of interest is not Christ but His mother, whose long soliloquy, full of despairing grief, is a kind of set piece stemming from the long convention of the *Stabat Mater*. But here grief is too facile, almost sentimental; it has no relation to the rest of the poem, just as the distraught woman imploring God to visit His wrath upon her has no relation to the poised and majestic queen of other passages. The will is not even invoked to check the violent outpouring of sorrow.

It is an irony typical of Rome in the early years of the Reformation period that the *De Partu Virginis* was hailed by Leo X as a potential weapon against the German heretics. He could not have understood that in all its essential qualities, the poem was calculated to alienate them: its studied classicism would offend their anti-Humanism, its stylistic smoothness their antiformalism, its emotional facility their stern integrity, its humanizing of God their Augustinian awe of Him, its high conception of man their tormented sense of human misery. Unaware of all these contradictions, Leo had his high hopes expressed in writing even before the poem appeared, hopes phrased for him by the great Bembo:

> We were awaiting your work eagerly and rejoice to see it completed. It would have been precious to us at any time, but at this moment it is particularly precious . . . We believe it to be the work of divine Providence that the divine Spouse, attacked by so many opponents and critics, finds in

> you such a defender; that while others exhaust their efforts against celestial matters, you alone have thought to prop up this edifice with every buttress and splendor of style, surpassed by none of the ancients. You are the devout David who combats with his sling a Goliath heavily armed.[12]

When the poem appeared several years later, it was welcomed by another letter from Clement VII, who nourished similar illusions.

The illusions may have been based upon a certain strain in the work which implicitly glorifies the church. The echoes of Jupiter's prophecy noted in Gabriel's speech at the Annunciation have an important function: they paragon the power and scope of Augustus' empire with the power and scope of Leo's church. The parallel was not, of course, Sannazaro's invention; as the ghosts of antiquity came to haunt all of Italy, the parallel was in everyone's mind. Thus the empire, which might have played the role of antichrist in the poem, is on the contrary treated respectfully. This consideration may explain the presence of a passage at the poem's precise center which has irritated some of its critics: a long roll call of all the nations in turn which comprised the Roman Empire. The interlude is a stylistic *tour de force,* naming a hundred-odd peoples and assigning some sort of geographical or ethnic characteristic to each; but it finds its true justification in the implicit comparison of empire and church. In its opening lines:

> Interea terra parta iam pace marique
> Augustus pater aeratis bella impia portis
> Clauserat et validis arctarat vincta catenis
> Imperii exhaustasque armis civilibus urbes
> Dumque suas Regnator opes viresque potentis
> Nosse cupit . . . [2.116–21] [13]

the chains and doors which contain war recall the cage where Virgil's Rome contains the "impius Furor," but "Augustus pater"

12. Quoted by Giuseppe Toffanin, in Italian translation, in *Il Cinquecento,* Storia Letteraria d'Italia (Milan, 1954), pp. 42–43.

13. "Meanwhile, earth and sea having been pacified, Father Augustus had shut up impious war behind bronze gates and bound it with firm bonds; and the Ruler desired to count the wealth and the population of his potent empire, and the cities pillaged by the armies of the state."

recalls rather the holy father to whom the poem was dedicated.[14] In a certain sense the task of the new-born Christ child would be to extend and deepen the accomplishment of Augustus. So if in the literal view there is joy for the decorative and graceful scene about the manger, and in the theological view joy for the return of man to angelic dignity, there is in the historical view joy that the political authority of Rome be perpetuated in a divinely sanctioned church. Thus Sannazaro's attempt to reconcile the classical and Christian traditions was conceptual as well as artistic. But it is always dangerous to base a work of art on a situation which history can alter. In the year which saw his poem published, Rome was sacked by the armies of another emperor.

iii.

Sannazaro's correspondence contains these remarks on the classical allusions in the *De Partu Virginis:*

> I did not choose to proceed nakedly as many have chosen to do and it would not please me to treat this material without a certain poetic sprightliness. Let it suffice that the Virgin is not called a nymph, nor Christ the son of Jove or Apollo as Petrarch calls him: "Lavit apollineos ad ripam fluminis artus"; I think that this would indeed be a mistake. But I have not refrained from things which do no harm to religion and which one can feign without scandal; on the contrary I have sought them with great care.[15]

14. Leo may be represented allegorically in a triumphal procession which follows Christ to heaven after the harrowing of hell:

> Et iuxta nemorum terror rexque ipse ferarum
> Magnanimus nitet ore Leo, quem fusa per armos
> Convestit iuba, pectoribus generosa superbit
> Maiestas . . . [1.419–22]

"And next gleams the terror of the forest, the very king of the wild beasts, magnanimous Leo, clothed by the flowing hair which covers his shoulders, whose noble majesty stirs the heart . . ."

15. *Un Divorzio ai tempi di Leone X da XL lettere di Jacopo Sannazaro,* ed. E. Nunziante (Rome, 1887), pp. 168–69. The Petrarchan phrase: "He bathed his Apollonian limbs by the river bank," is drawn from his first eclogue.

In his own mind Sannazaro thought that he was pursuing a middle course between the austerity of those who eschewed classical mannerisms and the excessive classicizing for which he condemns Petrarch. The expression he uses to describe his own course is striking—"feign without scandal"—*fingere senza scandalo.* "Scandalo" seems to have meant for him both desecration and offense to public taste; we learn from the same letter that, but for fear of public criticism, he would have alluded to passages by Latin poets other than Virgil, passages which he might have been able to twist into prophecies of the divine birth.[16] It is instructive that his poem was criticized by his contemporaries from both directions: by those who, like Erasmus, thought the imaginative dress too gaudy and the piety too thin:

> He would have deserved more praise if he had treated his sacred subject somewhat more reverently.[17]

but also by those like the saintly Cardinal Egidio da Viterbo who reproached the poet for not making more of the Muses. There were many other readers, however, who admired the poem, and only later in the century, when piety was less tolerant, was there a chorus of derogation. The poem crystallized for its century, as it may for us, an artistic problem which was even then a millenium old and which would persist to trouble epic poetry for another century and a half. Sannazaro had many predecessors who had chosen to feign fictions in writing religious poetry, and had done it, to their own satisfaction, "without scandal."

At the end of the fifteenth century two early Christian poems were brought to light in Italy which spurred considerably the zeal of Christian epic poets. These were the *Evangeliorum Libri Quattuor* by Gaius Juvencus (d. 337), a Spaniard who seems to have been Bishop of Salamanca, and the *Carmen Paschale* in five books

16. "I believe that I do not err if I maintain that God wished to be preached throughout the world, and if the same fear of giving offense did not restrain me, I would have found a place for more than six other prophecies of our people, and for one, that of Ovid speaking of Augustus: 'Prospiciet prolem sancta de vergine natam.' " Ibid., p. 167. The allusion is to the *Metamorphoses,* 15.836.

17. *Ciceronianus,* trans. I. Scott (New York, 1908), p. 118.

by Caelius Sedulius (fifth century A.D.), published in 494. Both poems were written in hexameters, both dealt with the life of Jesus, and both, but particularly Juvencus', derived from classical pagan poetry. In the example of these ancient works Renaissance poets found an authority for their own grafting of Christian branch to classical tree.

But in fact the propriety of such poetry would not have gone unquestioned in the patristic age. The proper attitude of Christianity toward classical culture was debated warmly by the early Church Fathers. That St. Augustine's position in this debate was liberal was a circumstance heavy with consequences for the future of poetry and indeed of occidental culture. Augustine's attitude is typified in a passage of the *De Doctrina Christiana* (Book II, chapter 40); the passage may remind us, incidentally, of the refined degree to which its author had brought the art of scriptural interpretation.

> If by chance those who are called philosophers have spoken truths which can be accommodated to our faith . . . these truths should, far from being rejected, rather be reclaimed by us for our own use as though from illegitimate owners. For just as the Egyptians had not only idols and hard work which the children of Israel detested and avoided, but also gold and silver vases and ornaments, and clothing, which the Hebrews claimed for their own better use as they left Egypt, not on their own authority but by the command of God . . . so all the beliefs of the Gentiles contain not only fables and invented superstitions and useless requirements of labor, which each of us must despise and shun as we follow Christ out of the pagan world, but also the liberal arts, which are more proper for the use of truth, and certain precepts useful in governing our lives, even verities which reveal the one God.

The charming analogy with the children of Israel made the chapter memorable; together with other passages and with Augustine's own example, it provided authority for the enjoyment within limits not only of pagan philosophy but other forms of culture.

This authority was heeded by Dante, whose employment of classical deities, heroes, ideas, and institutions in the *Commedia* was audaciously free. Not only did he place Charon, Minos, Cerberus, Pluto, and other mythological figures in the *Inferno* while placing Trajan in heaven; not only did he damn Capaneo for blaspheming Zeus and assign equal punishments to Brutus, Cassius, and Judas; not only did he address God as

sommo Giove
che fosti in terra per noi crucifisso.
[*Purgatorio,* 6.118–19] [18]

More significantly, Dante made one of the great structural principles of the work the complementary relation of classical and Christian, empire and church, Virgil and Beatrice, natural wisdom and divine inspiration, cardinal virtues and theological virtues, temporal power and celestial power, just as he carefully alternated classical and Judaic-Christian *exempla* on each terrace of Purgatory. Thus the author of the *Convivio* had not hesitated to write that Roman power was brought to its height at Christ's birth by Providence, that Aeneas and David were contemporaries by Providential plan, and that the "sacratissimo" Cato of Utica had been the most perfect image of God on earth.[19] In the *Commedia,* Cato, converted to Christianity, is the ideal example of the classical-Christian fusion and as such is made the overlord of Purgatory.

But despite Dante's profound Humanistic feeling, there is never any question in his work of the embarrassing lapses of taste into which later poets would blunder. This is because Dante's mind was in this respect solidly medieval, enlightened certainly beyond most of his contemporaries,[20] but restricted nonetheless by a medieval vision of antiquity. He assimilated and harmonized instinctively the alien antique culture to the values and images of his own. This restrictedness of vision was of great use; it permitted him to include a wide range of pagan material without violating the tonality and moral coherence of his poem.

The problem for Petrarch presented itself less simply and resolved itself less happily. The greater depth of Petrarch's erudition worked almost as a handicap for him, dividing his sensibility and

18. "Supernal Jove who wast crucified on earth for us.

19. *Convivio,* 4th treatise, chapter 5.

20. For example in the interpretation of Virgil's fourth eclogue, *De Monarchia,* 1.ii.

making him aware of cultural alternatives. It was no longer possible in his age to assimilate antiquity because too much of it was beginning to be known and its irreducible distinctiveness was too obvious. We have already seen evidence of Petrarch's bad conscience in the opening of the *Africa;* in the first Latin eclogue quoted by Sannazaro, Petrarch openly dramatized the conflict between piety and Humanist poetry in his own soul. The eclogue takes the form of a dialogue between two shepherds, Silvius and Monicus, who represent respectively Petrarch and his brother Gherardo, a Carthusian monk. Silvius is haunted by the memory of Parthenias (Virgil) and an unnamed stranger (Homer), whose songs have inspired him to emulation. Monicus prefers the song of another shepherd (David). At the conclusion of the debate, Silvius goes off to celebrate a stalwart youth (Scipio) who won renown long ago in Africa. Monicus chooses to spend his life in divine adoration. There is no true resolution of the conflict; there is simply the personal decision of Silvius, the poet, to follow his poetic bent. The eclogue suggests that the historical Petrarch did not follow his bent without qualms. These qualms constitute a historical fact of some importance and initiate a chapter of cultural history which will lack neither comedy nor profound significance. It was clear then as now what was at stake: the possibility of a Christian Humanism.

The third great poet of the *trecento,* Boccaccio, attempted like Petrarch to treat Christian subjects in the pastoral mode; his eleventh eclogue, the *Pantheon,* celebrates the Christian God and Christ through a veil of pastoral and mythological names. But more important for later centuries was his influential mythographical compilation, the *De Genealogia Deorum,* which mingled moral and Christian interpretations with summaries of ancient myths. Thus, for example, Boccaccio interpreted Perseus' combat with the dragon in terms of Christ's harrowing of hell and subsequent ascension. This procedure would be imitated and developed during the sixteenth century in such influential works as Comes' *Mythologiae* and Cartari's *Imagines Deorum,* works of international popularity and considerable authority among poets in many languages.

During the fifteenth century in Italy, the most grotesque mingling of classical and Christian elements appeared in pastoral poetry, although the many panegyrical Latin epics were far from free of it.[21] Thus the holy Egidio da Viterbo, he who reproached Sannazaro for neglecting the Muses, wrote Christianized eclogues which, to cite one example, justify Christ's supernatural birth by the precedent of Minerva's; and in the eclogues of one Antonio Geraldini, the Virgin is represented as Venus and Christ as a shepherd Dafni who is innocently condemned by his fellows because his sheep's fleece is whiter than that of the other sheep. But the most celebrated of Sannazaro's predecessors was the poet known in English as Mantuan (1448–1516), a Carmelite friar who has been beatified. Mantuan, whose real name was Battista Spagnoli, composed a volume of hagiographic poetry entitled *Parthenicae* which seems to have influenced a whole generation of religious poets. The first *Parthenice,* dealing with the life of the Virgin, draws heavily upon early apocryphal legends. One can reproduce only a few of the classical touches: the Virgin is bathed in the Jordan by the Graces, who swear to be eternal "sodales"; Thetis, Ceres, Aeolus, and other pagan divinities pay homage to her; she reads the stories of Hercules, Hippolytus, Helen, etc., reproving in each whatever offends her delicacy. In a later poem (*Fasti*), Mercury eavesdrops during the annunciation of Gabriel, understands confusedly that something wrong is afoot, and hurries off to bring the dismaying news to his fellow gods. All of these scenes seem to have been written without a grain of humor.

This brief review of Sannazaro's poetic precedents should suffice to show how little original was his quasi-Virgilian manner in the *De Partu Virginis.* It should be remembered that the authority of classical mythology was supported by age-old rationalizations and moralizations, older, in some cases, than Christianity itself. M. Seznec has demonstrated [22] how the memory of the pagan gods was never stamped out by the church fathers and how pagan conceptions persisted in unbroken if eccentric patterns throughout the Middle Ages and down to the Renaissance. This was possible because the ancient gods were regarded either as astronomical

21. Thus in the *Sphortias* of Francesco Filelfo, Venus accompanies a young girl to a Christian mass.

22. Jean Seznec, *La Survivance des Dieux Antiques* (London, 1940).

bodies, or as historical heroic human beings of the dim past, or as allegorical personifications of abstract qualities. It was this last assumption which permitted fourteenth century nuns to read Ovid with moral delectation and which produced in England Bacon's *Wisdom of the Ancients.* Although the moralizations of Ovid were placed on the Index by the Council of Trent, the Counter-Reform continued to encourage the allegorical interpretation of mythology.[23] The Jesuits gave exercises in such interpretations to schoolboys, and in Protestant England they were commonly taught in grammar schools.[24]

The mingling of traditions was at least as common in Renaissance plastic arts as in literature and could be traced to as ancient examples. Pagan subjects appear in the art of the catacombs, and in medieval art they are ubiquitous if often unrecognizable. But the Middle Ages had no sense of historical contrast and was incapable of feeling anomalies. In medieval dramatic processions, Virgil and the sybils marched among the Hebrew prophets as foretellers of Christ's coming, and sybils are even invoked in the *Dies Irae,* in the liturgy itself: "Teste David cum Sibylla." The mingling was more self-conscious in the Renaissance and so more significant. Raphael's stanza of the Signatura is only a single, and conservative, example, but there are no end of others: the mausoleum of the Venetian doge (in Saints Giovanni and Paolo) which bears representations of Christ, the Maries at the tomb, and Hercules; the charterhouse of Pavia where emperors and pagan gods alternate with prophets on sculpted medallions; the Colleoni chapel at Bergamo where Old Testament stories alternate with the labors of Hercules;[25] the apartments of Alexander VI at the Vatican, adorned with paintings of Isis, Osiris, and Apis; above all the church of San Francesco at Rimini, transformed by Alberti into

23. "Ainsi donc l'Eglise, en principe, condamne l'usage de l'allegorie; mais, en fait, elle le favorise. Précisément parce que la crise de la contre-Réforme a mis en lumière l'incompatibilité entre l'esprit païen et la morale chrétienne, elle a rendu plus urgent ce besoin de conciliation et de justification qui n'avait jamais cessé de tourmenter secrètement les lettrés et les artistes de la Renaissance." Ibid., p. 241.

24. Davis Harding, *Milton and the Renaissance Ovid* (Urbana, 1946), pp. 11–41.

25. As I state below, Hercules was often associated symbolically with Christ, and this may explain his frequent appearances in religious art.

what amounted virtually to a pagan temple for his divinified patron, Sigismondo Malatesta.

In the countries north of the Alps pagan myths were commonly rendered acceptable by the notion that they constituted deformations or prophecies of Biblical stories. Thus Ronsard's *Hercule Chrestien* elaborates the tradition viewing Hercules' labors as symbolic prophecies of the life of Christ. In England this notion was particularly common; it can be found in works as different as Raleigh's *History of the World* and the *Mythomystes* of that arrogant iconoclast, Henry Reynolds.[26] Joshua Sylvester echoes the notion in his interpolations in the translated text of Du Bartas, comparing Tubal with the Cyclops and the Biblical Tree of Life with the Homeric moly. Giles Fletcher was particularly fond of these parallels; in *Christ's Victorie and Triumph* he compares Christ to Pan and Ganymede, Judas to Orestes, Pentheus, and Oedipus, and goes on to crowd one analogy upon another with lavish ingenuity:

> Who doth not see drown'd in Deucalion's name
> (When earth his men, and sea had lost his shore)
> Old Noah? and in Nisus' lock, the fame
> Of Sampson yet alive; and long before
> In Phaëthon's, mine owne fall I deplore:
> But he that conquer'd hell, to fetch againe
> His virgin widowe, by a serpent slaine,
> Another Orpheus was then dreaming poets feigne.[27]

It is less surprising to find the tradition sustained in *Paradise Lost,* where Eve is compared to Pandora, Proserpina, Pomona, Ceres, and Eurynome, than in *Paradise Regained,* where Christ's rejection of classical culture is paradoxically followed by the conventional comparison of his victory with Hercules' over Antaeus.

All of these pseudo-syntheses have to be viewed, I think, as symptoms of a cleavage in the European consciousness at the beginning of the modern age, a cleavage which was felt and which

26. See J. E. Spingarn, *Critical Essays of the Seventeenth Century, 1* (Oxford, 1908–09), 171–76.

27. *Christ's Triumph After Death,* Stanza 46. For the other comparisons, see the same book, Stanza 14, and *Christ's Triumph Over Death,* Stanzas 47–48, 65–67.

troubled, if not the excellent Jacopo Sannazaro, many other men of his century. It is our good fortune that the cleavage was not allowed to widen and to split irrevocably the modern mind, that it was covered over even by such flimsy constructions as we have seen, until the time that a more complex consciousness could emerge, a distinctly modern and independent consciousness, to subsume Christian and classical in a sturdier synthesis. Throughout most of this long, subtle, and difficult process of emergence, the Christian epic (and virtually all epic poems through the seventeenth century show at least a tincture of Christianity) constituted a faithful mirror of the synthesis possible at any time and place. Perhaps no single epic poet ever effected a wholly successful reconciliation. But the nobility and power of the successive great attempts spring partly from the struggle of the imagination to overcome its duality, to see heroic action single and whole just as, in Frost's phrase, our two eyes make one in sight.

iv.

The *Christias* of Marco Girolamo Vida, bishop of Alba, appeared within a decade of the *De Partu Virginis* and resembles it in several superficial respects. Like his predecessor's, Vida's far more influential poem reflects papal patronage, boasts a correct and fluent Latin style, abounds in Virgilian echoes, and attempts to classicize Scripture. Despite these similarities, however, there are relative novelties in Vida which anticipate later developments in the religious epic and the climate of feeling gradually settling down over Italy. The *Christias* is a colder and less original poem than Sannazaro's, but it registered accurately the direction in which the literary winds were beginning to blow and doubtless hastened their advent by its own example.

If Sannazaro's sky remains uniformly blue and rose, in Vida there are darker clouds on the horizon. If Sannazaro, to be precise, virtually excludes a diabolic principle, Vida reintroduces Hell, Satan, devils, and a demonic council to set a long-standing and highly productive fashion. It is very important, whether for better or worse, that Vida's demonic machinery derives from Claudian (and from antique epic in general) rather than from Dante, whom

Vida patronizes in his *Ars Poetica;* it is important because Vida's treatment was to be imitated, among others, by Tasso, Hojeda, Marino, Phineas Fletcher, Cowley, and Milton. In addition to this innovation, Vida laid greater stress on sin and suffering than the serene Sannazaro, dwelling in particular upon the physical torment of Christ with an attentiveness which is not so much post-medieval as pre-Baroque. There is also strong emphasis upon the maleficent role of the Jewish priesthood, which is painted in still darker colors here than in the Gospels; in places the text seems to breathe that effluvium of religious hatred which was to hang over many later Christian epics. Pilate, on the other hand, is ennobled, so that his portrait may conform to the association made between imperial and Catholic Rome.

The *Christias* was one of those poems, like the *Africa* and the *Franciade,* too eagerly awaited for its own good. Like Ronsard, Vida tried to do too much. His six long books embrace not only the full life of Christ, from birth to crucifixion, harrowing of hell, resurrection, ascension, and the Pentecostal inspiration, but a great deal of Old Testament history as well. Vida did not know or did not heed Aristotle's praise of Homer for the delimitation of his subject; he wrote in an age almost entirely ignorant of the *Poetics* and imperfectly aware of Homer, and this neglect is highly significant in view of what was to come. His poem fails partly because it is not Aristotelian enough, has no beginning, middle, and end, and remains hopelessly episodic. And with all its superabundance of Biblical story, it succeeds far less happily than the *De Partu Virginis* in transmuting the dramatic values of the Bible. The last supper, for example, is held in apartments so richly furnished as to nullify the scene's impact. Some sections betray that Italian love of showiness for itself which is so un-Hebraic; this fault indeed mars the description of an angelic apparition to Joseph:

Nudus erat roseos humeros: tantum aurea laevo
Pendebat demissa chlamys, quam fibula subter
Ilia ter gemino mordebat rasilis auro,
Rubraque compactis pendebant cingula bullis,
Molles a tergo tractim succrescere plumae,
Ac sensim geminas humeris assurgere in alas:

Tum suras gemmis inclusit, caetera nudus.
Oris multus honos, gratique in corpore motus,
Haud nostri puerum generis testantur adesse,
Sed coeli sobolem, atque aulae stellantis alumnum.
Nec minus ipsa etiam mira spectabilis arte
Vestis erat baccis superas illusa per oras.
Textile maeandro duplici infra circuit aurum,
Admirabile opus . . .[28]

This excessive fullness of detail anticipates much later developments of the convention.

Vida must be regarded as a transitional figure from the high Renaissance to the Counter-Reformation. His proper nouns reflect something of Sannazaro's excesses: he refers to heaven as Olympos and hell as Tartarus, for example, and the angels he calls *superi;* he generally prefers to call his protagonist *Heros, Rex,* or *Deus,* rather than *Christus.* On the other hand he introduces no frankly pagan divinities. If Vida was transitional, however, at least one of his lesser-known contemporaries already prefigured much more strongly the tone and temper of the Counter-Reform. This was Teofilo Folengo, a converted reprobate who is best known for his macaronic mock-epic, the *Baldus.* The poem of Folengo's repentant old age, *L'Umanità del Figliuol di Dio,* is much inferior to his earlier, Rabelaisian work, but it possesses a certain historical interest because of its date (1533). Here the contrast with Sannazaro

28. The *Christiad,* translated from the Latin of Vida by J. Cranwell (Cambridge, 1768), p. 160. This edition contains facing texts.

"His beamy shoulders to the view were bare;
But bound with clasps of gold beneath his breast,
Down the left side depends a golden vest:
A crimson girdle richly wrought, and grac'd
With studs of gold, adorn'd his beauteous waste:
Smooth o'er his back, soft plumes in many a row
Rise by degrees, and on his shoulder grow
To two fair wings; his manly legs were dress'd
In starry gems, uncover'd all the rest:
His shining looks and graceful motion prove
The youth descended from the realms above.
Rich was his vest, and work'd with curious art,
Large rows of pearls adorn'd the outward part;
With gold neat woven in maeandring lines,
A wond'rous work . . ."

is already very marked in the descent of Gabriel to Zachariah, father of John the Baptist, to announce his son's future birth. The descent in both poems involves the idea of redemption, but whereas Sannazaro's stress on the release from sin approaches Pelagianism, Folengo's stress falls on the depravity Christ is to cleanse. The tone is set at the opening of the scene in heaven:

Sovenne a l'alto Padre onnipotente
compiuti esser già gli anni che 'l suo Figlio
fatt 'uom dé' sciôrre la perduta gente,
come di sciôrla fu tra lor consiglio
dal tempo che d'Adam l'ingordo dente
morse 'l vietato pomo, che 'n essiglio
cacciollo di miseria in questa valle;
cui dietro andavam tutti per un calle.

[2.5] [29]

Gabriel, having been summoned and instructed, begins his descent through a sky which is deliberately heightened beyond the comfortable proximity of the earlier descents, and once he has reached earth, the angel's further itinerary recalls a series of scriptural events which demonstrate the obduracy and frailty of the human heart:

. . . e la cagion del vento
passa veloce a la citá di Nino,
ove de la superbia l'argomento
vede la torre e temeraria massa;
la qual sdegnando, agli omeri si lassa.

Viene al petroso ed arido deserto,
radendo a man sinistra il mar sanguigno,
quel dove l'indurato re coverto
da l'onde fu col popol suo maligno;
vede fonte Marath che, amar' offerto,

29. Teofilo Folengo, *Opere Italiane,* 2 (Bari, 1912), p. 38. "The high omnipotent Father remembered that the year had already arrived when his Son, made man, must release the lost people, as it had been their design to release them from the time that Adam's greedy tooth bit the forbidden apple, which drove him into miserable exile in this valley, and we all were following him by a single path."

ratto addolcí nel porvi dentro il ligno;
ed Israel, cui l'esser tolto increbbe
di servitú, mormorator ne bebbe.

Poi giunge ove posâro le lor salme
quei degni di morir non anco nati
perfidi ebrei, fra le settanta palme,
da duodeci fontane dissetati . . .
[2.8–10] [30]

I have not quoted all of this dismal journey. The good tidings of the Annunciation are darkened by the memory of shame. The free and joyful will of the high Renaissance already begins to stiffen under a new pressure. And in the angel's speech to Zachariah there sounds an accent of the sensuous Baroque religiosity one associates with Crashaw, Bernini, and Saint Teresa:

Dal grembo di sua madre a l'ultim'ore
né sicera né vin d'alcuna foggia
berá giá mai, succiando quel liquore
ch'ebro fa l'uom e tutto a Dio l'appoggia.
[2.16] [31]

It is all the more curious, given Folengo's anti-Humanist bias (which other passages make explicit), that not even he chose to exclude the proper nouns of pagan mythology from his vocabulary. The First Person of the Trinity may still address the Second Person thus:

30. "The wind-maker speedily proceeds to the city of Ninus, an emblem of pride, where he sees the tower and foolhardy bulk, disdaining which, he leaves it behind his back.

He comes to the rocky and arid desert, following the bloody sea on his left where the hard-hearted king was covered by the waves together with his malevolent people; he sees the spring of Marath which, though bitter at first, soon grew potable when a tree was cast in it, and Israel, reluctant to be brought out of slavery, drank from it with discontented murmurs.

Then he arrives at the place where the perfidious Jews, who deserved to die before they were born, set down their burdens among seventy palm trees and quenched their thirst from twelve fountains."

31. "From his mother's womb to his last hour, he will never consume strong drink or wine of any kind, sucking instead that liquor which intoxicates man and causes him to lean wholly upon God."

Va', Figliolo,
va' slegar l'uomo nostro dal Cocito.
[2.6] [32]

And Zachariah may be described as offering incense to the true Jove—"al vero Giove." Such expressions appear in a work like this one almost like habitual poetic mannerisms which cannot be suppressed. Even by narrower standards of scandal, it would be hard to omit altogether the ingrained reflexes of traditional feigning.

32. "Go, my Son; go unchain man from Cocytus."

8. *THE COUNTER-REFORMATION*

i.

To trace with care the course of the epic in Italy during the forty years from Folengo to Tasso would be a complicated as well as ungrateful task, but one may acquire a rough idea of what was happening by tracing the convention of the celestial descent. I have already quoted a part of the first descent in Trissino's *L'Italia Liberata dai Goti*,[1] a poem historically important as the first major attempt in the vernacular to emulate the regularity and high style of classical epic. Trissino deliberately broke with the "irregular" romance tradition of Boiardo and Ariosto, and his failure to approach the quality of the *Furioso* resounded throughout Italy. Trissino did not enjoy the good fortune accorded most bad poets of seeing their blunders pass unnoticed. The reasons for his failure were debated by a generation of critics, including Tasso, but this debate did not in any case preclude the writing of more failures.

We may gauge the imaginative poverty of the epic poems of this period by noting how ineffectually they represent the mes-

1. See above, Chapter 7, p. 159.

senger's movement through space. In Folengo's poem and in *La Christiana Vittoria Maritima* of Francesco Bolognetti (1572), Sannazaro's swan simile is imitated, but deprived of its original grace. Thus Bolognetti:

Come d'alto veggiam scender veloce
Canoro Cigno, che l'amata sponda
Già del Meandro hà vista, o l'ampia foce
Del bel Caistro, o del Sangario l'onda;
Che senza mandar fuori o canto, o voce,
Perchè al desio l'effetto anchor risponda,
Se stesso accusa d'esser tardo, e tende
Le bianche penne, e l'aria, e l'aure fende.[2]

The proper nouns here are merly epic window-dressing, encumbrances upon a simile which is itself an encumbrance. It is hard to imagine this remorseful swan, blaming itself for its own delay. In the *Hercole* of Giovanbattista Giraldi Cinthio (1557) a comparison of Mercury to a rainbow loses the sense of speed without quite communicating the desired sense of radiance:

Vola Mercurio, e, al suo scender dal cielo,
Gli si fà intorno luminosa l'aria,
Si, ch'alcun non appar di nube velo,
Ovunque egli al volar l'ali sue varia,
Et quale à noi, poi che é passato il gelo,
Si mostra l'arco in ciel di forma varia,
Quando percuote il Sol nube, onde piove,
Di tale è cinto, ovunque l'ali move.[3]

2. Francesco Bolognetti, *La Christiana Vittoria Maritima* (Bologna, 1572), p. 7 recto. ". . . As we see the melodious swan descend swiftly, who has once seen the beloved shore of the Meander, or the broad mouth of the Caystros, or the wave of the Sangario; without emitting song or sound, that the result still correspond to the desire, it accuses itself of being tardy, and spreads its white wings, and fends the air and the breezes."

3. Giovanbattista Giraldi Cinthio, *Hercole* (Modena, 1557), p. 113. "Mercury flies off, and as he descends from the sky, he makes the air luminous about him so that he is not veiled by any cloud wherever he turns his wings in flight, and just as the rainbow displays itself in the sky to us in various forms, after the frost has passed, when the sun strikes the cloud, causing rain, thus is he surrounded by a nimbus, wherever he plies his wings."

Tasso was to succeed more happily in a compressed version of this simile. The passage is chiefly interesting because it displays a transference to the pagan god of light imagery commonly applied by Christian poets to angels. In certain respects the distinction between religious and secular poetry was growing progressively meaningless.

In other respects, however, the militant posture and moralistic temper of the post-Trentine Church made themselves felt with increasing force in the Italian epic as the century wore on. There is significance in the sudden fashion of Old Testament stories chosen for epic treatment toward the mid-century.[4] The earlier Biblical epics had been based almost exclusively on the gospels. Now, in a fragmentary Latin epic by Fracastoro, an angel descends to comfort the young Joseph, abandoned in a pit by his brothers.[5] But the new seriousness, even grimness, which accompanied this development was not the only effect of the Reformation upon the Italian epic. In Bolognetti's poem the angel descends precisely to warn Pope Pius V against the spreading heresy as well as to predict the victory of Lepanto. In a scene which skirts comedy the angel appears in the guise of a monk to the holy father, who is only momentarily discountenanced:

> Per quel giugner, che fece à l'improviso
> L'Angel beato, conturbosse alquanto
> Prima il sommo Pastor, ma poi con viso
> Lieto l'accolse, che'l conobbe in tanto;
> A cui, sorto dal seggio, or'era assiso,
> L'Angelo disse reverente. O Santo
> Padre, per grande, & necessario effetto
> Da DIO per suo Vicario in terra eletto.
>
> Saper ti fò per nome suo, che posta
> Da parte ogni altra, & sia pure grave, cura;

4. See Toffanin, *Il Cinquecento,* p. 54. Signor Toffanin interprets this fashion in terms of a quest for a more imaginative scope than the life of Christ permitted. I would associate it rather with that post-Trentine shift in theological emphasis away from redemption and toward original sin.

5. See *Ioseph,* Book I, in *Hieronymi Fracastorii Veronensis Opera Omnia* (Venice, 1574). See also chapter 12, note 9.

Solo habbi à discacciar l'alma disposta
L'Heresia, c'hor sen và lieta, & sicura;
Et se pur dianzi star solea nascosta
Ne gli antri, & ne le selve per paura,
Non pur lunge in Britannia hoggi dimora,
Ma frà l'Adria, e il Tirrheno, & l'Alpe ancora.[6]

Before he leaves, the angel odorizes the chamber with celestial vapor brought expressly from heaven.

Despite these reflections of an increasingly pious temper, the persistence of classical conventions like the celestial descent bears witness to the continuing prestige of Humanism among Christian poets. Chivalric romances, moreover, continued to be written in verse, works which remained detached in various degrees from both the Humanist and Christian tradition. But these lacked the invention and skepticism of Ariosto, and some contained a moralized allegory to justify their apparent frivolousness. One of these, the *Amadigi,* in exactly one hundred cantos, was composed by Bernardo Tasso, father of Torquato. The marks of all three traditions are indeed traceable in the *Gerusalemme Liberata,* toward which ambiguous masterpiece we may discern, from our vantage in time, many tangled lines of *cinquecento* literary history converging.

In the latter half of the century there became fashionable still another form of literary activity which was to affect the epic and Tasso in particular. This was the debate over literary theory. Vida had written his *Ars Poetica* as early as 1527, but the critical date was 1536, when Aristotle's *Poetics* was translated into Latin.[7]

6. *La Christana Vittoria Maritima,* p. 7 verso. "The supreme Pastor lost his composure somewhat at the unexpected entry of the blessed angel, but then received him with joyful countenance, having recognized him in the meanwhile; to whom, reseated now in the throne from which he had risen, the angel spoke with reverence: 'O Holy Father, chosen by God as his vicar for great and necessary ends, I bring you word in His name that you must put aside all other matters, however serious; your soul must be bent solely on driving away the Heresy which now circulates blithe and secure; and if it formerly was wont to remain hidden in caves and woods out of fear, today it no longer dwells far off in Britain, but also between the Adriatic, the Tyrrhenian, and the Alp.' "

7. By Alessandro de' Pazzi. An earlier Latin translation was published at Venice in 1498 but seems to have attracted little attention.

Commentaries on Aristotle quickly followed, and a flood of *Artes Poeticae,* all more or less deriving from him, followed in turn. The debates over theoretical issues and points of Aristotelian interpretation were intensified by the rising influence of literary academies, like the Accadèmia degli Infiammati at Padua and the Accadèmia della Crusca at Florence; both of these played important but very different roles in the personal history of Tasso. Academies had existed in Italy since the fifteenth century, but whereas they had been founded chiefly to study classical philology, during the latter sixteenth century they concerned themselves increasingly with the vernacular, with literature as well as language, and with theory as well as practice. The academies contributed to that growing Alexandrian self-consciousness of criticism which inhibited artistic freedom in Italy and rigidified the imagination. But this influence was only one of many upon Tasso; to distinguish the others, and to describe his contribution to epic poetry, will require a closer study of his poem.

ii.

Tasso is the most difficult of epic poets to judge with assurance. His gifts were distinguished and precocious; his ambition was lofty; his poem is celebrated; and yet one does not praise it as it deserves without a twinge of doubt. Few poems interweave so closely the genuine and the meretricious. Few poems admired so highly for so long have been denigrated so bitterly by their detractors. To this day Italian criticism remains divided regarding the value of the *Gerusalemme Liberata,* although recent decades have reversed the downward curve its reputation followed after its downgrading by De Sanctis, D'Ovidio, and other nineteenth century critics. One scholar has formulated the problem by alluding to its "valore poetico irrefutabile ma commisto a elementi spurii e difficile da identificare e definire criticamente." [8] There is probably very rough agreement today, however, that despite its debatable imperfections, its lapses into melodrama, its unconvincing

8. B. T. Sozzi, *Studi sul Tasso* (Pisa, 1954), p. 269. "An undeniable poetic value but mixed with spurious elements and difficult to identify and define critically."

religiosity, its sentimentality, its moral ambivalences, the *Liberata* remains an authentic achievement of a great imagination, to be judged only on the level of masterpieces.

It may be that the poem is so difficult to judge because it is a hybrid. Tasso's poetic genius was by nature synthetic, just as his critical position was always mediatory. It was his misfortune that this quality proved a handicap, in certain respects, as well as an asset. Perhaps it was a handicap because his age was itself divided, hypocritical, even to a degree emotionally false, unsure of the moral, social, and philosophic syntheses it had patched up to confront heresy. This uncertainty underlies the brilliant patchwork of the *Liberata*.[9] When it is moving and authentic, it is speaking out of its own imaginative reality; when it is hollow, it reverberates the emptiness of its time.

One could not say that Tasso's mind was unoriginal, but it was a Protean mind which produced original compositions out of elements already given. The elements which compose his poem are many. There is first of all a certain framework of history, stemming from the poet's close study of the chroniclers who participated in the first crusade. There are ubiquitous echoes and imitations of earlier poets—particularly Dante and Homer and above

9. See the dialogue *Il Malpiglio Secondo:* ". . . Né de la morte solo e de l'amore ho varie opinioni secondo la varietà de' tempi e de l'occasioni, ma de la sanità, de l'infermità, de l'aversa fortuna e de la prospera, de la povertà e de la ricchezza, de la gentilezza e de l'ignobiltà, de la possanza e de la debilezza, de la vita reale e de la privata e de l'attiva e de la contemplativa, e in somma di tutte le cose de la quali soglion parlar variamente i poeti, gli oratori e gli istorici: perché, s'in uno autore medesimo e s'intorno ad uno soggetto istesso troviamo alcuna volta gran diversità di pareri, quanta maggiore si può ritrovare in tanti scrittori e sì diversi, nati e cresciuti in sì diversi paesi e fioriti appresso così varie nazioni e celebrati in così varie lingue." Torquato Tasso, *Prose,* p. 130. ". . . Nor is it only of death and love that I hold various opinions according to the changes of times and occasions, but of health, of infirmity, of adverse and prosperous fortune, of poverty and wealth, of high birth and of base, of strength and weakness, of court life and of private and of the active and contemplative, and in short of all the things poets, orators, and historians are accustomed to discuss variously: wherefore, if we find sometimes such a great diversity of opinions in a single author regarding a single subject, how much greater a diversity can be found in so many and such different writers, born and reared in such different lands and flourishing among such various nations and celebrated in such various languages."

all Virgil. There is a lyricism, a feeling for sensuous beauty, a sensitivity to nature, a gracefulness and melancholy together which recall the Renaissance of two or three generations earlier—of Poliziano, Botticelli, Raphael, and Leonardo. There is the flavor of the court life at Ferrara, a flavor one detects in the characterization of the knight Tancredi, in episodes involving jealousy and flirtation at the Christian camp, and of course in the florid encomia devoted to Alfonso II and the d'Este family. There is the censorious moral climate of the Counter-Reformation, which subordinates love and glory to piety. There are even traces, in the Olindo and Sofronia episode, of the masochistic Baroque interest in martyrdom. There is the formal self-consciousness stemming from the Aristotelian literary climate, an influence which we can probably thank in part for the poem's superb architecture. There is a complementary Platonism, whose spirit lay closer to Tasso's true temperament. There is finally the very powerful influence of the *Orlando Furioso* and other romances in verse and prose at least as old as Heliodorus' *Aethiopica.* All of these elements were worked together by the youthful, ardent, book-nourished mind of the poet.

The amalgam which constitutes the *Gerusalemme Liberata* does not bear the definitive stamp of Tasso's final judgment. He was concerned with the poem, in one way or another, from early adolescence until the closing years of his life. He seems to have begun work on a poem entitled *Il Gierusalemme* at the age of 15, and the fragment of 116 octaves then composed was to be transmuted into the first canto of the mature poem. Although he interrupted this work in his eighteenth year to compose *Rinaldo,* a verse romance, he apparently continued to meditate his more ambitious poem. The *Arte Poetica,* probably written when he was 20, seems to have been a preliminary study for that poem. In 1566, at 22, he speaks of working on the sixth canto. A version substantially like the poem we now possess was concluded in 1575. But this, to Tasso's great misfortune, was not the end of the story. Apprehensive of offending the Inquisition on the one hand and the literate public on the other, he submitted his poem to censors, whose strictures delayed its publication and precipitated the poet's madness. The *Liberata* was first published in a pirated edition, and Tasso published his own corrected edition in 1581 with considerable reluctance. A large portion of his remaining life was devoted first to the defense of his poem against the polemics it aroused, and second to its "reformation" which resulted in the radically altered version entitled *Gerusalemme Conquistata.* His indecision and hesitations about the poem betoken the same interior uncertainty whose effects I have already discerned in the poem's contents.

There are two important and conventional descents of an angelic messenger in the *Gerusalemme Liberata.* The first of these appears at the opening of the first canto and initiates the action of the entire poem. The Eternal Father in heaven directs his regard to earth and considers in particular the progress of the crusade, now in the winter of its sixth year. Nicea and Antioch and Tortosa have been taken; battles have been won; but Jerusalem, the ultimate goal, remains unfallen. God looks within the hearts of the Christian leaders: in Goffredo he sees holy zeal; in Baldovin, the greed for human wealth; in Tancredi, the suffering of futile love; in Boemondo, the dream of founding an empire; in Rinaldo, the immoderate passion for honor. God then summons Gabriele,

> interprete fedel, nunzio giocondo

and dispatches him to earth:

> Disse al suo nunzio Dio:—Goffredo trova [10]
> e in mio nome di' lui: perché si cessa?
> perché la guerra omai non si rinova
> a liberar Gierusalemme oppressa? 92
> Chiami i duci a consiglio e i tardi mova
> a l'alta impresa: ei capitan fia d'essa.

10. All Italian quotations from Tasso's poetry are taken from Torquato Tasso, *Poesie,* ed. F. Flora (Milan and Naples, 1952). The verse translations are from *Jerusalem Delivered,* trans. E. Fairfax (London, 1749).

> To whom the Lord thus spake—Godfredo find,
> And in my Name ask him, why doth he rest?
> Why are his Arms to Ease and Peace resign'd?
> Why frees he not Jerusalem distrest?
> His Peers to Council call, each baser Mind
> Let him stir up; for Chieftain of the rest

Io qui l'eleggo: e 'l faran gli altri in terra,
già suoi compagni, or suoi ministri in guerra.—

Così parlogli, e Gabriel s'accinse
veloce ad esseguir l'imposte cose:
la sua forma invisibil d'aria cinse
ed al senso mortal la sottopose:
umane membra, aspetto uman si finse,
ma di celeste maestà il compose:
tra giovene e fanciullo età confine
prese, ed ornò di raggi il biondo crine.

Ali bianche vestì c'han d'or le cime,
infaticabilmente agili e preste:
fende i venti e le nubi, e va sublime
sovra la terra e sovra il mar con queste.
Così vestito, indirizzossi a l'ime
parti del mondo il messaggier celeste:

I chuse him here; the Earth shall him allow;
His Fellows late shall be his Subjects now.

This said, the Angel swift himself prepar'd
To execute the Charge impos'd aright;
In Form of airy Members fair imbarr'd,
His Spirits pure were subject to our Sight;
Like to a Man in Show and Shape he far'd,
But full of heav'nly Majesty, and Might;
A Stripling seem'd he, thrice five Winters old,
And radiant Beams adorn'd his Locks of Gold:

Of silver Wings he took a shining Pair,
Fringed with Gold, unweary'd, nimble, swift;
With these he parts the Winds, the Clouds, the Air,
And over Seas and Earth himself doth lift:
Thus clad, he cut the Spheres and Circles fair,
And the pure Skies with sacred Feathers cleft;
On Libanon at first his Foot he set,
And shook his Wings with rory May-Dews wet;

Then to Tortosa's Confines swiftly sped
The sacred Messenger with head-long Flight.
Above the Eastern Wave appeared red
The rising Sun, yet scantly half in Sight;

pria sul Libano monte ei si ritenne
e si librò su l'adeguate penne;

e ver' le piagge di Tortosa poi
drizzò precipitando il volo in giuso.
Sorgeva il novo sol da i lidi eoi,
parte già fuor ma 'l più ne l'onde chiuso,
e porgea matutini i preghi suoi
Goffredo a Dio com'egli avea per uso,
quando a paro co 'l sol ma più lucente,
l'angelo gli apparì da l'oriente:

e gli disse:— Goffredo, ecco opportuna
già la stagion ch'al guerreggiar s'aspetta:
perché dunque trapor dimora alcuna
a liberar Gierusalem soggetta?
Tu i principi a consiglio omai raguna,
tu al fin de l'opra i neghittosi affretta:
Dio per lor duce già t'elegge, ed essi
sopporran volontari a te se stessi.

Dio messaggier mi manda: io ti rivelo
la sua mente in suo nome. Oh quanta spene
aver d'alta vittoria, oh quanto zelo
de l'oste a te commessa, or ti conviene!—

Godfrey e'en then his Morn-Devotions said,
(As was his Custom) when with Titan bright
  Appear'd the Angel in his Shape divine,
  Whose Glory far obscured Phoebus' Shine.

Godfrey, quoth he, behold the Season fit
To war, for which thou waited hast so long!
Now serves the Time, if thou o'erslip not it,
To free Jerusalem from Thrall and Wrong:
Thou with thy Lords in Council quickly sit;
Comfort the feeble, and confirm the strong:
  The LORD OF HOSTS their General doth make thee,
  And for their Chieftain they shall gladly take thee.

I, Messenger from everlasting Jove,
In His great Name thus His Behests do tell;
Oh what sure Hope of Conquest ought thee move!
What Zeal, what Love should in thy Bosom dwell!

Tacque, e sparito rivolò del cielo
a le parti più eccelse e più serene.
Resta Goffredo a i detti, a lo splendore,
d'occhi abbagliato, attonito di core. 136

In its felicitous control of language, its glowing evocation of light and speed, its poetic power uninhibited by the convention it yet acknowledges, this passage distinguishes itself from the mass of spiritless imitations whose progress we have been tracing. The stylistic mastery is manifest in the restraint, the assurance, the absence of any stridency. In the *Arte Poetica,*[11] Tasso listed the rhetorical means by which the high style could reach that roughness, *asprezza,* he thought essential to it, and some of these means can be found in this descent. Most striking is the polysyndeton, the frequent use of connective conjunctions, employed in the third of the stanzas quoted; the Italian word "e" ("and") appears six times from lines 105 through 113, the lines devoted to Gabriele's flight, and this repetition, together with the long, brilliantly-chosen adverb "infaticabilmente," conveys admirably the impression of agility and speed. It draws out, moreover, the length of the sentences; this lengthening Tasso thought to be another means of creating *asprezza.* Notice, for example, that a single sentence runs from line 115 to 124, although logic would have suggested full stops after 116 and 120. There is also the frequent enjambment Tasso prescribed, and the discreet displacement of normal word order, as in the withholding of the verb *conviene* until the end of line 132. These devices are supplemented by such a traditional figure as the chiasmus in line 136.

But of course the art of this passage is not limited to devices a poorer poet could imitate. The speech of the deity is fittingly lacking in long periods; its clauses are clipped; and its brevity as a whole is dramatically correct, contrasting as it does with the

---

This said, he vanish'd to those Seats above,
In Height and Clearness which the rest excell:
  Down fell the Duke, his Joints dissolv'd assunder,
  Blind with the Light, and strucken dead with Wonder.

11. *Prose,* pp. 395 ff.

interminable harangues of many another epic divinity. The angel's radiance is achieved through the sustained imagery of gold: the blond hair, the golden tips of the white wings, the faint association with the rising sun in line 115 which is then made explicit in lines 119–20, where the angel, like the sun but brighter, appears to Goffredo from the east. The conventional simile at this point has been excluded in order to avoid any check upon the impression of swiftness. The freshness of the dawn hour is in subtle harmony with the freshness of the angel's aspect, for in spite of the "celestial majesty" attributed to him, he chooses to appear at an age between boyhood and youth. In touches like these, which mingle heavenly solemnity with an ephebic gracefulness, Tasso's debt to the earlier Renaissance, and particularly to painting, is manifest. Of all the earlier descents, this one with its lyrical poise and radiance and charm is closest to Sannazaro's. In a sense Tasso was spiritually most at ease in the age he missed by a birth two generations late. His poem might be considered in certain respects as a fulfillment of that age's ideals.

So reminiscent indeed is this passage of the Renaissance manner that the elements extraneous to that manner are muted, so to speak, and softened by its influence. There is in fact a good deal of Homer and Virgil here: the phrase

> . . . va sublime
> sovra la terra e sovra il mar con queste

derives from the *Aeneid* 4.240–41, and its Homeric antecedent; the pause on Mount Lebanon, the "Libano monte," imitates Mercury's pause on Atlas, and lines 112–14 imitate the Virgilian

> Hic primum paribus nitens Cyllenius alis
> Constitit; hinc toto praeceps se corpore ad undas
> Misit . . . [4.252–54]

Lines 135–36 imitate the corresponding passage in the *Aeneid:*

> At vero Aeneas aspectu obmutuit amens . . . [4.279]

Perhaps even in the Deity's use of interrogatives, repeated at lines 123–24 by Gabriele, there is a faint echo of Virgil (4.232 ff.). The classical imitations are indeed present but they have been transmuted.

A comparable process of transmutation or disguise has affected the sterner ideological content of Gabriele's descent. The poet says little about his poem within its pages, but one remark there is, in his opening invocation to the Christian muse, which suggests that he was quite aware of this process of disguise. To justify it, he borrows a simile from Lucretius:

> . . . tu perdona
> s'intesso fregi al ver, s'adorno in parte
> d'altri diletti che de' tuoi le carte.
>
> Sai che là corre il mondo ove più versi
> di sue dolcezze il lusinghier Parnaso,
> e che 'l vero condito in molli versi
> i più schivi allettando ha persuaso:
> così a l'egro fanciul porgiamo aspersi
> di soavi licor gli orli del vaso:
> succhi amari ingannato in tanto ei beve,
> e da l'inganno suo vita riceve.
>
> [1.14–24] [12]

Modern criticism would view this dualism as oversimplified, and doubtless we must not suppose too naively that Tasso actually conceived of his poetic composition in these terms. But if we grant a much more complex process to have in fact governed the composition, we need not deprive ourselves of whatever part of truth these lines contain. If they indicate a certain tension between two

12. The poet is addressing the Christian muse.

> . . . forgive the Thing,
> If fictions light I mix with Truth divine,
> And fill these Lines with other Praise, than thine.
>
> Thither thou know'st the world is best inclin'd,
> Where luring Parnass most it's Sweet imparts;
> And Truth, convey'd in Verse of gentle Kind,
> To read perhaps will move the dullest Hearts:
> So We, if Children young diseas'd we find,
> Anoint with Sweets the Vessel's foremost Parts
> To make them taste the Potions sharp we give;
> They drink deceiv'd, and so deceiv'd they live.

poetic elements—between what we could roughly call *image* and *idea*—let that suffice us. Such a tension does indeed emerge from the descent of Gabriele, though it is not so pronounced as to weaken the descent's effect.

Juxtaposed with everything one associates with Gabriele's splendor, the *splendore* of line 135, there is the message itself, *i detti.* The message is less characteristic of the high Renaissance than of the militant age which succeeded it. The key word is *dimora* (line 123) which means "delay." The human realm with its delays and indecisions contrasts with the divine realm, whose force is symbolized by Gabriele's speed, and whose unanimity by his obedience. In heaven there are no *neghittosi,* and in this passage that is the important difference. The emphasis is upon holy action, spurred by the zeal (*zelo,* line 131) to which Gabriele exhorts his auditor. Goffredo is discovered at prayers which demonstrate his piety, but one recalls Saint Ignatius' doctrine that prayer and meditation should lead to deeds. The medieval scale of values which led Dante to place the contemplatives above the militant in Paradise has been reversed. The God presented here sanctions or rather commands the shedding of blood in holy combat, the sort of combat tragically familiar to Europe in the latter sixteenth century.

The more active pursuance of the war is part of Gabriele's message; the other part concerns the election of Goffredo to command the Christian armies. This election, which follows the descent in the poem, is in fact at variance with history, and Tasso knew it. During the actual crusade, Goffredo was only one of several generals who acknowledged no supreme commander. Tasso did not pretend, of course, to chronicle history accurately, and the liberty taken here is less audacious than many of his other liberties. But one may ask nonetheless why he chose to take it, and what relation it bears to the spirit of his poem.

The answer lies in his authoritarianism. As a man, he was dependent upon a society headed by a single spiritual authority, the pope, and governed by a series of petty rulers, each absolute within his dukedom. Tasso's material existence as a courtier depended upon the power of his patrons, and throughout the complaints against Alfonso d'Este, Duke of Ferrara, which recur in his correspondence, he never questions the legal right of the duke to imprison or otherwise mistreat his subject. Tasso's temperament was one which found compliance to authority rather too congenial for modern taste. His respect for it was in harmony with the Counter-Reformation glorification of centralized power and hostility to northern individualism. The faith of both the poet and his age are reflected in God's election of Goffredo to command, and in Goffredo's subsequent characterization.

The most persuasive argument for authority is found indeed in the commander's wisdom, piety, clemency, and humility. As a character, Goffredo has been unpopular with many critics, but I have never been able to persuade myself that their derogations are justified. Tasso followed Virgil in giving his hero the thankless, lack-luster role, and there is a good deal of Aeneas in him: the weariness, the care-worn sense of responsibility, the loneliness, the refusal to be glamorous. He is the chief bearer of whatever explicit moral meaning the poem contains; he is a kind of saint who is not even permitted the luxury of charity, and such saints are destined to unpopularity. Although he is no more frequently on the poetic stage than many others, he remains at the center of the action, in control of the principal plot, and his character puts a stamp upon the poem as none other does. He is the only character who could not conceivably have appeared in the *Orlando Furioso,* despite certain resemblances to the traditional conception of Charlemagne. He is the benevolent personification of order throughout the poem.[13]

I want to make only one more observation on Gabriele's descent before quoting its complement in the ninth canto. In lines 98 to

13. For the reasons indicated here, and others below, I would take issue with John Arthros' comment that "In Tasso's universe there is no order. Even the hierarchy of society can be subverted and the Duke can fight as a private soldier, indeed feels morally compelled to . . . There is no chain of being." *On the Poetry of Spenser and the Form of Romances* (London, 1956), pp. 182–83. Goffredo can fight as a foot-soldier only because the paradox of his so doing is understood. Were his position less assured, he would have to remain commander. He "feels morally compelled" to fight as a soldier simply because he has taken a vow to this effect on setting out. His humility would be meaningless if his authority were in doubt. I shall have more to say below regarding the conception of the chain of being Tasso found in Ficino, and regarding the philosophical basis of his treatment of love, which Arthros would also deny.

100, Gabriele is represented as putting on a form visible to human sense, clothing, as it were, his invisibility. Tasso means to make it clear that heaven is not to be apprehended by mortals. He elaborates his meaning in a later dialogue entitled *Il Messaggiero* from which I quote, not only for its relevance to the poem, but for its use of a pagan poet to authorize metaphysical conclusions. The speaker is supposed to be the poet's familiar spirit, and he is explaining the two ways in which spirits reveal themselves to men:

> L'uno è . . . quando essi vi purgano in modo la vista che siate atti a sostener la luce loro; l'altro, quando si circondano di corpo che possa esser obietto proporzionato de' vostri umani sentimenti. Se gli vedete ne la prima maniera, voi vi transumanate, per così dire . . . Ma se l'immortali forme ne la seconda maniera a voi si dimostrano, non vi transumanate voi, ma esse si vestono d'umanità, cioè di corpo e di mote e di tutte quelle altre circonstanze che accompagnano la natura visibile e corporea. Questi due mode ben conobbe il tuo glorioso poeta: perché, dove Enea vede Venere e per sua grazia le idee e le intelligenze, vuole intendere ch'egli si solleva sopra l'umanità con la contemplazione; ma quando Venere gli appare sotto corpo fittizio o quando Mercurio gli è mandato da Giove, l'uno e l'altro di loro ricoprendo la divinità si fa vedere nel modo co'l quale da' mortali possono esser veduti . . . Poi, quando Mercurio sparisce, più chiaramente appare ch'egli s'era vestito di corpo aereo, in que' versi:
>
> . . . Tali Cyllenius ore locutus
> mortales visus medio sermone reliquit
> et procul in tenuem ex oculis evanuit auram.
>
> Parlo teco volentieri co' versi di questo poeta, perché l'hai in tanta venerazione ch'a la sua autorità, non altrimenti ch'a quella de' maggior filosofi, presti fede . . .[14]

14. *Prose,* pp. 11–12. "The one way is followed when they purge your vision in such a manner that you are capable of enduring their brilliance; the other, when they invest themselves with a body which can be adapted to your human senses. If you see them in the first manner, you are trans-humanized, so to speak. . . . But if the immortal forms are revealed to you in the second manner, you are not trans-humanized, but they themselves put on humility, that is to say, a body and movements and all those other cir-

Perhaps indeed it was the authority of Virgil which led Tasso to introduce into his epic what might be called a technical problem in angelology. One may ask in any case what purpose these three lines (98–100) serve. They permit, quite obviously, an easy transition to the description of the angel's appearance. But the suggestion that celestial creatures are not naturally apprehensible to earthly ones seems to me to do more; to remove heaven to a greater distance from earth, to render it more remote, more unlike, more ethereal, and so more awesome. One remembers the substantiality of Sannazaro's heaven, a substantiality which argued for the proximity of a benign God to Pelagian man. Tasso might well have found that conception attractive, but his age professed to worship a less comfortable deity. His reminder that heaven does not reveal itself easily to human eyes harks back to the more reverent imagination of Dante, from whom he may have borrowed the verb *transumanare*.[15] But Tasso's conception of heaven is still not to be confused with the more austere conception of Milton, for Milton thought all celestial action revealed to man was not only invisible but symbolic, not only beyond his senses but his intellect:

> To recount Almighty works
> What words or tongue of Seraph can suffice,
> Or heart of man suffice to comprehend? [16]

---

cumstances that accompany visible, corporeal nature. Your glorious poet knew these two ways well; since, when Aeneas sees Venus and by her grace the ideas and spirits, he means that he is raised above humanity through contemplation; but when Venus appears to him in an assumed body or when Mercury is sent to him by Jove, the one and the other conceal their divinity and render themselves visible in the way that mortals are visible . . . Then, when Mercury disappears, it is still more evident that he had clothed himself with an airy body, in these lines: 'After Mercury delivered his message, he suddenly left mortal view and vanished far from sight into thin air.'

I cite you expressly the lines of this poet, because you hold him in such veneration that you acknowledge his authority as you would that of the greatest philosophers."

15. *Paradiso,* 1.70.

16. *Paradise Lost,* VII.112–14. See also "Christian Doctrine" in *The Works of John Milton, 14* (New York, Columbia, 1933), 31. It is true that Milton is speaking specifically in both passages of the acts of God, not of angels.

Milton's Puritan heaven was in fact far more remote from earth than Tasso's, although we shall find the latter attempting more vigorously to elevate the heaven of his second descent.

iii.

The angel Michele, dispatched by God to earth in the ninth canto of the *Liberata,* descends not to admonish a human hero but to drive back to hell a legion of demons. The demons have sided with the pagan armies who are pressing the advantage of a night attack upon the Christian encampment outside Jerusalem. The crusaders, surprised and confused, are in serious peril when their plight draws the attention of the King of Heaven:

Sedea colà dond'Egli e buono e giusto [17]
dà legge al tutto e 'l tutto orna e produce
sovra i bassi confin del mondo angusto,
ove senso o ragion non si conduce;
e de la eternità nel trono augusto
rispondea con tre lumi in una luce.
Ha sotto i piedi il Fato e la Natura,
ministri umili, e il Moto e Chi 'l misura,

e 'l Loco, e Quella che qual fumo o polve
la gloria di qua giuso e l'oro e i regni,
come piace là su, disperde e volve,
né, diva, cura i nostri umani sdegni.

17. From whence, with Grace and Goodness compass'd round,
He ruleth, blesseth, keepeth all He wrought,
Above the Air, the Fire, the Sea and Ground,
Our Sense, our Wit, our Reason and our Thought;
Where Persons Three, with Pow'r and Glory crown'd,
Are all one God, who made all Things of Nought;
Under whose Feet, subjected to His Grace,
Sit Nature, Fortune, Motion, Time and Place.

This is the Place, from whence, like Smoke and Dust,
Of this frail World the Wealth, the Pomp and Pow'r
He tosseth, tumbleth, turneth as He lust,
And guides our Life, our Death, our End and Hour:

Quivi ei così nel suo splendor s'involve
che v'abbaglian la vista anco i più degni:
d'intorno ha innumerabili immortali,
disegualmente in lor letizia eguali.

Al gran concento de' beati carmi
lieta risuona la celeste reggia.
Chiama Egli a sé Michel, il qual ne l'armi
di lucido adamante arde e lampeggia,
e dice lui:—Non vedi or come s'armi
contra la mia fedel diletta greggia
l'empia schiera d'averno, e in sin dal fondo
de le sue morti a turbar sorga il mondo?

Va', dille tu che lasci omai le cure
de la guerra a i guerrier, cui ciò conviene,
né il regno de' viventi né le pure
piaggie del ciel conturbi ed avvenene:
torni a le notti d'Acheronte oscure,
suo degno albergo, a le sue giuste pene;
quivi se stessa e l'anime d'abisso
crucii: così comando e così ho fisso.—

No Eye, however virtuous, pure and just,
Can view the Brightness of that glorious Bow'r;
On ev'ry Side the blessed Spirits be,
Equal in Joys, though diff'ring in Degree.

With Harmony of their celestial Song
The Palace eccho'd from the Chambers pure;
At last He Michael call'd, in Harness strong
Of never-yielding Di'monds armed sure;
Then spake; Behold, to do Despite and Wrong
To that just Flock my Mercy hath in Cure,
How Satan from Hell's loathsom Prison sends
His Ghosts, his Sprites, his Furies and his Fiends.

Go, bid them all depart, and leave the Care
Of War to Soldiers, as doth best 'pertain:
Command them cease t'infect the Earth and Air;
To darken Heav'n's fair Light bid them refrain:
Bid them to Acheron's black Flood repair,
Fit House for them, the House of Grief and Pain;
There let their King himself and them torment;
So I command—go tell them my Intent.

Qui tacque, e'l duce de' guerrieri alati
s'inchinò riverente al divin piede:
indi spiega al gran volo i vanni aurati,
rapido sì ch'anco il pensiero eccede:
passa il foco e la luce, ove i beati
hanno lor gloriosa immobil sede;
poscia il puro cristallo e 'l cerchio mira
che di stelle gemmato in contra gira; 480

quinci, d'opre diversi e di sembianti,
da sinistra rotar Saturno e Giove
e gli altri, i quali esser non ponno erranti
se angelica virtù gli informa e move:
vien poi da' campi lieti e fiammeggianti
d'eterno di là donde tuona e piove,
ove se stesso il mondo strugge e pasce,
e ne le guerre sue more e rinasce. 488

Venia scotendo con l'eterne piume
la caligine densa e i cupi orrori:

This said, the winged Warrior low inclin'd
At his Creator's Feet with Rev'rence due,
Then spread his golden Feathers to the Wind,
And, swift as Thought, away the Angel flew:
He pass'd the Light and shining Fire, assign'd
The glorious Seat of his selected Crew,
  The Mover first, and Circle crystalline,
  The Firmament, where fixed Stars all shine;

Unlike in Working then, in Shape and Show,
At his left Hand Saturn he left, and Jove,
And those untruly errant call'd, I trow,
Since He errs not, who them doth guide and move;
The Fields he passed then, whence Hail and Snow,
Thunder and Rain fall down from Clouds above,
  Where Heat and Cold, Dryness and Moisture strive,
  Whose Wars all Creatures kill, and slain revive.

The horrid Darkness, and the Shadows dun
Dispersed he with his eternal Wings;

s'indorava la notte al divin lume
che spargea scintillando il volto fuori.
Tale il sol ne le nubi ha per costume
spiegar dopo la pioggia i bei colori;
tal suol, fendendo il liquido sereno,
stella cader de la gran madre in seno.

Ma giunto ove la schiera empia infernale
il furor de' pagani accende e sprona,
si ferma in aria in su 'l vigor de l'ale
e vibra l'asta, e lor così ragiona:
—Pur voi dovreste omai saper con quale
folgore orrendo il Re del mondo tuona,
o del disprezzo e ne' tormenti acerbi
de l'estrema miseria anco superbi.

Fisso è nel Ciel ch'al venerabil segno
chini le mura, apra Sion le porte.
A che pugnar co 'l fato? a che lo sdegno
dunque irritar de la celeste corte?
Itene, maledetti, al vostro regno,

The Flames, which from his heav'nly Eyes out-run,
Begild the Earth, and all her sable Things:
After a Storm so spreadeth forth the Sun
His Rays, and binds the Clouds in golden Strings;
  Or in the Stillness of a Moon-Shine Even
  A falling Star so glideth down from Heaven.

But when th' infernal Troop he 'proached near,
That still the Pagans Ire and Rage provoke,
The Angel on his Wings himself did bear,
And shook his Lance, and thus at last he spoke:
Have you not learned yet to know and fear
The Lord's just Wrath, and Thunder's dreadful Stroke?
  Or in the Torments of your endless Ill
  Are you still fierce, still proud, rebellious still?

The Lord hath sworn to break the iron Bands,
The brazen Gates of Sion's Fort which close;
Who is it, that His sacred Will withstands?
Against His Wrath who dares himselfe oppose?
Go hence, ye curst, to your appointed Lands,

regno di pene e di perpetua morte,
e siano in quegli a voi dovuti chiostri
le vostre guerre ed i trionfi vostri.

Là incrudelite, là sovra i nocenti
tutte adoprate pur le vostre posse
fra i gridi eterni e lo stridor de' denti
e 'l suon del ferro e le catene scosse.—
Disse, e quei ch'egli vide al partir lenti
con la lancia fatal pinse e percosse:
essi gemendo abbandonâr le belle
region de la luce e l'auree stelle,

e dispiegâr verso gli abissi il volo
ad inasprir ne' rei l'usate doglie:
non passa il mar d'augei sì grande stuolo
quando a i soli più tepidi s'accoglie,
né tante vede mai l'autunno al suolo
cader co' primi freddi aride foglie.
Liberato da lor, quella sì negra
faccia depone il mondo e si rallegra.

The Realms of Death, of Torments and of Woes,
And in the Deeps of that infernal Lake
Your Battles fight, and there your Triumphs make;

There tyrannise upon the Souls you find
Condemn'd to Woe, and double still their Pains,
Where some complain, where some their Teeth do grind,
Some howl and weep, some clink their iron Chains.
This said, they fled; and those that stay'd behind
With his sharp Lance he driveth and constrains;
They sighing left the Lands, his silver Sheep
Where Hesperus doth lead, doth feed and keep,

And towards Hell their lazy Wings display,
To wreak their Malice on the damned Ghosts:
The Birds, that follow Titan's hottest Ray,
Pass not in so great Flocks to warmer Coasts;
Nor Leaves in so great Numbers fall away,
When Winter nips them with his new-come Frosts:
The Earth, deliver'd from so foul Annoy,
Recall'd her Beauty, and resum'd her Joy.

To a greater degree than its predecessor, this passage is a *cento* of poetic fragments. Of these the *Aeneid* remains the most important source. Lines 465–66 imitate a line from the seventh book:

bella viri pacemque gerent quis bella gerenda

and the rest of the stanza probably derives from Neptune's rebuke to Aeolus (1.139–41). Lines 505–08 more or less imitate 10.6 ff. and 12.793 ff., passages in which Jupiter argues for the destined success of Aeneas. But the most explicit imitation appears in lines 523–26, in the two similes applied to the fleeing demons. These are virtual translations of the beautiful similes applied by Virgil to souls newly arrived in Tartarus:

quam multa in silvis autumni frigore primo
lapsa cadunt folia, aut ad terram gurgite ab alto
quam multae glomerantur aves, ubi frigidus annus
trans pontum fugat et terris immittit apricis.
[6.309–12] [18]

a passage first imitated by Dante in two analogous contexts.[19] Another of Tasso's similes (493–94) derives from a descent by Giraldi Cinthio I have quoted above (p. 177), while the simile immediately following echoes Dante, Poliziano, and Vida.[20] The description of God's throne, with the allegorical figures about it, expands a passage in Pontano's *Urania:*

Hic sedes augusta Dei, siquando vocatis
Dat leges superis, aut publica munera tractat.
In medio sedet ipse: astat Sapientia dextra,
Hinc Amor, et solio resident tria numina in uno;
Sub pedibus Natura potens, Tempusque, Locusque,
Et varians Fortuna, atque immutabilis Ordo;

18. "As many fluttering leaves fall in the forests at the first cold of autumn or as many birds gather on the land from the deep flood when the cold year puts them to flight across the sea and sends them to lands of sunshine."

19. *Inferno* 3.112–15 and 5.40–41. Milton in turn imitated one of these similes in *Paradise Lost* I.301–04, using it like Tasso in reference to devils. Also cf. above, pp. 140–41.

20. Dante: *Paradiso,* 15.13–14. Poliziano: *Stanze,* 2.17. Vida: *Christias,* ed. J. Cranwell, pp. 30–32.

Inde alii proceres et convenientia late
Numina.

[1.875–82][21]

Tasso's allusion to Fortune (449–52) is based on Dante (*Inferno,* 7.73–96), although the precise language used is not derivative, and line 455 is virtually identical with a line in Petrarch's *Trionfo d'Amore:*

D'intorno innumerabili mortali . . . [1.28]

Finally, lines 509–12 imitate a passage in Claudian's *De Raptu Proserpinae.*[22]

Even if some of these resemblances are dismissed as fortuitous, one must recognize that Tasso is here attempting a more recondite poetry, a poetry depending on the resonance of half-remembered phrases and the flashback of half-glimpsed images. It is learned poetry, moreover, which needs annotation. The uninstructed reader might not guess that the phrase *Chi 'l misura* in line 448 refers to time and *Quella* in the following line to Fortune; he would probably identify *il puro cristallo* in line 479 with the outermost crystalline sphere and *cerchio . . . di stelle gemmato* with the sphere of the fixed stars, but he might not understand why the second moved in opposition, *in contra* (line 480), to the first, or why the planets are said to rotate from the left (line 482). These abstruse details, like the poetic allusions, render the poetry more esoteric. Why should the poet have chosen to render it so? Because I think he wanted it to be more "sublime." He has tried to replace the spirit of the *De Partu Virginis* with the spirit of the *Divina Commedia.* I have already suggested that his imagination would in fact have been more at ease in a less elevated, more pictorial heaven—the heaven, say, of a Fra Angelico. Here he is straining, and calls upon his learning to support his inven-

21. "Here is the holy throne of God, whenever He dispenses laws or concerns Himself with general affairs. He Himself sits in the center; Wisdom stands at His right hand, Love at the other, and they constitute three deities in one. At His feet are puissant Nature, and Time, and Place, and variable Fortune, and immutable Order; then the other powers and divinities in a large assembly."

22. 2.216–22. Renaissance commentators suggest other derivations, but many of them seem to me far-fetched.

tion. It is the strain of the Italian Baroque attempting to imagine a more terrible God, like the God of Luther and Calvin.

The tension in Gabriele's descent between image and idea is relaxed in Michele's; both elements now express the sublimity of God, the frailty of man. The shift stems naturally from the traditionally different associations of Gabriel and Michael[23] and from the respective contexts of the two descents. Michele is a much more formidable figure than Gabriele. The metallic glitter of his adamantine arms outshines the warm radiance of Gabriele's blond hair, and his speed is evoked in images which almost surpass the imagination. He fends the air like a falling star, quicker even than thought itself:

> rapido sì ch'anco il pensier eccede.

His speed indeed is abstract; it is encumbered by so many comparisons (as Gabriele's is not), it traverses so many spheres, that we *think* the speed but we do not feel it. Gabriele's speed is not called so much to our attention, but his flight in fact seems much quicker. Tasso seems to have worked harder on Michele. Some of the lines, such as these, are very fine:

> s'indorava la notte al divin lume
> che spargea scintillando il volto fuori.

But the descent as a whole loses in ease and control what perhaps it gains in magnificence.

The God who dispatches Michele is Himself much more magnificent. He gives laws to all; He commands Fate and Nature (the two instruments of Providence), Motion, Time, Space, and Fortune; innumerable angels encircle His august throne; Michele kneels reverently at His feet, as Gabriele does not. The poet's language imitates the sound of his thunder:

> . . . con quale
> folgore orrendo il Re del mondo tuona . . .

And here the brilliance of celestial things—the mystic "tre lumi in una luce," the gleam of Michele's flight, the fiery realms of the

23. Michael was associated with warfare even by Biblical writers; see Daniel 10:21 and Revelation 12:7.

blessed—this brilliance is not reflected by the sunlit freshness of earth but rather intensified by earthly gloom:

> la caligine densa e i cupi orrori.

The earth appears as petty and contemptible:

> i bassi confin del mondo angusto
> ove senso o ragion non si conduce.

And this depth of gloom is exceeded by a still darker region, the realm where demons vent their fury uninterruptedly upon the guilty, among screams, the shaking of chains, the gnashing of teeth. To that realm the demons fly in order, writes Tasso in a powerful phrase, to aggravate the customary pain of the damned:

> ad inasprir ne' rei l'usate doglie.

Perhaps the most important contrast between the two descents lies in their implicit conceptions of the crusade and of all human endeavor. God speaks to Gabriele of the "high enterprise," "l'alta impresa," and that angel speaks to Goffredo of the "hope of high victory" he should entertain. Here human endeavor is free, dignified, and capable of success. But in Michele's descent the glory of human endeavor is like smoke or dust, governed as it is by the caprice of God's minister, Fortune:

> . . . Quella che qual fumo o polve
> la gloria di qua giuso e l'oro e i regni,
> come piace là su, disperde e volve,
> né, diva, cura i nostri umani sdegni.

The wars of this world are proofs of its vanity:

> . . . se stesso il mondo strugge e pasce,
> e ne le guerre sue more e rinasce.

It is in keeping with this conception that Michele's speech to the demons make no allusion whatsoever to the crusaders.

The severity and "sublimity" of Michele's descent are atypical of the *Liberata* as a whole. They represent one pole of Tasso's religiosity as the blond adolescence of Gabriele represents the other. The significance of each lies in its distance from the other.

This is not like the distance between the canticles of the *Commedia,* a paradoxical relation created and resolved by the controlling artistic mind. Tasso's shifts of tone, of moral feeling, esthetic distance, religious awe, literary tradition, betray the existence of real alternatives whose respective claims he would satisfy but cannot fuse as simply as Dante. Dante was one of the last great men to whom the monolithic unity of the medieval world was still accessible. Perhaps he was able to reach it only through the synthetic power and range of his extraordinary mind. Whatever unity was reached by Tasso's age resulted from the papering over of divisions, divisions which the poet was not original enough fully to resolve. But he *was* an immensely resourceful artist, and one can only admire the skill with which he bridged divisions, satisfied alternatives, pieced together a single poem whose unity is not factitious.

iv.

In his Preface to the early poem, *Rinaldo,* the 18-year-old Tasso already raised the critical issue which would preoccupy him all his life, as it preoccupied his age. In the same Preface he indicated his own compromise solution which, despite various tactical maneuvers, he defended all his life. To understand his own view of the *Gerusalemme Liberata* it is necessary to understand that issue. It was posed in the world of Italian letters, saturated as it was in Aristotelian poetics, by the great success of Boiardo and Ariosto. The difficulty was that the single poem composed by these two men violated all the classical canons. It possessed none of the unities; it disregarded verisimilitude; it was immensely long; it did not sustain the high style; it contained little *utile* to balance its irresistible *dulce.* Yet it was hugely popular, even among most men of taste. The history of Italian criticism from 1536 (date of the translation of the *Poetics*) to 1581 (when the *Liberata* appeared) is to a great extent a history of successive solutions to this critical dilemma. Many theoretical solutions were turned into practice by critic-poets, who then had to witness in the failure of their poems the most humiliating refutation of their systems. Tasso's practical solution in *Rinaldo* was different from his later one: it involved a series of episodes unified by the presence of a single hero. But theoretically, as I have said, he moved very little: he consistently defended a unity of action which left room for episodic diversity.

To see the alternatives in the simplistic way the sixteenth century saw them, you would have to make a list of opposites in facing columns. One column would be headed *epic* and the other *romance,* and under these respective genres would appear edification as against pleasure; history or verisimilitude against fantasy; the Latin and Greek languages against the less "austere," more lyrical Italian language; unity of the fable against diversity—that is to say, a single hero against many heroes, a single plot line against an episodic plot; the high style against a more flexible style; the authority of Aristotle against the applause of the multitude, and in particular of women. The *Gerusalemme Liberata* was criticized by readers aligned on either side: first, before publication, by the Humanist Sperone Speroni, and later, during the furious polemics which followed publication, by such admirers of Ariosto as the scientist Galileo and the secretary of the Accadèmia della Crusca, Salviati. In his two most important critical works, the youthful *Arte Poetica* and the late *Discorsi del Poema Eroico,* Tasso defended himself primarily against the admirers of romance. In the so-called *Lettere Poetiche,* written to those and about those, like Speroni, who were urging him to "regularize" the poem, Tasso's polemical posture faced in the opposite direction. But on this particular question of unity, the key question of the whole debate, he never really changed his opinion. He summarized it in a beautiful and famous sentence which I quote once again. An epic, he wrote, should have both the unity and the diversity of the world itself:

> Però che, sì come in questo mirabile magisterio di Dio, che mondo si chiama, e 'l cielo si vede sparso o distinto di tanta varietà di stelle; e, discendendo poi giuso di mano in mano, l'aria e 'l mare pieni d'uccelli e di pesci; e la terra albergatrice di tanti animali così feroci come mansueti, nella quale e ruscelli e fonti e laghi e prati e campagne e selve e monti si trovano; e qui frutti e fiori, là ghiacci e nevi, qui abitazioni

e culture, là solitudini ed orrori: con tutto ciò uno è il mondo che tante e sì diverse cose nel suo grembo rinchiude, una la forma e l'essenza sua, uno il modo dal quale sono le sue parti con discorde concordia insieme congiunte e collegate; e non mancando nulla in lui, nulla però vi è di soverchio o di non necessario: così parimente giudico che da eccellente poeta (il quale non per altro divino è detto se non perché, al supremo Artefice nelle sue operazioni assomigliandosi, della sua di divinità viene a partecipare) un poema formar si possa nel quale, quasi in un picciolo mondo, qui si leggano ordinanze d'eserciti, qui battaglie terrestri e navali, qui espugnazioni di città, scaramucce e duelli, qui giostre, qui descrizioni di fame e di sete, qui tempeste, qui prodigii; là si trovino concilii celesti ed infernali, là si veggiano sedizioni, là discordie, là errori, là venture, là incanti, là opere di crudeltà, di audacia, di cortesia, di generosità; là avvenimenti d'amore, or felici or infelici, or lieti or compassionevoli; ma che nondimeno uno sia il poema che tanta varietà di materie contegna, una la forma e la favola sua, e che tutte queste cose siano di maniera composte che l'una l'altra riguardi, l'una a l'altra corrisponda, l'una da l'altra o necessariamente o verisimilmente dependa: sì che una sola parte o tolta via o mutata di sito, il tutto ruini.[24]

24. *Prose,* pp. 387–88. "For, in this admirable realm of God called the world, the sky is seen to be scattered over and beautified with a great variety of stars, and descending lower and lower from region to region, the air and the sea are full of birds and fishes, and the earth harbors many animals both fierce and gentle, and in it we can see many streams, fountains, lakes, fields, plains, forests, and mountains, here fruits and flowers, there ice and snow, here dwelling and cultivation, there solitude and wild places. Yet for all that, the world, which includes in its bosom so many and so diverse things, is one, one in its form and essence, one the knot with which its parts are joined and bound together in discordant concord; and while there is nothing lacking in it, yet there is nothing there that does not serve either for necessity or ornament. I judge that in the same way the great poet (who is called divine for no other reason but that, because he resembles in his works the supreme architect, he comes to participate in his divinity) is able to form a poem in which as in a little world can be read in one passage how armies are drawn up, and in various others there are battles by land and sea, attacks on cities, skirmishes, duels, jousts, descriptions of hunger and thirst, tempests, conflagrations, prodigies; there are a variety of celestial and infernal councils, and the reader encounters seditions, discords, wanderings, adventures, incan-

This great summation, with its rhetorical fluency, its Olympian breadth, its fervent faith in the Poem as mirror and microcosm of creation, its vision of the imagination fusing all its creatures "con discorde concordia insieme," becomes itself a miniature image of that little world which is its subject.

But the most persuasive argument for Tasso's solution is the *Gerusalemme Liberata.* It is a triumph of firm, symmetrical, various but unobtrusive architecture. It balances brilliantly the main plot, the plot dominated by Goffredo which moves ever forward to the capture of Jerusalem, with the several secondary plots, which concern chiefly the loves of two Christian knights, Rinaldo and Tancredi, and three pagan women, Armida, Clorinda, and Erminia. The poet's capacity for interweaving main plot and subplots, war and love, is masterful; no one story is allowed to usurp all one's interest; each incident flows naturally into the next; each is told with all the vigor and color it needs, but none ever checks the central forward movement, which remains central in the reader's mind even when his attention is turned from it.

The poem consists of twenty cantos. If you divide it in half, you see that each block of ten begins and ends with a great turning point in the main plot. The descent of Gabriele in the first canto initiates the whole narrative; it leads to the election of Goffredo and the opening of the siege. In the ninth canto the Christians succeed in staving off the furious night raid led by Solimano, and the demons are driven from the field by Michele. In the eleventh canto, the first concerted attack is made upon Jerusalem, which is finally taken in two successive days of fighting described in the eighteenth through the twentieth cantos. Between these peaks of action, the great central movement is allowed to slacken and to branch off into the subplots. The first and last quarters tend to focus on the Armida plot, the second and third quarters on the Erminia and Clorinda plots. But so sophisticated is the interweav-

---

tations, works of cruelty, audacity, courtesy, and generosity, and actions of love, now unhappy, now happy, now pleasing, now causing compassion. Yet in spite of all, the poem that contains so great variety of matter is one, one is its form and its soul; and all these things are put together in such a way that one has relation to the other, one corresponds to the other, the one necessarily or apparently so depends on the other that if one part is taken away or changed in position the whole is destroyed."

ing that the reader notices no mechanical counterbalance, no geometric symmetry, only his own pleasure. Tasso succeeds superbly in fusing the single movement of antique epic with the variety of romance.

The romance tradition exercised a healthy influence on Tasso because it depended on visible, objective action. From Vida to Milton the risk always run by the Christian epic was the risk of too little objective action—too little, that is, to appeal to a certain naïve deep-rooted need which we all bring to long stories. Spenser contrived partly to satisfy that need without quite possessing the great, simple, primitive gift. Ariosto *did* possess it, to as high a degree, I suppose, as anybody ever did. Tasso's narrative gift was inferior to Ariosto's, but it was nonetheless sure, and it was abetted by his ability to organize a mass of complex material into an elegant whole. Had Tasso lacked his brilliant models, he might have tried to interiorize his poem excessively, and thereby have robbed it of its charm. As it is there are few deliberative episodes, few weak-image episodes, as there are few in Ariosto. In suppressing them, Tasso's instinct about his own genius was correct. He wrote best when adorning a tale. This tendency away from the deliberative is manifest in both angelic descents, where the speeches of God and of the angels are subordinated, quantitatively and dramatically, to the narrative context.

Adapting the magical elements of romance to the celestial machinery of classical epic, and adjusting both to Christianity was a particularly delicate task. Tasso's bold solution lay in what he called the *maraviglioso verisimile*. When he spoke of verisimilitude, Tasso meant that Christians are accustomed to believing in miracles and will accept anything supernatural as possible so long as God wills it. He carefully refrained from saying that *he* believed in miracles. But he went on to fill his poem with magicians and witches, enchantments, dream-visions, prophecies, as well as the angels and demons we have already encountered. Not even the devoutest readers have ever believed in the probability of Tasso's *maraviglioso,* but many have been grateful for its lurid wonders. One might want to quarrel with the taste of certain passages, but if all the magic were purged, the poem would be a poorer, duller thing. It appeals unabashedly to the storybook fancy no one really outgrows. In the finest of his magical fantasies, the enchanted wood, Tasso is very great indeed.

The pity is that he had to pay a price for his magic. The price is the credibility of his really serious flights of devotion. Tasso could not have it two ways. The fiction of the storybook is not the fiction of the *Paradiso*. This is why the "sublime" passages like Michele's descent are not truly sublime. You are not persuaded that his heaven is so lofty as the poet would have you imagine. It is a part of the fable, a part of the make believe, appealing enough but never "real," never impinging on one's actual spiritual life.

Thus in its weighting of the three elements—the epic, the Christian, and the romance, the *Gerusalemme Liberata* in effect gives shortest shrift to the Christian. Or more precisely, its subordinates the subjective to the objective; the edifying, the abstract, the didactic, the deliberative, to the delightful, the concrete, the marvelous, the executive. But I would not, however, leave the impression that Tasso wrote simply a more "regular" chivalric romance. There were stirrings of mature feeling in him, feeling which escaped the authorized, pious categories and which ennobles the romance conventions at those intermittent moments when it finds expression. There is also a skeletal substructure of neo-Platonism which lends firmness to the fable. To these less flamboyant strains in the poem I want to turn now. Let me first make brief mention of other ways in which the *Liberata* modifies its romance heritage. Tasso suppressed, for better or worse, the burlesque and satiric wild oats of Ariosto. He individualized his eight or nine major characters much more distinctively than the romances, so that, for example, you would never conceivably confuse his heroines. He even introduced a certain psychological finesse, as in the portrait of Erminia, which approaches, without resembling, Virgil's portrait of Dido. Finally, Tasso aimed at a limited historical accuracy and based several characters and events upon the chronicles at his disposal.

But actually his poem's historicity counts for little; in this respect the romance tradition proved too strong. The great weakness of second-rate literary epic ever since Apollonius Rhodius was that it cut itself off from history and became a closed system, relevant to nothing but itself. Ariosto avoided that risk by, on the one hand, accepting and delighting in the unreality while, on the other, touching the real world with personal allusions. Tasso tried much harder to be historic and failed. When his poem succeeds, it succeeds through the intensity of his imagination, unaware of the vacuum in which it is working. Historians have profited from the *Iliad;* they might conceivably profit from the *Aeneid* or the *Commedia,* but they could learn nothing from the *Liberata,* neither of the eleventh century nor of the sixteenth. That in itself does not matter. But there is a problem for Tasso's readers of esthetic distance. By introducing a kind of history, he tried to shorten the distance a little. And yet his story nonetheless remains in its fabulous irreality.

v.

Both of the angelic descents in the *Liberata* are made to further a single end, the conquest of Jerusalem. What meaning exactly does the conquest acquire? Very little, I fear. When God dispatches Gabriele, he speaks of a war to liberate "Gierusalemme oppressa." But this oppression is not dramatized enough to make the reader hope for its end. The isolated incident of Olindo and Sofronia, to be sure, hinges on the infidels' cruelty toward Christians within the city. But this incident is one of the most melodramatic and unlikely in the poem; it involves only two victims; and even these are pardoned in the end. What suffering *they* endure scarcely justifies the blood and agony of the rest. The fact is that we are shown Jerusalem from two very different perspectives. On one hand it is the holy goal of the crusaders whose very sight brings them to tears (3.7). On the other hand it is a community, neither holy nor unholy, of beleaguered men and women, some of them villainous and some admirable. This latter perspective is the one maintained through most of the poem. We feel the plight of the besieged much more acutely than the necessity of besieging them.

Is the whole enterprise then futile? Is there no moral or metaphysical principle to inform with meaning the conduct of Tasso's heroes? I think there is none if you stand very near his poem and consider it at close hand, as I have just done. If you draw back a little, you can discern the outlines of a systematic conception. The philosophy most congenial to the poet, particularly in his youth during the *Liberata's* composition, was neo-Platonism. Ficino was the Renaissance thinker with the greatest influence on Tasso, partly because Ficino seemed to have reconciled Platonism with Christianity. It may have been he who directed Tasso's attention to the passage in Plato's *Cratylus* suggesting a common etymology of *eros* and *heros* (hero). Tasso alludes to the etymological connection in his prose as though it were a fact.[25] This association of love and heroism seems to me to be a key to his ethic throughout the *Liberata.*

Neo-Platonism enters the poem at the outset, in a passage I have summarized above. Before dispatching Gabriele, the Eternal Father looks into the hearts of the chief crusaders:

> Mirò tutte le cose ed in Soria
> s'affissò poi ne' principi cristiani,
> e con quel guardo suo ch'a dentro spia
> nel più secreto lor gli affetti umani,
> vede Goffredo che scacciar desia
> de la santa città gli empi pagani,
> e pien di fé, di zelo, ogni mortale
> gloria, imperio, tesor mette in non cale.
>
> Ma vede in Baldovin cupido ingegno
> ch'a l'umane grandezze intento aspira:
> vede Tancredi aver la vita a sdegno,
> tanto un suo vano amor l'ange e martira:
> e fondar Boemondo al novo regno
> suo d'Antiochia alti principii mira,
> e leggi imporre ed introdur costume
> ed arti e culto di verace nume,
>
> e cotanto internarsi in tal pensiero
> ch'altra impresa non par che più rammenti:

25. *Prose,* p. 55. See the *Cratylus,* 398c. The etymology is of course false, as Plato probably knew.

scorge in Rinaldo ed animo guerriero
e spirti di riposo impazienti:
non cupidigia in lui d'oro o d'impero,
ma d'onor brame immoderate, ardenti:
scorge che da la bocca intento pende
di Guelfo e i chiari antichi essempi apprende.
[1.57–80][26]

At first glance this passage is puzzling because two of the five men named—Baldovin and Boemondo—play no role in the poem. This is odd, since these names are the first one encounters. But if one considers these five in Platonic terms, if one ranges the love of each on successive steps of a Platonic ladder, then the passage presents no problems. Goffredo, at the highest level, burns only with holy zeal, the active love of God and eagerness to do His will. All earthly glory, empire, wealth, he disdains. This sequence—"gloria, imperio, tesor"—is not fortuitous; it indicates three of the

26. All Things He view'd; at last in Syria staid
Upon the Christian Lords His gracious Eye:
That wond'rous Look, wherewith He oft survey'd
Man's secret Thoughts, which most concealed lye,
He cast on puissant Godfrey, who assay'd
To drive the Turks from Sion's Bulwarks high,
And, full of Zeal and Faith, esteemed light
All worldly Honor, Empire, Treasure, Might:

In Baldwin next He spy'd another Thought,
Whom Spirits proud to vain Ambition move:
Tancred He saw his Life's Joy set at nought,
So woe-begon was he with Pains of Love:
Boemond the conquer'd Folk of Antioch brought
The gentle Yoke of Christian Rule to prove;
He taught them Statutes, Laws, and Customs new,
Arts, Crafts, Obedience, and Religion true;

And with such Care his busy Work he ply'd,
That to nought else his acting Thoughts he bent:
In young Rinaldo fierce Desires He spy'd,
And noble Heart of Rest impatient;
To Wealth or sov'reign Pow'r he nought apply'd
His Wits, but all to Virtue excellent;
Patterns and Rules of Skill and Courage bold
He took from Guelpho, and his Fathers old.

steps below Goffredo in descending order. This sequence is reversed and increased by a fourth step in the series of names that follow—Baldovin, Tancredi, Boemondo, Rinaldo. Baldovin loves wealth and rank—"l'umane grandezze"; Tancredi loves a woman, Boemondo empire, Rinaldo honor. The love of each is ethically superior to his predecessor's, but all are inferior to the zeal of Goffredo. The two important words applied to Tancredi are "sdegno" and "vano"; his love for Clorinda is inferior because it brings him to despair and because it is futile. But it is still preferable to Baldovin's cupidity. Boemondo's passion for an empire of law and civilization is higher than either; it is Virgilian. It is only reprehensible because it leads Boemondo to neglect the high enterprise he has embarked upon:

> altra impresa non par che più rammenti.

Rinaldo is above all of these:

> non cupidigia in lui d'oro o d'impero

although he is not to remain above Tancredi's passion. His own dominant passion is honor, the highest aspiration of classical antiquity, the mark of Aristotle's magnanimous man. The glimpse of Rinaldo hanging upon Guelfo's heroic tales is attractive and shows that Tasso does not condemn the love of honor. His Christian qualification is implied by the adjective *immoderate.* The danger of immoderate ambition is its disregard of higher goals, a disregard Rinaldo will betray when he deserts the crusaders' camp. Neither romantic love nor the pursuit of honor is in itself evil, but each is reprehensible to the degree that it inhibits the full service of God.

This simplified form of neo-Platonism underlies the conduct of the Christian knights, although not that of the Saracens. Goffredo is chosen commander by God precisely because his form of love is highest. In his dialogue on love, *La Molza,* Tasso discusses the virtues of Goffredo (without naming him) as manifestations of love:

> . . . Ma se l'amor si volge a le cose create, produce la prudenza, la giustizia, la temperenza e la fortezza, la liberalità,

> la mansuetudine, la modestia e l'altre, le quali sono in guisa congiunte che l'una non può star senza l'altra . . .[27]

Goffredo's wearing of a common soldier's uniform underscores his freedom from a punctilious sense of honor. But if he rises above it, Tancredi's temptation is to fall beneath it; from *his* moral level, the pursuit of honor is elevating. He is twice diverted by love from honor in his duel with Argante—first, momentarily, when he is rapt into immobility by the sight of Clorinda on the field, and secondly, more gravely, when his misguided pursuit of her prevents him from appearing to continue the duel. Later his grief at her death destroys his usefulness as a soldier. Fully to play his true role and to overcome Argante, his love must be spiritualized by a dream-vision of his beloved:

> Quivi io beata amando godo, e quivi
> spero che per te loco anco s'appresti,
> ove al gran Sole e ne l'eterno die
> vagheggiarai le sue bellezze e mie.
>
> Se tu medesmo non t'invidii il Cielo
> e non travii co'l vaneggiar de' sensi,
> vivi e sappi ch'io t'amo, e non te 'l celo,
> quanto più creature amar conviensi.
>
> [12.733–40][28]

Rinaldo in turn abandons his true role as champion of God when he kills an insulting knight and flees rather than humble himself before Goffredo. His potential capacity for serving God

27. *Prose,* p. 214. "But if love is directed toward created things, it produces prudence, justice, temperance and courage, generosity, meekness, modesty and the others, which are mingled in such a way that one cannot remain without the other."

28. There will I love thee; there for Tancred fit
A Seat prepared is among the Blest;
There in eternal Bliss, eternal Light,
Thou shalt thy Love enjoy, and she her Knight,

Unless thy self thy self Heav'ns Joys envy,
And thy vain Sorrow thee of Bliss deprive:
Live; know I love thee, that I nill deny,
As Angels Men, as Saints may Wights alive.

is destroyed by his pride. This fall, both Christian and Platonic, is followed by a second, to the level of sensuality, when he is charmed and seduced by Armida. This second fall is repaired by the speech of Ubaldo, when he comes upon the dulled Rinaldo in Armida's garden. Ubaldo's appeal is not to holy zeal but to honor, the intervening step:

> Su, su, te il campo e te Goffredo invita:
> te la fortuna e la vittoria aspetta.
> Vieni, o fatal guerriero, e sia fornita
> la ben comincia impresa: e l'empia setta,
> che già crollasti, a terra estinta cada
> sotto l'inevitabile tua spada.
>
> [16.259–64] [29]

The earlier fall can only be repaired by Peter the Hermit and the grace of God. Rinaldo transcends the pursuit of worldly honor when, at Peter's bidding, he prays alone at dawn on Mount Olivet and recognizes the emptiness of earthly things. Purged and redeemed by this experience, he can offer himself without fear to the repentant Armida.

Perhaps this analysis will suffice to demonstrate Tasso's debt to neo-Platonism. But having demonstrated it, I would not want to exaggerate it. If I have interpreted him correctly, Tasso used a form of Ficino's system to pattern his fable, but he cannot be said to have written a Platonic poem. His debt is no greater than it is, I think, because Tasso was himself never able to reach, even in imagination, the higher sphere of Platonic love. The redemptions of Rinaldo and Tancredi occur by *fiat* of the omnipotent author, but they are not psychologically authentic; they are part of the *maraviglioso*. Goffredo is the only believable figure at the height of the scale, but Goffredo himself is joyless. The subtlest voice of the poem, and the most persuasive, whispers that there is no

29. Up, up, our Camp and Godfrey for thee send;
Thee Fortune, Praise, and Victory expect:
Come, fatal Champion, bring to happy End
This Enterprise begun, and all that Sect,
Which oft thou shaken hast, to Earth full low
With thy sharp Brand strike down, kill, overthrow.

rapture on earth for any lover. There is only the lover's restless and forlorn pursuit.

Just as the poet's own life was a long, anguished search for rest, so his poem betrays a nostalgia for serenity. The word *sereno* appears in both the angelic descents: Gabriele returns from earth to those regions of the sky "più eccelse e più serene," and Michele resembles a falling star "fendendo il liquido sereno." In both contexts serenity is a quality reserved for heaven. Goffredo's militant zeal wins him none, though he desires it. When he rises in a dream to the "sereno candido" of heaven and learns that his place awaits him there, he is eager to put off his mortality:

> —Quando ciò fia?—rispose—il mortal laccio
> sciolgasi omai, s'al restar qui m'e impaccio.
> [14.55–56][30]

It is characteristic of Tasso that in *La Molza* he defines the end of love as *quiete*. There is a moment of spiritual *quiete* during Rinaldo's redemptive experience on Mount Olivet. But it is only a moment. The poem does not really represent the serene fulfillment of spiritual love on earth. Rather than the junction of Idea and action, it represents their tragic separation. It denies serenity to our world. There is a pathetic prose passage, written much later than the poem, confessing the Platonist failure which was implicit but unarticulated earlier:

> Il trattar de le forme in tutti modi . . . apporta seco grande oscurità e gran malagevolezza: perciò che s'altri considera le forme separate, ch'idee sono state dette da' filosofi, può di leggeri esser persuaso ch'elle o non siano o nulla giovino a' nostri umani arteficii ed a l'operazioni de' mortali; e, se non persuaso, almeno da la contraria ragione é costretto di lasciar così alto contemplazione; ma, contemplando le forme ne la materia, trova ancora grandissima difficultà, perciò che la materia è cagione d'incertitudine e d'oscurità: laonde a le tenebre ed a gli abissi da gli antichi filosofi fu assomigliata; ma separandole con l'imaginazione, divien quasi bugiardo e,

30. Ah when, quoth he, these mortal Bonds unknit,
Shall I in Peace, in Ease and Rest, there sit?

> se pur non dice menzogna, non contempla a fine d'alcun bene.[31]

The contemplation of Ideas is difficult whether one seeks them in the shadowy obscurity of matter or whether one attempts to separate them from it. The *Liberata* dramatizes this *oscurità* of earthly endeavor, this abyss of flux and uncertainty that awaits Michele:

> ove se stesso il mondo strugge e pasce,
> e ne le guerre sue more e rinasce.

So the world appears to Goffredo in his dream vision of heaven, at the Dantesque moment when the spirit of Ugone directs his view downward:

> . . . l'altro in giuso i lumi
> volse quasi sdegnando e ne sorrise:
> ché vide un punto sol, mar, terre e fiumi,
> che qui paion distinti in tante guise;
> ed ammirò che pur a l'ombre, a i fiumi,
> la nostra folle umanità s'affise,
> servo imperio cercando e muta fama,
> né miri il ciel ch'a sé n'invita e chiama.
> [14.81–88][32]

31. *Prose,* p. 691. "To speak of the forms in any manner involves great obscurity and great difficulty: for if one considers separately the forms, which are called ideas by philosophers, one can easily be persuaded either that they do not exist or else that they are of no benefit to our human artificers and the activities of mortals; and, if one is not persuaded, at least he is forced to abandon such exalted contemplation by the opposing argument. But if one contemplates the forms in matter, he still meets with the greatest difficulty because matter is a source of uncertainty and obscurity, for which reason ancient philosophers compared it to shadows and chasms. But if one separates them with the imagination, it becomes virtually false and even if it does not lie, it leads the mind to no good."

32. . . . the other bended down
His looks to Ground, and half in Scorn he smil'd;
He saw at once Earth, Sea, Flood, Castle, Town,
Strangely divided, strangely all compil'd;
And wonder'd, Folly Man so far should drown,
To set his Heart on Things so base and vile,
Who servile Empire searcheth, and dumb Fame,
And scorn Heav'n's Bliss, yet proffers Heav'n the same.

Instead of true serenity on earth, the *Liberata* presents a simulacrum of it in the garden of Armida, one of the supreme arch-images of the Renaissance imagination. In this labyrinth of the senses, one form of love, the commonest, is given its perfect gratification. But paradoxically, it remains ungratified. The lover is suffocated with the sweetness of love; he can ask no more, can desire no absent thing; he is lulled into immobility by the luxuriance of beauty. But his desire remains avid in its very consummation:

> . . . i famelici sguardi avidamente
> in lei pascendo si consuma e strugge.
>
> [16.145–46] [33]

There is only the appearance of rest. The garden is a much more soporific, enclosing, inhibiting place than its closest model, Ariosto's island of Alcina. Its motionlessness seems the apotheosis of serenity. But the secret of its languor is rather the perpetual threat to serenity:

> . . . Cogliam la rosa in su 'l mattino adorno
> di questo dì, che tosto il seren perde,
> cogliam d'amor la rosa . . .
>
> [16.117–19] [34]

An alternative image of repose is the pastoral retreat discovered by the fugitive Erminia. Tasso describes it in a few octaves (7.5-22) which seem the distillation of a hundred forgotten eclogues. The tranquillity of this world is actually opposed to the torpidity of the garden, for it suppresses the desires which the garden surfeits, and all others as well. The shepherd's poverty is dear to him because he asks for nothing; it is . . .

> . . . a me si cara
> che non bramo tesor né regal verga,
> né cura o voglia ambiziosa o avara

33. His hungry Eyes upon her Face he fed,
And feeding them so pin'd himself away.

34. Oh, gather then the Rose, while Time thou hast;
Short is the Day, done when it scant began;
Gather the Rose of Love.

> mai nel tranquillo del mio petto alberga.
> Spengo la sete mia ne l'acqua chiara . . ."
> [7.73–77][35]

He has renounced all the possible forms of love. But Erminia, whose love is irrepressible, wins no repose and leaves. The shepherd's precious indifference is a rarity.

Does Tasso then leave altogether unmitigated the tragic separation of Idea and experience? Does he simply leave the will weary with its pursuit of unearthly fulfillment? Yes, in a sense he does; but there are moments in the poem which transcend his somewhat lachrymose anguish as they transcend the storybook fantasy. There are scenes whose tragedy is truly serious and virile and resigned. They tend to cluster about the figures of Argante and Solimano, the two principal Saracen champions. I do not have space to discuss these at length, but they are perhaps the most grandiose figures in the *Liberata.* Like the Christian champions, they are easily distinguished: Argante the titanic, the scornful, pitiless, arrogant, tireless, furious; Solimano the deposed king, regal and poised, he, too, splendidly vital but more somberly courageous, more reflective, more embittered. In his treatment of this towering pair Tasso abandons his Christian-Platonic categories and catches the appeal of sheer dynamism in itself. He achieves one of epic poetry's most difficult tasks—the creation of that heroic energy, that superabundant vitality whose touchstone is Achilles. Solimano fights, supposedly, to regain his kingdom, but both fight actually out of a passion for fighting, out of disdain for repose and serenity. As against the weary, Virgilian will of Goffredo and Rinaldo's abandonment of his will to Armida's dreamy enchantment, they embody the robust élan of the will, joyful in its own rugged freedom. Each is in love with his own life, and for each the only crushing loss is death. Each is killed.

Argante dies on the penultimate day of fighting at the hands of Tancredi, whom he has accompanied beyond the city walls in order that their duel be uninterrupted. They repair to a valley

35. Dearer to me than Wealth or kingly Crown!
No Wish for Honor, Thirst of others Good,
Can move my Heart contented with my own:
We quench our Thirst with Water of this Flood.

which resembles in shape a theatre or a tilting field. Before they renew their feud, Argante pauses and turns to view the beleaguered city with unwonted pensiveness. His enemy asks brusquely if he is afraid to begin. Whereupon Argante replies:

> Penso—risponde—a la città del regno
> di Giudea antichissima regina,
> che vinta or cade, e indarno esser sostegno
> io procurai de la fatal ruina:
> e ch'è poca vendetta al mio disdegno
> il capo tuo, che 'l Cielo or mi destina.
> Tacque, e in contra si van con gran risguardo.
> [19.73–79][36]

The speech is typical of him, in its taciturn and fierce pride, but it invests him with a tragic profundity he has not hitherto displayed. So Solimano, on the following day, viewing from the tower of David the final battle beneath him beyond the city walls, is granted an emblematic epiphany:

> Or mentre in guisa tal fera tenzone
> è tra 'l fedel essercito e 'l pagano,
> salse in cima a la torre ad un balcone
> e mirò, ben che lunge, il fer Soldano:
> mirò quasi in teatro od in agone,
> l'aspra tragedia de lo stato umano,
> i vari assalti e il fero orror di morte,
> e i gran giochi del caso e de la sorte.
>
> Stette attonito alquanto e stupefatto
> a quelle prime viste, e poi s'accese . . .
> [20.577–86][37]

36. I think, quoth he, on this distressed Town,
The aged Queen of Juda's antient Land,
Now lost, now sack'd, now spoil'd and trodden down,
Whose Fall in vain I strived to withstand:
A small Revenge for Sion's Fort o'erthrown
That Head can be, cut off by my strong Hand.
This said, together with great Heed they flew.

37. Between the Armies twain while thus the Fight
Wax'd sharp, hot, cruel, though renew'd but late,

He sees the tragedy "as in a theatre or arena," like the valley where Argante dies, and he wonders at it dazedly before his fury is rekindled and he rushes down to his death by Rinaldo's sword.

Nothing in the *Gerusalemme Liberata* is more beautiful or moving or majestic than this lonely image of a king on a balcony above a scene of carnage, surprised by the mystery of things. It subsumes both pagan fatalism and Christian *contemptus mundi.* The tragic repose of this moment, which is only a prelude to violence, contains perhaps the truest serenity any of Tasso's characters reach. In his profoundest passages—and there are others I have not quoted—Tasso regards the universe with a matured pessimism, a sober compassion more authentic than the fashionable, authorized severity of the Michele descent and its vision of hell. The color and variety and occasional naïveté of this patchwork poem do not frequently leave scope for the deeper intensity which could not, in any case, consistently have governed Tasso's volatile imagination. But the *soavi licor* of his romantic marvels leave a faint aftertaste of bitterness—the "astringent tragedy of the human condition." His fable is set in a theatre where fancy alone summons a presence from the seat of the King of Heaven, ruler of Space and Time, Fate and Nature and Fortune.

vi.

Tasso's poem, nourished by books and dreams, is complemented by the nearly contemporaneous *Os Lusíadas* by Luiz de Camoens, whose imagination was nourished by physical hardship, voyage, disease, and personal and national disillusion. If Tasso knew history and geography from the printed page, Camoens knew them to the marrow of his ravaged body. The history represented in his

---

Upclomb the Soldan to the Tower's Height,
And saw far off their Strife and fell Debate;
As from some Stage or Theatre, the Knight
Saw play'd the Tragedy of human State,
  Saw Death, Blood, Murder, Woe and Horror strange,
  And the great Acts of Fortune, Chance and Change.

At first astonish'd and amaz'd he stood,
Then burn'd with Wrath . . .

poem is authentic; he introduces few people who did not once exist, and he pronounces the exotic names of African and Indian places with the assurance of a man who has seen them. This sturdy spine of *wahrheit* amid the surrounding *dichtung* makes of the poem an historical artifact which is subject to the abrupt reverses of history, and thus *Os Lusíadas* today seems almost swamped by the twentieth century. Of the two great forces which animate it, imperialism and nationalism, the first is largely discredited in our time, and the second is beginning to be suspect.[38] The prickly critical problem which arises from this situation can scarcely be resolved on these pages, but I think it has to be confronted by any serious reader of the present day. The tarnishing of so admired a monument as this would constitute a great loss, and yet one can scarcely open Camoens' volume without questioning those principles he takes most instinctively for granted. Such a fate is not likely to befall the work of Tasso, which is virtually sealed off, so to speak, from history. Certainly the decline of Christian faith touches it far less deeply than the lost prestige of imperialism has blighted *Os Lusíadas.*

The only celestial descent of any amplitude appears in the second of the ten cantos. It follows a lengthy speech, imitated from the first *Aeneid,* in which Jupiter reassures Venus regarding the glorious future of her beloved Portuguese. Jupiter concludes with this prophecy:

> De modo, filha minha, que de jeito [39]
> Amostrarão esforço mais que humano,
> Que nunca se verá tão forte peito
> Do Gangético Mar ao Gaditano,
> Nem das boreais ondas ao Estreito,
> Que mostrou o agravado Lusitano,
> Posto que em todo o mundo, de afrontados,
> Ressuscitassem todos os passados. [2.55]

38. The name of Goa, for example, a place where the poet lived for some time and which he names more than once in his text, awakens uncomfortable associations in contemporary ears.

39. Thus, child, they'll show their manner and their state,
For more than man's their fortitude will be.
And never shall be seen courage so great

He then proceeds to dispatch Mercury to the fleet of Vasco Da Gama, which is in danger at this moment from a treacherous attack by the natives of Mombasa, on the East African coast. Da Gama, as will appear, has to be urged on to the friendly city of Malindi which lies upon his present northerly course:

Como isto disse, manda o consagrado [40] 56
Filho de Maia à Terra, por que tenha
Um pacífico porto e sossegado,
Pera onde sem receio a frota venha;
E, pera que em Mombaça, aventurado,
O forte capitão se não detenha,
Lhe manda mais que em sonhos lhe mostrasse
A terra onde quieto repousasse.

Já pelo ar o Cileneu voava; 57
Com as asas nos pés à terra dece;
Sua vara fatal na mão levava
Com que os olhos cansados adormece;
Com esta as tristes almas revocava
Do Inferno, e o vento lhe obedece;

From the Gangetic to the Cadiz Sea,
Nor from the Boreal Ocean to the Strait
Which the wronged Portugese found latterly,
Though all who ever knew peril and pain
Of old throughout the world should rise again.

40. All Portugese quotations are taken from Luiz de Camoens, *Obras Completas,* ed. H. Cidade (Lisbon, 1946–47). The translations are taken from *The Lusiads of Luiz de Camoens,* trans. Leonard Bacon (New York, The Hispanic Society of America, 1950).

So saying, he bade Maia's sacred son
Descend to earth, with the commandment clear
To find safe harbor and a pleasant one,
In which the fleet might enter without fear.
Lest in Mombassa some fresh risk be run
By the brave Captain if he lingered near,
He bade the god in dream to him disclose
The land where he might quietly repose.

Already the Cyllenian down the air
Was hurling. On wing'd feet to Earth he flies
And in his hand the fateful rod doth bear,
Wherewith he lulls to sleep outwearied eyes,
Or from Hell summons spirits that despair,
And the winds obey it. In his wonted guise

Na cabeça o galero costumado.
E desta arte a Melinde foi chegado.

Consigo a Fama leva, por que diga 58
Do Lusitano o preço grande e raro,
Que o nome ilustre a um certo amor obriga
E faz, a quem o tem, amado e caro.
Desta arte vai fazendo a gente amiga
Co'o rumor famosíssimo e perclaro.
Já Melinde em desejos arde todo
De ver da gente forte o gesto e modo.

Dali pera Mombaça logo parte, 59
Aonde as naus estavam temerosas,
Pera que à gente mande que se aparte
Da barra imiga e terras suspeitosas,
Porque mui pouco vale esforço e arte
Contra infernais vontades enganosas;
Pouco val' coração, astúcia e siso,
Se lá dos Céus não vem celeste aviso.

Mercury upon his head his helmet wore,
And thus descended on Melindè's shore.

And Rumor he took with him to proclaim
How worthy was the Portuguese and rare.
For favor hung on his illustrious name,
That made him loved and courted everywhere.
And thus was spread the legend of his fame
Among the friendly people here and there.
Already in Melindè will grows warm
To know us and our pressure and our form.

Then straightway to Mombassa did he go,
Where all the fearful ships at anchor lay,
And bade them from the harbor of the foe
And lands suspect at once to take their way;
For skill and valor make but a poor show
Against their hellish urge, who would betray.
Naught avail courage, subtlety, and sense,
Not guided by celestial Providence.

Meio caminho a noite tinha andado, 60
E as estrelas no céu co'a luz alheia
Tinham o largo mundo alumiado,
E só co'o sono a gente se recreia.
O capitão ilustre, já cansado
De vigiar a noite que arreceia,
Breve repouso então aos olhos dava,
A outra gente a quartos vigiava,

Quando Mercúrio em sonhos lhe aparece, 61
Dizendo: "Fuge, fuge, Lusitano,
Da cilada que o rei malvado tece,
Por te frazer ao fim e extremo dano!
Fuge, que o vento e o céu te favorece;
Sereno o tempo tens e o Oceano,
E outro rei mais amigo noutra parte,
Onde podes seguro agasalhar-te!

"Não tens aqui senão aparelhado 62
O hospício que o cru Diomedes dava,
Fazendo ser manjar acostumado

Half way along her road had gone the night,
While with strange fire the stars in Heaven keep
This world in its immensity alight,
And the one pleasure of mankind was sleep.
The famous Captain, overwearied quite
From night watch in anxiety so deep,
To give his eyes some little rest is fain,
While others at their posts their guard maintain.

In dream to him did Mercury appear,
Uttering these words: "Fly, Lusitanian, fly
From treachery the false King is weaving here
To work destruction and your death thereby.
Calm are the waters and the weather clear.
Fly now, for the wind favors and the Sky.
And elsewhere is a king of friendlier mind,
With whom in safety shelter you shall find.

"Here you are nothing but the feast arrayed
For his stallions by Diomedes the fell,
Who trained his beasts so that their meal they made

Da cavalos a gente que hospedava;
As aras de Busíris infamado,
Onde os hóspedes tristes imolava,
Terás certas aqui, se muito esperas.
Fuge das gentes pérfidas e feras.

"Vai-te ao longo da costa discorrendo, 63
E outra terra acharás de mais verdade,
Lá quase junto donde o Sol ardendo
Iguala o dia e noite em quantidade;
Ali, tua frota alegre recebendo,
Um rei, com muitas obras de amizade,
Gasalhado seguro te daria
E pera a India certa e sábia guia."

Isto Mercúrio disse, e o sono leva 64
Ao capitão, que com mui grande espanto
Acorda e vê ferida a escura treva
De ũa súbita luz e raio santo;
E, vendo claro quanto lhe releva
Não se deter na terra iníqua tanto,

On flesh of folk he entertained so well.
The altars where sad captives with the blade
Were slaughtered by Busiris horrible,
You will attain, if you delay too long.
Fly from these brutes and their perfidious wrong!

"Forthwith the length of all the coastline run
Till on a greener country you shall light,
Hard by the region where the flaming sun
Has equal made the length of day and night.
The King there, with kind acts in friendship done,
Will cheerly give the fleet a welcome right.
Safe shelter he will grant you, and beside,
To India, a wise and trusty guide.'

This Mercury said, from slumber rousing swift
The Admiral, who started up awake
And saw in cloudy darkness, through a rift,
A sudden ray of sacred sunshine break.
He thought how in that land of evil shift
Clearly it skilled not more delay to make,

Com novo esprito ao mestre seu mandava
Que as velas desse ao vento que assoprava.

"Dai velas (disse), dai ao largo vento, 65
Que o Céu nos favorece e Deus o manda . . ."
[2.56–65]

The "Deus" of the last line quoted is of course not Jupiter but the Christian God whom Da Gama repeatedly acknowledges. There is also a faint implication in the phrase "raio santo" (#64.4) that Mercury is an angel. The poem's cosmic confusion, the result of introducing pagan gods into a professedly Christian work, is the most naïve of its faults and has attracted a great deal of critical attack, particularly in view of the important roles played by Venus and Bacchus. The author's blunder is not really helped by the predictable identification of Jupiter with Christian Providence in the final canto, nor by a Euhemeristic explanation of the lesser gods. It remains a blunder, perhaps the most regrettable of all the attempts to risk pagan feigning without Christian scandal. The only wonder is that the poem does not collapse at once beneath it. If the poem does not, its resistance may be owing to the firmness of its focus upon this world, a focus which tends to render all the conventional interventions by the gods a little irrelevant to the poem's main business. In the descent of Mercury, the poet wastes no words on the god's passage through space; he is truly interested only in human action on earth, and the reader quickly learns that Camoens' firm but evocative sense of space in this world fades, once he leaves the earth behind, into insubstantial fancies that carry little conviction or weight.

Camoens is foremost among those Renaissance poets who were determined to introduce pagan machinery at whatever cost in coherence. He was so determined because he felt himself in competition with the poets of antiquity and his heroes in competition with the figures of antique history and legend. This feeling, which seems to have been more acute in Camoens than in any other

---

And bade the master, with a courage new,
Shake out the canvas to the gale that blew.

"Make sail," he said, "for the wind blowing wide,
Since the Skies favor and 'tis God's intent."

poet one can think of, finds expression in the conclusion of Jupiter's speech and in countless other more specific comparisons scattered through the poem. Thus Mercury, in his speech to Da Gama, compares the inhospitable natives of Mombasa to the despotic king of Thrace, Diomedes, and to Busiris, the Egyptian tyrant who sacrificed all foreigners to Jupiter. It is more surprising to discover the Moslem king of Malindi comparing the Portuguese audacity to that of Pirithous, Theseus, and Erostratus! The cumulative allusions to ancient legend, poetry, and especially history throughout *Os Lusíadas* bear witness to the poet's considerable learning, but they also come to constitute, as Portuguese history is made to surpass antiquity on page after page, a major theme of the poem. Like Milton after him, Camoens insists that his is a higher argument, the argument of truth which surpasses the marvelous fables of Homer and Virgil:

> Que por muito e por muito que se afinem
> Nestas fábulas vãs, tão bem sonhadas,
> A verdade, que eu conto, nua e pura,
> Vence toda grandíloca escritura! [5.89] [41]

The poet and his subjects are forever running a race and forever winning it. This acute sense of emulation explains, even if it does not justify, the use of pagan gods just as it renders more acceptable such classical imitations as the familiar lines on the caduceus.

If Mercury and the heavenly "Olympus" are a little hazy, it must be confessed that Da Gama too, the nominal hero, emerges as rather faceless. But this facelessness does not represent quite the artistic disaster it would in another poem, since Da Gama is relatively unimportant. The real hero is Portugal itself, and in particular the collective leaders who made it great. The first line lays deliberate stress on the difference from Virgil:

> As armas e os barões assinalados . . . [1.1] [42]

41. Though greatly they refine their fables vain,
And though theirs be imagined ne'er so well,
Mere truth I speak in naked purity
Triumphs over all high-flying poetry.

42. Arms, and those matchless chiefs who . . .

The traditional heroic awe for individual capacity is replaced by the impression of historical sweep, the living personality of a nation reincarnated in leader after leader, reaffirmed in crisis after crisis, and ultimately stamped upon the vast oriental world. Da Gama is weak dramatically because his human limitations are never felt, and the dialectic inherent in true heroism in him remains faint. But the dialectic in Portuguese history as a whole is made very powerful, and is sustained past the time of Da Gama's voyage to the poet's own age, in his appeals to the reigning king not to betray the nation's past.

As Camoens writes about his country, he leads one to feel repeatedly how difficult it is for a nation to be great in the face of the incertitude and imponderables of human life. One does not feel the difficulty of achievement quite so vividly in regard to Da Gama's voyage, in spite of the poet's reiterated reflections on the uncertainty of life and action. Even Mercury's descent gives him occasion to reflect on this (#59), and his concern for incessant vigilance appears just below in the detail of the sailors on watch (#60.8). Camoens' Christian sense of frailty does not actually conflict with his epic celebration of human achievement, but the two create a kind of tension by their very coexistence in the work, a tension that brings to it, under the surface, an enriching dramatic vitality. I am not sure that the poet was in control of this tension, but it clearly had its life in his own spiritual development and so got transferred inevitably into his poem. Thus he opens his first canto with a spirited and eloquent review of the splendor of Portuguese achievement, only to close it with a somber meditation on the frailty of human existence:

> Ó grandes e gravíssimos perigos,
> Ó caminho de vida nunca certo,
> Que aonde a gente põe sua esperança!
> Tenha a vida tão pouca segurança!
>
> No mar tanta tormenta e tanto dano,
> Tantas vezes a morte apercebida!
> Na terra tanta guerra, tanto engano,

Tanta necessidade avorrecida!
Onde pode acolher-se um fraco humano,
Onde terá segura a curta vida,
Que não se arme e se indigne o Céu cereno
Contra um bicho da terra tão pequeno?
[1.105–06][43]

At this most somber moment, even the hope of divine succor is withdrawn—that hope which mitigates the pessimism darkening Mercury's descent—and heaven itself is seen as hostile. The poem never quite provides an answer to this last bleak question, but it provides various perspectives upon human dignity and divine grace, which seem to reveal a mind wavering and grasping for truth with exemplary fortitude.

It is significant that the allegorical figure of Fama accompanies Mercury in his descent, because a great many of the poet's meditations center upon the ideas for which she stands. Once again we have a Virgilian adaptation, but here the transformation is real and important. *Fama* in Virgil can be roughly equated with "rumor" or "scandal," and is quite a disagreeable figure, anticipating Spenser's Blatant Beast. But Fama in Camoens (the Latin and Portuguese nouns are identical) is generally beneficent, as we have seen, and serves the gods. Her role at this point is relatively restricted; she is required simply to make known the valor of the Portuguese mariners at Malindi in order to ensure their friendly reception by these people. Elsewhere in the poem, however, the idea of fame or glory plays a far greater role; it comes to consti-

43. Oh, great and heavy perils without end!
Oh, road of life where nothing sure we meet!
For where we think our hope is most secure,
Life holds but little that can long endure.

At sea by such rough storms and griefs forespent!
So many a moment when Death stands alert!
Ashore such strife and treacherous intent,
Where horrible necessity can hurt!
How can weak man escape the harsh event,
And how misfortune from brief life avert,
Where calm Skies rage not nor take arms alway
Against so mean a creature of the clay?

tute the real justification for heroism, and in particular for Da Gama's voyage. Through glory, the poet writes, man transcends his frail condition and makes himself immortal and godlike, just as the pagan gods, according to the Euhemeristic doctrine, once did in the remote past. Camoens allegorizes the delightful recompense of glory through an enticing if somewhat inappropriate Island of Cupid, where Da Gama's weary followers can gratify all the pleasures of their senses. This climactic episode must have been intended to resolve whatever dialectical ambivalences had earlier emerged.

In actuality, however, the ambivalences remain, and the poem is the stronger for them. For this fabricated island of delights, with its ripe and affectionate nymphs, is not so heady that the reader altogether forgets those soberer passages in which the value of glory is questioned. The most explicit and the finest of these appears in the famous speech of an old man at the harbor as Da Gama's fleet sets sail. At this dramatic crux, the old man's voice is raised in protest against the senselessness of the pursuit of glory, against the risk of life for quixotic ends, against all the hubristic endeavor of mankind:

> Ó glória de mandar! ó vã cubiça
> Desta vaidade a quem chamamos fama!
> Ó fraudulento gosto que se atiça
> Co'ũa aura popular que honra se chama!
> Que castigo tamanho e que justiça
> Fazes no peito vão que muito te ama!
> Que mortes, que perigos, que tormentas,
> Que crueldades neles exprimentas!
>
> Dura inquietação de alma e da vida,
> Fonte de desemparos e adultérios,
> Sagaz consumidora conhecida
> De fazendas, de reinos e de impérios!
> Chamam-te ilustre, chamam-te subida,
> Sendo dina de infames viturpérios;
> Chamam-te Fama e Glória sobreana,
> Nomes con quem se o povo néscio engana! . . .

Oh! maldito o primeiro que no mundo
Nas ondas vela pôs em seco lenho!
Dino da eterna pena do Profundo,
Se é justa a justa lei que sigo e tenho!
Nunca juízo algum, alto e profundo,
Nem cítara sonora ou vivo engenho
Te dê por isso fama nem memória,
Mas contigo se acabe o nome e glória! . . .
[4.95, 96, 102][44]

In its general tenor and in specific phrases the speech sounds not so much the note of Christian humility as the skepticism of that least epic of ancient poets—Horace. In certain lines Camoens appears to have divined that imperialistic exploration had not only enriched his country but was on the point of exhausting it. It is immensely to his credit that he found room in his poem for this denial of Promethean heroism which is virtually a denial of

44. Glory of empire! Most unfruitful lust
After the vanity that men call fame!
It kindles still, the hypocritic gust,
By rumor, which as honor men acclaim.
What thy vast vengeance and thy sentence just
On the vain heart that greatly loves thy name!
What death, what peril, tempest, cruel woe,
Dost thou decree that he must undergo!

Dreadful disquiet of his life and soul!
Spring of adultery and abandonment,
Empires and realms and wealth consuming whole,
And, as we know, only too provident!
Thy powers for high and noble men extol,
More worthy of their curse malevolent,
And call thee fame and glory's plenitude,
Names whereby witless men their souls delude.

My curse on him who first on the dry tree,
In the waters of this world, set up the sail!
Worthy of the Deep's eternal pain was he,
If the just creed I trust in does not fail!
May no high judgment's wise authority,
Nor singing lyre, nor genius bright, prevail
To grant thee either memory or fame,
But with thee die the glory and the name!

epic poetry. For the very denial enlarges the heroism and the shadows it casts endow the action with a plastic relief.

Thus *Os Lusíadas* is a poem which turns back upon itself. The ideal of glory was bound up in the poet's mind with his own poetic act of praise, and when he writes that no poet should celebrate the first man who set sail, he is thinking of his own Promethean epic, which honors and shares a comparable audacity. In later cantos, his hopes for his poem's success are tempered by his despair at poetry's low estate in Portugal, and once again he has to qualify his ideal. Does the grandiose enterprise in any sphere truly attract that divine favor symbolized by Mercury's descent? The answer, it seems, is up to history, whose answers are never final.

vii.

Were one to read only Italian poetry of the Baroque era, one might suppose there to be some necessary link between the "artificial," convoluted, hyperbolic style of Marinism and the spiritual aridity it betrays. But of course there is no such link, as the contemporaneous poetry of other countries demonstrates. Both the metaphysical style in England and Gongorism in Spain—to choose only two examples—represent national variations of the same kind of poetry, but the finest examples of these styles utilize their rhetorical distortions to authenticate deep feeling. The English metaphysicals produced no important epic poetry, but an example of Gongorist or pre-Gongorist epic is found in *La Christiada* of Fray Diego de Hojeda, a Spanish-born Dominican father writing in Peru. Published at Seville in 1611, it has never attracted very much attention.[45] Readers may well have been discouraged by the kind of diffuseness, extravagance, bathos, and naïveté that are likely to vitiate poetry written with great fervor in cultural semi-isolation. Yet despite its vices *La Christiada* is the work of a splendidly inspired and visionary imagination, informing the conven-

45. But see Fray Justo Cuervo, *El Maestro Fr. Diego de Ojeda y "La Cristiada"* (Madrid, 1898); Sister Mary Edgar Meyer, *The Sources of Hojeda's "La Cristiada"* (Ann Arbor, 1953); Frank Pierce, "Hojeda's *La Christiada:* a Poem of the Literary Baroque," *Bulletin of Spanish Studies, 17* (1940), 203–18; also the anthology of the same scholar, *The Heroic Poem of the Spanish Golden Age* (New York and Toronto, 1947).

tions of the now stereotyped Christian epic[46] with a fresh and personal ardor.

Hojeda relates in twelve books the passion of Christ from the holy supper through the Crucifixion, composing reverently the scene of each successive, terrible event—the supper, Gethsemane, the judgment, the confrontation with Pilate, the flagellation, the procession to Calvary, the seven last words, the entombment. But interspersed with these familiar scenes Hojeda introduces others unauthorized by the Gospel—councils in heaven and hell, perspectives into the past and future, visions of allegorical personifications like Life and Death, Impiety and Fear—all of these punctuated by polemics, moral exhortation, didactic digressions. The structure is disconcertingly centrifugal; the tone is charged, intense, sometimes violent; the style is dense, highly wrought, hermetic, sprinkled with elegant *cultismos* which render its access thorny. But Hojeda is fortunate in possessing a theme which binds all his scattered leaves into one volume, a theme whose mystery and terror he finds inexhaustible. This theme is the enigma of Incarnation. It is of particular relevance in the first (and for our purposes the richest) of Hojeda's angelic descents.

This episode concludes the second book, but fully to understand it we must return to the first, which deals with the agony at Gethsemane. It is typical of Hojeda that he intensify rather than mitigate the anguish of this crisis. For if incarnation is to be apprehended at all, one cannot minimize its fearful paradoxicality; one must dwell both on God's ineffable grandeur and on the lowliness of His indignities. The poet is tireless, even pitiless, in describing realistically Christ's physical suffering. Alone in the garden of Gethsemane, Christ finds the weight of sin too great for him and is driven to pray his Father for mercy. There is no immediate answer, save the gigantic and repellent apparition of Death. This passes in turn, but after a long and bitter debate with himself, Christ renews his prayer. This Prayer (*Oracion*), metamorphosed into an allegorical figure, rises to the dazzling radiance

46. In an appendix to her edition of *La Christiada* (Washington, 1935), Sister Mary Corcoran lists Spanish religious narrative poems published between 1500 and 1700. Twenty-six of these antedate the publication of *La Christiada*. The editor regards her list as incomplete.

of heaven, there to plead for divine mercy, recalling the merits of the Son and picturing his present distress. But the Father's will is firm; Christ must die, and the only concession to mercy is the dispatching of Gabriel to comfort him:

"Ve, Gabriel, a mi Hijo, y con razones
Vivas a la batalla le conforta:
Declárale mis graves intenciones,
Y a seguillas con ánimo le exorta.
Y tú, espejo de santas oraciones,
Vete; que to despacho al mundo importa."
Dixo; y de sus concetos un abismo
Y un mar de gloria les mostró en sí mismo.
[p. 81, 11.1–8] [47]

The last two lines epitomize the poet's double response to the redemption. His sense of divine glory informs the entire poem but the story still remains for him lost in the abyss of God's wisdom. Gabriel will descend to encounter a mystery. For the moment, however, the poet is in no haste to reach that goal. He devotes four stanzas to the appearance Gabriel assumes as he prepares for flight, thus anticipating that shift of emphasis from narrative to description, verb to adjective, which strikes one increasingly in the descents of minor seventeenth century epics. I think these four stanzas need to be quoted in full:

Mas Gabriel del aire refulgente
Da la región más pura un cuerpo haze,
Y cércalo de luz resplandeciente,
Que las tinieblas y el orror deshaze:
Cuerpo umano de un joben excelente,
Gallardo y lindo que a la vista aplaze;

47. All Spanish quotations are from the M.H.P. Corcoran edition (Washington, 1935). All further references will be to this edition. The episode is based on Luke 22:43—"And there appeared an angel unto him from heaven, strengthening him."

'Go, Gabriel, to my Son, and comfort Him with forceful terms to ready Him for His battle. State my solemn intentions to Him and exhort Him to follow them with courage. And thou, mirror of sacred prayers, go; for thy departure is of concern to the world.' Thus He spoke, and showed them an abyss of thoughts and a sea of glory in Himself."

Mas bañada su angélica belleza
En una grave y señoril tristeza.

Lleva el roxo cabello ensortijado
Del oro fino qu'el Oriente cría,
Y en mil hermosas bueltas encrespado,
Que cada qual relámpagos embía:
De un pedaço del iris coronado,
Del iris, que con fresco umor rocía
El verde valle y la florida cumbre,
Quando entre nieblas da templada lumbre.

La vergonçosa grana resplandece
En las mexillas de su rostro amable;
Y aljófar de turbada luz parece
El sudor de su frente venerable:
Aspecto de un legado triste ofrece,
Que haze su ermosura más notable,
Qual invernizo sol en parda nube
Opuesta al tiempo, que al Oriente sube.

Prestas alas de plumas aparentes,
De color vario y elegante forma,
Y de vistosas piedras reluzientes
Puestas a trechos, en sus ombros forma.
Con la grave embaxada convenientes
Ojos, y trage y parecer conforma:
Es morado el vestido roçagante,
Y lagrimoso el jubenil semblante.

[p. 82, 1–32] [48]

48. "But Gabriel makes a body out of the shining air from the purest region and surrounds it with sparkling light which dispels darkness and horror: the human body of an excellent youth, graceful and attractive, inviting the gaze, but his angelic beauty bathed in a grave and lordly sadness.

He wears his red hair in ringlets of the delicate gold nurtured by the orient, twisted into a thousand curls that flash lightning as they fall; crowned with a part of the rainbow, the rainbow which bedews the green valley and the flowery mountain peak with moisture, emitting a tempered radiance among the mists.

The abashed scarlet shines in the cheeks of his kind visage and the sweat of his venerable brow appears to be pearls of troubled light. He makes the

Inasmuch as the angel puts on a form visible to human eyes, and the form is of a blond young man, the seed of this passage can be found in Tasso. But the respective effects of light make an important contrast. Tasso's Gabriel is compared to the sun half-risen from the sea at dawn; he is quick, fresh, radiant, and his gleaming white wings are tipped with gold. Hojeda qualifies his angel's youth with a "grave y señoril tristeza" which is reflected in the tempering of his physical brightness. There is nothing here of the melodramatic blacks and whites in Tasso's second descent and in several of Marino. The brightness is filtered through a haze of melancholy which, by a kind of celestial decorum, befits the purpose of the flight. The key phrase is *turbada luz*—"troubled light"—light which in its context refers with Baroque particularity to the beads of angelic sweat gleaming like misshapen pearls. Hojeda loses his modern readers at this point, but the rest of his description is unexceptionably harmonious. The image of filtered light appears first in the rainbow passage (lines 13–16), an image which qualifies and softens the lightning image it immediately follows.[49] The rainbow gives way to the pearl, and the pearl in turn to the wintry setting sun, half hidden by a dark cloud. The whole passage is governed by a dramatic idea: the need to cloak celestial brightness when heaven must descend to earthly tragedy.

> Con la grave embaxada convenientes
> Oyos, y trage y parecer conforma.

We find then, adumbrated in these preparations, that theme of Incarnation I have already described as the binding theme of the poem.

Gabriel's flight to earth is less successfully managed by Hojeda; it is marred by three similes which would persuade us abstractly

---

appearance of a sad messenger, and this renders his beauty more marked, like the winter sun from the dark cloud set in that part of the sky opposite to its place of rising in the east.

He makes quick wings with visible feathers, of diverse colors and elegant form, and with handsome gleaming gems placed at intervals upon his shoulders. He suits his eyes and gown and aspect to his grave embassy. The billowing dress is purple and the youthful countenance is tearful."

49. Compare Revelation 10:1: "And I saw another mighty angel come down from heaven, clothed with a cloud: and a rainbow was upon his head, and his face was as it were the sun."

of the angel's speed but do not permit us to see or feel it. These are followed in turn by a characteristic Gongoristic conceit whose hyperbole seems today more forced than clever:

> Ala no mueve, pluma no menea,
> Y las espaldas de las nubes hiende;
> Seguille el viento bolador dessea,
> Y en vano el impossible curso emprende:
> Déxale de seguir, la vista emplea,
> Y a celebrar su ligereza atiende;
> Y acierta en conceder justa alabança
> A quien con fuerças y valor no alcança.
>
> [p. 83, 9–16] [50]

The verb *hiende,* which means "to fissure" or "to cleave," gives force to the first two lines, and the clouds whose backs are cleft by the angel's flight are of interest because they provide a kind of continuity between the "parda nube" above and the terrifying mist—"pavorosa niebla"—enveloping Gethsemane. This shadowy mist and the murmur of muted sounds are the first impressions, synaesthetically equivalent, the angel receives as he reaches the garden.

> El aire ve de pavorosa niebla
> Y de sombra confusa rodeado;
> Opaca, triste y órrida tiniebla
> Lo tiene de ancha oscuridad cercado:
> De assombro y miedo, y de terror se puebla
> El huerto, ya de espinas coronado:
> Detiénese Gabriel, y atento escucha
> Y mira a Dios, que con la muerte lucha.
>
> Del cielo puro el cristalino aspecto,
> Del espantado arroyo el lento passo,
> Del aire mudo el proceder secreto,

50. "He neither moves a wing nor flutters a feather, and cleaves the backs of the clouds; the flying wind wishes to follow him, and attempts the impossible race in vain: it ceases to follow and relies on its sight, and waits to celebrate his swiftness; and it does well in conceding just praise to one whom it cannot equal in might and valor."

Y del manso favonio el sopio escasso,
D'aves y fieras el callar discreto,
Y de ver triste a Dios el grave caso,
Como caso tan grave comprehende,
Las plumas y la lengua e suspende.
[p. 83, 25–32; p. 84,1–8] [51]

The agony of the Son is all the more poignant as the reader returns to it from the gleaming gates of heaven, apprehending that central quiescent drama only gradually as he pierces through its solemn setting. A kind of horror tempered with awe filters through the dusky air, portentously empty of speech. The *turbada luz* of the preceding passage is intensified and as it were interpreted. The angel is dumb and can only meditate with wonder at his God

por el ombre inobediente
Sobre la tierra con dolor postrado . . .
[p. 84, 21–22] [52]

Hojeda has the discretion to leave this scene without breaking its silence, and only much later in the third book does he return to Gabriel's long speech of comfort. Here he concludes the descent with the paradox of the incarnation unplumbed. Only the angel, who fully knows heaven and earth alike, can measure the breadth of the paradox and simultaneously understand it.

The speech by which Gabriel restores the courage of Christ dwells upon the immensity of good accruing to mankind from the redemption. This speech is necessary because it reminds the reader of the justification for Christ's terrible suffering. But although this justification is attempted in three or four passages, the weight of

51. "He sees the air filled with a terrifying mist and surrounded by a confused shadow; the opaque, sorrowful, and fearsome gloom encloses him in the widespread darkness; the garden, already crowned with thorns, is peopled with astonishment, fear, and terror. Gabriel pauses and listens attentively, and contemplates God struggling with death.

The crystalline aspect of the pure heaven, the slow flow of the fearful brook, the secret movement of the silent air, the faint breath of the gentle breeze, the discreet silence of birds and beasts, and the solemn situation of sorrowfully beholding his God,—he understands all these to be so solemn that his feathers and tongue are suspended."

52. "Prostrated with sorrow over the earth for disobedient man."

the poem falls not upon the achievement but the agony. This is important because it shows Hojeda resisting the suppositious epic tradition of a triumphal ending.[53] In spite of Gabriel's consolation, the dramas of incarnation and redemption remain inexhaustibly mysterious and Hojeda does not really pretend to pierce them with logic. His poem is not a theodicy; it does not explain suffering away, and for this it is a better poem. Most of the poems considered in this chapter are concerned in various ways with the degree of solicitude mankind merits from heaven. Hojeda's Deity is more severe than any of the Italian poets', but He is perhaps easier to accept because His severity is contemplated meditatively rather than defended sophistically or assumed unconvincingly.

With Hojeda we first encounter a kind of heroism which becomes increasingly common in the Baroque era: the lonely and passive heroism of the afflicted saint, Milton's "better fortitude of patience and heroic martyrdom unsung." The Baroque epic tended in general to place progressively heavier demands upon the human will. The nostalgia and weariness of Tasso's Goffredo give way to the trepidation of Hojeda's Christ and the tortured desperation of d'Aubigné's Huguenots. The concluding books of *Paradise Lost* fit easily into this pattern, and if Marino's *Adone*

53. In fact there is little of the classical spirit in Hojeda, despite some Homeric similes and other derivative elements. The quality of his Humanism can be gauged by the following curious allusion in the description of Gabriel's descent:

> Paró su luz con improviso espanto
> Más tarde el rubio padre de Faetonte
> A la oración del capitán hebreo,
> Que a la de Christo el celestial correo.
> (p. 83, 21–24)

("The blond father of Phaeton, with sudden fright, stopped his light more slowly at the prayer of the Hebrew captain [Sisera] than the celestial messenger to that of Christ.") The clumsiness of this juxtaposition of Apollo and Sisera may constitute evidence of the poet's thin classical training, although such evidence is far from compelling. Little is known of his schooling, but we do know that he began his novitiate in Peru before he was 20. Had Hojeda felt the classical spirit more intimately, his poem might have been more "regular," more decorous and symmetrical, less violent and diffuse, but it might well have lost the originality and power it contains. Both *La Christiada* and d'Aubigné's *Les Tragiques* are examples of epics relatively free from classical influence, and both display the advantages as well as the liabilities of this freedom.

does not, the collapse of the will it represents is explicable in these terms. In *La Christiada* the angelic messenger sustains a will which feels itself too weak for its destiny. Not only are the demands great but man is frail and the world is contemptibly pitiful—

la tierra y el polvo y la baxeza . . .

The will is weak but there is hope for grace.[54] D'Aubigné and Milton are less concerned with the pathos of that weakness. But the tone of all these poems is intensified by the effort of the will caught up in a universal war almost too vast and fierce for it to bear.

viii.

The work of Giambattista Marino contains three extended celestial descents, all of which are demonstrably indebted to Tasso's ninth canto. They appear in his most ambitious poem, *Adone,* in the briefer Biblical epic, *La Strage degl' Innocenti,* and in the fragment of an incomplete *Gerusalemme Distrutta.* Of these descents, the second is perhaps the most interesting, but I want first to speak of the others.

Adone (1623) must be one of the longest poems modern Europe has produced; it is substantially longer than *Orlando Furioso* or *The Faerie Queene,* and is spun out with considerably less action than either. It does not pretend to be an epic. Like Paris, whose choice is described in one of his innumerable digressions, Marino prefers "la vita voluttaria" (Venus) to "l'attiva" (Juno), to say nothing of "la contemplativa" (Minerva). This preference is in itself of historical importance. Few poems were written in the high style during the sixteenth century without greater or lesser epic pretensions. Those romances without pretensions did not sustain a high style. But *Adone,* written for the most part in an unmistakably inflated style and containing any number of epic conventions, remains well outside the mainstream of the Virgilian tradition. It is rather a mythological, descriptive, didactic, erotic fable, in the Ovidian vein, even if burdened with an alle-

54. The descent of Gabriel in Book Two is not the only instance of divine intercession to console and encourage. Christ and Mary are visited at least four times in the poem by angelic comforters.

gorical-ethical level so palpably irrelevant, so transparently hypocritical, that it is confined to prose summaries at the opening of each canto where it can be conveniently ignored. Stripped of this pseudo-meaning, *Adone* has very little to do with human life at all; its chief characters are gods, witches, nymphs, personified abstractions, with a bare sprinkling of apotheosized humans like the hero Adonis. The only historical people who figure in the poem—the royalty and nobility Marino chose to flatter—are so elevated by extended panegyric as to be unrecognizable and unrecognizably human. If epic descends from mythical narrative on a suprahuman plane,[55] it here returns to that plane, or to a vulgarization of it.

Marino's first version of a celestial descent appears in the opening canto. Amore, smarting from a whipping administered by his mother, Venus, is counselled by Apollo to take revenge by enamoring her with Adonis. Amore's descent to Adonis is described in this way:

> Come prodigiosa acuta stella,
> Armata il volto di scintille e lampi,
> Fende dell' aria, orribil sì, ma bella
> Passeggiera lucente, i larghi campi.
> Mira il nocchier da questa riva e quella,
> Con qual purpureo piè la nebbia stampi,
> E con qual penna d'or scrive e disegni
> Le morti ai regi e le cadute ai regni.
>
> Così mentre ch'Amor dal ciel disceso
> Scorrendo va la region più bassa,
> Con la face impugnata e l'arco teso
> Gran traccia de splendor dietro si lassa.
> D'un solco ardente e d'auree fiamme acceso,
> Riga intorno le nubi ovunque passa,
> E trae per lunga linea in ogni loco
> Striscia di luce, impression di foco.
>
> [1.38–39] [56]

55. See Chapter 2, pp. 12–14.

56. All quotations are drawn from *Adone,* ed. Balsamo-Crivelli (Turin, 1922).

The first of these stanzas typifies Marino in several ways. First of all, it expands an image he might have found in the *Liberata* (although as we have seen it has a longer history). This kind of expansion is the first principle of Marino's art. He seems to have produced very few original images, although in this he was scarcely unique. His special gift was in dilating the images he found to hand and in coloring them with his own characteristic tonality. He was a virtuoso at blowing up a given motif; once he began to work upon a fertile subject, his inventiveness seems to have been inexhaustible. *Adone* was first projected as a much shorter poem, in three cantos instead of twenty. It grew by excrescences and by the spinning out of each episode in its slender plot. Thus the simile of the falling star, to which Tasso had given two lines, receives eight from Marino.

This dilation allows one to study more closely the contrast of sensibility between the two. That there is a contrast nobody will dispute, although it is equally true that the germ of *Marinismo* can be found in Tasso. If you reread him after reading his successors, you are surprised to see how much of the Marinistic has already taken root in his work. But this quality is still embryonic in him and intermixed with older elements. Marino was clever enough to take from Tasso just those things his contemporaries admired. So it is in this image of the falling star. In the *Liberata* it had struck a brief flash of limpid, untroubled brilliance:

> Tal suol, fendendo il liquido sereno,
> stella cader de la gran madre in seno.

although in its context, the descent of Michele, one does sense faintly the hectic, melodramatic, portentous quality which Marino heightens. In the *Liberata* this quality is not unnatural, since the

---

"As a prodigious, pointed star, its visage armed with sparks and flashes, cuts through the broad fields of the air, truly a fearful but beautifully radiant traveler; the pilot wonders from this shore and that with what scarlet foot it prints the cloud, and with what golden pen it writes and depicts death to kings and falls to kingdoms:

So while Love, having descended from heaven, goes scouring the lowest region, with brandished torch and drawn bow, he leaves behind him a great trail of brilliance. Lit with a burning furrow and golden flames, he streaks the clouds about him wherever he flies, and draws in a long line everywhere a stripe of light, an impression of fire."

figure of the angel is awesome, the situation critical, the hour nocturnal. In *Adone* the hour is dawn and the figure is Cupid. No matter; Marino knows the effect he wants. The key word in his passage is *prodigiosa*—"ominous," and even more striking—*orribil*—"terrible." *Orribil sì, ma bella*—"terrible yes, but beautiful" (beautiful, we understand, because terrible)—this fusion of disparate impressions is the secret of Marino's *frisson nouveau*. The beauty which seems his sole concern, toward which he bends all the resources of his formidable craft, is a beauty fascinating for its canker, disturbing because it is sinister. Not only does his art admit the disagreeable and the diseased; it feeds upon them.

The preciosity of Marino's own language corresponds to this disturbing presence with an analogously uncomfortable ingenuity. By one of his characteristic "turns," Amore is made to follow

> Più che vento leggier le vie de' venti. [1.37] [57]

The star is made far larger than it appears in Tasso by the subimages which find their way into the longer simile. If Amore is a star, the star is possessed of a face (*volto*); it is a traveler (*passeggiera*); its scarlet foot imprints the cloud; it is a feather pen (recalling perhaps the wings of Amore) inscribing ominously the fall of empires. In English poetry, we are accustomed to mixed metaphors and jumbled images, but these are far less common in the Romance languages, and their effect upon the native reader is proportionally more unsettling. Marino's poetic power seems to lie partly in the wedding of the beautiful and the exotic with the disturbing. It is a method which diverts the attention from such flaws as the unnecessary repetition "scriva e disegni."

The preciosity, the melodramatic *chiaroscuro,* the agreeably sinister elements in Marino's verse are complemented by his genuine descriptive mastery. His fondness for painting, his celebrations and imitations of specific painters, and his conception of poetry as "pittura parlante" are clichés of criticism. We are still lacking, however, an analysis of the precise way he has transmuted these sister arts. It is not so easy for painting to acquire speech. Such an analysis would need to pursue many problems, but the brief pas-

57. "Quicker than wind the paths of the winds."

sage before us leads to one incidental observation. It seems to me that Marino's scenes acquire the vividness and plasticity of good painting through his ability to describe a thing several times in expressions which reinforce each other. By this technique he leads us to dwell upon an image which then acquires increasingly sharp focus with successive reformulations. He is not content, for instance, to write:

> Gran traccia di splendor dietro si lassa.

He must then find a new expression:

> D'un solco ardente e d'auree fiamme acceso,
> Riga intorno le nubi ovunque passa . . .

and then still another:

> E trae per lunga linea in ogni loco
> Striscia di luce, impression di foco.

This last line is typical of the wit, or pseudo-wit, by which Marino tends to round off such a repeated description, striving for a paradoxical twist which in this case is not actually very paradoxical. But his finest effects are usually not those in which the language parades itself, but those where verbal resourcefulness serves pictorial ends.

This descriptive genius is less rewarding in the fulsome portrait of Adonis which follows Amore's descent and which I shall not quote. Here the vulgarity and incipient voyeurism of Marino's eroticism betray themselves. The descent in the *Argonautica* is the closest classical model for these qualities, and it is clear that Marino owes Apollonius a good deal. They share a common estheticism, an artificial style, a cult of prettiness, although Marino lacks the Alexandrian flair for pretty *little* things; all of his pretty things, as we have seen, are pitilessly expanded. Above all, both poets are interested in the breakdown of the will before passion, and to this end both send the god of passion to earth. In Marino, to be sure, there is very little will to be overcome. The strain of the Counter-Reformation will, typified by Tasso—the unsatisfied striving for sublimity, the nostalgia for rest—these find their sequel in Marino's open hedonism. *Adone* might have been written in the garden of Armida.

The most interesting question to be asked about this poem is "What is its subject?" One might be likely to put it down first as eroticism, but on reflection this turns out to be inadequate. In the last analysis Marino seems bored with sex as such, and his description of the lovers' consummation is rather perfunctory, centrifugal, and unexciting. I should say rather that the subject of the poem is its form—by which I mean all that it brings to bear on its meager plot, the elaborate artifice, the ostensible excrescences, the peculiarities of imagery and diction, the swirl of words and impressions that blur sexuality even as they heighten it, everything in short that stems from an individual and recognizable sensibility. The sensibility contemplates itself; the epistemological subject becomes object. Poetry has become a reflexive and narcissistic exercise.

It might have been expected that an age of rigidified piety would censure poetry so formalistic and so morally ambiguous. But in fact there were aspects of Marino and Marinism calculated to please the church as well as the laity. The great merit of such poetry lay precisely in its lack of any serious subject, a negative merit, doubtless, but weighty nonetheless during an era of intellectual constriction. Toffanin has explained the paradoxical entente between the Counter-Reform and the new estheticism in terms of the church's need for an antiseptic literature, "that which was most disinterested in the alarming inspirations of the mind and of nature, and showed itself disposed to be quarantined from their contagion."

> Little by little *secentismo* and *spagnolismo* . . . began to reveal . . . the benefit to be gotten from them with their intellectual fatuity, their indifference to the great problems of the spirit, their love of the fanciful considered as a toy. Then the Counter Reform, driven by its prejudices and its forms of fanaticism, came to an understanding with the *secentismo* and, in literature, merged with it and mastered it with its own Aristotelianism.[58]

58. Giuseppe Toffanin, *La Fine dell' Umanesimo* (Turin, 1920), pp. 227–28.

Bruno was a contemporary of Marino possessed of a far more profound religious temperament but lacking a certain intellectual decorum. Between two such men the choice was easy, not only for the institutions of the Counter-Reform but for the secular Italian nation beneath its shadow, a nation for the most part weary of dispute and cynical regarding truth.

The compatibility of Marinism with contemporaneous Catholicism is demonstrated by those late poems of Marino based upon religious subjects. I shall not quote much from the fragmentary *Gerusalemme Distrutta,* which was either unfinished or lost in its greater part. The descent of Michele in its only extant canto is remarkable chiefly for the magnificence of the preceding scene in heaven:

> Quasi teatro luminoso e grande
> Al trono intorno, ove il gran Re s'adora,
> Popolo innumerabile si spande
> Che di lui sol si pasce e s'innamora . . .
>
> Qui cento Orfei, cento Arioni e cento
> Ninfe e mille Sirene e Muse mille,
> Di dolce infaticabile concento
> S'odon l'aure ferir sempre tranquille . . .[59]

The scene in its entirety creates precisely the sort of luminous and grandiose arch-image best suited to Marino's talent, and doubtless to look for any religious feeling would be beside the point. It is typical of him to contrast as he goes on to do the gold, red, and white of the angels' garments with the scarlet, green, and purple of the saints'. It is also typical of him to bring together these Arions and sirens and Muses in the hundreds and thousands. Such epithets might remind one of Sannazaro, but the older poet would never have permitted himself such gross treatment of the myths

59. *Opere,* ed. G. Zirardini (Naples, 1861), p. 493, #66, 68. "As in a large and luminous theatre, an innumerable multitude is scattered about the throne where the great King is adored, feeding upon and enamored of Him alone. . . .

Here a hundred Orpheus and a hundred Arions and a hundred nymphs and a thousand Sirens and Muses are heard wounding the ever-tranquil breezes with sweet, indefatigable harmony."

he loved. The liberties Marino took throughout his work represent a real decline in the prestige of the classics, no longer quite the living presence they had been a century earlier. I think that Sannazaro would also have avoided such a verb as *si pasce,* at once more strenuous and more distasteful than anything in his vocabulary. The disparity in this scene between God and His heavenly creatures, the flushed and slightly hectic ardor which colors it, a certain flickering and unquiet intensity, are characteristically Baroque and very distant from the symmetrical coolness of Sannazaro's empyrean.

The descent of an unnamed angelic messenger in *La Strage degl' Innocenti* (published posthumously in 1632) tends to reproduce qualities of Marino's art we have already encountered, and yet I am tempted to quote from it because it is probably as a whole the finest of the three. If Marino appears to us as a charlatan, this passage is evidence of how very accomplished a charlatan he nonetheless was. The descent appears in the second book of the four which comprise the poem. When the massacre is imminent, the figure of Pity (Pietà) prostrates herself before God's throne and pleads for the lives of the innocent children. The answer she receives is ambiguous. On the one hand, the holy family will be warned and permitted to flee. But the remaining innocents must die, in a massacre whose barbarity the Deity does not succeed in mitigating. When He concludes, an unnamed angel—"una pennuta luce della beata famiglia" [60]—descends to warn Joseph of his family's danger.

> Leggiadra spoglia in breve spazio ammassa
> D'aure leggiere e di color diversi,
> Poi dal colmo del ciel volando lassa
> Precipitosamente in giú cadersi:
> Pria della sfera immobile trapassa
> I fuochi e i lampi fiammeggianti e tersi,
> Indi de' corpi lubrici e correnti
> Gli obbliqui calli e i lievi giri e lenti.
>
> Viensene là dove 'l piú basso cielo
> Di bianca luce i suoi cristalli adorna,

60. "A feathered light of the blessed family."

Né dell' umido cerchio il freddo gelo
Sente, e sen va fra l'argentate corna.
Giunge ove 'l foco il rugiadoso velo
Asciuga della Dea, che l'ombre aggiorna;
Né l'offendon però gli ardor vicini,
O le fulgide penne, o gli aurei crini.
[2.94–95][61]

The angel wears a light tunic of blue and gold and crimson which leaves his shoulders uncovered, a tunic which

Mentre vola ondeggiando e si dilata,
Morde con dente d'or fibbia gemmata.

Spunta del vago tergo in su i confini
Gemina piuma e colorata e grande;
Sazio d'amomo il crespo oro de' crini
Trecciatura leggiadra all' aura spande.
Di piropi immortali e di rubini
Fascian l'eburnea fronte ampie ghirlande;
Chiude il bel piè, che mena alte carole
Tra gemme, che son stelle, oro ch' è Sole.
[2.96–97][62]

Once again we must return to Tasso to measure the lesser poet's originality. It will be clear to the reader how sharply the influence

61. Giovanbattista Marino, *Dicerie Sacre e La Strage degl' Innocenti,* ed. G. Pozzi (Turin, 1960). "In a short time he forms a graceful garment of varied colors out of the light breezes, and then flying from the summit of the sky, lets himself fall precipitously downward; first he passes the bright, flaming fires and flashes of the immobile sphere, then the oblique paths and quick and slow courses of the fleeting, racing bodies.

He comes to the place where the lowest heaven adorns its crystals with white light, nor feels the cold frost of the moist sphere, and passes through the silvery horn. He arrives at the fire which dries the dewy veil of the goddess who brings day to the shadows. Nor does the nearby heat offend him, neither his refulgent wings, nor his golden locks."

62. ". . . a bejewelled buckle bites with a golden tooth while it ripples and billows.

Twin plumes, tinted and large, spring from the attractive back above the tunic's edge; wearied of a clasp, the curled gold of the locks spreads its graceful tress upon the breeze. Abundant garlands of immortal garnets and rubies bind the ivory forehead; the beautiful foot that leads celestial dances is tipped, among jewels that are stars, with gold that is the sun."

of Virgil, heretofore dominant, has declined. Among the ancient poets, Marino was drawn temperamentally far more to Ovid, whose style was partly responsible for the wit and artifice of his own. But the celestial descents in Marino all look back to the *Liberata.* One follows this dandyish angel, like Tasso's Michele, through the successive spheres of the created universe, and the flight of each involves a contrast of heavenly radiance with earthly darkness:

> . . . del mondo, ch'eterno arde e riluce
> verso il fosco e caduco il cammin piglia.

Like Gabriele in the *Liberata,* this angel composes a visible semblance "leggiadra spoglia"—out of the air. But whereas Tasso's concern with movement is reflected by the primacy of his verbs:

> *s'indorava* la notte al divin lume
> che *spargea scintillando* il volto fuori.

Marino's concern with description leads to a poetry of adjectives:

> Pria della sfera *immobile* trapassa
> I fuochi e i lampi *fiammeggianti* e *tersi,*
> Indi de' corpi *lubrici* e *correnti*
> Gli *obbliqui* calli e i *lievi* giri e *lenti.*

These last two lines adumbrate, moreover, a new conception of space, a space complicated by the intersecting obliquities of astral movements and by their unequal velocities. It is to this spiralling Baroque cosmos that Milton likens the dance of his angels:

> . . . Mystical dance, which yonder starry Sphere
> Of Planets and of fixt in all her Wheels
> Resembles nearest, mazes intricate,
> Eccentric, intervolv'd, yet regular
> Then most, when most irregular they seem.
>
> [*Paradise Lost,* V.620–24]

Tasso's cosmos by comparison is a model of a more obvious, Renaissance symmetry:

> . . . da sinistra rotar Saturno e Giove
> e gli altri, i quali esser non ponno erranti
> se angelica virtù gli informa e move . . .

The convolution of Marino's space complements the convolution of his language and underlies his daring shifts of visual perspective. He has a tendency to shift from broad description to minor detail, from a sweeping and theatrical whole to an intimate or miniscule part. So he shifts in the allusion to Dawn, which seems to me almost a touchstone of his art at its most arresting:

Giunge ove 'l foco il rugiadoso velo
Asciuga della Dea, che l'ombre aggiorna.

The reader's eye is led from the great sphere of fire to the dewy veil of Dawn dried by its warmth. So, analogously, Marino shifts from the general effect of the flight to the tunic and thence to the buckle which nibbles it with golden tooth, finally to the foot which is set against the sun and stars. These shifts of focus are sometimes coupled with something like the pathetic fallacy, the animation and personification of the inanimate; thus the nibbling of the golden tooth, the hair weary of its clasp, or in *Adone* the scarlet foot of the star leaving its print on the cloud.

Once he has touched upon these details, Marino returns to the general effect, suggesting in four lines the brilliance of the angelic passage seen from a distance.[63]

E, ventilando i vanni, in sé raccolta,
Lungo solco di luce in aria stampa.
Ingannato il pastor lascia le piume
Al tremolar del mattutino lume.

[2.98] [64]

This last touch of the shepherd's awakening is admirably expressive, and its felicity is enhanced by the delicate suggestions of *tremolar*. Taken as a whole, this descent represents a poetry which knows itself, its capacities and limitations, which aims at nothing more than it achieves, but which raises fancy, ingenuity, visual magnificence, almost to the level of the imagination. I say "almost" because even the best work of Marino lacks the vital center, the living warmth, which a genuine imagination engenders. He is after all best represented by such a method as we have here been

63. Compare the use of the *nocchier* in the passage quoted above, p. 240.

64. "And fanning his pinions, gathering himself in closely, he prints a long furrow of light upon the air. The shepherd leaves his bed deceived by the flicker of morning brightness."

following. Any one of his episodes studied in isolation is likely to seem more individual and more richly decorated than another poet's. But his longer poems are simply accretions of episodes. Marino described *Adone* as a "gonnella rappezzata," a skirt patched together. I have spoken of the *Gerusalemme Liberata* as patchwork too, but the stitching there is very different. Tasso's seams are invisible, but Marino's are grossly obvious. Thus the angel's descent in *La Strage degl' Innocenti* is patched together with another set piece, a visit to the realm of Sleep. It too is described with elegant virtuosity, but it is not harmonized artistically with what precedes or follows. Marino remains at his best a fabulous extemporizer. And because he aims simply at spectacle, because he never enters his world but remains merely its impresario, all his figures seem inhuman. His world is not a landscape but a museum.

Inhuman in several senses are the climactic scenes of *La Strage*. These are devoted to the massacre, which is described in detail and with relish. In scenes like these, the quasi-sadistic taste of the age fuses with another of its preoccupations—the dialectic of severity and mercy. The same fusion can be found in a common Baroque motif—the figure of the beseeching female suppliant—which is repeated in *La Christiada, La Strage degl' Innocenti,* and *Gerusalemme Distrutta.* How is this motif, frequent in Baroque painting, related to the dialectic I speak of? The Counter-Reformation involved on the one hand a stiffening of moral rigor, sometimes genuine, sometimes hypocritical, but in the face of heresy at least, pitiless. On the other hand, at certain social levels the rigor tended to be purely formal and concealed a generous tolerance of frailty. This ambivalence pierces to the heart of the age, and it was reflected in epic poetry. The figure of the suppliant generously beseeching the Deity for mercy toward others serves this ambivalence by heightening the appearance of severity but by winning Him nonetheless to leniency.[65] This is what happens

65. Marino's use of the suppliant may be contrasted with d'Aubigné's use in *Les Tragiques.* The descent in that poem is also preceded by a speech of Pieté (see below, p. 258). But pity for D'Aubigné means pity for God's martyred lambs, the Huguenots, and thus in effect greater severity toward most others. (There is no debate between his Pity and Justice, who rather plead for identical vengeance.) Pity serves to intensify moral rigor. D'Aubigné's

in *Gerusalemme Distrutta,* where God is persuaded by the Virgin to spare Jerusalem. The ambivalence in *La Strage degl' Innocenti* is cut a little finer. When Pietà appeals to God for mercy, the justification of the divine refusal is particularly sophistic. God replies first, that the massacre is not His own will but that of Justice (a figure conventionally complementary to Pity or Mercy in debates before God's throne), although He accepts her will without demur; secondly, that the Church soon to be founded requires the adornment of these lives; thirdly, that the outrage of the infants' deaths will turn against its Satanic source and change to immortal glory. In this speech the massacre is somehow made to appear as a victory for heaven, and so it is again at the close of the poem, where David sings a hymn of joyful welcome to the innocent souls entering Limbo. Their entrance is hailed as an omen of deliverance by Christ and so the poem ends on a note of ostensible triumph. But the sickening brutality of the preceding scenes must modify for most readers any real sentiment of triumph. Severity and mercy remain confused. The classical epic form, which was thought to require a triumph, fits clumsily with the unheroic Biblical incident. This ambivalence will recur in not so very different form at the close of a very different poem—*Paradise Lost.*

Deity would be incapable of the melting tenderness ascribed to Him more than once by Marino.

9. *D'AUBIGNÉ*

i.

The fashion of classical imitation reached France approximately at the midpoint of the sixteenth century, one of those deceptively convenient dates which beguile the literary historian. The break with the immediate past was not so sharp as we are inclined to think, or as the poets of the Pléiade thought, but it is true that imitation became increasingly common in the latter half of the century. The gifts of the Pléiade poets did not favor epic poetry, and with the exception of one experimental epyllion based on a Biblical story, by Du Bellay,[1] the first writing in anything like the epic mode by this group appeared only in 1572—the date of Ronsard's *Franciade* and of Belleau's epyllion, *Les Amours de David et de Bersabee*. The first of the *Franciade*'s four completed books contains a celestial descent which brings Mercury to Epirus as a spur to the departure of the hero Francus, destined founder of Gaul. I quote the description of his flight alone:

1. "La Monomachie de David et de Goliath," in *Oeuvres Poétiques,* ed. H. Chamard, *4* (Paris, 1931), 119 ff.

A peine eut dit que Mercure s'apreste:
Sa capeline affubla sur sa teste,
De talonniers ses talons asortit,
D'un mandillon son espaule vestit,
A frange d'or à mi-jambe escoulée,
Prist sa houssine à deux serpens aeslée,
Puis se plongeant de son long, en avant
Dedans la Nue, à l'abandon du vent
Fendoit le Ciel, ores planant des aesles,
Ores hachant coup sur coup des aisselles,
Ores à poincte, et ores d'un long tour
Environnoit le Ciel tout à l'entour:
Ainsi qu'on voit aux rives de Meandre
L'oyseau de proye entre les airs se pendre,
Puis s'eslancer à pointes de roydeur
Sur les canards herissez de froideur,
Tremblans de voir le gerfault qui ombrage
D'un corps plumeux tout le haut du rivage.
[1.305–22] [2]

This passage can demonstrate as well as another Ronsard's limitations as an epic poet. His great failing was that he was concerned with *ornaments,* with prettiness and gracefulness exhibited in a series of tags; he strung out pieces of poetry, fragments of his classical study, in a mosaic of shards. This failing is abundantly

2. *Oeuvres Complètes,* ed. P. Laumonier, *16*[1] (Paris, Marcel Didier, 1950), 44–45. "He had scarcely finished speaking when Mercury made his preparations: he set his little hat on his head, attached his wings to his heels, garbed his shoulders in a small coat with a gilt border that fell to his knees, took his winged rod with its two serpents, then plunging into the cloud at full length, cut through the sky at the mercy of the winds; now coasting on his wings, now chopping with his arms one stroke after another, now moving directly, now he circled the sky all about in a long sweep: thus one sees on the shores of the Meander the bird of prey hang in the airy region, then dart with rigid plumage upon the ducks stiffened with cold fear, trembling to see the falcon shadowing all the crest of the bank with his feathery body."

This does not represent Ronsard's first celestial descent, since as early as 1551 he had tried his hand at one in the "Hymne Triumphal sur le Trespas de Marguerite de Valois, Royne de Navarre," ed. Laumonier, *3,* 67–71, ll. 289–360.

evident in the prose prefaces with which he introduced his poem.[3] He lacked the moral seriousness and sustained imaginative vision ever to write a whole epic poem. Thus when he describes Mercury, he tries to make the god merely decorative; he prettifies the cap with the diminutive *capeline,* provides an elegant, gold-fringed little coat, and turns the caduceus into a *houssine,* a riding switch. Then, wanting to restore the god his lost dignity, he produces a simile which recalls the classical models but, as developed here, proves irrelevant. The same interest in decoration is manifest in Belleau's poem, where the angelic messenger is even prettier:

> Il a dessus le dos
> De cent et cent couleurs deux ailes bigarrees,
> Comme on voit en esté és nueuses contrees
> Un arc qui ceint le ciel: jusques à ses talons
> Un crespe blanc et net comme en petits sillons
> Flottoit à longs replis, une perruque blonde
> A l'entour de son col, s'esgaroit vagabonde.[4]

The serious moral imagination which these men lacked as epic poets is to be found in the pair of Huguenots who appeared in the next generation—Du Bartas and d'Aubigné: the one an uneven, prolix poet, encyclopedic and didactic; the other a crude but great poet who merits esteem and study.

3. Thus, speaking of epic verse, Ronsard writes that it must be wrought by "la main d'un bon artisan, qui les face autant qu'il luy sera possible hausser, comme les peintures relevees, & quasi separer du langage commun, les ornant & enrichissant de Figures, Schemes, Tropes, Metaphores, Phrases & periphrases eslongnees presque du tout, ou pour le moins separees, de la prose triviale & vulgaire . . . & les illustrant de comparaisons bien adaptees de descriptions florides, c'est à dire enrichies de passements, broderies, tapisseries & entrelacements de fleurs poëtiques, tant pour representer la chose, que pour l'ornement & splendeur des vers." "Preface sur La Franciade," ed. Laumonier, *16²*, 332.

4. *Oeuvres Poëtiques,* ed. C. J. Marty-Laveaux, 2 (Paris, Lemerre, 1878), 148. "He has two wings on his back of hundreds of variegated colors, such as one sees in a bow that bands the sky during summer in cloudy regions; a white and immaculate garment of crepe floated to his heels in long folds as in little furrows; his blond locks wandered unbound about his neck."

ii.

Agrippa d'Aubigné is one of the few epic poets who was himself a hero with the sword. His biography is very close to incredible, so full is it of precocious violence, of mortal danger, of romantic peripety, of famous personalities, most of it acted downstage on the theatre of French history. However distinguished a poet, historian, and satiric novelist he was, d'Aubigné seems to have considered himself—quite rightly—as a soldier first of all, and as a leader of the Huguenot cause which he served for forty years. Intellectual prodigy at 6, orphan at 15, officer and hero at 18, courtier and Petrarchan poet at 21, later counselor and spiritual guide of Henri de Navarre, Humanist, diplomat, marshal of the Huguenot armies, he lived in the high style at least as consistently as he wrote in it. Even in old age when, like Milton, he saw his cause definitively defeated, he refused to yield altogether and published his youthful, partisan poem, *Les Tragiques,* already badly outdated and of interest to none but the authorities who were ultimately to drive its author out of France. It is the poem for which we read him chiefly today.

Published in 1616, it was written for the greater part in the 1570s, with cumulative additions accruing well into the seventeenth century. How is one to categorize it, for the reader who has not had the occasion or the courage to confront it at full length? Into what pen of sheep does one herd a maddened bull? Enormous, furious, apocalyptic, strident, repetitious, it has no continuous epic action and yet it has, in its misshapen way, something of the physical, intellectual, and spiritual dimensions of the epic. It is concerned, certainly, with heroism, and in its most ambitious moments it reaches for the grand style. It was born of violence. Historically its author composed it, as he writes at the outset, between campaigns and battles, in peaceful interludes, or when recovering from wounds. It is the work of a man whose element is violence, whose stomach is strong, whose sensibilities are so exacerbated that only the wildest horrors, the most glaring effects touch him. If epic is the genre by which violence is accommodated most commonly in literature, then here epic accords violence its apotheosis. Torture, martyrdom, massacre, auto-da-fé, starvation, infanticide, cannibalism, perversion—there is room for it all, and room to dwell on it all with attentive detail. Violence finds its apotheosis and ultimately reaches satiety. The reader who cannot make the effort to close the book feels presently as though he had himself been hit sharply on the back of the head.

If you consider the mass of brutality which the poem contains, you are surprised that it succeeds in being literature at all. But I think it must be accorded nonetheless a place of considerable distinction. It is the product of a powerful imagination, capable of visionary intensity, and supported by inexhaustible verbal inventiveness, by terrible moral earnestness, and by rich personal experience. And despite its continuous violence, *Les Tragiques* is a poem of impressive range: it gives us searing satirical passages as well as moving personal confession, Biblical meditation, and historical interpretation; it mixes pamphleteering and metaphysics, allegory, polemic, and prophecy. It has the encyclopedic scope of other famous literary monsters—the *Roman de la Rose, Gargantua et Pantagruel, The Anatomy of Melancholy*. But it lacks, as they do, a controlling sense of form, and it lacks much more than they a sensitivity to most of the realms of experience in which most people lead their lives. It bears the strangeness born of nightmare. It is marred because its author was incapable of lowering his voice. It is perhaps the most exhausting of great poems, but it is undeniably great all the same.

Les Tragiques has only recently been well considered in France, for important historical reasons. D'Aubigné as a poet took a direction which ran counter to the direction taken by subsequent French poetry. He did not have his say, like so many of his successors, in exactly the right number of words, but rather in three times too many. He is seldom elegant, seldom delicate, never, in this poem, graceful. So the reader must forget Malherbe, Racine, and Valéry, and remember rather Ezekiel, Milton, and Hugo. There are minor poems by d'Aubigné which suggest some sort of kinship with the former poets also. But in his one major poem, the heat is too glaring for fragile flowers to grow. For d'Aubigné to come into his own it required, in France, the advent of Hugo to restore to the language a certain vitality which had disappeared a little after Malherbe. It required, contemporaneously, the advent of Sainte-Beuve who renewed French interest in the literature of the sixteenth century and specifically in d'Aubigné. It required, finally, the edition of his complete works, some of them previously unpublished, which appeared late in the nineteenth century. But not until the last few decades has d'Aubigné begun to receive the appreciation he merits. The charge of obscurity which hurt his reputation for so long has been largely refuted by a critical edition of *Les Tragiques* in which the historical allusions are clarified and the Biblical echoes identified.[5] D'Aubigné is in fact no more obscure than Dante.

If as I have said the poem follows no continuous epic action, its seven books do nonetheless fall into a kind of rough pattern. The first book, *Misères,* is devoted primarily to the suffering of the French people during the religious wars, although it contains also a long, savage digression upon Catherine de Médicis and her counselor, perhaps her lover, the Cardinal of Lorraine. *Princes,* the second book, satirizes Catherine's three sons, two of them kings, and the effeminate, debauched court of flatterers and favorites which they gathered about them. After these contrasting pictures of the countryside and the court, d'Aubigné opens his third book, *La Chambre Dorée,* in heaven, where God enthroned receives the souls of Protestant martyrs with terrible anger at their persecutors. Having chosen to descend Himself to earth, to view human iniquity at closer hand, he happens first upon the Palace of Justice in Paris. The *chambre dorée* is the hall where Huguenot victims are judged, before a bench composed of Injustice, Envy, Madness, Drunkenness, and several other colleagues, each described in considerable, often brilliant detail. There is a digression evoking an auto-da-fé at Seville, followed by the description of an imaginary mural at the Palace of Justice, in which the great judges of history march in a kind of triumph with the victims of injustice. The fourth book, *Les Feux,* is perhaps the weakest; it rehearses Protestant martyrology from Hus and Wyclif up to the opening of the religious wars. Book Five, *Les Fers,* reveals God once again in heaven, understandably sated with the sight of so much human

5. Edition critique avec introduction & commentaire par A. Garnier & J. Plattard (Paris, 1932).

cruelty. Hidden among the ranks of angels is Satan who, when recognized, proposes a bargain like the one in Job, involving however in this case the whole body of the Huguenot elect. God consents that his faithful be tested, not only by the fires of martyrdom, as heretofore, but in the far more trying conditions of civil war. Thus the greater part of *Les Fers* is devoted to the wars of religion, and in particular to the St. Bartholomew massacre. The sixth book, *Vengeances,* involves another sort of historical pattern: opening with an eloquent prayer for supernatural illumination, it recalls the frightful punishments with which God has visited the oppressors of the innocent through the centuries—first, in early Jewish history, second, under the Roman Empire, and finally in the poet's own era. These testimonies of divine wrath serve as preliminaries to the final book, *Jugement,* where after more preliminaries (including a digression on pagan theories of immortality) a grandiose vision of the end of the world is evoked, that quickly approaching end when God's patience will be ultimately exhausted, Satan bested, and the righteous finally justified. With the evocation of their near-unimaginable bliss, so long delayed, the poem triumphantly concludes.

I quote here part of the scene in heaven from *La Chambre Dorée,* with the subsequent description of God's descent to earth. It is dissimilar to any of the descents encountered thus far, and one could argue in fact that it owes nothing at all to the Homeric-Virgilian convention. But it may serve to exemplify, by its very dissimilarities, a certain form which the epic conception assumed in Renaissance France.

> Là les bandes du ciel, humbles, agenouillees,[6]
> Presenterent à Dieu mil ames despouillees
> De leurs corps par les feux, les cordes, les couteaux,
> Qui, libres au sortir des ongles des bourreaux,
> Toutes blanches au feu volent avec les flammes,
> Pures danz les cieux purs, le beau pays des ames,

6. All French quotations from *Les Tragiques* are from the Garnier and Plattard edition. "There, the heavenly companies, humble and kneeling, presented to God a thousand souls stripped of their bodies by fire, rope, and knife, souls which, freed by their passage from the nails of their executioners, all white from the pyre, mount up with the flames, pure in the pure heavens,

Passent l'ether, le feu, percent le beau des cieux.
Les orbes tournoyans sonnent harmonieux:
A eux se joinct la voix des Anges de lumiere,
Qui menent ces presens en leur place premiere.
Avec elles voloyent, comme troupes de vents,
Les prieres, les cris & les pleurs des vivants,
Qui, du nuage espais d'une amere fumee,
Firent des yeux de Dieu sortir l'ire allumee.
  De mesme en quelques lieux vous pouvez avoir leu,
Et les yeux des vivans pourroyent bien avoir veu
Quelque Empereur ou Roy tenant sa cour planiere
Au milieu des festins, des combats de barriere,
En l'esclat des plaisirs, des pompes; & alors
Qu'à ces princes cheris il monstre ses thresors,
Entrer à l'improvis une vefve esploree
Qui foulle tout respect, en deuil demesuree,
Qui conduict le corps mort d'un bien aimé mari,
Ou porte d'un enfant le visage meurtri;
Fait de cheveux jonchee, accorde à sa requeste
Le trouble de ses yeux qui trouble cette feste:
La troupe qui la void change en plainte ses ris,
Elle change leurs chants en l'horreur de ses cris.
Le bon Roy quitte lors le sceptre & la seance,
Met l'espee au costé & marche à la vengeance.

---

the beautiful homeland of souls, pass through ether and fire and penetrate the beauty of the heavens. The turning spheres chime harmoniously; with them are joined the voices of the angels of light, who lead these arrivals to their original places. With them were flying, like troops of winds, the prayers, cries, and tears of the living, which, by a thick cloud of bitter smoke, made the enkindled anger start from the eyes of God.

Thus in certain places you may have read and the eyes of living men could well have seen, some emperor or king holding full court amidst banqueting and tourneys, surrounded by the brilliance of pleasure and pomp; and then, as he displays his treasures to these beloved princes, a widow in tears enters abruptly, in uncontrolled mourning, who tramples all forms of respect, leading the dead body of a beloved husband or bearing the bloodied countenance of a child. Her hair disheveled, she conforms to her petition the troubled expression of her eyes, which troubles this festivity. The company, on seeing her, changes its laughter to lament; she changes their songs into the horror of her cries. The good king leaves behind him sceptre and assembly, buckles his sword to his side and sets out for vengeance.

Dieu se leve en courroux & au travers des cieux
Perça, passa son chef; à l'esclair de ses yeux
Les cieux se sont fendus; tremblans, suans de crainte,
Les hauts monts ont croullé: cette Majesté saincte
Paroissant fit trembler les simples elements,
Et du monde esbranla les stables fondements.
Le tonnerre grondant frappa cent fois la nuë;
Tout s'enfuit, tout s'estonne, & gemit à sa veuë;
Les Rois espouvantez laissent choir, paslissans,
De leurs sanglantes mains les sceptres rougissans:
La mer fuit & ne peut trouver une cachette
Devant les yeux de Dieu; les vents n'ont de retraitte
Pour parer ses fureurs: l'univers arresté
Adore en fremissant sa haute Majesté.
Et lors que tout le monde est en frayeur ensemble,
Que l'abysme profond en ses cavernes tremble,
Les Chrestiens seulement affligez sont ouïs,
D'une voix de loüange & d'un pseaume esjouïs,
Au tocquement des mains faire comme une entree
Au roy de leur secours & victoire asseuree:
Le meschant le sentit, plein d'espouventement,
Mais le bon le connut, plein de contentement.
Le Tout-Puissant plana sur le haut de la nue
Long temps, jettant le feu & l'ire de sa veue
Sur la terre, & voici: le Tout-Voyant ne void,

God rises in anger, passed his head through the heavens and cleft them; at the lightning from His eye, the heavens divided; the high mountains, trembling and sweating with fear, crumbled; this sacred Majesty appearing made the basic elements tremble and rocked the steady foundations of the world. Thunder struck the clouds a hundred times in reproof; everything flees, everything is stunned and moans at the sight of Him. Kings, terrified, ashen, drop the red sceptres from their bloody hands; the sea flees and can find no hiding place before the eyes of God; the winds have no shelter to ward off His fury; the paralyzed universe adores, quaking, His high Majesty. And then when all the earth is unified in its terror, and when the deep abyss trembles in its caverns, only the Christians in their afflictions are heard, gladdened by a song of praise and a psalm, greeting the King of their help and their certain victory with a beating of hands, as in a triumphal entry. The evil man, filled with terror, felt Him, but the good man, filled with satisfaction, knew Him.

The Almighty hovered long on the crest of the cloud, casting the flame and ire of his regard upon the earth, and behold: the All-Seeing sees nothing,

En tout ce que la terre en son orgueil avoit,
Rien si pres de son oeil que la brave rencontre
D'un gros amas de tours qui eslevé se monstre
Dedans l'air plus hautain. Cet orgueil tout nouveau
De pavillons dorez faisoit un beau chasteau
Plein de lustre & d'esclat, dont les cimes pointues,
Braves, contre le ciel mipartissoyent les nues.
Sur ce premier object Dieu tint longuement l'oeil,
Pour de l'homme orgueilleux voir l'ouvrage & l'orgueil.
Il void les vents esmeus, postes du grand Eole,
Faire en virant gronder la girouette folle.
Il descend, il s'approche, & pour voir de plus pres
Il met le doigt qui juge et qui punit apres,
L'ongle dans la paroi, qui de loin reluisante
Eut la face & le front de brique rougissante.
Mais Dieu trouva l'estoffe & les durs fondements
Et la pierre commune à ces fiers bastimens
D'os, de testes de morts; au mortier execrable
Les cendres des bruslez avoyent servi de sable . . .

[*La Chambre Dorée,* 109–82]

This is one of those passages of *Les Tragiques* wherein the grandiosity of the imagination is partially abrogated by a stylistic crudity. The poet would have needed to be a Milton or an Ezekiel to find the language conformable to his vision's sublimity. As it is, a certain roughness, an impression of haste, the repetitions which are not always artful, qualify, although they do not destroy, this sublimity. The third verse paragraph in particular typifies

---

throughout all that the earth in its presumption presented, so near his eye as the splendid spectacle of a thick cluster of towers displaying their elevation in the proudest region of the sky. This brand new presumption of gilded pavilions made a fine castle full of brilliance and eclat, whose brave pointed tops divided the clouds against the sky. God fixes his eye upon this first structure for a long time, to see the work and pride of prideful man. He sees that the excited winds, couriers of the great Aeolus, make the mad weathercock scold by their veering. He descends, he draws near, and to see the better he places the nail of the finger that judges and later punishes upon the battlement, whose facade of reddish brick shone to a great distance. But God discovered the material and hard foundations and the stone common to these proud structures to be bones and skulls; the ashes of burned martyrs had been used as sand in the ghastly mortar . . ."

that Hebraic majesty which d'Aubigné introduced into French poetry, and in its command of cosmic space, its magisterial marshalling of kingdoms and elements, it manifests an awesome control of apocalyptic forces.

One is struck first in reading this poetry by the syntactic disorder. In Ronsard, the syntax is generally simpler, certainly easier to follow; it offers no resistance as one reads and it adheres to certain principles of clarity, moderation, and decorum. The poetry of *Les Tragiques* impresses us rather with a kind of Dionysian disregard for syntax, an impression which may have been intended. It is not, in any case, typical of d'Aubigné's other verse. Here the lack of balance or symmetry in the sentence structure, the dishevelled way in which phrases and clauses shoulder one another, is a stylistic constant. There are certain passages of the poem in which syntactic relations become absolutely mysterious. The function of *entrer* in line 129 of the quotation is not quite obscure, because one supposes that it depends upon "avoir leu" and "avoir veu" in lines 123–24, although in line 125 these are followed not by an infinitive (like *entrer*) but a participle—*tenant.* But if the syntax is not altogether chaotic here, it is at least vague.

A favorite syntactic form of d'Aubigné is the series of nouns, verbs, adjectives, or relative clauses which he likes to accumulate without a connective conjunction.[7] In the first sentence of the quotation, for example, the habit is obvious enough, although there are none of the much longer series that one frequently finds. The two adjectives of the first line, separated by a comma rather than a conjunction, would not be unusual in themselves, but the pattern begins to be manifest if we note the series of nouns in line three:

> les feux, les cordes, les couteaux . . .

and the parallel adjectives in the following three lines—"libres," "blanches," "pures," which however are not quite parallel because the second introduces unexpectedly a verb—"volent"—of the rela-

7. This element in d'Aubigné's style has been commented upon by Imbrie Buffum in his study *Agrippa d'Aubigné's Les Tragiques* (New Haven, 1951). It is impossible to write at length about the style of the poem without alluding to elements Buffum has treated, and I shall have occasion to do so more than once.

tive clause which contains them. But before we are through we discover that "volent" itself is only the first in a parallel series which is concluded in line 115 by "passent" and "percent." "Passent" in its turn takes two objects—"l'ether" and "le feu"—again separated by a comma. You have the impression that the syntax is improvised, that the sentence, like any given series, might be extended indefinitely or cut off at an earlier point. We seldom know where we are being led, whereas in the hands of a master of syntax like, say, Pope, we always know pretty well. Each sentence in d'Aubigné is an enterprise, an adventure, almost a risk, and some end in a swamp of confusion. But many others, including perhaps the sentence I have analyzed, are powerfully effective in their very disorder, and I would not be understood to wish *Les Tragiques* very much more tidy in this regard. In any case it is suggestive that the metric unit, the alexandrine, is not treated with a great deal more respect than the syntactic unit, the sentence. Enjambment is frequent, and syntactic breaks frequently occur in the middle of the line:

> Dieu se leve en courroux & au travers des cieux
> Perça, passa son chef; à l'esclair de ses yeux
> Les cieux se sont fendus; tremblans, suans de crainte,
> Les hauts monts ont croullé: cette Majesté saincte
> Paroissant fit trembler les simples elements . . .

In the rush of language the smaller units lose their effectiveness as brakes, and the only true unit of division is the verse paragraph, whose flexibility permits the rush to spend itself momentarily before pausing. The impetuosity of d'Aubigné's language, in its heaping up of words pell mell, seems always to risk saying too much, but it implies that no language, however excessive, can possibly convey the excesses of the subject matter itself.

The passage I have quoted is dense with stylistic effects which violate the decorum approved by the Pléiade. Ronsard would have permitted the treatment of adjective as noun, audacious for that age:

> . . . percent le beau des cieux . . .

or of verb as noun:

. . . au sortir des ongles des bourreaux . . .

but he would certainly have reprobated the turns upon words which seem to move slightly toward the paradox or pun:

. . . Pures dans les cieux purs . . .
Le trouble de ses yeux qui trouble cette feste . . .
Pour de l'homme orgueilleux voir l'ouvrage &
    l'orgueil . . .

as well as the Biblical antithesis in lines 159–60, the excessive shifting of verb tenses, the bold use of the pathetic fallacy in lines 139 ff., and the uncomfortable images which close the quotation. Behind all these syntactic and stylistic departures, behind the welter, confusion, and excitement of the poetic texture throughout the poem, lies an original conception of heroic language. The demonic properties of language are given freer play in *Les Tragiques* than in any other Renaissance epic—one would almost say in any Renaissance poetry. The restraining rhetorical rules, carefully shored up in the Renaissance *Artes Poeticae,* have been deliberately forgotten. Doubtless one could find all the textbook devices of the rhetorical manuals in this poetry, but their emotional impact has been heightened by several orders of magnitude. The description of God's anger and descent is in this respect atypically restrained; in comparison with the rest of the work it constitutes a relative lull in the storm. The greater part of the work is written quite unambiguously to inflame, and the distinctions of style levels, the criteria of "good taste," the very rules of grammar come to appear pedantic flim-flam in the face of that purpose. Traditionally the epic poet wrote for truth as well as delight, but here the very conception of truth has changed; it has become an instrument of aggression.

Preste moi, Verité, ta pastorale fonde,
Que j'enfonce dedans la pierre la plus ronde
Que je pourray choisir, & que ce caillou rond
Du vice Goliath s'enchasse dans le front.

[*Princes,* 45–48] [8]

8. "Loan me, Truth, your pastoral sling, so that I may bury in it the roundest stone I find, and that this round pebble fix itself in the forehead of the vice Goliath."

The sense that there are limits to the proper exploitation of language fades before the hope that language *engagé* can render service to a cause. Now the only limits will lie with the poet's own capacity.

D'Aubigné alludes in several passages to the originality of his poetic manner. He wrote that he had to find a "stylle inconnu" to match the unprecedented horror of his subject, and he intended his style as a kind of provocation of his enemies.

Enfans de vanité, qui voulez tout poli,
A qui le stile sainct ne semble assez joli,
Qui voulez tout coulant, & coulez perissables
Dans l'eternel oubli, endurez mes vocables
Longs & rudes. [*Jugement,* 361–65] [9]

Variations of the significant phrase "stile sainct" appear elsewhere:

La sainte fureur de mes vives chansons.
[*Vengeances,* 68] [10]

It may allude in part to the influence of the Old Testament prophetic books, which every reader feels, and to the pervasive echoes of Biblical imagery. D'Aubigné read the Bible in the original and his imagination was in fact saturated with it. But the "stile sainct" must also allude to the moral motive which animates his poem, the need to denounce abomination which imposed itself like a sacred duty. He writes in his verse Preface:

Amis, en voyant quelquefois
Mon ame sortir de ses loix,
Si pour bravement entreprendre,
Vous reprenez ma saincte erreur,
Pensez que l'on ne peut reprendre
Toutes ces fureurs sans fureur.
[*Préface,* 355–60] [11]

9. "Children of vanity, who prefer everything polished, to whom the sacred style seems insufficiently pretty, who prefer everything smooth and smoothly slide into eternal oblivion, morals, suffer my long and harsh phrases."

10. "The holy fury of my passionate songs."

11. "Friends, in witnessing sometimes my soul rapt from its laws, if you take my sacred delusion to task with your brave raillery, remember that one cannot rebuke all these frenzies without frenzy."

and again in *Princes:*

Le temps a creu le mal; je viens en cette sorte
Croissant avec le temps de style, de *fureur,*
D'aage, de volonté, d'entreprise, & de coeur:
Et d'autant que le monde est roide en sa malice,
Je deviens roide aussy pour guerroyer le vice.
[*Princes,* 50–54] [12]

Fureur is the word which recurs to justify the stylistic excesses and to excuse what would appear a multitude of artistic sins to the pedant or the moral indifferent.

The muse d'Aubigné invokes is Melpomene, the muse of tragedy.

D'ici la botte en jambe, et non pas le cothurne,
J'appelle Melpomene en sa vive fureur . . .

Fureur appears again, and in the passage which follows, it emerges as the proper expression of the tragic:

J'appelle Melpomene, en sa vive fureur,
Au lieu de l'Hypocrene, esveillant cette soeur
Des tombeaux rafraichis dont il faut qu'elle sorte,
Eschevelee, affreuse, & bramant en la sorte
Que faict la biche après le faon qu'elle a perdu.
Que la bouche luy saigne, & son front esperdu
Fasse noircir du Ciel les voutes esloignees;
Qu'elle esparpille en l'air de son sang deux poignees,
Quand espuisant ses flancs de redoublez sanglots,
De sa voix enrouee elle bruira ces mots:
"O France desolee! o terre sanguinaire!
Non pas terre, mais cendre . . ." [*Misères,* 78–90] [13]

12. "The age has heightened the evil; thus I appear heightening along with the age my style, my fury, age, will, determination, and heart: and to the degree that the world is rigid in its malice, I too become rigid to make war on vice."

13. "From here, booted rather than buskined, I summon Melpomene in her passionate rage, waking this sister not from the Hippocrene but from the cool tombs which she must leave behind, disheveled, frightful, and moaning like the doe for her lost fawn. Let her mouth bleed, and her frenzied fore-

I need not quote the rest of the lament. The muse is invoked not from Mount Helicon but from the tombs freshly opened to receive more bodies. She appears raving, bloody, in disarray, frantic, like a woman in Picasso's *Guernica*. She has a prototype in the suppliant widow of the simile, lines 123–38 of my quotation. She is no Sophoclean muse. I think we are meant to take her as a kind of divinity of suffering, of pathos and violence, and to take the word *tragique* to mean *pathetic* in an extreme sense.[14] So the poem's title implies that pathos born of unnatural violence is the element which gives it unity. Confronted with such pathos, the poet can only write with uncontrollable rage, with *fureur*. That is his implication. Something of Juvenal is here and something of Roman tragedy; the innovation consisted in using the *rant* as the normal manner of a long, quasi-epic poem.

Fureur has two senses in French; it can mean violent anger or it can mean a temporary loss of reason amounting virtually to madness. D'Aubigné's usage implies both senses, and I think we can find instruction in this duality. For his uniqueness as a poet lies in this: that the stunning energy of his verse, the eternal freshness of his indignation, the unflagging quest for epithets, as well as the stylistic roughness, asymmetry, unconventionality, the improvisational manner, all that is "Dionysian," spring from a

---

head blacken the distant vaults of Heaven; let her sprinkle upon the air two handfuls of blood as, exhausting her sides with redoubled sobs, she mutters these words hoarsely: 'O desolate France! O bloody earth, not earth, but ashes . . .' "

14. This reading is supported by d'Aubigné's use of *tragique* or *tragedie passim*. In describing a massacre of Huguenots he writes:

> Là les tragiques voix l'air sans pitié fendoyent . . . *Fers,* 615
> ("There the tragic voices pierced the pitiless air . . .")

And referring elsewhere to martyrs:

> Dieu receut en son sein les ames infinies
> Qu'en secret, qu'en public trainoyent ces tragedies . . . *La Chambre Dorée,* 581–82.
> ("God received to his breast the infinite numbers of souls which were drawn into these tragedies, in secret and in public.")

In the introductory *Aux Lecteurs,* four of the seven books (first, fourth, fifth, and seventh) are designated as written in a "style tragique," and these are in fact the books which dwell most upon pathos and violence.

single, precise, and limited emotional source, which is religious hatred. One could study in *Les Tragiques,* almost in a clinical way, the rhetorical forms which that awesome passion assumes when it possesses a man of talent to the depth of his soul. It is the most fearsome kind of hatred because it is the blindest and the most unappeasable. It darkens the Old Testament; it recurs in the epic in Camoens and Tasso, and it even touches Milton. But nowhere in modern literature does religious hate motivate a work so purely and so nakedly as it does this; the whole poem is sustained by a lyricism of rage.

It is a terrible passion, and we do not need the poem to tell us with what nightmares it has afflicted history. What the poem can teach us, what we might not otherwise have supposed, is that it is rich enough soil in itself for an extended work of art. It is conceivable that d'Aubigné as a poet might never have made such happy claims upon his talent, never fulfilled it to a comparable degree, without the animus which his public and military life provided.

But on the other hand his passion did not sustain him without a price. If the poem is as exhausting as it is, the cause may lie partly in the sense of frustration it communicates. For no verb is violent enough, no epithet abusive enough, to destroy by itself the poet's enemies. The appeals to heaven and earth to damn the iniquitous are made in vain, because language is being asked to do something which in fact only history can do, or else the day which will end history. And history, as we know, did not damn the objects of these terrible imperatives:

> Empuantissez l'air, ô vengeances celestes,
> De poisons, de venins & de volantes pestes . . .
> Vent, ne purge plus l'air; brise, renverse, escrase,
> Noye au lieu d'arrouser, sans eschaufer embrase . . .
> Terre, qui sur ton dos porte à peine nos peines,
> Change en cendre & en os tant de fertiles plaines,
> En bourbe nos gazons, nos plaisirs en horreurs,
> En soulfre nos guerets, en charongne nos fleurs.
>
> [*Vengeances,* 277–78, 281–82, 285–88][15]

15. "Foul the air, celestial avengers, with poison, venom and winged plagues . . . Wind, cease to cleanse the air; destroy, overturn, crush, drown

Language is no substitute for the sword, but it is used here as a kind of weapon. Language cannot in itself conjure the last day, although d'Aubigné uses it as though it could.

> Leve ton bras de fer, haste tes pieds de laine,
> Venge ta patience en l'aigreur de la peine,
> Frappe du Ciel Babel . . .
>
> [*Misères,* 1377–79] [16]

The poet would make poetic language into a transitive instrument, but it remains pitilessly intransitive. The robust Catholic frames could only be broken by sticks and stones. And so the poem is divided between its natural function as a work of art to be contemplated, and its impossible function as a weapon.

iii.

The contemplation of the poem is itself a very different experience from the contemplation of Sannazaro's or Tasso's poem. For in the first place no attempt has been made to woo the reader's eye with imagery that pleases in the same naïve, immediate way that theirs does. In the episode of God's descent, the angels are not ravishing, glorious creatures who please us simply in the beholding. Nor is heaven any longer so resplendent. There are, to be sure, allusions to the 'beau des cieux" and the "Anges de lumiere," and there is the fine line:

> Les orbes tournoyans sonnent harmonieux.

But the brilliance is palled by the bitter cloud rising from earth, and the scene as a whole fades to grey. The sensuous Renaissance pleasure in color and light has no place.

On the contrary the reader's senses are assaulted by the painfulness of the imagery. The episode in heaven begins with allusions not only to "les feux, les cordes, les couteaux" of martyrdom but more precisely to the "ongles des bourreaux," an image we

---

instead of sprinkling, burn without heating. Earth, you who can scarcely bear our suffering on your back, transform so many fertile fields into ashes and bones, into mire our lawns, our pleasures into horror, into sulphur our meadows, to carrion our flowers."

16. "Raise thy iron arm, hasten thy woolen feet, avenge thy patience through the bitterness of punishment, strike Babel from heaven."

might have wanted to be spared. And the passage closes with the equally painful allusion to the bones and blood which have served to build the palace.[17] There is something in the poet's sensibility which finds pleasure in the revolting and the painful, something in his nature that is almost sadistic. It is this which colors the simile of the suppliant widow, which causes the poet to exaggerate and theatricalize her gestures of despair. The southern, pre-Reformation delight in the senses has given way to subtler delights.

The theatrical exaggeration of the imagery casts a lurid light upon the whole episode. If the language of hatred seems always on the brink of overstatement, the poem's phenomenology acquires thereby a certain melodrama: the bloody sceptres fall from royal hands palsied with terror; the anger of God's eye rips open heaven. Nature itself runs to excess: the thunder strikes the cloud a hundred times; the mountains sweat and crumble when God appears. Wind, sea, and sky imitate human passion.

But despite its melodrama the poetic universe remains mysteriously static. God's descent is remarkable for its lack of dynamism. The verbs of movement are weak.

> Dieu se leve en courroux et au travers des cieux
> Perça, passa son chef . . .
> Il descend, il s'approche . . .

These are the only indications of movement we are given. The descent is suggested rather by three successive images or scenes: first the enthronement in heaven (lines 109–22); second God's wrathful apparition in the sky, with the earth's ensuing terror (lines 139–60); and third the observation of the Palace of Justice from a cloud (lines 161–82). These images are complemented by the simile (lines 123–38) which gives an alternate, analogous image to the enthronement. So we are able to see that God has moved without really seeing him moving. Throughout the episode nothing occurs that could not be represented in painting: the angels' presentation of the martyred souls; the entrance of the suppliant widow; the sceptres falling from the kings' hands. Each act is frozen as it were at the critical moment.

The analogy with painting is not fortuitous. In the composition

17. I have deliberately omitted the lines which follow and which are still more offensive by conventional standards of taste.

of all these scenes one feels the influence of the visual arts. The third scene in particular, with its division into terrestrial and celestial planes, the use of the cloud as a vantage point, the serried towers reaching into the sky, the sense of broad, indefinite space, might have been copied from some Baroque engraving. Buffum has analyzed at length d'Aubigné's relation to the visual arts and these considerations of cultural history will not preoccupy us here. But the picturesqueness has a poetic effect which needs to be remarked: it helps to freeze whatever initiatives to action seem to be gathering; it helps to create the curious impression of motionlessness. For all of the whirl of violence in *Les Tragiques* never seems to shift from a single fixed point. Deep hatred is too obsessive to leave its object behind. There are scarcely any changes of relationship before the concluding judgment. The part of the action which would presumably have required the highest narrative gifts—the action of *Les Fers*—is narrated by means of imaginary paintings done by angels and hung in heaven. The successive battles and the St. Bartholomew are reduced to stasis by descriptions of the angelic paintings.

The fixed point which anchors the action is a simple, persistent historical situation: the disparity between the worldly deserts of the elect, the lambs of God, and of the iniquitous, the wolves of men. The elect suffer although they are good; the iniquitous triumph although their evil is unfathomable. But eternity will reverse the injustices of time, as soon as the long patience of God is exhausted. These articles of faith govern d'Aubigné's imagination so narrowly that his images tend to resemble emblems. The moral implications of the image are felt so strongly that the image loses its freshness *as* image. The poetry hurries up out of the literal level of contemplation, where hatred is at a loss, on to the moral and anagogical levels, where hatred takes its nourishment. The felicitous line:

Faire en virant gronder la girouette folle

succeeds because the heavy moral content is conveyed in a vivid and immediate fashion. But very often the immediacy is threatened by the image's crushing moral burden. This is the weight which fixes the poem in its immobility.

It is significant that God descends to no human individual, that the earthly terminus of His descent is rather an institution with symbolic meaning. For there are almost no individuals as such in *Les Tragiques,* although there are many names. Heroism is the virtue of a group, the lambs of God, and so is iniquity, of another, larger group. We never quite *see* Henri III or Catherine de Médicis or Coligny, although there are moments when we think we are about to see them. We are given facts about their appearance. But they tend always to resemble allegorical personifications of perversion or treachery or nobility. This is Henri III:

> L'autre fut mieux instruit à juger des atours
> Des putains de sa Cour, & plus propre aux amours;
> Avoir raz le menton, garder la face pasle,
> Le geste effeminé, l'oeil d'un Sardanapale:
> Si bien qu'un jour des Rois ce douteux animal,
> Sans cervelle, sans front, parut tel en son bal:
> De cordons emperlez sa chevelure pleine,
> Sous un bonnet sans bord, faict à l'Italienne,
> Faisoit deux arcs voutez; son menton pinceté,
> Son visage de blanc & de rouge empasté,
> Son chef tout empoudré, nous monstrerent ridee,
> En la place d'un Roy, une putain fardee . . .
>
> [*Princes,* 773–84] [18]

The observation is sharp but we have no sense of the divided, hesitant, complex man that Henri must have been. It may be that hatred necessarily sees men only in generalities, or sees only the details it chooses. On the other hand—and this is d'Aubigné's strength—his imagination never quite loses touch with the concrete. If men have suffered in their muscles and bones, then their enemies must suffer so too. If their accusing lips are perjured,

> Brise leurs grosses dents en leur puante bouche . . .
>
> [*La Chambre Dorée,* 1032] [19]

18. "The other was more accomplished in judging the embellishments of the court whores, and readier for amours, good at keeping his chin shaven and his complexion pale, his gestures effeminate and his eye like Sardanapalus'; so that one Epiphany this uncertain animal, lacking both brains and shame, appeared at his ball as follows: his head-dress decked with strings of pearls, under a rimless bonnet, Italian style, made two sweeping arches; his ruffed chin, his face plastered with white and rouge, his powdered head exhibited, instead of a king, the wrinkles of a painted whore."

19. "Break their thick teeth in their stinking mouth . . ."

The pages are dense with physical things. But no man ever stands before us as a clear, apprehendable entity, as does, for example, the Odysseus of Homer.

It is among inanimate and invisible presences that the imagination possessed by hate begins to find itself, to look about with assurance and care. Among these heavenly or allegorical creatures of its own fantasy, corresponding to its own purposes, it can take its ease. Here the sense of the concrete will serve doubly well.[20] The scene in heaven we have examined is equalled or surpassed in visionary realism by several passages: by the later scene of Satan's bargain, by the apocalyptic conclusion, and by the powerful series of allegorical caricatures composing the bench of the *chambre dorée.*

In this last section the picturesqueness, the immobility, the gift for detail, the theatricality, and the moral obsessiveness of d'-Aubigné's vision are happily fused. Everything is vivid and incisive; everything has dramatic depth. Each hideous grotesque is peculiarly compelling, beginning with Avarice:

> A gauche avoit sceance une vieille harpye
> Qui entre ses genoux grommeloit accroupie;
> Contoit & recontoit, approchoit de ses yeux
> Noirs, petits, enfoncez, les dons plus precieux
> Qu'elle recache aux plis de sa robbe rompue,
> Ses os en mille endroicts repoussans sa chair nue . . .
> [*La Chambre Dorée,* 249–54] [21]

and next to her:

> La jeune Ambition, folle & vaine cervelle,
> A qui les yeux, flambants, enflez, sortent du front

20. The faculty of rendering physical the inanimate seems to be proper to most Baroque art. It appears strikingly in that curious image Crashaw might have admired (lines 119–22 of the quotation) which pictures the divine eyes smarting from a bitter vapor of prayers, cries, and tears.

21. "To the left was seated an old Harpy who was muttering between her knees in a squat; she was counting and recounting, bringing up to her little, black, sunken eyes her most precious gifts, which she then hides in the folds of her tattered dress, her bones protruding from the bare flesh in a thousand places . . ."

Impudent, enlevé, superbe, fier & rond,
Aux sourcils rehaussez . . .
[262–65][22]

There are places also for Passion:

Qui n'attend pas son tour à dire sa sentence . . .
[386][23]

for 'cette seiche, tremblante, pasle" figure of Hypocrisy:

Qui parle doucement, puis sur son dos bigot
Va par zele porter au buscher un fagot.
[327–28][24]

and for the unnamed figure whose identity dawns on us more slowly:

On connoist bien encor ceste teste sans front,
Poinctue en pyramide, & cet oeil creux & rond,
Ce nez tortu, plissé, qui sans cesse marmotte,
Rid à tous en faisant de ses doigts la marotte.
[283–86][25]

It is the grinning face of Folie—Madness. At the end of the bench is seated Ignorance:

Ses petits yeux charnus sourcillent sans repos,
Sa grand bouche demeure ouverte à tous propos,
Elle n'a sentiment de pitié ni misere:
Toute cause luy est indifferente & claire;
Son livre est le commung, sa loy ce qu'il luy plaist:
Elle dit, *ad idem,* puis demande que c'est.
[363–68][26]

22. "Young Ambition, a vain madcap, whose eyes, flaming and protruding, start from a forehead impudent, bold, arrogant, haughty, and round, with raised brows . . ."

23. "Who doesn't wait her turn to give her opinion."

24. "Who speaks softly and then goes off in her zeal to carry on her bigoted back another fagot to the stake."

25. "We know well also this head without a brow, pointed like a pyramid, and this hollow, rounded eye, this wrinkled, twisted nose, which gabbles ceaselessly and grins at everyone as it makes a bauble with its fingers."

26. "Her little fleshy eyes blink without rest, her wide mouth stays open whatever is said; she has feelings neither of pity nor of misery; all issues to her are indifferent and obvious; her book is public opinion, her law is her caprice; she says 'I think the same,' and then asks what it's about."

In a single line of this—"Toute cause luy est indifferente & claire" —what a world of lucid malice! There are twenty odd portraits in all, and in virtually every one, whatever else is noted, the eyes are individuated with remarkable descriptive power. It is a stunning *tour de force.* Although some of the portraits give away the abstract name immediately, many others withhold it to the end, so that the accumulated details add up to a kind of riddle. One seldom guesses, but the answer, when finally given, bursts upon one with triumphant necessity. When the gallery is completed, one is faced with a seething, febrile crew whose unmatchable ugliness is punctuated by two dozen eyes, repellent and distinct. The section has been neglected even by admirers of the poem because, I think, we have lost the taste for allegory. It is a pity that inventiveness of so high an order should be lost upon us for want of modernity. We are accustomed to admiring other poetry which renders no more graphically things which are no more real.

The best of d'Aubigné's poem reveals an ambition common to the greatest imaginations—the ambition to create a new heaven and a new earth, and to intuit afresh the place of man between them. It happened more than once that the poet's pen betrayed his high design. But whatever value one puts on the poetry of *Les Tragiques,* its creative independence is undeniable. To be sure there are medieval prototypes for these allegorical caricatures as there are Biblical and classical models for other passages. But the existence of models cannot obscure the revolutionary conception of the work as a whole. Seen in the perspective of the epic tradition, it appears as a monumental attempt to reinvigorate, even to recreate the heroic poem, to free it from academicism, to win a new vision of the mysteries which had brought it into being. Such a defiance of Humanistic precept could only have been made by a poet habituated to spiritual revolt. By refusing the traditional epic form he threw open his poem to formlessness and immobility. We may regret the blemishes that ensue, but we must be grateful to a poet who insists on seeing in his own way, with his own fearful passion, for whom the divine could not possibly be replaced by machinery, for whom heroism could not be a matter of convention. One may speculate, futilely, on the course the Renaissance epic might have taken had *Les Tragiques* appeared thirty years earlier, when most of it was already written and when its impact might have equalled its power. As it happened, it was the weaker Du Bartas who became the most notorious Calvinist poet and whose influence was to mark the epic imagination.

iv.

Is d'Aubigné truly a Calvinist poet? The question may well be posed. For despite its polemical aggressiveness, *Les Tragiques* touches astonishingly little upon the issues of theology. However many other things it accommodates, it does not accommodate these, although written in an age which saw nothing unpoetic in theology. It contains much less doctrine than the *Divina Commedia* or *Paradise Lost* or even Ronsard's *Discours des Miseres de ce Temps,* which is the closest Catholic approach to a counterpart. To be sure it contains the speech of the martyr Montalchine (*Les Feux,* 647–705) which resumes cursorily the doctrinal issues, but the poet seems interested by the audacity of Montalchine's ruse and by his mechanical wit rather than by the issues themselves, which in any case he grossly oversimplifies. One may wonder moreover whether the exuberance and grandiloquence of d'Aubigné's style are truly in the Calvinist spirit. Calvin himself had written in a far more sober manner, and during his lifetime Huguenot poetry had taken Marot's chaste translations of the Psalms as models.[27] There are passages in the *Institution Chrétienne* which seem to authorize a plain simplicity as the highest eloquence. In the first chapter of the 1541 edition Calvin had written that the simplicity and rhetorical bareness of Scripture serve to prove its authenticity as God's word. He admitted that the rhetoric of pagan writers may be ravishing, but the fact the the Scriptures moved him more, without rhetoric, was a sure sign that they contained the truth. Calvin chose to ignore the parts of Scripture which are heavily rhetorical (even if they do not conform to classical rhet-

27. "A l'époque de la Pléiade, les poètes calvinistes, ou influencés par les idées protestantes—Bèze et Riveaudeau, Tagault, Babinot, Grèvin lui-même (bien que celui-ci fût plus 'élaboré')—étaient esthétiquement des puritains, qui répudiaient les beautés païennes et les ornements pour user d'un style dépouillé—le langage du vrai, disaient-ils, dont les Psaumes de Marot leur donnaient l'example." Marcel Raymond, *Génies de France* (Neuchatel, 1942), p. 80.

oric) and so betrayed his own taste for plainness. It is a quality for which *Les Tragiques* has never been reproached.

Still less Calvinist is the abrupt metaphysical digression (*Jugement,* 361–542) which precedes directly the concluding vision of the last judgment. Indefensible on structural grounds, it is equally out of place theologically. It falls into two parts, the first devoted to conceptions of immortality current in the thought of classical antiquity (361–478) and the second (479–542) devoted particularly to the thought of Hermes Trismegistus. The justification of the first part lies in the presumed agnosticism of the poet's audience, which can only be persuaded of immortality by its own idols, the "philosophes vains" of the pagan ages. By such a justification d'Aubigné protects himself against the imputation that *he* accepts the philosophers' authority. But in the second part he refers openly to the "axiomes vrais" of Hermes Trismegistus and thus adopts them as his own. The point is important because the "axioms" he goes on to paraphrase from Hermes' book violate flagrantly the spirit and letter of Calvinism. Hermes propounds a doctrine of reincarnation which would have repelled Calvin; Hermes asserts the immortality of the physical world, which by common Christian belief (including d'Aubigné's elsewhere, cf. *Jugement,* 903 ff.) was to be destroyed on the last day; most significantly Hermes emphasizes the nobility of man in terms which contrast with Calvin's insistence on human frailty. So we find d'Aubigné, paraphrasing Hermes, referring to man as:

> Le prince estably au terrestre pourpris
> [*Jugement,* 526] [28]

and:

> Du premier animal le chef d'oeuvre eminent [530] [29]

and:

> Un tesmoin de Nature a discerner le mieux,
> Augmenter, se mesler dans les discours des dieux.
> [501–02] [30]

28. "The heir apparent of the terrestrial realm."
29. "The foremost masterpiece of the first animal."
30. "A witness of Nature to discern the best, to improve and mingle in the discourses of the gods."

It may be supposed that d'Aubigné inwardly reserved these distinguished titles for God's elect. But for Calvin even the elect were subject to the frailty and misery of human life on earth. No amount of logic-chopping could truly harmonize the two conceptions of man and of nature.

Is one then to consider d'Aubigné as a Calvinist poet only by accidental adherence to a party? I am inclined to think that it is rather the divergences which are superficial, and that in most important regards *Les Tragiques* is the purest example we possess of great Calvinist poetry. The interest in Hermes Trismegistus, which leaves no traces on most of the poem, ought doubtless to be considered as the aberrant product of a spiritual restlessness to which even the austerest Calvinist spirit might occasionally be driven. The theological bareness of the poem need not in itself prejudice our estimate of the religious attitude which colored the poetic imagination. The rhetorical overlay of the style, moreover, was not peculiar to d'Aubigné among Calvinist poets in the late decades of the century; one finds comparable stylistic elements, *mutatis mutandis,* in Du Bartas and Sponde.[31] If an historical explanation were necessary for the movement away from Calvin's ideal simplicity, it might be found perhaps in the turbulence of the bloody age itself, which imposed spiritual as well as physical struggle and which may well have rendered Marot's Christian mildness insipid.

The episode of God's descent is itself deeply infused with the Calvinist spirit. Typical of that spirit is the majestic, awesome Deity who dominates the composition of each successive scene, who troubles the foundations of the earth by the anger of his glance, and to whom even the angels kneel with submission.

> Là les bandes du ciel, humbles, agenouillees . . .

Heaven has receded from earth, has grown more remote, less accessible, and less jocund. The rosy-cheeked angels of Sannazaro would seek in vain their gleaming mansions here. The Jehovah of

31. After alluding to the plainness of Huguenot style at mid-century (see above, p. 276, note 27), Raymond goes on to write: "Vingt-cinq ans après, ce sont les huguenots, plus libres dans leur style et autrement ambitieux, qui échellent les cieux et font retentir les hauts-lieux, niant par là souverainement les bassesses courtisanes de la Muse de Desportes." Raymond, *Génies,* p. 80.

the Old Testament has replaced the deified Renaissance prince. He is a God who sends no messenger to earth for the instruction or guidance of man. For according to Calvinist doctrine man needs no intermediary with the divine beyond his individual conscience and the word of Scripture. God's message is already available and woe to him who does not heed it! Thus the absence from the poem of a divine messenger, which might appear to imply a lack of divine pressure upon man, bears witness rather to the most intense pressure. God descends, de post facto, to observe and to judge.

Calvin altered the Christian tradition by minimizing the theological virtue of charity and the doctrine of atonement. This deformation too is operative in *Les Tragiques;* it is what permits an avowedly Christian poem to base itself on hatred. It is clear enough from the manner of God's descent what forgiveness can be hoped for by the persecutors of His faithful. The poet feels no anomaly when he prays God to harden His heart:

> Que ceux qui ont fermé les yeux à noz miseres,
> Que ceux qui n'ont point eu d'oreille à noz prieres,
> De coeur pour secourir, mais bien pour tormenter,
> Point de mains pour donner, mais bien pour nous oster,
> Trouvent tes yeux fermez à juger leurs miseres;
> Ton oreille soit sourde en oiant leurs prieres;
> Ton sein serré soit clos aux pitiez, aux pardons,
> Ta main seiche, sterile aux bienfaicts & aux dons.
>
> [*Misères,* 1357–64] [32]

There is no room for softness, *douceur,* on the part of God, just as there is no delicacy, gentleness, *douceur,* on earth. The pain and agony which oppress the reader in *Les Tragiques* reflect accurately the Calvinist conception of human life. And if the faithful suffer more than most, that distinction is willed by God to test and purge them.

The Job-like bargain struck between God and Satan, at the

32. "May those who shut their eyes to our misery, those who had no ears for our prayers, no heart to assist but only to torment, no hands for giving but for taking away, may they find Thy eyes closed in judging their misery, Thy ear deaf in hearing their prayers, Thy jealous heart closed to pity or pardon, Thy hand dry and sterile in its benefactions and gifts."

opening of *Les Fers* (see above, p. 258), depends upon several Calvinist doctrines. It depends first upon the doctrine of the elect, those whom we have seen at God's descent, isolated from the rest of mankind and from nature, welcoming Him with psalm and praise. It depends secondly upon the Calvinist conception of the devil, or rather devils, who serve God involuntarily by molesting the elect.

> Or d'autant que Dieu conduit ça et là les esprits immondes comme bon luy semble, il ordonne et modere en telle sorte ce gouvernement, qu'ils molestent fort les fideles . . . les tourmentent de divers assauts . . . mesme jusques à les navrer, mais le tout pour les exercer, non point pour les opprimer ni vaincre.[33]

It depends thirdly upon the importance assigned by Calvinist psychology to the will. This doctrine will need ampler illustration.

Satan challenges the fidelity of the elect with wonted malice. He would have it that the fires of martyrdom constitute no true trial.

> Aux cachots estouffez on les va secourir
> Quand on leur va donner un peu d'air pour mourir.
> La pesanteur des fers, quand on les en delivre,
> Leur est quelque soulas au changement de vivre:
> L'obscur de leurs prisons à ces desesperez
> Faict desirer les feux dont ils sont esclairez.
>
> [*Fers,* 123–28] [34]

This devil, like Milton's, has his peculiar wit. Let him but have his way with the faithful and God shall see them falter.

33. Calvin, *Institution de la Religion Chrétienne* (Philadelphia, 1936), Book I, chapter 14, #18. "While God directs the courses of unclean spirits hither and thither at his pleasure, he regulates this government in such a manner that they exercise the faithful . . . harass them with incursions . . . and sometimes wound them, yet never conquer or overwhelm them." J. Allen translation of Calvin's original Latin.

34. "One assists them in exchanging their stifling dungeons for a little air to die in; the deliverance from the weight of their chains gives the change of life a certain solace; the darkness of their prisons makes these desperate wretches wish for fires to light them."

Mais si tu veux tirer la preuve de ces ames,
Oste les des couteaux, des cordeaux, & des flammes:
Laisse l'aize venir, change l'adversité
Au favorable temps de la prosperité,
Metz les à la fumee & au feu des batailles,
Verse de leurs haineux à leurs pieds les entrailles:
Qu'ils manient du sang, enflamme un peu leurs yeux
Du nom de conquerans ou de victorieux . . .
Qu'ils soient solliciteurs d'honneur, d'or & de bien,
Meslons l'estat des Rois un peu avec le tien.
Le vent de la faveur passe sur ces courages,
Que je les ploie au gain & aux macquerelages;
Qu'ils soient de mes prudents, & pour le faire court,
Je leur montre le Ciel au mirouer de la Court:
Puis après tout soudain, que ta face changee
Abandonne sans coeur la bande encouragee,
Et lors pour essaier ces hauts & braves coeurs,
Laisse les chatouiller d'ongles de massacreurs,
Laisse les deschirer, ils auront leur fiance
En leurs Princes puissants, & non en ta puissance.
Des Princes les meilleurs au combat periront,
Les autres au besoing lasches les trahiront,
Ils ne connoistront point ni la foy, ni la grace,
Ains te blasphemeront, Eternel, en ta face.
Si tout ne reussit, j'ay encor un tison
Dedans mon arcenal, qui aura sa saison,
C'est la guerre d'argent qu'après tout je prepare . . .
C'est alors que je tiens plus seure la deffaicte.
[*Fers*, 129–36, 139–57, 161] [35]

35. "But if you want to put these souls to the test, take knives, ropes and pyres away from them; permit the advent of ease, transform adversity into an auspicious period of prosperity; place them amid the smoke and fire of battles, pour the bowels of their hated enemies at their feet; let them handle blood; inflame their eyes a bit with the name of conquerors or victors . . . let them be solicitous of honors, gold, and property; let's mingle the estate of kings a little with yours. Wait till the wind of royal favor blows upon these courageous souls, till I bend them to profit and pandering; let them be numbered among my prudent—to sum it up, let me show them heaven in the mirror of the court. Then, suddenly, let your face be altered and heartlessly surrender the now encouraged band, let the nails of massacrers tickle

This is the formidable trial to which God assents, knowing that those of the flock predestined for salvation will not fail Him. He is proved right, of course. There will be no theodicean questions, of the sort Job asks, pondered by the lambs of God. There will be rather a heroic constancy of purpose, supported by the unshaken will. The test which Satan and God alike foresee depends uniquely upon the will, the will *not* to falter; in this respect it differs sharply from the testing of Job, of *Paradise Lost,* and of *Faust.* And although we are told that the will of the elect is incapable of weakening, we are led rather to feel the inhuman effort required to withstand the test.

The Calvinist psychology underlying this drama is simple. It divides the soul into two parts.

> Il y a deux parties en notre âme: *intelligence* et *volonté.* L'intelligence est pour discerner entre toutes choses qui nous sont proposées, et juger ce qui nous doit être approuvé ou condamné. L'office de la volonté est d'élire et suivre ce que l'entendement aura jugé être bon, ou au contraire rejeter et fuir ce qu'il aura réprouvé . . . Toutes les vertus de l'âme humaine se réduisent à l'un de ces deux membres. En cette manière nous comprenons le sens sous l'entendement.[36]

This is the familiar psychology on which *Paradise Lost* is based and which makes of temptation the only human drama worthy of interest. Eve's is a sin of the understanding, Adam's of the will.

---

these high, brave hearts to try them; let them be torn apart; they will put their trust in their powerful princes, and not in your power. The best of the princes will perish in combat; the others will betray them in time of need. They will know neither faith nor grace, and so will blaspheme you, Eternal, in your face. If all this doesn't succeed, I shall still have some tinder in my arsenal, which will have its season: the war of money which I'm preparing for later. That is the time I'm surest of their defeat."

36. *Institution,* Book I, chapter 15, #7. "The human soul has two faculties, the understanding and the will. Now, let it be the office of the understanding to discriminate between objects, as they shall respectively appear deserving of approbation or disapprobation; but of the will, to choose and follow what the understanding shall have pronounced to be good; to abhor and avoid what it shall have condemned . . . No power can be found in the soul, which may not properly be referred to one or the other of these two members. But in this manner we comprehend the sense in the understanding."

But Milton subordinated the will to the understanding, or reason, which he respected more than Calvin. In the *Institution* the two parts are theoretically equal. D'Aubigné chose rather to subordinate the understanding to the will, at least for the dramatic needs of his poem. In this sense his psychology is to be distinguished slightly from the heavily intellectual Calvin's. But he remains orthodox, far more than Milton, in the denial or perversion of the sensuous which has already been remarked. He is orthodox also in his negative conception of the will.

The *Institution* describes Christian life on earth with sober eloquence:

> Puisqu'il n'est ni terrien ni charnel, pour être sujet à corruption, mais spirituel, le royaume de Christ nous attire là-haut et introduit à la vie permanente, afin que nous passions doucement et en patience le cours de cette vie, sous beaucoup de misères, faim, froid, mépris, opprobres, toutes fâcheries et ennuis, nous contentant de ce bien seul, d'avoir un Roi qui ne nous défaudra jamais qu'il ne nous subvienne en nos nécessités, jusqu'à ce qu'ayant achevé le terme de guerroyer, nous soyons appelés au triomphe . . . Puisqu'il nous arme et munit de sa puissance, qu'il nous pare de sa beauté et magnificence, qu'il nous enrichit de ses biens: de là nous avons très ample matière de nous glorifier, même nous sommes fortifiés en fiance, pour guerroyer sans crainte contre le diable, le péché et la mort.[37]

The conception is heroic, depending as it does on the Pauline metaphor of warfare. It was this powerful and fertile conception of Christian heroism which permitted d'Aubigné to reinvigorate

37. *Institution,* Book II, chapter 15, #4. "Since it is not terrestrial or carnal, so as to be liable to corruption, but spiritual, the kingdom of Christ elevates us even to eternal life, that we may patiently pass through this life in afflictions, hunger, cold, contempt, reproaches, and other disagreeable circumstances; contented with this single assurance, that our King will never desert us, but will assist our necessities, till having completed the term of our warfare, we shall be called to the triumph . . . Now, since he furnishes and arms us with his power, adorns us with his beauty and magnificence, and enriches us with his wealth, hence we derive most abundant cause for glorying, and even confidence, to enable us to contend with intrepidity against the devil, sin, and death."

the epic. But it lacks the element which had been essential to classical epic—the element of achievement. The necessary conflict between the classical and Christian traditions which troubled all Christian epics finds its compromise in d'Aubigné with this conception of passive heroism. It is a conception which sacrifices much more of the classical than the Christian. For unlike almost all previous epics, *Les Tragiques* offers no possibility of individual victory or self-fulfillment. A man is not expected to shape his circumstances, to win through against obstacles; the best he can do is to resist evil with integrity. The highest virtue becomes obstinacy. "Remets entre mes mains ces Chrestiens obstinez," says Satan. But obstinacy is a collective virtue. And so if there are individual antagonists in *Les Tragiques* who emerge with a kind of personality, there is virtually no protagonist. There is not even any hope of deliverance by human means. Calvinist man is too miserable to achieve that kind of dignity. Rather, the only achievement which matters, for which the whole poem yearns, is the achievement reserved uniquely for God—judgment and retribution. *Les Tragiques* is the epic above all of divine vengeance, and secondarily of the faceless and formless group which preserves its purity with tenacious but negative courage.

v.

There is one more respect in which d'Aubigné typifies the Calvinist movement and indeed all of Protestantism: in his use of the Bible. There are few pages of *Les Tragiques* which do not echo, more or less directly, passages of Scripture. For the scene of God's descent which I have quoted, the editors suggest no less than eight Biblical echoes.[38] One need not assume that the poet himself could have identified all of these with precision. It is much more likely that they fell from his pen almost without his seeking them, or identifying exactly their provenience. Even in his deliberate allusions to a Biblical episode one feels the instinctive reflex of a mind for which Hebrew feeling and thought had become second nature. So saturated was his mind with them that Biblical situations and

38. The most important are Isaiah 54:10, 24:18; Psalms 18:8; Revelation 16:20.

characters became symbolic counters which his wit could manipulate at will, juxtapose, and interweave. Thus, after the opening lines of *Vengeances* have compared the most secret part of God to the inner altar of His temple:

> Ouvre tes grands thresors, ouvre ton sanctuaire,
> Ame de tout, Soleil qui aux astres esclaire,
> Ouvre ton temple sainct à moy, Seigneur, qui veux
> Ton sacré, ton secret enfumer de mes voeux.
>
> [1–4] [39]

the lines which follow compare the poet's relation to God vis-a-vis the worldly great with the situation of the shepherds at Bethlehem, whose offerings were not scorned for those of the Magi.

> Si je n'ay or ne myrrhe à faire mon offrande
> Je t'apporte du laict: ta douceur est si grande
> Que de mesme oeil & coeur tu vois & tu reçois
> Des bergers le doux laict & la myrrhe des Rois.
>
> [5–8] [40]

The altar of God's sanctuary is assimilated with the Christ child's manger. But in a further enrichment of the theme of offering, both of these are assimilated with the altar raised by Elijah on Mount Carmel, where the supernatural fire which consumed Elijah's offering confounded the priests of Baal before their own fireless altar.

> Sur l'autel des chetifs ton feu pourra descendre
> Pour y mettre le bois & l'holocauste en cendre,
> Tournant le dos aux grands, sans oreilles, sans yeux
> A leurs cris esclatans, à leurs dons precieux.
>
> [9–12] [41]

39. "Open thy great treasure, open thy sanctuary, Soul of all, Sun that shines as far as the stars, open thy holy temple to me, Lord, who wish to scent Thy sacred, secret place with my vows."

40. "If I have neither gold nor myrrh with which to make my offering, I bring Thee milk; Thy mildness is so great that with equal eye & heart Thou seest and receivest the sweet milk of shepherds and the myrrh of kings."

41. "Thy fire can descend to the altar of the weak to reduce the wood and the sacrifice to ashes, turning thy back upon the great, without ears, without eyes for their clamorous cries, for their precious gifts."

These twelve lines are dense, but they are not obscure or tortured; they bear witness to a creative mind which finds intuitively its analogies between Biblical and modern history.

Les Tragiques is full of such analogies, manifold threads which bind together the present and the past in a network of resemblance. Henri of Navarre is perhaps a Gideon:

> Rend toy d'un soin continuel,
> Prince, Gedeon d'Israel;
> Boi le premier dedans l'eau vive . . .
> [*Préface,* 307–09] [42]

But after his conversion, which the poet blamed upon Henri's mistress, Gabrielle d'Estrées, Henri becomes rather a Samson duped by Delilah:

> J'ay peur qu'une Dalide fine
> Couppe ta force & tes cheveux,
> Te livre à la gent Philistine
> Qui te prive de tes bons yeux.
> [*Préface,* 315–18] [43]

Charles IX is a Herod (*Fers,* 1300). Elizabeth of England is a Deborah (*La Chambre Dorée,* 993). La Rochelle is Bethulia (*Fers,* 1277), Paris is Babel (*Fers,* 392), and the Valois court is Sodom and Gomorrah (*Princes,* 1503). The queen mother Catherine is Jezabel (*Misères,* 747, etc.). The full meaning of these analogies is made manifest only in the penultimate book, *Vengeances,* where the Biblical stories are interpreted as virtual prefigurations of modern and future history. Or rather, the poet seems to have conceived of history as perpetually repeating itself, so that the Bible could serve in any period to help one scrutinize and prophesy events. The analogies which had previously seemed to be rhetorical mannerisms begin to assume in *Vengeances* the consistency of a system. Cain's murder of Abel contains the perennial truth, for those who understand, that the church must suffer violence on earth.

42. "Prince, make yourself a Gideon of Israel through continual effort; be the first to drink of the living water . . ."

43. "I fear that a subtle Delilah will sever your strength and your hair, and deliver you to the Philistines who will deprive you of your good eyes."

Le premier sang versé on peut voir en eux deux:
L'estat des agneaux doux, des loups outrecuideux.
En eux deux on peut voir (beau portrait de l'Eglise)
Comme l'ire & le feu des ennemis s'attise
De bien fort peu de bois & s'augmente beaucoup.
[*Vengeances,* 159–63] [44]

But if Abel represents in some sense the church, Cain represents its persecutors, and in the curse upon him one may read God's anger against all persecutors. Upon his shoulder will fit any number of sixteenth century faces. So it is with the deluge, which might serve as a secret warning to the impious of latter days were they not blinded by their pride. Scripture is not simply a compendium of moral wisdom, as Homer had been for the Greeks (although d'Aubigné's faith in analogy led him, like many Protestants, to look to Scripture for solutions to practical problems.[45]) Scripture is more than this; it constitutes a series of symbolic prophecies which, properly interpreted, permit the initiate to read the present and future in their deepest sense.[46] Such, to a lesser degree, is the rest of Christian history. *Vengeances* is an exercise in historical interpretation, and the secret truth it reveals is the imminent destruction of the enemies of the faithful. If Cain and Jezabel and Nebuchadnezzar suffered, and Herod and Nero and Domitian, surely living tyrants would fare no better. Already God's purpose had been revealed in the deaths of Charles IX, the

44. "One sees in these two the first blood shed: the condition of mild lambs and ambitious wolves. One sees in them (an apt portrait of the Church) how the anger and fire of enemies are kindled with very little wood and spread greatly."

45. In his *Devoir Mutuel des Roys et des Subjects,* for instance, the example of David and Saul is invoked to support the argument, surprisingly temperate, that subjects can legitimately revolt against their sovereign only after they have patiently endured the most virulent persecution. See *Oeuvres Complètes,* ed. E. Réaume and F. de Caussade, 2 (Paris, Lemerre, 1877), 42–45.

46. "La Bible est pour lui la Loi et les Prophètes, la vérité et l'histoire. Oui, pour d'Aubigné, sa propre histoire et celle de ses contemporains, celle de l'Eglise de Dieu et du nouveau peuple élu, *a déjà été écrite,* figurativement. Il n'est que de considérer "ce qui se passe" en suivant du doigt dans le livre sacré les phrases des prophètes et de l'Apocalypse pour mettre au jour un réseau de correspondances, pour déceler de profonds symboles, pour voir clair dans l'obscurité des choses." Marcel Raymond, anthology of d'Aubigné's *Prose* (Neuchâtel, 1943), p. 14.

marshal de Retz, and others. Not by accident does d'Aubigné's Palais de Justice resemble his description of the tower of Babel.

But analogies can be made with the lives of the holy as well as the iniquitous. So it is not surprising that the most powerful and the fullest of the Biblical analogies appears in a prayer for divine inspiration and is applied by the poet to his own past. It first appears in an introductory section of *Vengeances,* where an allusion is made to the prophet Jonah which looks incidental. In the catalogue of persecutors to follow, says the poet to the curious reader, you will find no mirage or esoteric fancy, but rather the simple facts of history. You would like a sign, but rather you will have Jonah returned from the depths.

> Ainsi dit le Sauveur: Vous n'aurez point de signe,
> Vous n'aurez de nouveau (friands de nouveauté)
> Que des abysmes creux Jonas ressuscité.
>
> [*Vengeances,* 82–84]

The allusion is to Matthew 12:38–40.

> Then certain of the scribes and of the Pharisees answered, saying, Master, we would see a sign from thee. But he answered and said to them, An evil and adulterous generation seeketh after a sign, and there shall no sign be given to it but the sign of the prophet Jonas. For as Jonas was three days and three nights in the whale's belly: so shall the son of man be three days and three nights in the heart of the earth.

There is an interval of sixteen lines before the analogy returns. But as its significance is gradually deepened in the meditation which follows, the correspondences demand increasingly serious contemplation. It is clear finally that the poet takes himself, and asks the reader to take him, as a kind of Jonah figure.

> Encor faut-il Seigneur, ô Seigneur qui donnas
> Un courage sans peur à la peur de Jonas,
> Que le doigt qui esmeut cet endormi prophete
> Resveille en moy le bien qu'à demi je souhaite . . .
> Je m'enfuyois de Dieu, mais il enfla la mer,
> M'abysma plusieurs fois sans du tout m'abysmer.

J'ay veu des creux enfers la caverne profonde;
J'ay esté balancé des orages du monde;
Aux tourbillons venteux des guerres & des cours,
Insolent, j'ay usé ma jeunesse & mes jours . . .
J'ay esté par les miens precipité dans l'onde,
Le danger m'a sauvé en sa panse profonde,
Un monstre de labeurs à ce coup m'a craché
Aux rives de la mer tout souïllé de peché;
. . . Le doigt de Dieu me leve & l'ame encore vive
M'anime à guerroyer la puante Ninive,
Ninive qui n'aura sac ne gemissement
Pour changer le grand Dieu qui n'a de changement.
[*Vengeances,* 99–102, 115–20, 125–28, 137–40] [47]

My quotation omits many of the details which fill out the comparison. This passage displays a reverent wit which is highly individual, combining medieval typology with the newer meditative practices introduced by the poet's despised Jesuits. There is more than ingenuity involved; there is meditation upon a divine and mysterious pattern, whose understanding brings self-knowledge. This kind of wit, informed with religious humility, anticipates Donne's *Holy Sonnets* and Herbert's *The Temple.* For a few decades English literature perpetuated a taste for poetry comparable to *Les Tragiques*—a taste already dying in France when the poem appeared.

Although Biblical history was richest, it was not alone in containing analogies with later ages. *Princes,* the satirical book, de-

47. The Garnier-Plattard critical edition explicates in detail the autobiographical sense of the passage.

"It is still required, Lord—O Lord who gave a courage without fear to Jonah's fear—that the finger which disturbed that sleeping prophet wake in me the good that I half desire . . . I fled from God but he raised up the sea, overthrew me many times without altogether overthrowing me. I have seen the abysmal cavern of the hollow depths; I have been hurled about by the tempests of the world; in the windy vortices of wars and courts I have insolently worn out my youth and my days . . . I have been thrown to the waves by my own people; danger saved me in its deep maw; at this a monster of labors vomited me upon the shore, smirched with sin . . . The finger of God raises me up and the still living soul enheartens me to make war upon stinking Niniveh, Niniveh which shall have neither sackcloth nor outcry to alter the great God who knows no alteration."

pends upon repeated comparisons with Nero and Caligula as touchstones of moral perversion. There are references scattered through the poem to Messalina, Sardanapalus, and Domitian. Here again the precision and frequency of the analogies imply that they are more than fortuitous. In the prose work, *Les Avantures du Baron de Faeneste,* the same conception is developed more amply. The Baron's description of a tapestry depicting the triumphal procession of Impiety proves once more the repetitious pattern of history. Not only today are the valiant defeated, says the Baron.

> De tout pareil ordre marchoit l'Eglise primitive, Apostres, Martyrs & Confesseurs, menez rudement par Neron, Domitian, Adrian, Severe & les autres pareils, jusqu' à Julien l'Apostat. Ces meschants tapissiers l'ont tiré sur un pourtraict de ce temps que je n'ose dire; comme celui de Libanius a les traicts de Monsieur le Convertisseur; comme aussi le visage de Papinian, qui mourut plustot que de vouloir escuser le forfait de Caracalla, est tout semblable au feu Chancelier de l'Hospital.[48]

The contemporary face woven upon the body of Julian the Apostate belongs to Henri IV. The head of Libanius (the pagan rhetorician who was Julian's friend) belongs to the Cardinal Du Perron ("Monsieur le Convertisseur") who gave Henri Catholic instruction. In essence the two apostasies are identical, and one must not lose heart at the latter because the earlier proves it might have been expected, that it forms a part of God's plan, that it is *natural* to life on earth. And if it is natural, it is no cause for discouragement.

There is a seed of this conception in the prefatory epistle of

48. *Oeuvres Complètes,* ed. Réaume-Caussade, 2, 636. "In quite the same order proceeded the primitive Church, Apostles, Martyrs and Confessors, harshly led by Nero, Domitian, Hadrian, Severus and others like them, including Julian the Apostate. These mischievous weavers had represented him with the head of a modern personage whom I dare not identify, as Libanius had the features of Monsieur the Converter; and also as the face of Papinian, who chose to die rather than pardon the crime of Caracalla, resembled closely the late Chancellor de l'Hospital."

Calvin's *Institution*.[49] Calvin had written there that the Huguenots might take comfort and guidance from the example of the apostles, and he compared the various attitudes confronting the righteous in both ages. Comparisons of this sort must have been common enough. But for d'Aubigné the search for analogies was a matter of reverent ingenuity which could not be taken lightly; it provided a mystical key to the hidden wisdom of God. It stemmed doubtless from the medieval search for anticipations of Christ's mission in the stories of the Old Testament, a search which took inspiration in such allusions as Jesus had made to Jonah. Medieval interpreters thought, for example, that the derivation of Eve from Adam's side foreshadowed the growth of the church from Christ's wound on the cross. But these interpreters disregarded secular history and limited the field of their ingenuity to the Bible. D'Aubigné's field was the total of human action as he knew it.

The effect of his historical conceptions upon *Les Tragiques* is important. Earlier epic poets of the Renaissance—Ariosto, Tasso, Ronsard—had followed Virgil (as Spenser would later) in postulating a hereditary link between past and present which informed history with continuity and direction. Rather than being meretricious bombast, extrinsic to the respective poems, this use of history provided a necessary, "ennobling" frame for the poetic action. D'Aubigné sacrificed the Virgilian frame for the Christian. He rejected the traditional panegyrical pattern of history, based on an ideal of dynastic power, for a Christian pattern of recurrences with fixed terminal limits—creation and judgment. The two patterns are mutually exclusive and no poet ever attempted to fuse them, for they involve different estimates of human capacity. The orthodox Christian pattern (which, as we have seen, not all Christian poets employed) implied that no individual action could essentially alter human destiny. The Virgilian pattern implied that a man might so alter it, as Aeneas was supposed to have done. It implied that the divine might effectually intervene in human affairs, because human affairs were capable of progress. The Christian pattern limited direct divine intervention to the two termini

49. "Epître au Roi," ed. La Société Calviniste de France, *1* (Geneva, 1955), xxxvi.

of history and to the incarnation (which plays no role in *Les Tragiques*). No more was necessary because God's will ultimately controlled a man's role and limited his capacity for earthly transcendence.

So *Les Tragiques* remains a poem of anguished anticipation, in which action receives its form only from the future. If the present is only a shabby copy of a fruitless past, then the present is empty duration. If history is always repeated, then in itself it is meaningless. The fascination or reassurance of its secret analogies cannot truly relieve its monotonous cruelty. We have always the poetry of a pre-epiphanous world. Each of the first six books of *Les Tragiques* concludes by calling for the Deed which will justify history, the Deed which is accomplished at the end of the seventh book. The episode of God's descent is simply a rehearsal of it. With what infinite jubilation, with what release, are the solemn words pronounced which make known Its imminence!

> Voici le Fils de l'homme & du grand Dieu le Fils,
> Le voici arrivé à son terme prefix.
> Des-jà l'air retentit & la trompette sonne . . .
> [*Jugement,* 697–99] [50]

The whole poem lies behind to render the trumpet peal its full significance, to inform with joy the brilliant radiance which floods the sky.

> L'air n'est plus que rayons tant il est semé d'Anges.
> [*Jugement,* 120] [51]

Upon the certainty of this fulfillment the faithful have wagered their temporal felicity. *Les Tragiques* is the monument to their wager.

In the deformation of the epic tradition which the poem represents, one discovers those tensions emerging from which modern literature was to take its profoundest themes. Out of the epic tradition which could only render its narrowest disciples sterile,

50. "Behold the Son of Man and of great God the Son, behold Him arrived at the predestined term. Already the air reverberates and the trumpet sounds . . ."

51. "The air has become one beam of light, so thick is it sown with angels."

there was developing *something else,* something which defied the tradition as it was using it. The oppositions that the epic engendered helped to form, as their result, that new entity which is the modern consciousness. Modern literature was to find its drama in the disputed area between these frontiers: between language as demonic and geometric; between the tension and relaxation of the will; between the indulgence and denial of the senses; between time as progressive movement and time as fixed whirl; between history as capable and incapable of transcendence; between man as governor and as servant of his destiny; between awe for his strength and disgust for his wretchedness. No previous literature ever ranged between frontiers so widely spaced, nor was any so complicated and rich, so various and disorderly. It is strange to think in how few decades, essentially, these frontiers were defined. It gives pause to think of the men who first measured the breadth of the gaps between them, and saw how difficult such distances are to narrow.

10. *SPENSER*

i.

To return to the English Renaissance, after reading the continental literature which partly inspired it, is to be struck with the relative weakness of early English Humanism. Needless to say, that weakness did not prejudice the quality of English poetry; it might even be regarded as beneficial, in a negative way, since it allowed the native English genius to develop without radical distortion. In any case, this weakness is a fact, and a crucial one for our purposes. Some Greek was taught in English universities before the opening of the sixteenth century, but after considerable and spirited advances during that century's opening decades, its study languished, and Bruno, after visiting Oxford in 1583, had occasion to joke about the dons' poor command of the language they professed.[1] It has been noted that Spenser, who spent seven years at Cambridge, never alludes directly to a Greek text not available in Latin translation. Classical Latin did, of course, form the basis of public school education. But despite the ardor of a few propa-

1. Giordano Bruno, *Opere Italiane,* ed. G. Gentile, *1* (Bari, 1907), 14–15.

gandists, and the warm sympathy of a much larger number, England was never *hit* by the excitement of Humanism, as Italy and France were; it never became an intoxication and a mania. Not only did sixteenth century England produce far fewer editions of the classics than the continental countries; she also produced a body of neo-Latin poetry which was inferior in bulk and quality. The Scotsman Buchanan, the most notable Latin poet of Tudor Britain, significantly lived for several years in France.

The rise of English Humanism was impeded by the political and religious unrest of the century's middle decades, by the hostility and strength of Puritanism, by the geographical distance from the centers of printing and scholarship, and perhaps by the heightening of English insularity due to religious differences with the continent. England was to absorb gradually, as she has so often, a movement she would ultimately make her own. But she never turned scornfully upon her own medieval past, like the poets of the Pléiade, in a kind of mistaken humility before the monuments of antiquity.

This moderation is quite evident in Elizabethan literary criticism. The critical issue largely defined itself on the continent around the propriety of imitating classical models. In France the influential voice of Du Bellay, prescribing close imitation, acquired great authority,[2] and among reputable poets only the heretical pens of Du Bartas and d'Aubigné, Protestants cut off from Paris and the court, dared to disobey. The imitation enjoined of the heroic poet was of course particularly strong, since Homer and Virgil dominated the Humanist Pantheon of poets. Ronsard's *Preface sur La Franciade, touchant le Poëme Heroïque* (1587), spells out the procedure of epic imitation in considerable detail. But in Puttenham's *Arte of English Poesie,* published two years later, the term *imitation* is directed only toward nature or life and never toward literary texts. Earlier, Ascham in *The Scholemaster* (1570) had advocated the imitation of models within certain limits. But Ascham's interests were chiefly pedagogic; he was concerned much more with prose than poetry and clearly subordinated the skill gained by imitation to individual originality and taste. Thus he attacked Sallust because his writing was "more Arte than nature,

2. See *La Deffence et Illustration de la Langue Francoyse, 1,* chap. 8.

and more labor than Arte." [3] Puttenham has comparable passages [4] and so does Sidney, who dismisses imitation in a sentence:

> But these, neyther artificiall rules, nor imitative patternes, we much cumber our selves withall.[5]

Campion, attacking rhyme as less noble than the quantitative hexameter, invokes antique usage with the mildest sort of praise: "Old customes, if they be better, why should they not be recald . . . ?" [6], only to be answered with Daniel's magnificent plea for cultural independence:

> Me thinks we should not so soone yeeld our consents captive to the authoritie of Antiquitie, unless we saw more reason: all our understandings are not to be built by the square of Greece and Italie. We are the children of nature as well as they, we are not so placed out of the way of judgment, but that the same Sunne of Discretion shineth upon us; we have our portion of the same vertues as well as of the same vices . . . It is not the observing of Trochaiques nor their Iambiques, that will make our writings ought the wiser: All their Poesie, all their Philosophie is nothing, unlesse wee bring the discerning light of conceit with us to applie it to use. It is not books but only that great booke of the world, and the all-overspreading grace of heaven that makes men truly judiciall. Nor can it but touch of arrogant ignorance, to holde this or that Nation Barbarous, these or those times grosse, considering how this manifolde creature man, wheresoever hee stand in the World, hath alwayes some disposition of woorth, entertaines the order of societie, affects that which is most in

3. "The Scholemaster," in *Elizabethan Critical Essays,* ed. G. Gregory Smith, *1* (Oxford, 1937), 40.

4. "Peradventure also it will be granted, that a man sees better and discernes more brimly his collours, and heares and feeles more exactly by use and often hearing and feeling and seing, and though it be better to see with spectacles then not to see at all, yet is their praise not egall nor in any man's judgement comparable: no more is that which a Poet makes by arte and precepts rather then by naturall instinct: and that which he doth by long meditation rather then by a suddaine inspiration . . ." George Puttenham, *The Arte of English Poesie,* ed. G. D. Willcock and A. Walker (Cambridge, 1936), pp. 305–06.

5. "Apologie for Poetrie," in Smith, *Essays, 1,* 195.

6. "Observations in the Art of English Poesie," in Smith, *Essays, 2,* 330.

> use, and is eminent in some one thing or other, that fits his humour and the times.[7]

Both Puttenham and Sidney admit the inferiority of earlier English authors to the classics but treat them nonetheless with respect.

The English theory of epic in the sixteenth century betrays a comparable conservatism. This is partly due to English ignorance of Aristotle's *Poetics,* which was not edited in England throughout the century and which left little mark on Tudor criticism. Although Aristotle had relatively little to say about the epic, he did stimulate other people to say a great deal. In England, however, Elizabethan epic theory clung rather to the medieval conception of the poem as an exemplary portrait.[8] Thus William Webbe, in his *Discourse of English Poetrie* (1586), writes of Virgil that he . . .

> performed the very same in that tongue which Homer had doone in Greeke . . . Under the person of Aeneas he expresseth the valoure of a worthy Captaine and valiaunt Governour, together with the perrilous adventures of warre, and polliticke devises at all assayes.[9]

and later he opens a chapter by writing:

> Nowe will I speake somewhat of that princelie part of Poetrie, wherein are displaied the noble actes and valiant exploits of puissaunt Captaines, expert souldiers, wise men, with the famous reportes of ancient times . . . such as the *Iliad, Odyssey, Aeneid.*[10]

Among the chapters devoted by Puttenham to the various genres, there is none for the epic, but one is devoted to a genre which clearly subsumes it; the title will indicate its content and its underlying theoretical assumptions:

7. "Defence of Ryme," in Smith, *Essays, 2,* 366–67.
8. A short history of this conception is given by E. M. W. Tillyard in *The English Epic and its Background* (New York, 1954), pp. 191–213.
9. Smith, *Essays, 1,* 237.
10. Ibid., *1,* 255.

> Of historicall Poesie, by which the famous acts of Princes and the vertuous and worthy lives of our forefathers were reported.[11]

Sidney distinguishes heroic poetry as "the best and most accomplished kinde," but goes on to speak of it in terms not unlike Puttenham's:

> For as the image of each action steyrreth and instructeth the mind, so the loftie image of such Worthies, most inflameth the mind with desire to be worthy, and informes with counsel how to be worthy. Only let Aeneas be worne in the tablet of your memory, how he governeth himselfe in the ruine of his Country . . .[12]

Spenser's letter to Raleigh introducing and describing *The Faerie Queene* is based on an identical theory, here employed to assert greater homogeneity between the poet and his predecessors than in fact existed:

> I have followed all the antique Poets historicall, first Homere, who in the Persons of Agamemnon and Ulysses hath ensampled a good governour and a vertuous man, the one in his Ilias, the other in his Odysseis: then Virgil, whose like intention was to doe in the person of Aeneas: after him Ariosto comprised them both in his Orlando: and lately Tasso dissevered them againe, and formed both parts in two persons, namely that part which they in Philosophy called Ethice, or vertues of a private man, coloured in his Rinaldo: The other named Politice in his Godfredo. By ensample of which excellente Poets, I labour to pourtraict in Arthure, before he was king, the image of a brave knight, perfected in the twelve private morall vertues, as Aristotle hath devised, the which is the purpose of these first twelve bookes: which if I finde to be well accepted, I may be perhaps encoraged, to frame the other part of pollliticke vertues in his person, after that hee came to be king.[13]

11. *Arte of English Poesie,* p. 39.
12. Smith, *Essays, 1,* 179.
13. All quotations from Spenser are from *The Poetical Works of Edmund Spenser,* ed. J. C. Smith and E. de Sélincourt (3 vols. Oxford, 1909–10). The passage here quoted appears in vol. 3, p. 485.

As a description of his poem, Spenser's letter is inadequate. Happily, a great deal of *The Faerie Queene* cannot be reduced to the scheme of exemplified virtues. But on the other hand, the scheme is not altogether irrelevant. The *exemplum* theory fits Spenser's poem better than it fits Ariosto's or Tasso's or any other Renaissance poem we have considered. *The Faerie Queene,* in other words, was profoundly affected by the lag in critical theory, theory being less sensitive to foreign influence than most poetic practice.

In many other respects as well—in style and structure as well as in conception—Spenser's poem has to be situated on the far edge of the Renaissance, at a stage where new forms and ideas and techniques were still filtered through a late medieval atmosphere. Spenser was stirred by those intimations of the Renaissance which reached him—doubly removed as he was in Ireland—but we must not attribute to him, as man or poet, the suavity and self-consciousness of the continental authors he meant to imitate. He did not share their sharp sense of a gulf between the enlightened present and the Gothic past, nor did he share the depth of their veneration for antiquity. If he sometimes echoed Homer and alluded to Virgil, he paid warmest homage to Chaucer. Even his irony—for Spenser was quite capable of irony—is blurred for us by its unclassical temper. All this being so, one must not look to him for the classical virtues of poise, clarity, economy, and shapeliness. His poetry rather is penetrated by other virtues whose names one scarcely knows, virtues which take their definition from his placid, earnest, ceremonious voice. One grasps those virtues, and all the charm and profundity they bring into being, only by accepting Spenser's poetic mode—a mode whose obvious attributes are quaintness and naïveté. Naïve perhaps Spenser is, but you must be careful not to apply the word unguardedly, lest it return to mock your wisdom. For heading the list of Spenser's insidious virtues are his intractability to useful categories and his impermeability to worldly condescension.

ii.

Spenser's longest account of a celestial messenger's descent appears not in *The Faerie Queene* but in a much shorter poem, *Proso-*

popoia, or Mother Hubberds Tale, included in a volume of *Complaints* published in 1591. I want to consider it first since, despite great differences, it makes a good introduction to the major poem in several important ways. Its very form, the beast fable, demonstrates that affinity with medieval art of which I have been speaking. The story is both traditional and typical of its author. The ape and the fox make common cause as unscrupulous adventurers, scorning the subjection to which they are born and setting up as lords of their own destiny, choosing to

> wander free
> Whereso us listeth, uncontrolled of any . . .

They pass through successive roles as soldiers, priests, and courtiers (permitting the poet to satirize each class in turn) finally to mount the throne itself. This they achieve by making off with the lion's skin as he lies sleeping in the forest. The ape dons the skin and passes himself off as the veritable monarch, but is himself controlled by the fox who acts as his first minister. Their injustice and misrule ultimately attract the notice of Jove, who dispatches Mercury to rectify matters. Mercury verifies the impostors' wickedness and wakens the still sleeping lion, who quickly regains his usurped kingdom.

The poem poses many historical and bibliographical problems which ought to be mentioned even if they are not completely solved. There is internal evidence of revision, hastily or clumsily done, and there is external evidence that the poem, either in a separate edition or in the *Complaints,* was "called in," censored or suppressed in some way. It is likely that some of the beasts are meant to represent historical figures, particularly in the closing section, and it has even been conjectured that these allusions were pointed enough to lead to Spenser's quasi-exile in Ireland.[14] It may well be that the fox as first minister should be identified with Burghley, and the ape as king with Elizabeth's French suitor, the Duc d'Alençon, and/or his agent Simier. (The threat of this marriage worried many Englishmen, particularly Sidney and other patrons of Spenser, during the late 1570s when this poem was

14. Edwin Greenlaw, "Spenser and the Earl of Leicester," *PMLA,* 25 (1910), 535–61.

probably first drafted.) The misrule of ape and fox would then constitute a prophetic warning to the queen against a French marriage, and the lion's sleep would suggest her apparent blindness to the evil involved. Although there is considerable reason to accept a reading along these lines, the equations can not always be made to fit, and we would do well to heed the remark of a shrewd editor:

> We must not press interpretation [i.e., identification of beasts with historical figures] too far. Spenser shifts his ground frequently, and the reader requires a certain agility to follow him.[15]

In speaking of *The Faerie Queene* I shall revert to this crucial point. But it is time now to quote Mercury's descent.

The scene on Olympus opens with a majestic portrait of Jove:

> . . . in whose almightie hand
> The care of Kings, and power of Empires stand,
> Sitting one day within his turret hye,
> From whence he vewes with his blacklidded eye,
> Whatso the heaven in his wide vawte containes,
> And all that in the deepest earth remaines,
> The troubled kingdome of wilde beasts behelde . . .
> [1225–31]

Spenser's readers would have remembered the first description of Jupiter in the *Aeneid* (1.223–26) although one detail of this description—the "blacklidded eye"—may possibly derive from the *Iliad* (1.528). Perceiving the ape's subversion of the animal kingdom, Jove's first impulse is to launch a thunderbolt. But choosing on reflection to pursue the offenders with shame rather than violence, he directs Mercury to investigate, to re-establish the lion, and to punish the pair of traitors. Mercury thereupon takes his leave:

> The Sonne of Maia soone as he receiv'd
> That word, streight with his azure wings he cleav'd
> The liquid clowdes, and lucid firmament;

15. W. L. Renwick, in his edition of the *Complaints* (London, 1928), p. 231.

Ne staid, till that he came with steep descent
Unto the place, where his prescript did showe.
There stouping like an arrowe from a bowe,
He soft arrived on the grassie plaine,
And fairly paced forth with easie paine,
Till that unto the Pallace nigh he came.
Then gan he to himselfe new shape to frame,
And that faire face, and that Ambrosiall hew,
Which wonts to decke the Gods immortall crew,
And beautefie the shinie firmament,
He doft, unfit for that rude rabblement.
So standing by the gates in strange disguize,
He gan enquire of some in secret wize,
Both of the King, and of his government,
And of the Foxe, and his false blandishment:
And evermore he heard each one complaine
Of foule abuses both in realme and raine.
Which yet to prove more true, he meant to see,
And an ey-witnes of each thing to bee.
Tho on his head his dreadfull hat he dight,
Which maketh him invisible in sight,
And mocketh th'eyes of all the lookers on,
Making them thinke it but a vision . . .
That on his head he wore, and in his hand
He tooke Caduceus his snakie wand,
With which the damned ghosts he governeth,
And furies rules, and Tartare tempereth.
With that he causeth sleep to seize the eyes,
And feare the harts of all his enemyes;
And when him list, an universall night
Throughout the world he makes on everie wight;
As when his Syre with Alcumena lay.
Thus dight, into the Court he tooke his way,
Both through the gard, which never did descride,
And through the watchmen, who him never spide:
Thenceforth he past into each secrete part,
Whereas he saw, that sorely griev'd his hart,
Each place abounding with fowle injuries . . .

Having verified the extent of misrule, Mercury discovers the lion and arouses him from his death-like sleep. The enraged lion easily regains his throne and exposes the impostors. Of Mercury and Jove we hear no more.

E.K., the annotator of *The Shepheardes Calendar,* praised Spenser for the "dewe observing of decorum everywhere," a compliment echoed by Professors Renwick and Bush,[16] but the passage I have just quoted constitutes in fact an extraordinary breach of decorum. The beast fable by definition required the low style, and Spenser so describes his style at the outset:

> No Muses aide me needes heretoo to call;
> Base is the style, and matter meane withall.
> [43–44]

In his dedicatory letter he writes "Simple is the device, and the composition meane." And indeed the style throughout most of *Mother Hubberds Tale* remains plain, unpretentious, relatively unadorned, and syntactically uncomplicated, if enlivened with a marvelously fluent and understated irony. But the description of Jove suddenly introduces a momentary loftiness coupled with an unwonted syntactic amplitude; I have quoted above (1225–31) only part of a sentence which runs for thirteen lines before it reaches a colon, and twenty-two before a period. The whole episode, as we have reason to know, stems from that genre which Spenser would have considered most unlike the one in hand. Moreover he has not, let it be noted, reduced the epic device to mock-epic; he has suppressed his irony. It is irrelevant, for our purposes, if the shift constitutes further evidence of revision. The fact is that Spenser did choose to mingle genres and flout decorum, and that such a mingling is typical of, even essential to, his art.

I spoke above of Tasso and Marino as patchwork poets, and perhaps I shall appear to be saying the same things about Spenser. But there is a vast difference between the late Renaissance syncretism of these Italians, and the post-medieval syncretism of Spenser. The Englishman's historical sense was much less devel-

16. E. K., *Epistle to Harvey, 1,* 416. W. L. Renwick, *Edmund Spenser* (London, 1925), p. 74. Douglas Bush, *Mythology and the Renaissance Tradition* (Minneapolis, 1932), p. 87.

oped and so too the sense of his "sources' " cultural distinctiveness. In *The Faerie Queene* he lumps together romance, philosophy, Scripture, folk tale, chronicle, saint's legend, allegory, myth and personal vision with the freedom of a Dante. And when he adopts some traditional element, Spenser makes no effort to retain its original spirit and flavor; he annexes rather than imitates. Thus the Jove of *Mother Hubberds Tale,* despite his provenience, has much less of Virgil about him than has, say, Tasso's "Padre eterno," and the mermaids who sing to Sir Guyon recall Homer's sirens only to point the contrast. The chaotic machinery of *The Faerie Queene* involves both angels and pagan gods, but they are somehow subsumed and reconciled. The "naïveté" of Spenser's syncretism, which might be expected to split his work in pieces, actually leads to homogeneity. One can say of Spenser's poetry, as of few Renaissance poets', that everything in it is his own.[17]

It was a kindred sense of freedom that led him to manipulate classical myth as he chose. Spenser's Mercury owes a little to Virgil, more to such Renaissance mythographers as Natalis Comes and Vincenzo Cartari, but a bit as well to the poet's own creative intuition. It was Spenser himself who first attributed to the caduceus the capacity of ruling the furies (a capacity mentioned again in *The Faerie Queene,* II.12.41; see also IV.3.42, quoted below), and to Mercury's hat the capacity of rendering him invisible. It was Spenser who introduced into this conventional episode the unexpected allusion to Jove's seduction of "Alcumena." And if he found the basic symbolism of the caduceus in the mythographers, it was nonetheless he who thought to introduce it into such an unlikely context as this poem.

Fully to understand this symbolism and the covert meaning of Mercury's descent, you must understand the poem's half-concealed metaphysical implications. These might be suggested by asking the question: "What place has *Mother Hubberds Tale* in a volume entitled *Complaints*?" The other eight poems of this volume are quite plainly concerned in one way or another with a single subject, which is indeed Spenser's great and only subject, the one

17. An example of Spenser's technique of poetic appropriation is studied by Robert Durling in "The Bower of Bliss and Armida's Palace," *CL, 6* (1954), 335.

underlying everything he ever wrote. This subject is the nature of *process.* In his first published work, *The Shepheardes Calender,* process is seen as the orderly round of months and seasons, a round presenting and symbolizing the successive human emotions appropriate to each phase. But the *Complaints* lay stress rather upon the destructiveness of process, which now is seen as mainly linear and downward rather than cyclical. The tone now is elegiac and nostalgic, and the order implied by the very arrangement of *The Shepheardes Calender* is implicitly denied. But what has *Mother Hubberds Tale* to do with this denial, and what has its subtle malice to do with elegy?

The first hint of an answer lies in its opening lines:

> It was the month, in which the righteous Maide,
> That for disdaine of sinfull worlds upbraide,
> Fled back to heaven, whence she was first conceived,
> Into her silver bowre the Sunne received . . .

The maid is Astraea, symbol of justice, through whose constellation, Virgo, the sun passes in August. Astraea fled back to heaven at the end of the Golden Age, when strife and injustice first corrupted human society. In this particular August, the Dog Star Sirius—"the hot Syrian Dog"—

> Corrupted had th'ayre with his noysome breath,
> And powr'd on th'earth plague, pestilence, and death.
> [7–8]

The narrator is himself stricken with the plague, and the body of the tale is told by a friend (Mother Hubberd) to relieve the irksomeness of his malady. But of course these opening lines are not simply pedantic indications of the season; the misrule symbolized by Astraea's flight and the plague symbolized by the corrupting start constitute the real subject of the old woman's story.[18] Moreover they adumbrate a metaphysical dimension which one is likely to overlook.

This dimension however is hinted at repeatedly in the telling of the story. The poem is really concerned not only with the abuses from which an opportunist profits but also with the Lucretian

18. See *The Faerie Queene,* Proem to Book V, 9–10.

universe of undirected process in which abuses flourish. The fox indeed counts upon chance in order to make his way:

> Wide is the world I wote and everie streete
> Is full of fortunes, and adventures straunge
> Continuallie subject unto chaunge.
>
> [90–92]

The upstarts will succeed by disdaining rank, tradition, and degree, the social equivalents of metaphysical order:

> Let us all servile base subjection scorne
>
> [134]

Rank is unnatural anyway, argues the democratic or communist fox, and with unconscious irony invokes as example that Golden Age whose passing he helps perpetuate. Thus they shall wander free, "uncontrolled of any." After their first experience as soldiers turned shepherds, they are left again "unto their fortune's change to toss" (342). When later they make their appearance at court, they reach the heart and center of slippery instability, the capital of Chance. There "Courtiers as the tide doo rise and fall" (614), and a beast without a patron "as a thistle-downe in th'ayre doth flie . . ."

> So vainly shalt thou too and fro be tost.
>
> [634–35]

This is the unprincipled palace of fluid appearances, where one must act

> That men may thinke of you in generall,
> That to be in you, which is not at all:
> For not by that which is, the world now deemeth,
> (As it was wont) but by that same that seemeth.
>
> [647–50]

This is the sanctum of fashion and novelty ("there all fashions beene") and the ape succeeds through his Protean capacity for imitation:

> Yet he them in newfanglenesse did pas
>
> [675]

He contrasts with the gentle mind that will not juggle with itself:

> Ne will be carried with the common winde
> Of Courts inconstant mutabilitie [722–23]

When the pair finally reach the throne, taking "the good which their owne happie chaunce them freely offred" (962–63), they set about more deliberately to undermine those forces which oppose continuity to flux. Now the fox is the more egregious culprit:

> Justice he solde injustice for to buy. [1147]

> No statue so established might bee,
> Nor ordinaunce so needfull, but that hee
> Would violate . . . [1161–63]

> . . . The whiles the Princes pallaces fell fast
> To ruine (for what thing can ever last?)
> And whilest the other Peeres for povertie
> Were forst their auncient houses to let lie,
> And their olde Castles to the ground to fall,
> Which their forefathers famous over all
> Had founded for the Kingdomes ornament,
> And for their memories long moniment.
> But he no count made of Nobilitie . . .
> [1175–83]

All of the passages I have quoted confer a breadth of significance upon these rascals' adventures by linking them to a certain philosophy of process. In a sense their power depends upon the truth of that philosophy. In the other *Complaints* the exquisite sarcasm of that parenthesis ("What thing can ever last") would lose its irony, for this idea constitutes their burden. But in this poem Mercury's intervention exposes the impostor and his philosophy, demonstrates continuity by the lion's restoration, and offers a victorious alternative to the principle of flux.

There is a little more in the presentation of Mercury than meets the eye, and here we return to the caduceus. If the hat betokens the god's extraordinary powers, the staff betokens his particular role. According to Comes, the caduceus, which had the property of appeasing quarrels, was a symbol of peace and was given to Mercury by Apollo. Mercury once threw it between two quarreling snakes who made up at once. Thus the intertwined snakes upon it stand for amity. In *The Faerie Queene* the bloody fight between Cambell and Triamond is halted by Cambina, another peacemaker, who also bears a caduceus:

> In her right hand a rod of peace shee bore,
> About the which two Serpents weren wound,
> Entrayled mutually in lovely lore,
> And by the tailes together firmely bound,
> And both were with one olive garland crownd,
> Like to the rod which Maias sonne doth wield,
> Wherewith the hellish fiends he doth confound.
> [IV.3.42]

Comes also writes that Mercury was the first inventor of alliances and armistices. In all these respects the god and his staff symbolize Concord, that state of universal order and rest and mutual love allegorized in *The Faerie Queene* with religious veneration (IV.10.31 ff.). Concord, or the hope of it, or the faith in its hidden presence, is Spenser's answer to the philosophy of chance and flux.

The language by which the caduceus is described clarifies its meaning. It is the wand

> With which the damned ghosts he *governeth,*
> And furies *rules,* and Tartare *tempereth.*

These three verbs carry great weight in Spenser. (Virgil's corresponding verbs are quite different: "evocat . . . mittit.") He did not share the fox's democratic ideas. He thought rather in terms of three analogous kinds of absolute authority: the *universal* government of God, or Love, or Concord, for which Mercury is here agent; the *individual* government of the self, whose conflicts are represented in Book Two (Of Temperance) of *The Faerie Queene;* and the *political* government of a realm, based on that concept of hierarchy which inspired the scornful phrase "that rude rabblement" of line 1270. All three governments are threatened by their respective furies, but the furies in turn are governable, theoretically and hopefully, by the caduceus.[19] Spenser's freedom with the myth is even clearer in the ensuing lines, wherein the Virgilian phrase "dat somnos adimitque" is altogether recast by the introduction of a new element:

> With that he causeth sleep to seize the eyes,
> *And feare the harts of all his enemyes . . .*

Mercury is no longer the passive instrument of fate or divine will, but himself an aggressive moral force. The "Alcumena" allusion which follows [1297–99] is more puzzling, and here one can only speculate. Spenser himself does nothing with it to help us, and yet it is unlike him to introduce such allusions just as stuffing. He had learned from the mythographers the art of moralizing pagan myth, although I have not found this particular story to have been explicated by them. It seems to me likely that Spenser had in mind the offspring of Jove and Alcmene—Hercules, who had become for the Renaissance an exemplum of heroism and glory. To introduce the allusion here was to draw an oblique equation between concord and glory, that greatness of individual and nation which only a just people at peace with itself can achieve. An equation something like this is also hinted at in the description of Cambina.[20]

19. The Furies in Spenser are spirits of Discord, not retribution. See *F.Q.*, II.2.29. See also Boccaccio's *De Genealogia Deorum,* Book III:

> "When events prove contrary to our desires, it follows that we become unreasonable, so that of necessity there arises in us a perturbation of mind which, like a mental darkness, persists, and persisting grows, and finally gives rise to unreasonable and furious behavior. This is why the Furies are said to be the daughters of Acheron and Night. They are also known as dogs or bitches by the inhabitants of the infernal regions; for men of base estate, when they are disturbed in their minds, not being able to restrain their fury, fill the air with their cries, like barking dogs." Quoted by C. W. Lemmi, "The Symbolism of the Classical Episodes in *The Faerie Queene,*" *PQ*, *8* (1929), 271.

20. Cambina holds the rod of peace in one hand; in the other a cup of Nepenthe, described as

> a drinck of soverayne grace,
> Devized by the Gods, for to asswage
> Harts grief, and bitter gall away to chace,
> Which stirs up anguish and contentious rage:
> In stead thereof sweet peace and quiet age

To the degree that Mercury's intervention is something more than an optative *deus ex machina, Mother Hubberds Tale* ceases to be a "Complaint." But one can speak only of degree, because the intervention *is* a bit arbitrary, *is* partly optative rather than prophetic. (The Alençon flirtation was history, to be sure, when the *Complaints* appeared in the edition we know, but it was not yet history, we may presume, when most of the poem was written. In any case, more is at issue than Alençon.) To complicate matters, Comes identified Mercury with reason, both human and divine, as well as with peace.[21] If we interpret the descent in these terms, it comes to mean both the queen's awakening by reason to a specific menace, and a human awakening to generalized injustice. As Spenser knew well, the latter process is necessarily incomplete, and leaves the issue forever undecided. The emphasis in this poem falls less on the victory over evil than on its anatomy. Spenser had scarcely exhausted the conflict or even found its definitive formulation. For that he would need the immense scope of *The Faerie Queene.*

We must turn now to contemplate that huge, irregular, motley bulk, and to search for the perspective glass which will take it all in. This reading of a shorter poem will have been useful if it shows how difficult Spenser is to exhaust. In the last analysis he defies interpretation because he always means something subtler and broader than one says he does. His mind moves intuitively at once on all the corresponding planes it commands. It is not enough to see that by beasts he means men; he also means in some places the corrupting voices within each man, and in other places he reaches out to involve forces of cosmic breadth. This procedure of

---

It doth establish in the troubled mynd . . .
Such famous men, such worthies of the earth,
As Jove will have advaunced to the skie,
And there made gods, though borne of mortall berth,
For their high merits and great dignitie,
Are wont, before they may to heaven flie,
To drincke hereof . . . [IV.3.43–44]

21. Spenser may have intended Mercury to represent the invisible passage of divine reason into the human mind. This would explain the putting off of his heavenly appearance described in lines 1266–70. Divine reason can only be apprehended dimly by men, just as the face that beautifies the shiny firmament cannot reveal itself on earth.

moving vertically from one plane to another or to several at once might be called *transvaluation.* Spenser complements it with the sort of sideways movement by which the ape ceases to be Simier in order to be Alençon or both, and by which Mercury as concord comes also to represent reason. We might call this procedure *metamorphosis.* Both procedures operate constantly in *The Faerie Queene,* and have engendered many a weary scholarly debate. Through these procedures Spenser's art reaches a curious harmony with his fundamental subject. In representing Proteus he becomes Proteus.

iii.

Spenser and d'Aubigné were exactly contemporary Protestant epic poets, but they have very little in common. The religious hatred which animated the Huguenot darkens Books One and Five of *The Faerie Queene* as it would darken a few pages of *Paradise Lost* (to say nothing of Hojeda's *Christiada*). But one has only to compare Spenser's pages on Henri IV's conversion (*F.Q.* V.11.43–65; 12.1–2) with d'Aubigné's (*Préface,* 307–36) to measure the artistic gulf that sundered them. The more rewarding comparison is with the Italians—Boiardo and Trissino, from whom Spenser may have borrowed trifles, and Tasso, from whom he took more, and Ariosto, from whom he took almost immeasurably.[22] It is quite possible that he misunderstood the spirit of Ariosto, but he must have felt a considerable affinity with the idealism, the Platonism, the bookishness, the courtliness, and even the peculiar pessimism of Tasso, not much more than eight years his elder.[23] Even so, they make a paradoxical contrast. Of the two, Tasso, by his innate brilliance, by his parentage and training, and by the sophisticated culture of his society, would have appeared far more likely to write a great heroic poem. The precocious adolescent who composed the *Rinaldo* with *sprezzatura* would not have taken for a serious rival the laborious author of the plodding *Shepheardes Calender.* But

22. See R. E. N. Dodge, "Spenser's Imitations from Ariosto," *PMLA, 12* (1897), 151–204, and S. J. McMurphy, *Spenser's Use Of Ariosto for Allegory,* University of Washington Publications, *2,* 1924.

23. Tasso's *Rime* seems to be the most important "source" for Spenser's *Amoretti.* See Janet Scott, *Les Sonnets Élizabéthains* (Paris, 1929), pp. 163 ff.

now that they have written and died, it is not so easy to choose between their major poems. Spenser is much cruder; his structure is uncertain, his narrative gift slender, and even his celebrated style a little inflexible. But whatever he creates has a radical integrity; it is authentic; it has been weighed and it rewards meditation. Tasso is not consistently authentic; his imagination is sometimes content to work for grandiose but empty effects. He is willing to paper over the gaps in his building, gaps which betray imaginative fatigue. Spenser seldom does that. His invention is astonishingly sustained, but when it flags there is no mistaking the lapse. And if his poem is a great storeroom of old images, they become at his touch solidly Spenserian, and render delightful his angular, rambling palace of wisdom. His unobtrusive quietness is the source both of his neglect and his following, for those who remain loyal discover with time that he has always bestowed more than he seemed to do. Truly to like him betokens a maturity of taste, as liking Tasso need not. No one is likely to pay the *Liberata* C. S. Lewis' compliment: "I never met a man who *used* to like *The Faerie Queene*."

Josephine W. Bennett has argued against grouping the work of Pulci, Boiardo, Ariosto, Tasso, and Spenser into a single genre.[24] Many historians have done so, but Mrs. Bennett insists that the supposed genre of epic-romance is non-existent. She may exaggerate a trifle the moral emptiness of Ariosto, but of course she is quite justified in stressing the vast disparities between the five poems. I am not sure, though, that such an emphasis settles the matter. For it is demonstrable that each poet had his predecessors in his head as he wrote; if he was being different, he was different *from them.* The genre recreated itself with each important new example, but if you deny *any* continuity you miss the interest of the recreation.

Whatever terms befit the Italian poems, *The Faerie Queene* can only be regarded as an amphibian. Mrs. Bennett herself in an earlier work [25] has shown that Spenser hesitated between the fanci-

24. Josephine Waters Bennett, "Genre, Milieu and the Epic-Romance," *English Institute Essays, 1951,* ed. Alan S. Downer (New York, 1952).

25. *The Evolution of The Faerie Queene* (Chicago, 1942).

ful imitation of Ariosto mentioned by Harvey [26] and a severer Virgilian poem. In many respects Spenser's poem straddles the two genres. Romance, as we have seen,[27] sacrifices epic amplitude for the mystery of the unilluminated, and forsakes the vision of heaven and hell to heighten the inexplicable wonders of their interventions on earth. Spenser creates three different versions of hell (I.5.31 ff.; II.7.21 ff.; IV.1.20 ff.) and a kind of heaven (VII.6.15 ff.), but he achieves that romantic sense of mysterious wonder by hinting at other powers, both higher and deeper, remaining in the shadow. Romance evokes awe for the world around the hero rather than for the epic dimension of his deed. In Spenser the sense of epic achievement struggles to free itself from the context of Christian romance. Romance isolates the hero from his community to exaggerate his bewildered loneliness, but Spenser's isolated heroes, in their emblematic ideality, still keep a link intact with the universal City. The pleasure of romance depends on its pure freedom from Important Issues, while epic seems naturally to adumbrate conflicts of universal resonance. *The Faerie Queene* somehow succeeds in imaging those conflicts without surrendering the delight of free invention. Mrs. Bennett notes acutely that romance depends upon surprise, moving as it does "toward an end foreseen from the beginning," whereas epic depends upon recognition, but she is surely wrong to add that "Unlike the romancers, Spenser does not surprise his reader." [28] Spenser rather leads us to an end partly foreseen via paths of his own delightful discovery. Romance contains few scenes of the kind I have called "deliberative," while epic seems to require them in regular rhythm. Spenser is chary of deliberative scenes but uses allegory to serve their function.

Both Ariosto and Tasso were occasional allegorists, but they were too "emancipated" from the Middle Ages to remain so for long. Spenser was not emancipated, and the reader who is drawn to him must make his peace with allegory, with *Spenser's* allegory, which is not always like anyone else's. To learn to read him is a

26. *Poetical Works of Edmund Spenser,* p. 628.
27. See above, Chapter 6, p. 112.
28. Bennett, *English Institute Essays,* pp. 104–05, 119.

matter of getting the feel of his mind, a feel which is not easy to acquire and very hard to describe. But you must avoid from the outset two disastrous and opposed ways of misreading him. One of these is to regard him simply as a romancer. This is Hazlitt's way: "If people do not meddle with the allegory, the allegory will not meddle with them." [29] Hazlitt was most struck with Spenser's descriptions, with his "voluptuous pathos, and languid brilliancy of fancy," and he went through the poem picking out for his readers' convenience those set passages he thought best represented it. He had an anthologizing regard for Spenser, an impressionistic hazy sense of the fable; he was bored by anything speculative, or anything like the wisdom Milton admired, but he had an acute sense of the atmosphere and tonality and imagery and what he called "sentiment." That is one misguided or fragmentary approach to *The Faerie Queene,* and the other I want to distinguish is that which misguidedly denies romance for "epic seriousness," which meddles *only* with allegory, and turns everything else into it. This approach cannot be associated with any name so distinguished as Hazlitt's, because of the two it is probably the more mistaken and dangerous. The greatest poverty, for the life of poetry as for our own, is not to live in a physical world. You must suppose that there *is* a knight pricking across the plain, a visible plain even if not much described, with a lady in a black wimple, and a dwarf, and a lamb. They really are there, and the reader must never make allowances for them and see through them to their abstractions. He would do better to close the book.

To arrive at a sounder approach we had better look at the text itself. The one conventional example of a celestial messenger's descent in *The Faerie Queene* is a brief, transitional passage, not truly representative of the poem's poetic richness. But the larger unit in which the descent appears—The Cantos of Mutabilitie [30] —forms one of the great dense nexuses of the whole work, as well as its (unintended) conclusion. These two cantos (with two stanzas of a third) are concerned with the rebellion of the Titaness Mutabilitie against the rule of Jove. Having established her dominion

29. *Complete Works, 5* (London, 1930), 38.

30. Published posthumously in what appears to be a self-contained fragment of an unfinished seventh book.

on earth, she ascends to the circle of the moon, there to claim the throne of Cynthia. When she attempts to secure the throne by violence, the earth and sky are deprived of light, and their inhabitants brought into consternation:

> Fearing least Chaos broken had his chaine,
> And brought againe on them eternall night . . .
> [VII.6.14. 6–7]

Mercury, whose planet lies closest to the moon, is particularly alarmed, but all the gods together call upon Jove for an explanation:

> All ran together with a great out-cry,
> To Joves faire Palace, fixt in heavens hight;
> And beating at his gates full earnestly,
> Gan call to him aloud with all their might,
> To know what meant that suddaine lack of light.
> The father of the Gods when this he heard,
> Was troubled much at their so strange affright,
> Doubting least Typhon were againe uprear'd,
> Or other his old foes, that once him sorely fear'd.
>
> Eftsoones the sonne of Maia forth he sent
> Downe to the Circle of the Moone, to knowe
> The cause of this so strange astonishment,
> And why shee did her wonted course forslowe;
> And if that any were on earth belowe
> That did with charmes or Magick her molest,
> Him to attache, and downe to hell to throwe:
> But, if from heaven it were, then to arrest
> The Author, and him bring before his presence prest.
>
> The winged-foot God, so fast his plumes did beat,
> That soone he came where-as the Titanesse
> Was striving with faire Cynthia for her seat:
> At whose strange sight, and haughty hardinesse,
> He wondred much, and feared her no lesse.
> Yet laying feare aside to doe his charge,

At last, he bade her (with bold stedfastnesse)
Ceasse to molest the Moone to walke at large,
Or come before high Jove, her dooings to discharge.

And there-with-all, he on her shoulder laid
His snaky-wreathed Mace, whose awfull power
Doth make both Gods and hellish fiends affraid:
Where-at the Titanesse did sternely lower,
And stoutly answer'd, that in evill hower
He bid her leave faire Cynthias silver bower;
Sith shee his Jove and him esteemed nought,
No more then Cynthia's selfe; but all their kingdoms
sought.

The Heavens Herald staid not to reply,
But past away, his doings to relate
Unto his Lord; who now in th'highest sky,
Was placed in his principall Estate,
With all the Gods about him congregate . . .

[VII.6.15–19]

The divine council is presently interrupted by the presumptuous entrance of the rebel herself, who astonishes the gods with her beauty, her disdainful rejection of their authority, and her appeal for a higher judge to arbitrate the quarrel:

. . . To the highest him, that is behight
Father of Gods and men by equall might;
To weet, the God of Nature, I appeale.

[VII.6.35]

Jove seems forced to agree, and on the appointed day Nature appears (of indeterminate sex, but now called a goddess), introduced by the poet with fervent veneration and esoteric symbolism. The Titaness discourses at length upon the extent of her dominion, but her plea is rejected in a momentous and celebrated judgment:

I well consider all that ye have sayd,
And find that all things stedfastnes doe hate
And changed be: yet being rightly wayd

They are not changed from their first estate;
But by their change their being doe dilate:
And turning to themselves at length againe,
Do worke their owne perfection so by fate:
Then over them Change doth not rule and raigne;
But they raigne over change, and doe their states main-
    taine. [VII.7.58]

In the Cantos of Mutabilitie Spenser treats most conclusively and explicitly that theme of process which unceasingly obsessed him and which was also the commonest and greatest of Elizabethan themes. Its philosophical formulation here makes so skilful and eclectic a blending of earlier systems that a host of commentators have failed to agree on its "sources." The Cantos keep their freshness—and more, their enigmatic elusiveness—in spite of their theme's familiarity, in spite of exhaustive research and a crushing burden of interpretation. They remain intrinsically difficult and, in their conclusion, characteristically ambivalent.

They are difficult in part because the debate they present hinges on *two* areas of dispute, upon both of which collectively *two* distinct judgments are made—by Nature and by the poet. It seems to me that the former of these dualities has not been sufficiently stressed. The two areas disputed by Mutabilitie and Jove are the terrestrial and celestial worlds, areas which Spenser carefully distinguishes throughout the fragment. At the opening of the action, Mutabilitie is already *de facto* suzerain on earth. From the outset of her enterprise, she has planned to subdue the whole universe (VII.6.4.1–4), but as yet she has succeeded only in the lower world:

At first, *on earth* she sought it to obtaine;
Where she such proofe and sad examples shewed
Of her great power, to many ones great paine,
That not men onely (whom she soone subdewed)
But eke all other creatures, her bad dooings rewed.

For, she the face of earthly things so changed,
That all which Nature had establisht first
In good estate, and in meet order ranged,

She did pervert, and all their statutes burst:
And all the worlds faire frame (which none yet durst
Of Gods or men to alter or misguide)
She alter'd quite, and made them all accurst
That God has blest; and did at first provide
In that still happy state for ever to abide.

. . . O pittious worke of MUTABILITIE!
By which, we all are subject to that curse,
And death in stead of life have sucked from our Nurse.
[VII.6.4–6]

Whatever the moral or legal rights of this conquest, no one is inclined to dispute it; the quarrel arises only when Mutabilitie attempts to extend it into heaven:

And now, when all the earth she thus had brought
To her behest, and thralled to her might,
She gan to cast in her ambitious thought,
T'attempt the empire of the heavens hight,
And Jove himselfe to shoulder from his right.
[VII.6.7]

The immediate point at issue is control of heaven, and thus Jove defines the quarrel in terms of an encroachment into *his* realm by an earthly power:

Harken to mee awhile yee heavenly Powers;
Ye may remember since th'Earths cursed seed
Sought to assaile the heavens eternall towers,
And to us all exceeding feare did breed:
But how we then defeated all their deed,
Yee all doe knowe, and them destroied quite;
Yet not so quite, but that there did succeed
An off-spring of their bloud, which did alite
Upon the fruitfull earth, which doth us yet despite.

Of that bad seed is this bold woman bred,
That now with bold presumption doth aspire

To thrust faire Phoebe from her silver bed,
And eke our selves from heavens high Empire . . .
[VII.6.20–21]

There is no question at this stage of Jove's power on earth. Earth, it would seem, has little to do with "heavens high Empire," and exists for Jove chiefly as a source of upstart nuisances. When presently the upstart makes her appearance, Jove immediately asks his uppermost question:

What idle errand hast thou, earths mansion to forsake?

Mutabilitie answers by reference to her mixed parentage: although her mother is Earth, her father is Titan, rightful ruler of heaven. Thus she inherits the government of both realms. But Jove denies the claims of Titan and continues to speak of Mutabilitie as a creature of earth:

Will never mortall thoughts ceasse to aspire,
In this bold sort, to Heaven claime to make,
And touch celestiall seates with earthly mire?
[VII.6.29]

Whereupon Mutabilitie appeals to the God of Nature, whose authority embraces *both* mortal and immortal, earth and heaven:

Father of Gods and men by equall might.

The trial moreover is to be attended by the inhabitants of both realms:

. . . All, both heavenly Powers, and earthly wights,
Before great Natures presence should appeare . . .
[VII.6.36]

As well those that are sprung of heavenly seed,
As those that all the other world doe fill . . .
[VII.7.3]

Thus throughout these preliminary scenes Spenser repeatedly distinguishes the two realms concerned and focuses the dispute only upon the higher.

This focus is enlarged once Mutabilitie begins to plead at the opening of the trial. Now for the first time she imputes to Jove a claim to the entire universe:

> To thee therefore of this same Jove I plaine,
> And of his fellow gods that faine to be,
> That challenge to themselves the whole worlds raign . . .
> [VII.7.15]

only to enter her own rival claim and to assert that the two realms are actually one:

> For, heaven and earth I both alike do deeme,
> Sith heaven and earth are both alike to thee;
> And, gods no more then men thou doest esteeme:
> For, even the gods to thee, as men to gods do seeme.
> [VII.7.15]

From what precedes and follows, this argument would appear to be specious. Ultimately, continues Mutabilitie, the universe is Nature's, but each "principality" belongs to her. Her ensuing demonstration of her right—i.e. of vicissitude as a universal principle—falls not surprisingly into two parts. The first, devoted to the earth . . .

> And first, the Earth (great mother of us all) . . .
> [VII.7.17]

contains an analysis of the ever-changing elements and a procession of the personified seasons, the Hours, Day and Night, and Life and Death—all creatures of this terrestrial realm. Mutabilitie concludes this first part of her discourse (VII.7.14–47) by summing up:

> . . . Wherefore, this lower world who can deny
> But to be subject still to Mutabilitie?
> [VII.7.47]

Jove interposes an objection here, revealing for the first time that he does lay claim to a kind of hegemony over earth at two removes. But he is quickly answered, and Mutabilitie proceeds to the second part of her discourse by turning upon him with the crucial question:

> Yet what if I can prove, that even yee
> Yourselves are likewise chang'd, and subject unto mee?
> [VII.7.49]

Her argument is now based on the inconstancy of the planetary courses, and secondarily on the earthly birth of Jove and Cynthia. This second part is much shorter than the first (thirty-four stanzas to six), although it is this part alone which seemingly touches upon the original point at issue. Having concluded this argument, she turns to the goddess-judge to make her final plea:

> Now judge then (O thou greatest goddesse trew!)
> According as thy selfe doest see and heare,
> And unto me addoom that is my dew;
> This is the rule of all, all being rul'd by you.
> [VII.7.56]

Nature proceeds to her verdict that all things reign over change by employing change to perfect themselves. She then addresses Mutabilitie:

> Cease therefore daughter further to aspire,
> And thee content thus to be rul'd by me:
> For thy decay thou seekst by thy desire;
> But time shall come that all shall changed bee,
> And from thenceforth, none no more change shall see.
> [VII.7.59]

The upshot of the debate hinges on the word *further*. Does Nature mean: "No longer aspire to overthrow my rule?" Nominally, Mutabilitie has never so aspired but has rather repeatedly acknowledged Nature's superior power ("That is onely dew unto thy might . . ."; ". . . all being ruled by you"). Does Nature mean that Mutabilitie aspires to overthrow her, as the embodiment of order, without realizing that this is the ultimate result of her enterprise? Or does she mean, laying stress on *thus:* "Aspire no higher than earth. Be content to remain my viceroy *here?"*

Or again: "Remain on earth. Be content to accept my verdict." The latter two alternatives would accord better with what follows. Perhaps in this passage, as in so many of Spenser's, we must accept a certain vagueness which permits the synthesis of several meanings.

In any case there is no doubt about the poet's own resolution in the following stanza, the first of the unfinished eighth canto, the penultimate stanza of the poem. The rueful melancholy of that resolution is too frequently passed over for the concluding prayer, and yet without it the prayer loses its terrible pathos. The poet is unconvinced by Mutabilitie's claim to, or rather her fitness for the celestial throne, but he is sadly convinced of her rule on earth:

> When I bethinke me on that speech whyleare,
> Of Mutability, and well it way:
> Me seemes, that though she all unworthy were
> Of the Heav'ns Rule; yet very sooth to say,
> In all things else she beares the greatest sway.
> [VII.8.1]

The first part of her discourse may have been irrelevant to the legal issue, but it is only too relevant to the poem. The metaphysical reply of Nature is little consolation to the individual in the existential desolation of his *contemptus mundi:*

> . . . Which makes me loath this state of life so tickle,
> And love of things so vaine to cast away;
> Whose flowring pride, so fading and so fickle,
> Short Time shall soon cut down with his consuming sickle.
> [VII.8.1]

At the very end of his immense poem, Spenser can no longer "find the mortal world enough," and the slow, familiar, meditative voice breaks with unwonted poignance into a final cry for deliverance:

> Then gin I thinke on that which Nature sayd,
> Of that same time when no more Change shall be,
> But stedfast rest of all things firmely stayd
> Upon the pillours of Eternity,

That is contrayr to Mutabilitie:
For, all that moveth, doth in Change delight:
But thence-forth all shall rest eternally
With Him that is the God of Sabbaoth hight:
O that great Sabbaoth God, graunt me that Sabaoths sight.
[VII.8.2]

Professor Bush writes: "In Mutability . . . the philosophic assertion of permanence behind the flux is not enough for a poet who is Christian and medieval. He turns from such cold consolation to the refuge of faith . . . In a moment of intense revulsion and spiritual insight, all things seem dross except God."[31] If faith is indeed a refuge here, it is a lonely and bitter one. For the poet has no sight of God or of that hearsay Sabbath. He invokes and he waits, but he affirms only the reality of the Titaness. If she has been checked in heaven, she never dreams of surrendering earth, and the whole fragment breathes with the energy of her vital being. Even if she aspires no *further,* her present dominion is sufficiently awesome.

Although the *Cantos* differ sharply from the rest of the poem, they also epitomize it. The authority of the title assigned to the fragmentary seventh book by its first publisher—*Of Constancy*—is uncertain. But in a larger sense this title might be assigned to each of the foregoing six books, whose nominal virtues—Holiness, Temperance, Chastity, Friendship, Justice and Courtesy—are all interpreted in terms of constancy. Underlying the fairy tale adventures against a dragon, an enchantress, a wizard, a tyrant, a monster—adventures in which good and evil are comfortably separated—underlying these is the profounder, darker, wearier conflict with vicissitude, which contains all adventures and engulfs them. That mightier antagonist is the stronger for its invisible ubiquity—like Nature, "unseene of any, yet of all beheld." It is to be found in the self, in history, in nature, in the cosmos. Against vicissitude little is achieved of true permanence: Red Cross and Arthur continue to wander; Artegall is recalled to face detraction; Calidore's Beast regains its freedom; Britomart awaits her marriage and the loss soon to follow. The motif of human insecurity is reiterated with obsessive insistence:

31. *Renaissance Tradition,* p. 122.

Blisse may not abide in state of mortall men.
[I.8.44]

Nothing is sure, that growes on earthly ground.
[I.9.11]

No earthly thing is sure. [II.9.21]

But what on earth can alwayes happie stand?
[V.3.9]

So feeble is mans state, and life unsound,
That in assurance it may never stand,
Till it dissolved be from earthly band.
[II.11.30]

Moreover the drama of each principal hero hinges upon the insecurity of his dedication. Of these six heroes (Cambell and Triamond do not merit to be ranked with them) only Britomart and Arthur remain unambiguously constant, and even Arthur's constancy is momentarily questioned (III.1.19.1–2).

By thus setting his nominal fable, with its somewhat obvious victories, against the muted but fundamental conflict with flux, Spenser resembled a poet whose work he may or may not have understood—the poet of the *Iliad.* But as a Christian Platonist he was not disposed to resolve that conflict with the heroic tragedy of the *Iliad*'s conclusion. His own resolution is presented in the Mutabilitie Cantos with significant ambivalence; a succincter, perhaps a clearer resolution might be isolated in such a stanza as the following, even though its apparent purpose is simply to indicate the hour:

By this the Northerne wagoner had set
His sevenfold teme behind the stedfast starre,
That was in Ocean waves yet never wet,
But firme is fixt, and sendeth light from farre
To all, that in the wide deepe wandring arre:
And chearefull Chaunticlere with his note shrill
Had warned once, that Phebus fiery carre

In hast was climbing up the Easterne hill,
Full envious that night so long his roome did fill.
[I.2.1]

By repeating certain images throughout the poem, Spenser endows them with accretions of meaning. A chapter could be written about each of the five great images in this stanza—the star, the ocean, the wanderer, day, and night. In particular, the image of the wanderer guided by a celestial light is so common in Spenser's poetry as to become archetypal.[32] But a very summary paradigm of these images' interrelations must suffice here. The stanza quoted presents sunrise as a reassuring, "chearefull" occurrence, instinct with the jocund bustle of Protestant zeal. But the sun in itself can neither maintain its advantage over night nor guide the wanderers. Rather the ocean and the "deepe" consist precisely of that flux which alternates day and night, good and evil, joy and sorrow, endlessly. This particular sun rises on an action which is anything but auspicious—Red Cross' misguided abandonment of Una. This day will see the beginning of his moral and literal

32. See III.1.43:

As when faire Cynthia, in darkesome night,
Is in a noyous cloud enveloped,
Where she may find the substaunce thin and light,
Breakes forth her silver beames, and her bright hed
Discovers to the world discomfited;
Of the poore traveller, that went astray,
With thousand blessings she is heried . . .

See VII.6.9:

And by her side, there ran her Page, that hight
Vesper, whom we the Evening-starre intend:
That with his Torche, still twinkling like twylight,
Her lightened all the way where she should wend,
And joy to weary wandring travailers did lend.

Epithalamion: (To Vesper) (288–91)

Fayre childe of beauty, glorious lampe of love
That all the host of heaven in rankes doost lead,
And guydest lovers through the nightes dread,
How chearefully thou lookest from above . . .

Epithalamion (409–12)

And ye high heavens, the temple of the gods,
In which a thousand torches flaming bright
Do burne, that to us wretched earthly clods,
In dreadful darknesse lend desired light . . .

See also *F.Q.*, I. Proem, 4; I.12.21.

wandering. But even when hero and heroine are reunited, when Red Cross is purged, and the dragon slain, he must continue to wander in a universe ostensibly Manichean. The dark principle of that universe is personified by Night, who appears three cantos later as a Satanically regal and awesome divinity, the "most auncient Grandmother of all." She is addressed, in a memorable phrase, as one who

> . . . sawst the secrets of the world unmade

and she is altogether magnificently sinister. In Book Three Arthur apostrophizes her in his great hymn (III.4.55–60) as the source of all suffering, evil, and death. Only the star is capable of piercing night and guiding the errant mortal, that star so firmly fixed that it remains above flux and is "in Ocean waves yet never wet." The star is the Platonic Good and the Christian God of Sabbaoth, that which dwells apart and transcends the good or evil of this world. Red Cross on the Mount of Contemplation is permitted a vision of that transcendent sphere, but not the experience of it; he must wait, as the poet waits and the reader waits. On earth he can hope at best for the sunlight of grace, the sunlight of Arthur's shield.

Thus *The Faerie Queene* is set in a divided world, a dualistic world waiting to be monistic.[33] The poem itself alternately celebrates and grieves the vicissitude it represents. But the burden of the whole is too somber to permit heroism its unwithering garland of enduring achievement. The one momentous event which the present withholds is out of human hands. The Day of Judg-

33. I had better quote the incisive remarks of C. S. Lewis on this subject, since, without refuting my own remarks, they place emphasis differently: "It is characteristic of him that the constant pressure of this day and night antithesis on his imagination never tempts him into dualism. He is impressed, more perhaps than any other poet, with the conflict of two mighty opposites—aware that our world is dualistic for all practical purposes, dualistic in all but the very last resort: but from the final heresy he abstains, drawing back from the verge of dualism to remind us by delicate allegories that though the conflict seems ultimate yet one of the opposites really contains, and is not contained by, the other. Truth and falsehood are opposed; but truth is the norm not of truth only but of falsehood also . . ." *Allegory of Love* (Oxford, 1936), pp. 314–15. This is quite true, and Lewis' ensuing examples prove it cogently. But to say it, and to know it, in Spenser's world is a little like listening to Nature's verdict; it is comforting certainly but it doesn't help one to flounder less in one's own personal situation.

ment, which d'Aubigné and Milton regarded as a settling of moral scores, meant to Spenser a period to vicissitude, a release from wandering, the advent of the star. Until that day, until "the stedfast rest of all things firmely stayd Upon the pillours of Eternity," all victories will appear as pseudo-victories, for they stand to evil as morning stands to evening. Despite appearances and the scholastic verdict of Nature, the mongrel Titaness is the true victress of the poem, and the time of her fall is not yet.

iv.

The stanza form which Spenser contrived, and which has earned him deserved praise, influenced inevitably the syntax and the style of his poem. In three obvious ways his stanza differs from the *ottava rima* of his models: it is longer; its rhyme scheme is more intricate; its last line is a foot longer than the others, and so more final. The effect of these innovations is first of all to isolate the stanza, to make of it much more of a separate, self-contained thing. The *ottava rima,* by its very flexibility and simplicity, its failure to call attention to itself, is far better adapted to narrative. It adjusts itself to two sentences as well as to one, and if the poet chooses to continue a sentence into the following stanza (as Ariosto and Tasso do, to say nothing of Pulci) that liberty does not really violate the form. But in Spenser the syntactic unit—the sentence—tends to be fitted to the prosodic unit—the stanza. Occasionally Spenser fits two sentences into a single stanza, but he is invariable in ending the stanza with a full stop. I should say also that he places some other mark of punctuation after many more lines than the Italians do.

The effect of these changes is to render Spenser's syntax more complex and more sinuous, to slow the reader's pace as he moves through a maze of clauses, and to create a faint sense of release when he finds his way to the last line's tranquil resolution. The slowness and sinuosity of his style, and the soft melancholy of his falling rhythms, suggest that image of wandering which is almost essential to romance and certainly to *The Faerie Queene.* But the last line, which is often syntactically independent or partly independent, and prosodically distinct, seems to re-establish a momentary order. The syntax is quite different from the "improvisational" syntax of d'Aubigné, who was confined by no stanza form at all, because Spenser's sentences must always be rounded off neatly at the foreseen moment. But before that end, his syntax is likely to be open, loose, asymmetrical, and repetitive.

Consider for example the stanza in which Jove despatches Mercury:

> Eftsoones the sonne of Maia forth he sent
> Downe to the Circle of the Moone, to knowe
> The cause of this so strange astonishment,
> And why shee did her wonted course forslowe;
> And if that any were on earth belowe
> That did with charmes or Magick her molest,
> Him to attache, and downe to hell to throwe:
> But, if from heaven it were, then to arrest
> The Author, and him bring before his presence prest.
>
> [VII.6.16]

The main verb is *sent,* but five other verbs depend upon it as vague infinitives of purpose—*knowe, attache, throwe, arrest, bring.* Of these the last four appear in the closing three lines of the stanza, separated from the main verb by six or more lines, and by the semicolon in line four. A second semicolon in line seven separates off the last two infinitives still further. The objects of the infinitive *to knowe*—a noun and a clause—are related in an awkward, nonparallel coupling, to say nothing of their redundancy. Moreover the *if* clause in the following line is briefly confusing because one expects it to be parallel to the *why* clause above it (instead of modifying *attache*). The *if* clause contains a further subordinate clause (line six) which increases the complexity. Finally the reference of the pronoun *it* in line seven is a little mystifying, given the use of *him* in line six; *it* must probably be referred to *cause* in line three, but the reader is unlikely to grasp the reference immediately. Spenser's use of pronouns is repeatedly vague. Of course he was in part reflecting the looser syntax of his age, but he is consistently and outstandingly loose even among his contemporaries.

These features of Spenser's style influence his poem in two

important ways. First of all the tangled and circular sentence structure, together with the melancholy and deliberation of his manner, deprive his language of that puissant energy which is common to most epic poetry. To say this is not to disparage Spenser, but it is to limit the kind of experience his poem affords. Subtle and seductive his language is, but it lacks the virile directness and natural force which inform even those great epics born of artificial, aristocratic tradition. This lack modifies whatever heroic achievement *The Faerie Queene* contains.

The second influence is more difficult to describe, but it leads to a quality which is basic to the poem and which is insidiously ubiquitous. This is the *blurring* of Spenser's language and even of his mind. To demonstrate it, I would begin by pointing to his use of the conjunction *and.* We have already seen how, in the stanza quoted above, the *and* in the fourth line connects two nonparallel elements, and in the fifth appears to connect clauses while in fact it connects infinitives. Analogously, in the line

> At whose strange sight and haughty hardinesse

the *and* connects two nouns which do not quite fit one another. *Hardinesse,* meaning *effrontery,* is a moral quality. But by "strange sight" Spenser means something altogether different—not simply "strange appearance," because Mutabilitie is later described as beautiful; her very being there is strange, and her untoward set-to with Cynthia. Thus *sight* and *hardinesse* are not coupled without wrenching. But the coupling does not lack a certain logic. The strangeness and the hardiness make up a single experience of Mercury, muddled together in his mind as they are in the reader's. Nothing is more typical of Spenser—in treating large elements as well as these minuscule ones—than the muddling together of the slightly unlike, the dissolution of contours, the blurring of meaning, the sacrifice of precision to the larger, vaguer aura. Today such a sacrifice is unfashionable, but I fear it cannot better be defended than by pointing to such an example as *The Faerie Queene.* If it seems to you unpardonable, then you had better give Spenser up.

We have already encountered an analogous sort of blurring in the ambiguity of the Mutability Cantos' conclusion. But in other respects it operates from their opening—for example in the associations we are led to attach to the major figures. Jove is partly the god of Homer and Hesiod, partly the planet, partly the principle of order in the celestial universe, and perhaps a little bit the Christian God. But then that God also appears as a separate power —the God of Sabbaoth—in the final stanza. He also enters into the figure of Nature through a simile (VII.7.7) which compares her to the transfigured Christ. God "enters into" the conception of Nature, but she cannot be equated with Him as simply as Lewis suggests; [34] the imagery connects her with the great Venus of Book Four, and thus with Lucretius' Venus; she has something of Concord as well, and the Nature of Alanus ab Insulis, whom Spenser names, and perhaps the Nature of Cicero. In the neo-Platonic scheme she is equivalent to the Anima, the World-Soul, which imparts form and being to matter.[35] Her most recent incarnation is in Joyce's ALP, the "Annyma" of *Finnegans Wake.* But above and beyond all these equivalences, she is the great mythical divinity of Spenser's own seventh book, evoking now one and now another of her counterparts, but remaining her own integral self through the continuity of her name and presence in the action.[36]

The most distinctive, the most original and inimitable quality of the whole poem lies in this perpetual *becoming* of its characters. Just as the associations of Nature shift, just as Mutabilitie is partly the Titaness daughter of Earth, partly Mary Stuart chal-

34. Op. cit., pp. 355–56.

35. See Josephine Waters Bennett, "Spenser's Venus and the Goddess Nature of the *Cantos of Mutabilitie," SP, 30* (1933), 160–92.

36. See the excellent introduction of Henry G. Lotspeich to his *Classical Mythology in the Poetry of Edmund Spenser,* Princeton Studies in English, *9* (1932). Lotspeich writes: "Spenser . . . does not have the habit of making clear distinctions. Rather, his mind seems to have been of a kind which synthesizes without analyzing, which tends to break down distinctions and to fuse together things originally separate" (p. 23). He writes later of Spenser's Venus: "She has an earthly house and a heavenly house. She is physical and spiritual, a symbol large enough to include within herself . . . elements and ideas assembled from the Roman elegists, from Lucretius, from Plato and Neo-Platonism, from medieval courtly love, and from the poet's own realization of fruitfulness and beauty, physical and spiritual, in the world and in human life. And this many-sidedness is possible because Spenser is using Venus as a mythological symbol. Without the mythology, such a synthesis would not have been achieved" (pp. 25–26).

lenging Cynthia-Elizabeth, partly the Christian Satan who introduced original sin, partly a natural principle, partly a philosophic doctrine, so the status and meaning and concreteness of all the manifold figures of the poem shift and fade and recombine. The Red Cross Knight is now Holiness, now simply a holy man, now Leicester, now Saint George, now Everyman, now the typical errant Christian, now Christ himself, or most commonly some fusion of several of these, so that one needs perpetually to take a cross-section in order to apprehend him. Elsewhere, moreover, he is none of these; he is merely the individual, Red Cross, whom we know as we know any other individual in fiction. Modern allegorical reading of Spenser has remained regrettably faithful to such eighteenth-century editors as Upton and such nineteenth-century critics as Ruskin, men whose contributions were valuable but who foisted upon their author those habits of mind characteristic of their times, habits which suit Spenser very badly. It was the eighteenth century which really fixed most of the static allegorical labels on Spenser's characters and led his readers to believe in them. It is time now to return his allegory to its own century, to that Protean changefulness, that volatile subtlety conjunct with syncretic naïveté I have already mentioned. Fortunately some recent critics have begun to throw off the neoclassic rigidity of two centuries' interpretation.[37]

Many vexed problems of Spenserian scholarship disappear at a stroke if we regard the characters as constantly gaining or losing moral and political and metaphysical meaning, turning into something different just as we think we grasp them. Considered in this way, a name like Red Cross or Britomart or Mutabilitie is not so much an arrow pointing to a single, familiar concept or quality or concrete universal; it is rather a cloak which provides the illusion of continuous essence, while behind it proceeds a ceaseless

37. See W. B. C. Watkins, *Shakespeare and Spenser* (Princeton, 1950): "It is impossible to make any lengthy allegory conform to strict, unqualified definition. Just as poetic intensity varies in any long poem, so allegorical significance will vary—now explicit, now implicit; now close to the abstract, now so concrete as to be lost to sight. Being dynamic, allegory is constantly changing before our eyes; it ebbs and flows . . ." (p. 125). See also Harry Berger, Jr., *The Allegorical Temper* (New Haven, 1957), esp. pp. 161–207, and M. Pauline Parker, *The Allegory of The Faerie Queene* (Oxford, 1960), especially pp. 34 ff.

transmutation. The reader's problem is to intuit what the cloak covers at any given point, without dragging the intuition with him if later it seems no longer to serve. He must pack it away somewhere without altogether discarding it, in case it will be needed again, perhaps in conjunction with other intuitions. Above all he should tread lightly, intuit delicately, never pounce, and never cling. For some minor characters, a single intuition, a single "meaning," may see one through their respective adventures, but this is not always true of the minor characters and never of the major ones. Those who change least are those who move least through space, those like Caelia and Phaedria and Malecasta who are anchored allegorically to a single place.

If this approach is valid, it follows that the names of the characters are of great importance. As Archimago appears and reappears under various guises, embodying no trait he does not share with others, the most constant and distinguishing thing about him is his name. It is well that *that* does not change, or we should be in danger of losing him altogether. It is well that we know from the outset Fidessa's true name to be Duessa.

The Faerie Queene is a ballet of images, motifs, situations, allusions, and characters woven and interwoven in ever-changing patterns, never altogether constant and never altogether new, "eterne in mutabilitie." The poet himself gives the key to his method in the letter to Raleigh, when he explains that Elizabeth figures in his poem as "two persons, the one of a most royall Queene or Empresse, the other of a most vertuous and beautifull Lady." The eighteenth century never could have conceived of "shadowing" Elizabeth as both Gloriana and Belphoebe. Spenser does not add that he shadows her in other characters too—in Mercilla, in Tanaquill, in Una, and in the Cynthia of the Mutabilitie Cantos. The shadow of Elizabeth hovers around each corner of the poem, finding partial embodiment here and there, apostrophized in the Proems, transvalued in numberless ways, but never fully and definitively realized any more than that Sabbaoth which is to dispel all shadows. Just as the fictive characters are fragmented into parts, so the historical figure is fragmented into characters.

Spenser's technique can best be understood in terms of the neo-

Platonic hierarchy as distinct from the Christian hierarchy. In the latter, the correspondences do not blur the reality of each plane. The king of a realm may "correspond" to the head in relation to the body, to reason in relation to the soul, to the sun in relation to the cosmos, and so on, but he remains nonetheless quite unmistakably and solidly a king. The symbolism of medieval Scriptural interpretation regarded many events of the Old Testament as prefiguring those of the New in mysterious configurations, but it did not for this diminish the historical factuality of the Old Testament. In medieval realism, analogues tend rather to reinforce the fitness of each thing for its place, its distinctiveness and importance, in a universe of sharp contours and neat categories. But in a neo-Platonic hierarchy the levels of reality tend to blur below one as one mounts. Spenser writes in the *Hymne in Honour of Love:*

> Such is the powre of that sweet passion,
> That it all sordid baseness doth expell,
> And the refyned mynd doth newly fashion
> Unto a fairer forme, which now doth dwell
> In his high thought . . . [190–94]

The new form edges out the old one. Similarly the ultimate reality on the highest level is blurred and faint before one reaches it. Wherever one stands upon the ladder, the levels above one are indistinct, and the things below are too contemptible to matter much as distinct entities. They never disappear altogether but they fade, fall out of focus, or are subsumed. Spenser's allegory is far from closed to the orthodox conception, but it is deeply influenced by the neo-Platonic. As it rises and falls from one level to another, the other levels tend to hover, as it were, a little out of focus.

It is hard to ascribe Spenser's technique either to artistic naïveté alone or to a subtle self-consciousness. Both perhaps contribute to his profound but easily overlooked originality. For of all the great poems which achieve epic amplitude, *The Faerie Queene* is one of the freest of convention. It contains scores of conventional passages, but it is superbly untrammeled by them. This freedom is precisely the opposite of the reader's first impression, because the poem first *looks* as though it were rigidly conventional. But in this respect too it is Protean; it moves boldly up and down the hierarchy of genres. It requires a bit of reading to discover that Spenser's bow to decorum is the emptiest of rituals; he makes his rules and chooses his modes, altering them as suits his absolute pleasure.[38] Thus *The Faerie Queene* is a much more unpredictable poem than one expects, and so much more delightful. With familiarity one becomes attuned to Spenser's fancy and grasps the harmony beneath the apparent disorder. But the principle of continuity is a living, internal force, scarcely to be articulated. The Mutabilitie Cantos are a quintessence of all of Spenser, but they also constitute an abruptly new beginning.

The only literary work whose organization remotely resembles *The Faerie Queene*'s is that whose heroine I have already called Spenserian—*Finnegans Wake*. Joyce, like Spenser, wrote a dream vision of history, fitting the techniques of metamorphosis and transvaluation and fragmentation to the operations of the liberated fancy, liberated in the one case by allegory as in the other by sleep. Both heightened the vision with experimentally evocative and unfamiliar language. Joyce's theme was identical with Spenser's —the nature of historical process, and each treated it with that mingling of courage and resignation which imitates the profoundest responses to life. Each sweetened his orthodox Aristotelian heritage with a measure of Plato or of Plato's wayward stepchild, Giordano Bruno.[39] The one had had a lover's quarrel with Ireland

38. "L'allégorie chez lui enfle les proportions hors de toute règle, et soustrait la fantasie à toute loi, excepté au besoin d'accorder les formes et les couleurs. Car, si les esprits ordinaires reçoivent de l'allégorie un poids qui les opprime, les grandes imaginations reçoivent de l'allégorie des ailes qui les emportent. Dégagées par elle des conditions ordinaires de la vie, elles peuvent tout oser, en dehors de l'imitation, par delà la vraisemblance, sans autre guide que leur force native et leurs instincts obscurs." Taine, *Histoire de la Littérature Anglaise,* quoted in the Variorum Spenser, *2,* ed. Greenlaw et. al. (Baltimore, 1934), p. 250.

39. Joyce's interest in Bruno and Bruno's importance in *Finnegans Wake* are well-known. Spenser's interest in him is less demonstrable, although we know that Bruno was in contact with Sidney during his English stay, and dedicated to him two major works. One of these, the *Spaccio de la Bestia Trionfante,* contains suggestive but inconclusive parallels with the Mutabilitie Cantos. If Spenser knew Bruno's work, it is unlikely that he fully understood it, and he certainly did not reflect it unmodified. But on the other hand Bruno

and the other felt for her an enemy's affection. Both made parables of the simplest things: earth, water, and sky, day and night, seasons, years, and generations, drawing their evasive wisdom from the gnomic circles of nature. Both celebrated a marriage of waters, and the sweet joy of the Medway's bridal day anticipates the Liffey's wearier union, "rolling down the lea" to her perpetual and renewing death. Only their tone is different: the tragic gaiety of *Finnegans Wake* in its roguish astringency sounds in harsher consonance than Spenser's untremulous serenity.

---

was the thinker of Spenser's age who dealt most systematically with the age-old problems that preoccupied him. It would have been natural for Spenser to read him and inevitable that, once having begun, he be interested. See Oliver Elton, "Giordano Bruno in England," *Modern Studies* (London, 1907); Ronald B. Levinson, "Spenser and Bruno," *PMLA, 43* (1928), 675 ff.; B. E. C. Davis, *Edmund Spenser* (Cambridge, 1933), pp. 232 ff.

11. SAINT-AMANT AND FRENCH NEO-CLASSICISM

The early seventeenth century in France produced little epic poetry; neither the taste for extravagance and buffoonery nor the taste for preciosity and refinement was conducive to that nobly decorous elevation which was increasingly associated with epic. But as the classical spirit grew stronger, as criticism gained self-consciousness, as the shadow of Aristotle lengthened and the example of Corneille's drama sobered and "ennobled" the literary consciousness, epic poetry gained a popularity which the harassed historian can hardly bring himself to applaud. The dam really broke in the sixth decade of the century, but of the twenty or thirty long poems produced in the ensuing decades, scarcely two are readable. This deluge can be channeled artificially into two streams—those based on Biblical or apocryphal stories (Lesfargues' *David,* Coras' *Ionas,* Desmarets' *Esther*) and those based on post-Biblical history or legend (Le Moine's *Saint Louis,* Scudéry's *Alaric,* Chapelain's *La Pucelle*). The division is artificial because the two streams are one in their pompous, rigid, tediously correct style and their sterile invention. The mice born of these laboring mountains are not even alive.

The only poem to escape even partially this common disaster is the gentlest and quietest of epics—the *Moyse Sauvé* of Saint-Amant. It is an unlikely poem from the pen of this roistering, ill-educated *bon vivant,* drinking companion to nobility, libertine connoisseur of low-life color, whose shorter poems mingle the grotesque, the sensual, the meditative, and the bizarre into curiously harmonious patterns. His longest poem has not received even the inadequate attention accorded the shorter ones,[1] and I am aware that this heroic idyll—*idyle heroïque,* as its author described it—will not appeal to many tastes, will seem in actuality the contradiction which that descriptive title suggests. And it will seem dull to boot. It must be read, I submit, in a very quiet place, with a quiet mind and heart, that the delicate shadings of tone and language be distinguished. Even thus, I fear that only a few will admire its refined whimsy, its mild irony, its genial preciosity. It is scarcely the poem for our own dishevelled times, and many will think that the dryer passages, which are interspersed with the felicitous ones, are too frequent and too long.

Saint-Amant's Preface to his poem belongs to that small class of prefaces which say something important about the work they introduce. The poet there records his belief, reflected in the poem, in the difficulty of writing verse well without knowing music and painting; he speaks of his attraction to small and modest things:

> La pluspart du temps je ne m'amuse à faire que des bouquets de simples fleurs tirées de mon propre parterre; la description des moindres choses est de mon appanage particulier.[2]

1. See, however, the essay of Remy de Gourmont in *Promenades Littéraires,* 3me série (Paris, 1916). Gourmont writes: "De tous les grands poèmes français modernes, le *Moïse Sauvé* est le seul qui ait gardé quelque fraîcheur"; and again: "C'est, en somme, le plus grand effort poétique, de Ronsard à Victor Hugo" (pp. 223–24).

2. All quotations from Saint-Amant are taken from the *Oeuvres Complètes,* ed. C. L. Livet (Paris, 1855). This passage appears in vol. 2, p. 143. "Most of the time I amuse myself merely in making bouquets of common flowers culled from my own plot; the description of the smallest things is my special prerogative."

He refers with confidence to his recent radical revisions without seeming to notice the structural awkwardness for which they are apparently to be blamed. He defends his use of the phrase *idyle heroïque:*

> Je sçay ce que demande l'epopée. Je n'ay ni principal heros agissant, ni grandes batailles, ni sieges de villes à produire; mon ouvrage n'est que d'un jour entier, au lieu qu'il faut que l'epique soit d'un an ou environ. Le luth y eclatte plus que la trompette; le lyrique en fait la meilleure partie, et neantmoins, comme presque tous les personnages que j'y represente sont non seulement heroiques, mais saints et sacrez; comme . . . j'ose y representer Dieu mesme en sa gloire et en sa magnificence . . . je croy que quand je luy aurois donné le titre de divin, il y auroit eu plus de justice que de presomption à le faire.[3]

He seems to believe, or pretends to believe, that the sacred is an extension of the heroic, and thus justifies a poem which remembers intermittently the epic tradition but whose most vivid combat pits two shepherds against a crocodile. The phrase he applies to a fishing expedition could serve for most of the violence in the poem:

> Une guerre sans coup, sans desordre, sans bruit . . . [4]

Elsewhere the Preface asserts an independence of Aristotle on the one hand:

> Sans m'arrester tout à fait aux regles des anciens, que je revere toutesfois et que je n'ignore pas, m'en faisant de toutes nouvelles à moy-mesme, à cause de la nouveauté de l'invention, j'ay jugé que la seule raison me seroit une authorité assez puissante pour les soutenir; car, en effet, pourveu qu'une

3. 2, 140. "I know what the epic requires. I can produce no central hero in action, nor great battles, nor sieges of cities; my poem takes up no more than a full day, whereas the epic needs approximately a year. The lute sounds through it more than the trumpet; the greater part of it is lyric; and yet, since almost all the characters I introduce in it are not only heroic but holy and sacred; since . . . I dare to represent God Himself in his glory and magnificence . . . I think that even if I had given it the title of *divine,* there would have been more justice than presumption in so doing.

4. 2, 250. "A war without blows, without tumult, without noise."

> chose soit judicieuse, et qu'elle convienne aux personnes, aux lieux et aux temps, qu'importe qu'Aristote l'ait ou ne l'ait pas approuvée? [5]

and of binding fidelity to Scripture on the other hand:

> Si, selon quelque Peres, l'histoire de Job n'est qu'une parabole sainctement inventée par Moyse mesme . . . il semble qu'il me doit bien estre permis d'inventer quelque chose dans la sienne . . . Au reste, autre chose est d'escrire en historien, autre chose est d'escrire en poëte . . . Qui osteroit la fiction à la poesie lui osteroit tout.[6]

Saint-Amant admits his heavy reliance on the Jewish historians Josephus and Philo, who introduced new incidents and characters into the reticent Biblical account of Moses' early life; but he leaves it to the reader to discover how profoundly he has altered the Biblical tone in filling out details and episodes, how he has softened and domesticated the Pentateuch at the expense of awe and terror. He invokes the example of Sannazaro (compared to whom his liberties are venial) for the use of pagan proper names applied to Hebraic-Christian places and personages, and goes on to pronounce himself on the central thorny issue created by the Christian epic:

> Comme certaines estoffes, pour avoir esté tissues par des mains payennes, ne laissent pas d'estre employées à l'embellissement des autels chrestiens, ainsi se peut-on servir de tout ce que l'antiquité a laissé de rare et de beau pour le convertir en un usage saint et legitime.[7]

5. *2*, 140. "Without subscribing altogether to the rules of the ancients, which I nonetheless revere and of which I am not ignorant, I have made quite new rules for myself, because of the novelty of the fiction, judging that reason alone would be authority sufficiently strong to defend them; for, indeed, if a thing be judicious and if it conform to the characters, places, and times, what does it matter whether Aristotle approved it or not?"

6. *2*, 141. "If, according to certain Fathers, the story of Job is only a parable devoutly composed by Moses himself . . . it would seem that I should be permitted to invent something in telling his story . . . Moreover, it is one thing to write as an historian, another thing to write as a poet . . . Whoever denied fiction to poetry would deny it everything."

7. *2*, 142. "Just as certain cloths, even if woven by pagan hands, are still used to embellish Christian altars, so one can use whatever antiquity has left that is precious and beautiful in order to convert it to a sacred and legitimate end."

In fact, neither the Christian nor the classical spirit colors Saint-Amant's sensibility very strongly; he pays his respects to each, but he really constitutes an individual, somewhat isolated, even eccentric presence in literary history, who invoked tradition only when he truly needed it and could absorb it. More familiar with the modern languages—Italian, Spanish, and English—than with Latin and Greek, he introduced an independent and modern transformation of the epic tradition, but his work remained without successors and without influence.

The celestial descent in *Moyse Sauvé* is introduced by an episode of a questionable Marinistic taste unusual for Saint-Amant. The infant Moses, hidden in his ark among the reeds bordering the Nile, is assailed by a tempest engendered by hostile demons. His mother Jocabel, driven at first to hysterical terror for her child, is reassured by a divine portent, regains her composure, prays heaven for forgiveness, and sheds tears of remorse. Her tears are caught by an angel who bears them to heaven in a golden vase and presents them at the throne of God. There they are miraculously transformed into a liquor to sustain the abandoned infant, and as one angel is dispatched to succor him, another is sent to the allegorical personage Calme to command an end to the tempest. I omit the scene in heaven, in which Saint-Amant is derivative and ill at ease, and cite only the descent itself with its ensuing descriptions. After a modified version of a simile which we recognize only too readily, Saint-Amant chooses to follow the second angel and to imitate Ariosto's fusion of two ancient and distinct conventions: [8]

Comme au plus beau des nuits, à ce qu'à l'oeil il semble,[9]
Deux astres destachez partent du ciel ensemble,
L'un à droit, l'autre à gauche, et d'un chemin divers
Precipitent leur cours en ce bas univers
Ainsy des deux courriers, qu'un beau devoir embrase,
L'un tire vers l'Egipte avec le riche vase,

8. See above, Chap. 3, pp. 26–27.

9. VI, 236–38. In this and the following verse quotations from *Moyse Sauvé* the roman numeral indicates the book, the arabic numeral the page number of Livet, vol. 2.

"As when, at the most beautiful time of night, it seems to the eye that two distinct stars leave the sky together, one to the right, the other to the left, and hasten their course to this lower universe by different paths, so one of

Et l'autre va trouver, d'un vol au sien pareil,
Le paisible demon qu'adore le sommeil.
 Il n'a pas un moment sillonné sur la nue,
Qu'il arrive en une isle aux mortels inconnue,
Où, bien loin des objets ennemis du repos,
Au sein d'un antre obscur, antre fait à propos
Par les puissantes mains qui formerent le monde,
Le Calme se retire, à l'instant que de l'onde
Les tyrans des vaisseux, d'un souffle impetueux,
Changent la face unie en monts tumultueux . . .
 Là, sur un trosne d'algue et de mousse et d'esponges,
Cet amy du silence et du pere des songes
Parloit avec effroy de l'orage excité
A ses soeurs la Bonace et la Tranquillité.
Là, ces aymables soeurs, pareilles à luy-mesme,
Taschans à r'ajuster son rare diadême,
Fait par leurs propres doigts de plumes d'alcions,
Montroyent de leur amour les tendres passions,
Quand le courrier divin, s'avançant dans la grotte,
Par l'honneur chevelu qui sur ses ailes flotte,
Par l'eclat de ses yeux et par le vestement
Dont son corps immortel s'ornoit augustement,
Dissippa l'ombre humide, illumina la voye,
Remplit tout de respect, de merveille et de joye.

---

the two couriers, fired by his noble mission, proceeds toward Egypt with the rich vase, and the other seeks in similar flight the peaceable spirit worshipped by sleep.

He has scarcely streaked through the cloud an instant when he arrives at an isle unknown to mortals, where, far from all things inimical to rest, in the heart of a dark cavern, a cavern expressly created by the powerful hands that shaped the world, Calm retires, the moment that the tyrannous lords of ships alter the even face of the wave into tumultuous hills with their impetuous breath . . .

There, seated on a throne of kelp and moss and sponges, this friend of silence and of the father of dreams spoke with terror of the aroused tempest to his sisters, Quiet and Tranquillity. There, these kind sisters, just like their brother, were trying to readjust his precious diadem, made from kingfishers' wings by their own hands, and so were revealing the tenderness of their love, when the divine courier, penetrating the grotto, by the glorious locks floating above his wings, by the radiance of his eyes, and by the garb majestically adorning his immortal body, dissipated the damp shadows, brightened his path, and filled all the place with respect, wonder, and joy . . .

The angel briefly communicates his commands and we are given a charming account of their execution:

. . . le Calme et ses compagnes
Prennent soudain leur vol sur les molles campagnes;
L'ange brille à la teste, et des flots applanis
Les vents seditieux aussi-tost sont bannis;
Zephyre et le beau temps, suivant leur course ailée,
D'un branle agile et doux rasent l'onde salée,
Desembarrassent l'air de nuages espais,
Et de leurs doigts serains partout sement la pais.
Les nageurs escaillez, ces sagettes vivantes
Que nature empenna d'ailes sous l'eau mouvantes,
Montrent avec plaisir en ce clair appareil
L'argent de leur eschine à l'or du beau soleil.
Enfin l'ange et sa trouppe en un moment se rendent
Sur la terre où du Nil les rivages s'estendent;
Borée, à leur abord de l'Egipte chassé,
S'en retourne en prison sous le pole glacé;
Le fleuve est un estang qui dort au pié des palmes
De qui l'ombre, plongée au fond des ondes calmes,
Sans agitation semble se rafraischir,
Et de fruits naturels le cristal enrichir;
Le firmament s'y voit, l'astre du jour y roule;

Calm and his companions suddenly take their flight over the fluid plains; the angel gleams at their head, and the seditious winds are immediately banished from the smoothened billows; Zephyr and fair weather, following their winged course, skim the salt wave with agile and gentle movements, clear the air of thick clouds, and disseminate peace everywhere with serene fingers. The scaly swimmers, those living arrows that nature endowed with wings beneath the water, display with pleasure the silver of their backs to the gold of the beautiful sun amidst this bright scene. Finally the angel and his troop reach in an instant the land where the banks of the Nile extend. Boreas, driven from Egypt by their approach, returns to his prison under the frozen pole; the river is a pool sleeping at the foot of the palms whose shadows, sunk to the bottom of the calm stream, seem to cool themselves without movement, and enrich the crystal water with natural fruits; the whole firmament can be seen in it; the luminary of the day passes through it, admiring himself and glittering in this flowing mirror; and the hosts of the air, in their various plumage, flying from one side to the other swim in it upside down."

Il s'admire, il eclate en ce miroir qui coule,
Et les hostes de l'air, aux plumages divers,
Volans d'un bord à l'autre, y nagent à l'envers . . .

I abbreviate the entire passage with some regret.

One is first struck by the mannered style which gives so much place to the circumlocutions endemic in an age of preciosity. If the English metaphysical style tends to remain at the "substantive level," the level of common, unqualified names for things,[10] the *précieux* style tends to hover one or two levels of generality higher. The sun is "l'astre du jour"; the birds are

les hostes de l'air, aux plumages divers . . .

the fish are

Les nageurs escaillez, ces sagettes vivantes
Que nature empenna d'ailes sous l'eau mouvantes . . .

the tempestuous winds are "les tyrans des vaisseaux"; Calme himself is

Le paisible demon qu'adore le sommeil.

This periphrastic generality is a constant feature of the poem's style; it is much more striking here than in most of Saint-Amant's shorter pieces. It can be tiresome and colorless, as the phrase "l'astre du jour" is colorless, but to those with a taste for it, the finer examples constitute part of the poem's seductiveness. Moses' ark is placed

Dans la verte espaisseur de ces fragiles plantes
Qui poussoyent hors du Nil leurs testes chancelantes.[11]

The serpent into which Moses' rod is changed appears as

. . . un beau monstre affreux
Qui, traisnant lentement ses jeunes flancs poudreux,
Laisse sur le sablon une trace ondoyante,

10. W. K. Wimsatt, "The Substantive Level," in *The Verbal Icon* (University of Kentucky Press, 1954), pp. 133–51.

11. I, 163. "In the green density of these fragile plants which raised their nodding heads from the Nile."

Aiguise sa prunelle obscure et flamboyante,
Hausse le noble orgueil de son chef couronné . . .[12]

Pharaoh's daughter amuses herself with her swans:

Qu'elle sentoit son ame et ses peines charmées
Lorsque ces beaux vogueurs à voiles emplumées
Se laissoyent emporter, au gré des dous zephirs,
Sur le paisible eclat des liquides saphirs!
Mais avec quels propos son aise exprimeray-je
Lors qu'elle contemploit cette vivante neige
Flotter sans se dissoudre et venir privement
Exiger de sa main l'heur de quelque aliment? [13]

or prepares to bathe:

Telle que le pinceau fabuleux et prophane
Depeint auprès de l'onde une belle Diane,
Quand, au retour des bois où ses pas mensongers
Suivent les pas craintifs des animaux legers,
Elle s'en vient noyer sa chaleur et sa peine
Dans l'humide plaisir d'une claire fontaine,
Et veut qu'en mesme temps toutes les vierges soeurs
Plongent leur lassitude en ses fresches douceurs.
Telle apparut la nimphe avecques ses pucelles . . .[14]

In descriptions like these, French poetry is enriched by a quiet but distinctive and mature art which no other French poet has quite contrived, and which is unthinkable in any other language.

The periphrastic style affects deeply the tone and pace of the

12. IV, 202. "A beautiful and horrific monster which, slowly dragging his dusty young sides along, leaves an undulating track behind him on the sand, sharpens his dark and flaming eye, raises the noble pride of his crowned head."

13. X, 294. "How her soul and her cares were charmed when these beautiful vessels with winged sails let themselve be blown over the peaceful sheen of the sapphire liquid at the will of the gentle zephyrs! But in what terms shall I express her delight when she beheld this living snow float without dissolving and come covertly to exact the good fortune of some nourishment from her hand?"

14. XII, 315–16. "As the fabulous and pagan brush portrays a beautiful Diana by the water when, at her return from the wood where her deceptive steps follow the fearful steps of agile beasts, she proceeds to drown her warmth and fatigue in the moist pleasure of a clear fountain, and has her virgin sisters plunge their lassitude as well in its cool delights; thus appeared the nymph with her maidens."

whole poem. For in this elegant cultivation of the ornate, this leisurely retardation, this decorative and aristocratic artifice, periphrasis is the graceful toy of a suavely untroubled quietude, examining without hurry its own picturesque fancies. And this quietude, it seems to me, is the secret subject of *Moyse Sauvé*. Le Calme, "cet amy du silence et du pere des songes," appears only in this one episode, but he is the true reigning divinity of the poem, and this finely detailed landscape with its ideal serenity, far from constituting an irrelevant excrescence, serves as the still point at the heart of the gently turning whole. For Saint-Amant succeeds in metamorphosing the severe and terrible stories of his sources into a celebration of pastoral tranquillity, wherein the strongest feelings less often find their way to heaven than they remain below to cling to a husband or wife, a brother, a pretty shepherdess, or a son. He is only affecting when he paints the quietest sentiments, the half-disclosed, the banal; everywhere else he remains without his story, and we with him, as connoisseurs to savor its cool delight.

All of the threats to tranquillity in this pastel Palestine serve to heighten the ensuing pleasure of rediscovered security. This is not perhaps completely true of the more serious threats which occur in the various interwoven stories—the stories of Jacob, of Joseph, of Moses' maturity. But it is true of those occurring in the main narrative, which moves from the infant's concealment in the morning to his discovery the same evening; for these are only minature threats—from a crocodile, a tempest, a swarm of wasps, and a vulture—threats the more empty in view of preceding celestial assurances of protection. The reader is not aroused to serious concern but he participates in the naïve joy which follows the pseudo-perils. This joy without real fear, this relief without danger is precisely, I imagine, what the poet intended. It reappears a little modified in two of his best known shorter poems, *La Solitude* and *Le Contemplateur,* poems which play with the dangerous and the macabre to titillate one's nerves and increase the delicious sense of safety. He writes in *La Solitude:*

> Tantost, sortant de ces ruines,
> Je monte au haut de ce rocher,
> Dont le sommet semble chercher

En quel lieu se font les bruïnes;
Puis je descends tout à loisir,
Sous une falaise escarpée,
D'où je regarde avec plaisir
L'onde qui l'a presque sappée
Jusqu'au siege de Palemon,
Fait d'esponges et de limon.[15]

The key phrase *tout à loisir* underscores the careless ease with which the poet skirts his annihilation, under the cliff *presque sappée,* and leads to the pleasure of the next stanza:

Que c'est une chose agreable
D'estre sur le bord de la mer,
Quand elle vient à se calmer
Après quelque orage effroyable! [16]

In *Le Contemplateur* the toying with danger climaxes with a vision of the day of judgment, followed by a prayer, less than impassioned, for exemption from the hideous torments of the damned. The prayer is a spiritual equivalent to the calm after the storm of *Moyse Sauvé.*

An esthetic equivalent to these effects is the interest in ugliness, or rather in the beauty within ugliness. There is already a touch of the grotesque, if not the comic, in the portrait of Calme, seated on "un trosne d'algue et de mousse et d'esponges," his upset feelings soothed by the sisters trying to readjust his crown. Saint-Amant was remembering Ariosto when he imagined this. Elsewhere he cultivates the grotesque and even the repellent more seriously. I have already quoted the passage referring to the serpent as "un beau monstre affreux." That revealing phrase is echoed by the remark that the serpent

Offre je ne sçay quoy d'horrible et d'agreable [17]

15. Livet, vol. 1, 25. "At times, leaving these ruins behind me, I climb to the top of this rock, whose summit seems to seek out the source of mists. Then I descend at my leisure under a precipitous cliff whence I contemplate with pleasure the wave which has almost undermined it, down to the throne of Palemon, made of sponges and mud."

16. Ibid. "How pleasant it is to be on the shore of the sea when it grows calm after some frightful tempest!"

17. IV, 202. "Presents I know not what of the sinister and the pleasurable."

and by Moses' response in

> Un mouvement confus de crainte et de plaisir.[18]

Later Saint-Amant refers to "une giraffe, en un belle et difforme." [19] And in the very closing lines he invests the darkness of the oriental night with the same paradoxical allure:

> Dejà les rossignols chantoyent sur les buissons;
> On oyoit dans le Nil retomber les poissons;
> Le silence paisible et l'horreur solitaire
> Contraignoyent doucement les hommes à se taire.[20]

The silence and the horror which is not really horrible together seduce us to a repose all the sweeter for its silken hint of fear.

The ending is typical of the rest, for the poem as a whole invites one to relax the will. *Moyse Sauvé* is not only profoundly antiheroic and anti-epic, it is also opposed to the voluntarism which its age brought both to art and to philosophy. The heroism of Corneille's protagonists objectifies Descartes' psychology; Polyeucte and Horace exemplify that strenuous victory of the will over the passions analyzed in the *Traité des Passions*. That fierce screwing up of the will which is common in Baroque art and which we have already encountered in d'Aubigné, seems to have engendered an opposite ideal, which would find its best known form in the quietism of Fénelon. The successors of Saint-Amant who attempted epic poetry tried to appropriate Corneille's voluntarism and failed. Saint-Amant had the courage of his own pensive sensibility, and produced a unique success. We shall discover both poles of this opposition in *Paradise Lost*.

If asked what gives life to the unturbulent action of *Moyse Sauvé,* one could answer, the poet's flair for the exotic, his whimsy, his eye for painterly detail, and the subdued but sustained delight of his language. The action itself is not of much interest; the stories, imperfectly fitted together, form a hodge-podge. There is no suspense and little narrative momentum; there are a few

18. IV, 202. "A gesture of mingled fear and pleasure."

19. XI, 313. "A giraffe, at once beautiful and misshapen."

20. XII, 328. "Already the nightingales were singing in the copses; one could hear the fish leaping in the Nile; the tranquil silence and solitary dread compelled mankind to be still."

strokes of psychological insight but, with the possible exception of the princess Termuth, no single character with any complexity or magnetism.[21] One has to fall back upon the local texture, page by page. Saint-Amant's greatest gift was for the curiosities of life, the caprices, the *exotica.* Of all the conscientious versifiers of Scripture, he was almost alone in catching the exoticism of its oriental setting. No poet of his century, neither Théophile nor Racan nor Scarron nor La Fontaine, would have combined whimsy with pastoralism by speaking of the birds reflected in the river who

Volans d'un bord à l'autre, y nagent à l'envers.

Whimsy there was in other men, and pastoralism in quantity, but in few could the two fuse without mutual destructiveness.

The sweeping and majestic gestures of the traditional epic were beyond Saint-Amant; the angelic descent itself is brief and ineffective. He appears to have known his limits; his preface seems covertly to refer to them. And in at least one passage, he permits himself some reflexive irony which anticipates the mock-heroic. This occurs when he describes the combat between his shepherds and a swarm of wasps threatening to attack the infant Moses. Here the formal preciosity becomes increasingly out of key with the subject:

Un coup en abbat mille, et sur les gazons vers
Leur orgueil ecrasé se remue à l'envers.[22]

and turns finally into comedy:

Qu'estes-vous devenus, anges doux et propices?
Voicy l'extremité, voicy les precipices . . .
Quoy doncques, sur les eaux vostre noble courage
Aura pour luy fait teste aux demons de l'orage;
Vostre bras valeureux les aura terrassez,
Et comme de l'Olympe en l'Averne chassez,

21. *Moyse Sauvé* would lend itself for once to that inveterate malady of French letters, the *morceaux choisis.* But heretofore it has been spared even the honor of being excerpted. The only exception is the Vérane edition of the *Oeuvres Poétiques* (Paris, 1930), in which the excerpts are depressingly brief and the commentary in general hostile.

22. VII, 255. "One blow brings down a thousand, and their crushed pride flutters upside down upon the green grass."

Pour souffrir qu'à ce coup, ressortans des tenebres,
Ces premiers scelerats, par leur crime celebres,
Viennent persecuter d'un orgueil travesty
L'enfant qui contr'eux tous prendra vostre party?
  Ha! m'arrive la mort plustost qu'en ma pensée
De cette oppinion l'erreur se soit glissée . . .[23]

The smile which is generally half-suppressed broadens as it turns upon the poet's own epic pretensions.

The marble solemnity of the epic was not quite unscarred, of course, even before Saint-Amant wrote. We have already noticed Ariosto's glancing hits, and cruder (if less effectual) blows were struck by Folengo in his mock-epic *Baldus*. The assault was sustained in *seicento* Italy by Tassoni's *Secchia Rapita* (1622) and Bracciolini's *Scherno degli Dei* (1618), to mention two of the better known efforts. In France the best-aimed shots came from the sling of Scarron, whose *Typhon* (1644) and *Virgile Travesti* (1648–52) (this latter inspired by an Italian counterpart) gave rise to a swarm of third-rate imitations within and outside of France. The popularity of this mode was not so much a cause as a symptom of the sinking epic vitality, and the appearance of Boileau's *Lutrin* (1672) and Dryden's *MacFlecknoe* (1682) can be regarded as signalling the final submersion of the whole vast bulk.

The seventeenth century made a distinction, which has since become blurred, between burlesque and mock-heroic. The passage quoted last from Saint-Amant is mock-heroic; so are *Le Lutrin* (whose author ridiculed the burlesque), *MacFlecknoe,* Butler's *Hudibras,* and *The Rape of the Lock.* Bracciolini and Scarron wrote burlesque—that is to say, they reduced a potentially heroic story by the triviality of their treatment. Mock-heroic reduces the heroic style by applying it to a trivial story. Both

23. VIII, 256–57. "Where are you, kind and propitious angels? Now is the crisis, here is the precipice . . . What! your noble courage will have confronted the demons of the tempest for him? Your valorous arms will have crushed them and driven them as it were from Olympus to Avernus, only to permit them now, these original villains, notorious for their crime, to re-ascend from the shades to persecute with disguised arrogance the child who is to take your side against them all?

Ah, let me die before this mistaken opinion steals into my thoughts!"

procedures are difficult to bring off well; both attract precisely those who are too self-consciously vulgar to succeed. A stanza from Bracciolini should suffice to suggest his qualities; the ruffian Mars, bickering with Vulcan, descends to Lemnos to pursue his quarrel, and the thump he makes as he lands is given its epic simile:

> Immagina, lettor, che un elefante
> Sopra d'un campanil fosse montato,
> E lassù dal battaglio di Morgante
> Pria sbalordito, eppoi precipitato:
> Tale il sanguigno Dio dal ciel tonante
> Tombolando scendea grave ed armato;
> O forse tal, ma con più scarsa mole,
> Cadde dal carro il Guidator del Sole.[24]

Scarron was the only poet with enough wit and grace not to abuse the burlesque; he alone gave it a distinction of sorts which renders his retelling of the *Aeneid* readable today. He began, like Dryden, Boileau, and Pope, with a genuine if unsentimental respect for the classics and a facility in reading them. In the seven and a half books of his *Virgile* completed before his death, he does not misread the Latin once. Perhaps it was his appreciation of Virgil which kept his version within the limits of taste and wit. Generally he knew where to stop. He knew moreover how to turn a serious situation into farce with the least expense of mockery; out of a longish sentence or two, the flicker of a word or phrase sufficed him. He had an ear for the popular turn of language; it came to him easily, and all he needed to do was to translate the Latin into the patter of his gossippy garrulity. The patter never seems to dry up, never seems forced, never even seems malicious, but it unfailingly reduces the epic action to the simplifying formulas of a lower bourgeois *commère.*

Thus when the liaison of Aeneas and Dido is bruited about, Scarron tells us that they "scandalisoient les gens de bien," and his Iarbas complains to Jupiter that "cet Enee . . .

24. Francesco Bracciolini, *Lo Scherno degli Dei* (Milan, 1804), p. 6. "Imagine, reader, that an elephant had climbed to the top of a bell tower, had first been stunned by Morgante's clapper, and then thrown off; so the bloody god of the thundering heaven tumbled down, weighty and armed; or perhaps thus, but with less bulk, the driver of the sun fell from his chariot."

Avec cette Sidonienne
Tout ouvertement fait dodo
Et, comme on dit, vit à gogo.[25]

Jupiter himself appears as a sturdy *père de famille:*

Cette harangue bien sensée,
Ainsi chaudement prononcée,
Fit tout l'effet qu'elle devoit.
Seigneur Jupiter, qui tout voit,
Vit le monsieur et la madame
Qui s'appeloient: Mon coeur, mon âme,
Et l'un de l'autre embéguinés
Sans cesse se rioient au nez,
Sans se mettre beaucoup en peine,
Autant Aeneas ou la reine,
S'ils faisoient les gens caqueter.
Cela fâcha bien Jupiter.
Il appela son fils Mercure,
Bâtard de gentille nature,
Et bien aussi morigéné
Qu'un garçon sans offense né:
Il est vrai qu'il aimoit à prendre,
Mais on en est quitte pour rendre . . .[26]

Jupiter dispatches his son to this "vaurien," this "miroir à putain," and concludes:

Qu'il cesse donc de me déplaire;
Qu'il navigue et me laisse faire,

25. All of the quotations from Scarron are from *Virgile Travesti,* ed. V. Fournel (Paris, 1858), pp. 138–40.

"This Aeneas goes to Slumberland with the Sidonian woman, and is living it up, as they say."

26. "This sensible harangue, expressed so warmly, had all the required effect. Lord Jupiter, who sees everything, saw the gentleman and the lady who addressed each other as "My heart" and "My soul," and who, each of them infatuated with the other, made eyes constantly, without caring much, either Aeneas or the queen, if they made people chatter. That annoyed Jupiter greatly. He called his son Mercury, his good natured bastard, just as well brought up as a boy born according to the rules. It's true that he liked to pilfer, but you just had to return the things later . . ."

Et, s'il dit qu'il n'en fera rien,
Qu'il s'aille, vous m'entendez bien;
Je ne veux point dire le reste.
Vole donc, mon fils, adieu, preste. [27]

Scarron has less apt material for his needs in Mercury's sandals and staff and the description of Atlas. But the passage which follows these is notable for its deliberate two-fold breaking of the narrative frame. He has been describing Aeneas' sumptuous apparel, and concludes:

Enfin, il étoit ce jour-là
De ceux dont l'on dit: Les voilà!
Elle près de lui, lui près d'elle,
Regardant une citadelle
Qu'on bâtissoit diligemment,
Ils ordonnoient du bâtiment;
Tout beau! tout beau! je me mécompte
Si fort, que j'en rougis de honte:
Didon n'étoit pas avec lui;
J'ai pensé donner aujourd'hui
A mes envieux à reprendre,
Et dire de moi pis que pendre.
  Retournons au dieu, qui surprit
Messire Aeneas, dont l'esprit
Ne songeoit alors qu'à Carthage,
Et bien moins à faire voyage
Que moi, cul-de-jatte follet,
Ne songe à danser un ballet.
La harangue du dieu fut telle:
"Ah! Dieu vous gard,' mademoiselle.
Car, vu l'habit que vous portez,
Semblable nom vous méritez.
Vous faites donc de l'architecte . . ." [28]

27. "So let him stop displeasing me; let him sail and allow me to do as I like, and if he says he won't, he can go . . . You understand my point; I won't say any more. So fly away, my son; quick; goodbye."

28. "In a word, this day he was one of those who make you say "Look at that." She next to him, he next to her, watching a tower that was going up

Scarron's references to his own infirmity and to his momentary error, real or pretended, in reading the original, represent artistic liberties of a still greater breadth than those to which he has accustomed one. But these too find their place; everything is harmonized by the unceremonious bonhomie. How disarming is that greeting:

Ah! Dieu vous gard', mademoiselle!

The epic of monumental tradition would scarcely withstand for long such winning and disingenuous debasement.

I shall not impose upon the reader with citations from the subsequent epics of the seventeenth century in France, although many contain celestial descents.[29] When these strive for even a modicum of poetic color, they dwell upon the angel's elaborate preparations. The passage from Cowley quoted in the next chapter can serve as an example of this new but unhappy fashion. On the whole one can follow the development of the French epic by following its theory: there was a general movement toward "utility" and morals at the expense of pleasure; toward a particular stress on civic and political morality; toward the use of allegory; toward the rapprochement of epic and tragedy, and such collateral stipulations as the unity of epic time—frequently limited to one year; [30] toward further purifications of epic style, and the proscription of such an ignoble procedure as Homer's comparing Ajax to a donkey.[31] Above all the freedom of the imagination was sharply cur-

---

with hard work, they were giving orders from the building. Oops, just a minute! I'm so badly mistaken I'm blushing with shame. Dido was *not* there with him. I thought I'd give my jealous rivals a chance to reproach me and stab me in the back.

Getting back to the god, he astonished Milord Aeneas, whose mind was dreaming only of Carthage, and even less of taking a trip than I, fanciful cripple as I am, dream of dancing a ballet. This was the god's speech; 'Ah, God keep you, Mademoiselle! For seeing the clothes you wear, that's the name you deserve. So now you've turned to architecture! . . .'"

29. See Chapelain's *La Pucelle* (Paris, 1656), pp. 13–15; Scudéry's *Alaric* (Paris, 1655), pp. 6–8; Desmarets' *Clovis* (Paris, 1666), pp. 45–46.

30. Ronsard had been the first to suggest this limit in his preface to the *Franciade*. Seventeenth-century criticism tended to confirm it and in some cases to shorten it.

31. A convenient summary of French neo-classic epic theory can be found in R. A. Sayce, *The French Biblical Epic in the Seventeenth Century* (Oxford,

tailed. "Machinery" and magic were not outlawed but they were confined, by some at least, to events explicable in terms of natural causes. Chapelain, for example, criticized the *Clovis* of Desmarets de Saint-Sorlin (published in 1657) for not adhering to this rule:

> Ce qu'il y a principalement à dire dans l'emploi de la magie, c'est qu'il la rend instrument des évènements sans qu'ils puissent être attribués à une autre cause naturelle . . . On peut dire la même chose de l'enlèvement de Clotilde au ciel par la Vierge, et de son transport du ciel par la même dans Vienne, qui sont des miracles formels introduits sans être appuyés de la renommée et qu'on ne peut attribuer à aucune cause naturelle, ce qui rend l'aventure improbable, et par cette improbabilité choque les principes de l'héroïque qui n'admet guère de merveille sans vraisemblance. Et bien que quelques poètes anciens et beaucoup de modernes se soient servis de l'effet de ces machines célestes et infernales pour le dénoûment ou pour le noeud de leurs entreprises, l'example mauvais ne justifie pas la mauvaise imitation; et Aristote et la raison n'y donnent pas les mains pour cela.[32]

In his earlier commentary on Marino's *Adone* (1623) Chapelain had excused the far greater improbabilities of this poem. His shift of position is typical of the century.

Boileau's attack upon the Christian marvelous in his *Art Po-*

1955), a study to which I am indebted. Longer studies can be found in R. Bray, *La Formation de la Doctrine Classique en France* (Dijon, 1926), and in R. C. Williams, *The Merveilleux in the Epic* (Paris, 1925).

32. Jean Chapelain, *Opuscules Critiques* (Paris, 1936), pp. 324–25. "The principal thing to be said about the use of magic is this: that he makes it the instrument of events in such a way that they cannot be attributed to any natural cause . . . The same thing can be said of the Virgin's carrying Clotilde off to heaven, and of her conveyance by the former to Vienne; these are unequivocal miracles which are introduced without any basis in legend and which cannot be attributed to any natural cause. This makes the adventure improbable, and by this improbability shocks the principles of the heroic which will scarcely permit the marvelous without verisimilitude. And although some ancient poets and many moderns have availed themselves of the effect of this celestial and infernal machinery for the untieing or the tieing of their action, the bad example does not justify the bad imitation; and neither Aristotle nor reason condone the practice."

étique (1674) hastened the end of the epic in France by curtailing the imagination still further.[33] He objected to the fashionable wedding of Christian divinities with classical forms and proposed a return to the Olympian divinities which almost nobody wanted. He was attacked vigorously by the same Saint-Sorlin who attracted Chapelain's criticism, but the negative half of his position quickly prevailed. The spate of epics abated, and the marvelous abated still more.

I am not really competent to discuss the one continental poem after Saint-Amant which would appear to distinguish itself from the general mediocrity—the *Joannes de Boetgezant* (1662) of the great Dutch poet Joost van den Vondel. But I do not want to leave it without mention. It was written in the poet's age, after the burning of his half-finished epic on Constantine, after most of the dramatic masterpieces, after the translations from Sophocles, Virgil, and Tasso, and after his conversion to Catholicism. It is not regarded by Dutch critics as the equal of Vondel's dramas, but it is still of interest for its substantial merit, for its possible influence on Milton,[34] and for its rarity as an example of the northern Catholic epic. The first of the six books contains a descent to the hero John the Baptist (*boetgezant* means "preacher of repentance") by Gabriel, who is directed by God to summon the saint to his mission of preparation:

33. C'est donc bien vainement que nos auteurs déçus,
Bannissant de leurs vers ces ornements reçus,
Pensent faire agir Dieu, ses saints et ses prophètes
Comme ces dieux éclos du cerveau des poètes,
Mettent à chaque pas le lecteur en enfer,
N'offrent rien qu'Astaroth, Belzébuth, Lucifer.
De la foi d'un chrétien les mystères terribles
D'ornements égayés ne sont point susceptibles;
L'Evangile à l'esprit n'offre de tous côtés
Que pénitence à faire et tourments mérités;
Et de vos fictions le mélange coupable
Même à ses vérités donne l'air de la fable.
Et quel objet enfin à présenter aux yeux
Que le diable toujours hurlant contre les cieux,
Qui de votre héros veut rabaisser la gloire,
Et souvent avec Dieu balance la victoire!
(*Art Poétique*, III.193–208)

34. See George Edmundson, *Milton and Vondel* (London, 1885), especially p. 94 ff.

> . . . Go to the world; descend straightway to the place where you twice faithfully assumed your mission, where the water of the Jordan bathes the holy landscape, long defended by David when he shone on earth. Exhort the desert-dweller in his rocky cavern to enter into the office ordained for him, as the spirit teaches him, and, impressing discipline and morals upon mankind, to witness undauntedly to the hero who comes to save them from the power of the abyss. The night of the law disappears, and requires that, without hesitation, before the stronger light comes to shine, he immediately meet the son of equity and justice.[35]

It is a token of Vondel's creative maturity that these lines from God's directive speech—conventionally a poetic flatland—introduce most of the motifs in the richly developed passage which follows. Desert, rock, water, light and darkness, discipline, heroism, contemplative mysticism (in the reference to the instructing spirit)—all of these elements reappear in the ensuing passage which, despite its length, cannot be cut without serious damage:

> Thus spoke the Almighty, and the archangel prepares[36] hastily, unfolds his wings, beautiful as phoenix feathers, shaded with heavenly blue and gold and purple, in the light where the divinity dwells. The colors can be seen to change or vary,

35. I, 112–23.

Ga naer de weerelt toe: stijgh neder regelrecht,
Daer gy nu tweewerf trou bekleede uw afgzantschap,
En 't water der Jordaene omspoelt het heiligh lantschap,
Van David langh beschut, toen hy op d'aerde blonck.
Gy zult den woestynier, in zijne rotsspelonck,
Aenmaenen in het ampt, hem toegekeurt, te treden,
Gelijck de geest hem leert, en, 't menschdom tucht en zeden
Inscherpende, onvertsaeght te tuigen van den helt,
Die hen verlossen komt van 's afgronts erfgewelt.
De nacht der wet verdwijnt, en eischt, dat, zonder draelen,
Hy daetlijck aenblicke, eer het stercker licht koom' straelen,
De zon van billijckheit en van rechtvaerdight.
[*De Werker van Vondel,* ed. J. F. M. Sterck (10 vols., Amsterdam, 1936), *9,* 691–94.]

36. I, 125–207.

Zoo sprack d'almaghtige, en d'aertsengel, om te rennen,
Bereit zich, en ontvout, zoo schoon als fenixpennen,
Zijn vleugels, geschakeert van hemelsch blaeu, en gout,

like the rainbow or beautiful peacock feathers, in the light of the sun just opposite. Ready to set off upon his flight, he rises and strikes his wings together three times, so that the choirs of angels look about and accompany his flight with their gaze. In the meantime the flier descends and swings from circle to circle, and descending descries Jerusalem, that lifts its crowned hilltops up to heaven out of the surrounding dunes, by which the royal city seemed entirely encircled. Then he set out in a direction which led past the royal stream where lay a waste desert, bare of any growth. Here the archangel, hovering with his wings, descends to the desert-dweller's cave: like an eagle which from its height finally makes out a spring and gliding down, quenches its thirst at the splashing of the fresh waterfall with the heart-quickening water.

Here the cave of prayer plunges downward which Gabriel has been seeking, a miracle, a true chapel of God, in the service of Jacob's God, either given to him by nature or hewn from the rock by the hammer of God's word. One descends by steps into the bowels of the earth; it receives the light through

---

En purper, in het licht daer zich de godtheit houdt.
Men ziet de verwen zich verandren en schakeeren,
Gelijck de regenboogh, of schoone paeuweveêren,
In 't licht der zonne, die recht tegens over staet.
Reisvaerdigh in zijn vlught verheft hy zich, en slaet
De pennen tegens een wel drywerf, dat de reien
Der englen ommezien, en zijne vlught geleien
Met hun gezicht; terwijl de vlieger nederstijght,
En zwaeit van ronde in ronde, en onder 't daelen krijght
Jerusalem in 't oogh, dat zijn gekroonde kruinen
Ten hemel opwaert heft uit d'omgelege duinen,
Waer van de koningsstadt in 't ronde omcingelt scheen.
Toen volghde hy de streeck, die naer den rijxstroom heen
Hem 't woest Quarente wees, niet rijck van groente en lover.
Hier hing d'aertsengel op zijn pennen, streeck voor over
Op 's woestijniers spelonck: gelijck een adelaer,
Die uit de hooghte in 't ende een springbron wort gewaer,
En nederzwevende den dorst lescht, op 't geklater
Des verschen watervals, aen 't hartverquickend water.
  Hier duickt de bidtspelonck om laegh, van Gabriël
Gezocht, een wonderwerck, een rechte godtskapel,
Ten dienst van Jakobs Godt, hem door natuur geschoncken,
Of met den hamer van Godts woort uit rots gekloncken.
Men stijght by trappen neêr. van onder sluitze dicht,

an opening above, when the sun shines at the meridian and causes the shadows to change and disappear. At the eastern end stands a table, also hewn only from stone. In the doorway God's prophet rests his limbs upon a mat of rushes twisted by his own hand. A garment of camel's hair, closed by a leather belt, clothes the tempted one against cold and rain. Hunger sometimes drives him out in the bad weather. The wild honey and the meager locust supply his food. A spring dripping from the rock provides drink. He tells the hours of his life, narrowly bounded and short and uncertain, by the movements of shadows. He hears no cock crowing, nor dog barking, but the roaring of lions who are shy and afraid to wound him. Sometimes his foot treads on the neck of the hissing serpent. The lions wag their tails and lick him as though they were spellbound by the faith of the pious hero. A lamp hung at the arched roof of this chapel of God and shone whenever he lighted it, striking sparks out of pebbles to burn foliage and dry and arid leaves. So in alert prayer to God he passed his years in solitude, and waited, humble

---

En om en in den buick. van boven scheptze licht
Door eene kloof, wanneer de zon op 't hooft komt schijnen,
Waer voor de schaduwen verwandlen, en verdwijnen.
Een tafel staet in 't ooste, al mede uit louter steen
Gehouwen. in 't poortael rust Godts profeet de leên,
Op eene biezemat, met zijne hant gevlochten.
Het kemelshaeren kleet bekleet den aengevochten
Voor koude en regen, daer de leêren riem op sluit.
De honger jaeght by wijl hem in het onweêr uit.
De wilde honigh en de magre springkhaen decken
Den disch. de bron schaft dranck, die uit een rots komt lecken.
Hy rekent d'uuren van het leven, naeu beperckt,
En kort en onwis, by de schaduwe afgemerckt.
Hy hoort geen' haenekraey, noch geen gebas van honden,
Maer leeuwen brullen, schuw en ang van hem te wonden,
Gelijck de veltslang, die hier schuifelt met den beck,
By wylen met zijn' voet getreden op den neck;
Terwijl de leeuwen hem aenquispelen en licken,
Als ofze voor 't geloof des vroomen helts verschricken.
Een lamp hing aen 't gewelf der godtskapelle en blonck,
Als hyze ontstack, en vier uit keizelsteenen klonck
In tonder van het loof, en drooge en dorre blaêren.
Zoo sleet hy, waeckende en Godt biddende, zijn jaeren
In eenzaemheit, en wachte, ootmoedigh en bereit

and ready to follow God's summons, where the Spirit might bring him. Now he was meditating Elijah's way of life, and Isaiah's word, and that which Malachi so long before had foretold; and stood transported and enraptured, stockstill, dumb as an image that does not move.

Who can understand how his senses wandered through all of heaven, and what visions of God and His son enlightened the ravished hero! Just as in the Chaldean fields, by the rushing of the Euphrates, visions appeared to Ezekiel, one more beautiful than the other, disappearing at once. Returning to himself at last, he called loudly: "Hallowed be God's name and the divine plan! Blessed is he who appears in honor of God's name. May the Savior come! That is all I desire." As he spoke the heavenly ambassador appeared. He halted in the cave just before the young man, upright as he was, and his radiance illumined the hermit; the dreariness and shadow disappeared; the lamp lost its glow. The desert-dweller considered the angel carefully, from head to foot, and the flickering light that usually shone above his crown seemed dark in comparison with the luster and brilliance of God's

---

Te volgen op Godts roep, waer hem de geest geleit.
Nu overleide hy den wandel van Helias,
En Izaïas woort, en wat hem Malachias
Zoo lang had voorgespelt, en stont verruckt, vervoert,
Stockstijf, en stom, gelijck een beelt, dat zich niet roert.
Wie kan begrijpen hoe de zinnen weiden gingen
Door alle hemels heene, en wat bespiegelingen
Van Gode en zijnen zoon den opgetogen helt
Verlichtten! eveneens als in 't Chaldeeusche velt,
Op 't ruisschen der Eufraete, Ezechiël verscheenen
Gezichten, elck om 't schoonste, en die terstont verdweenen.
Ten leste tot zich zelf gekomen, riep hy luidt:
Geheilight zy Godts naem, en 't goddelijck besluit.
Gezegent is hy, die verschijnt, Godts naem ter eere.
De heilant koom'. dat's al en 't een dat ick begeere.
Op zulck een stem verscheen de hemelsche gezant,
En hielt in dees spelonck recht voor den jongling stant,
Zoo reizigh als hy was, en lichte met zijn klaerheit
Den afgescheiden toe: waerop terstont de naerheit
En schaduwe verdween, de lamp haer' glans verloor.
De woestijnier bezagh den engel door en door,
Van boven tot beneên, en 't flonkren van den luister,
Gewoon op zijne kruin te lichten, scheen nu duister

> herald, entrusted with this high task by the supreme power. John shrank back when he first saw this high creature, but the envoy's agreeable fragrance filled the chapel of God and strengthened his heart.
>
> At length the angel spoke: "My son, you behold Gabriel, who descended thirty years ago from heaven's gate and announced your coming birth to your father at the altar. Take courage and fear not . . ."

I am unable to say anything about the style of this episode, but even to a reader with no Dutch it is remarkable in at least three respects. First, the treatment of heaven and of the angel's appearance is done with a ceremonious sumptuosity which one does not quite expect from a north European in the seventeenth century. Critics of Vondel's conversion have suggested that it resulted chiefly from an esthetic preference for ritual, color, and pomp, attractions more compatible with his native temperament than the austere Mennonite worship of his forebears. Whatever the truth of that insinuation, Vondel's celestial imagination shows his gift for gorgeous but formal sensuosity: in the resplendent description of the angel's wings, which vary their tints as the divine radiance plays over them; in the mysterious gesture, repeated thrice, of striking the wings together; in the original conception which has the angelic hosts turning in unison to follow the messenger in his flight; and in the angelic fragrance which fills John's cave. This last detail, like others, recalls Sannazaro and will reappear in Milton, who seems to have known Dutch and may well have read Vondel. The phoenix simile, here barely suggested, is further developed by Milton in a celestial descent which shows as much affinity with Vondel's as with any single predecessor's. But Vondel lacks Milton's capacity to suggest cosmic vastness.

Te worden, by den glans en 't licht van Godts herout,
Wien 't opperste gezagh dien hoogen last betrout.
Joannes zwichte in 't eerste, als hy die hoogheit merckte:
Maer d'aengenaeme geur des afgezants versterckte
Hem 't hart, en spreide zich rondom de Godtskappel.
  Ten leste sprack hy: zoon, gy ziet hier Gabriël,
Die dertigh jaer geleên, gedaelt uit 's hemels poorte,
Uw vader aen 't altaer verkuntschapte uw geboorte.
Schep moedt, en vrees niet . . .

The second remarkable thing in this descent is its mysticism, a form of religious experience which the epic had scarcely cultivated. It is true that Tasso attributed visionary raptures to two of his characters, Piero and Goffredo, and that his example had some influence. (Compare, for example, Spenser, III.3.50). But these episodes were unconvincing literary inventions, often introduced for encomiastic purposes (as in the *Liberata,* 10.73–77). In fact, mysticism is not altogether congenial to the epic imagination because it attributes a miraculous uniqueness to the kind of celestial vision which the epic takes for granted. One has only to think of such a mystical poem as the *Paradiso,* and the tremulous awe of Dante before the ineffable, to measure the difference between that extraordinary vision and the unabashed assurance of a Virgil or a Tasso or a Milton depicting the celestial boldly and commandingly. In Vondel the beautiful but conventional view of heaven is complemented by hints of more mysterious wonders, vouchsafed the hero John beyond the reach of the poet's own vision, and these hints are fortified by allusions to Old Testament mysticism which a poet of Catholic Europe, less intimate with Scripture than Vondel, might not have used so freely.

His northern temper is also apparent in a third remarkable feature, the virile realism of his physical description, a freedom which French purists might have found indecorous but which creates a dramatic authenticity not wholly out of tone with the Gospels. There is nothing in the New Testament to authorize the tame lions and the treading on the serpent (with its typological symbolism), but the description of the cave itself, with its mat and stone table and spring and lamp burning leaves, the portrait of the grizzled hermit himself—all of this is finely reconstructed, recalling some Dutch master painter rather than the paralyzed Christian epic. The effects of light are particularly painterlike, especially when the angelic radiance eclipses the flickering glow of the saint's halo (197–99). All of the light effects are carefully differentiated—the blinding sunlight of the Deity, the varicolored reflections of His winged court, the desert sun which pierces briefly the prophet's cave (153–54), the moving shadows which regulate the brief hours of his life, the lamp, the halo, the angel's sudden brightness.

Nothing in the descent is irrelevant or perfunctory. The eagle simile, which seems at first a mere reworking of Sannazaro, gains its effect from the imagery of sand and stone which frames it; in *this* context the splashing of water is a true relief. The whole passage is under magisterial control, alternately sober and lyrical, and it presents an affecting image of heroism consonant with a prevalent Northern view of life as "narrowly bounded and short and uncertain." Had Vondel written earlier and in a language of wider access, the expiring epic genre might have been temporarily restored at his *hartverquickend springbron,* the heart-quickening spring of his art.

12. MILTON

i.

Most of the important epic poetry of the sixteenth century was written by Humanist authors working at a court or, like Spenser, under the long shadow of a court. Boiardo, Ariosto, and Tasso wrote for the dukes of Ferrara as Pulci had written for Lorenzo de' Medici. Ronsard, the very model of a court poet, received not only the encouragement of Charles IX and the benefice to afford him leisure, but found himself obliged to follow the royal preference for a decasyllabic line. D'Aubigné spent several years at the court of Henri III and remained the confidant of Henri IV until the latter's conversion. Even Sannazaro and Vida wrote with the patronage of the papal court. Camoens, to be sure, wrote much of *Os Lusíadas* in the Orient, but part of his youth was spent at court, and he received a small royal pension after his epic was published. In all these sixteenth century courts, with the possible exception of the papal, a balance of sorts was maintained between soldiering and learning, the camp and the library, a balance which naturally led the Humanist poet to subjects involving warfare.

The ancient duality of *sapientia* and *fortitudo* was perpetuated, as Curtius has shown,[1] by the Renaissance coupling of "arms and studies." The courtly interest in epic action was thus not simply antiquarian. The immediate audience of the epic pursued an equilibrium of valor and refinement not utterly unlike the equilibrium reflected in the *Odyssey.* The finest Christian epics of the sixteenth century—those of Tasso, Spenser, and d'Aubigné—mostly eschewed Biblical subjects in preference for those of interest to an educated professional soldier.

In seventeenth century France the military caste tended to detach itself from the court, although the separation never became complete. As early a poem as Marino's *Adone,* written at the court of Louis XIII, signaled the taste for subjects which had nothing to do with violence. But Marino's mythographical eroticism was not influential. Epic poetry in the succeeding decades was divided, as we have seen, between tired perpetuations of the quasi-military epic (Scudéry's *Alaric,* Desmarets de Saint-Sorlin's *Clovis,* etc.)—poems which really betray the growing gap between courtier-poet and soldier—and on the other hand, bourgeois Biblical epics in the tradition of Sannazaro, Vida, and Du Bartas. The Pléiade had experimented with Biblical poetry—as in Du Bellay's *Monomachie de David et de Goliath,* but had only shown spasmodic interest in it. Now, with the growth of a middle class reading public, a bastard form of Biblical epic enjoyed a wide popularity.[2]

The socio-literary development of England was very different. There a Humanist literary movement comparable to the continental explosion gathered force only after the court ceased to be a literary center. This fact is of great importance. The first thorough-going neoclassical epic in England—Cowley's *Davideis*—was not published before 1656, although it was probably written a decade or more earlier. In 1656, continental epic poetry was expiring, and there existed in England no audience devoted to "arms and letters," no audience as variously accomplished as the court

1. E. R. Curtius, *European Literature and the Latin Middle Ages,* trans. Willard Trask (New York, 1953), pp. 178–79.

2. These poems are described at length in R. A. Sayce, *French Biblical Epic.*

for which Spenser wrote. This meant that the nature of heroism represented in the English epic was obliged to change, to idealize the efforts of will comprehensible to a devout bourgeois public. In 1656, moreover, the wind of prosaic rationalism was beginning to blow strong, that wind which was soon to wither epic poetry. Gusts of it flutter the pages of Cowley's poem, and its steady draft altogether blights the decorous quatrains of Davenant's *Gondibert.* Given this milieu, great epic poetry in seventeenth century England was an historical anomaly. *Paradise Lost* is only less anomalous than the Arthurian epic Milton planned to write. That poem would have had no *raison d'être,* no fit audience at all. *Paradise Lost* still had the dwindling core of an audience, but only the massive, proud, and isolated independence of a Milton could have brought even this poem into being.[3]

In sixteenth century England a movement had arisen which opposed the imitation of classical modes in all genres, and which substituted in each case sacred subjects and modes. Rather than attempt the *mélange coupable* of classical and Christian, this program enforced a strict segregation which, in epic poetry, broke down completely only with Cowley and Milton.[4] It is not remarkable that the pious and pedestrian Quarles betrays so little classical influence in his Biblical narratives (*Job Militant, The Historie of Samson*), but it is perhaps a little odd that a poet like Drayton (in his *Moses, David and Golia, Noah's Flood*) should not betray a great deal more. Giles Fletcher's underestimated *Christ's Victorie and Triumph* (1610), a poem somewhat more allegorical than Biblical, contains a celestial descent of sorts, in the passage of Mercie into Christ's breast (*Christ's Victorie on Earth,* 1–16), but for an extended conventional descent to represent the English epic before Cowley one would have to search out a forgotten poem by Thomas Robinson, *The Life and Death of*

3. J. B. Broadbent, in *Some Graver Subject* (London, 1960), pp. 47–65, discusses more fully the unpropitiousness of mid-century England for Christian epic. Broadbent remarks (p. 55) that "Milton's genius was irrevocably bent on a divine epic which the public no longer wanted."

4. This movement has been studied by Lily B. Campbell, *Divine Poetry and Drama in Sixteenth-Century England* (Berkeley, 1959).

Mary Magdalene (1569).[5] In any case, the important landmark, historically if not artistically, is Cowley's *Davideis.*

The angelic descent in that poem is memorable chiefly because of the criticism by which Dr. Johnson singled it out. It appears oddly at the very end of a book—the second of the twelve Cowley planned and of the four he completed. David, while still a young man and before taking the throne, has been vouchsafed a prophetic dream by heaven, a dream which summarizes Jewish history from his own lifetime to the advent of Christ. The account of this dream, which occupies over three hundred lines, is tedious. But if the the reader concludes it with pleasure, David awakes with doubt about its import, and Gabriel must descend to explain and reassure:

> When Gabriel (no blest Spirit more kind or fair)
> Bodies and cloathes himself with thickned ayr.
> All like a comely youth in lifes fresh bloom;
> Rare workmanship, and wrought by heavenly loom!
> He took for skin a cloud most soft and bright,
> That e're the midday Sun pierc'ed through with light:
> Upon his cheeks a lively blush he spred;
> Washt from the morning beauties deepest red.
> An harmless flaming Meteor shone for haire,
> And fell adown his shoulders with loose care.
> He cuts out a silk Mantle from the skies,
> Where the most sprightly azure pleas'd the eyes.
> This he with starry vapours spangles all,
> Took in their prime e're they grow ripe and fall.
> Of a new Rainbow e're it fret or fade,
> The choicest piece took out, a Scarf is made.
> Small streaming clouds he does for wings display,
> Not Vertuous Lovers sighes more soft then They.
> These he gilds o're with the Suns richest rays,
> Caught gliding o're pure streams on which he plays.
> Thus drest the joyful Gabriel posts away,
> And carries with him his own glorious day

5. Thomas Robinson, *The Life and Death of Mary Magdalene,* ed. H. O. Sommer (London, 1899), pp. 25–28.

Through the thick woods; the gloomy shades a while
Put on fresh looks, and wonder why they smile.
The trembling Serpents close and silent ly,
The birds obscene far from his passage fly.
A sudden spring waits on him as he goes,
Sudden as that by which Creation rose.
Thus he appears to David, at first sight
All earth-bred fears and sorrows take their flight.
In rushes joy divine, and hope, and rest;
A Sacred calm shines through his peaceful brest.
Hail, Man belov'ed! from highest heav'en (said he)
My mighty Master sends thee health by me.
The things thou saw'est are full of truth and light,
Shap'd in the glass of the divine Foresight.
Ev'n now old Time is harnessing the years
To go in order thus; hence empty fears;
Thy Fate's all white; from thy blest seed shall spring
The promis'd Shilo, the great Mystick King.
Round the whole earth his dreaded name shall sound,
And reach to Worlds, that must not yet be found.
The Southern Clime him her sole Lord shall stile,
Him all the North, ev'en Albions stubborn Isle.
My Fellow-Servant, credit what I tell.
  Straight into shapeless air unseen he fell.[6]

I fear that nothing can be said for the flatness of Cowley's unheroic couplets; his use of them is reminiscent of the uninspired Joshua Sylvester, from whom he may well have taken his lead. One must equally regret the bland coyness of his manner:

Of a new Rainbow e're it fret or fade.

the pleasantness substituted for energy:

Where the most sprightly Azure pleas'd the eyes . . .

the empty neoclassical generality of the vocabulary:

All like a comely Youth in lifes fresh Bloom . . .

6. Abraham Cowley, *Poems,* ed. A. R. Waller (Cambridge, 1905), pp. 304–05.

the gloomy shades a while
Put on fresh looks . . .

when, as in the use of *obscene* (817) to mean ill-omened, his vocabulary is not pedantically mannered. But it is graceless to belabor a dead author for the immature failures of his youth, and I shall not dwell long upon those of Cowley's shortcomings which were peculiar to himself alone. Dr. Johnson's strictures on lines 796–807 can scarcely be improved upon:

> This is a just specimen of Cowley's imagery: what might, in general expressions, be great and forcible, he weakens and makes ridiculous by branching it into small parts. That Gabriel was invested with the softest or brightest colours of the sky, we might have been told, and been dismissed to improve the idea in our different proportions of conception; but Cowley could not let us go, till he had related where Gabriel got first his skin, and then his mantle, then his lace, and then his scarf, and related it in the terms of the mercer and tailor.[7]

Cowley could not remember that epic poetry requires the subordination of part to whole; he constantly diverts the reader from his poem's main business by ornaments (like the fading rainbow or the lovers' sighs) for which, were they more truly witty, a lyric might find organic place, but which only clog heroic action.

This shortcoming is related to Cowley's lack of structural intelligence. For it is difficult finally to ascertain the "main business" of the poem at all, so divided is it into unlike episodes. In its unfinished form the plot has no shape or outline, and one wonders whether the completed poem would have acquired them. The poet explains in his preface that he intended to write the life of David only up to his elegy upon Saul and Jonathan, but it is evident from the text that he wanted to incorporate into his account most of Old Testament history. In this disastrous intent he was probably misled not so much by the older English history poems—Daniel's *Civil Wars* and Drayton's *Barons' Wars*—as by

7. *Works* of Samuel Johnson, Literary Club Edition, *3* (Troy, 1903), 330.

Vida and above all by Du Bartas' *Judit,*[8] a poem of undistinguished literary merit but great historical influence. Cowley's vast design was further weakened by his lack of dramatic sense, a shortcoming which led him to introduce this anticlimactic and superfluous descent of Gabriel with extended description. The account of the angel's preparations and the miraculous "sudden Spring" which attends him (inspired perhaps by Sylvester's Fracostoro [9]) would have befitted an event of high moment, but the effect of this descent is dissipated in its pointlessness.

Apart from Cowley's personal failings, the *Davideis* betrays other shortcomings—or as it seems to me, confusions—which are almost endemic to the Christian epic and with which Milton would also have to come to terms. The first of these involves the question of truthfulness. In the preface to his *Poems* (which included the epic), Cowley dwelt enthusiastically upon the Scriptures' unmined riches for poetry, and indignantly upon mythology's meretricious falsity:

> When I consider this, and how many other bright and magnificent subjects of the like nature, the Holy Scripture affords and proffers, as it were, to Poesie, in the wise managing

8. Translated by the indefatigable Sylvester as *Bethulia's Rescue* (1614).

9. The Italian Girolamo Fracastoro was a neo-Latin poet who left uncompleted a work entitled *Ioseph,* first published in 1555 and translated by Sylvester under the title *The Maidens Blush.* In the first book an angel descends to comfort Joseph after his brothers have thrown him into a pit. The passage which seems to have attracted Cowley reads thus in Sylvester's version:

> Such was the speed of this Celestiall Bird
> (To prosecute, and execute the Word
> Of his great Master) towards Dothan Down,
> Alighting first upon Mount Tabor's Crown,
> Amaz'd to see his Groves so sodain green,
> And Lawns so fresh, with flow'ry tufts between.
> The Hill-Born Nymphs with quav'ring warbles sing
> His happy Well-Come: Caves and Rocks doe ring
> Redoubled Ecchoes; Woods and Winds withall,
> Whisper about a joyfull Madrigall.

Complete Works of Joshua Sylvester, ed. A. B. Grosart, 2 (Edinburgh, 1880), 108, ll. 343–52. Cowley's apparent debt to Sylvester was first pointed out by J. M. McBryde, "A Study of Cowley's *Davideis,*" *JGP, 3* (1901), 24–34. It is of course conceivable that Cowley knew Fracostoro's Latin poem, but given his unquestionable familiarity with Sylvester, his indebtedness to the English version is much more likely.

> and illustrating whereof, the Glory of God Almighty might be joyned with the singular utility and noblest delight of Mankind; It is not without grief and indignation that I behold that Divine Science employing all her inexhaustible riches of Wit and Eloquence, either in the wicked and beggerly Flattery of great persons, or the unmanly Idolizing of Foolish Women . . . or at best on the confused antiquated Dreams of senseless Fables and Metamorphoses.
>
> There is not so great a Lye to be found in any Poet, as the vulgar conceit of men, that Lying is Essential to good Poetry.[10]

In the invocation to the *Davideis* he underscores his poem's veracity as its highest originality:

> But Thou, Eternal Word, hast call'd forth Me
> Th'Apostle, to convert that World to Thee;
> T'unbind the charms that in slight Fables lie,
> And teach that Truth is truest Poesie.
>
> [I.39–42]

But in practice Cowley departs from the truth, or from his own beliefs regarding the truth, and records the departures in his exhaustive notes. Thus he follows a debate on the location of the Queen of Sheba's realm with the tell-tale confession: "In fine, whatever the truth be, this opinion makes a better Sound in Poetry." [11] And on the question of the harmony of the spheres he writes:

> In this, and some like places, I would not have the Reader judge of my opinion by what I say; no more than before in diverse expressions about Hell, the Devil, and Envy. It is enough that the Doctrine of the Orbs, and the Musick made by their motion had been received very anciently.[12]

The issue of epic truthfulness which troubled Cowley can be related to issues which had been subject to international critical controversy for decades when he penned these various opinions.

10. *Poems*, pp. 12–13.
11. Book II, note 53.
12. Book I, note 24.

Critics were not agreed as to whether the heroic action should be based on actual history, or how closely it should follow history, or with how much of the marvelous it might be colored. Despite continuing debate, the cause of historical fidelity was markedly gaining ground on the continent by the mid-seventeenth century, at the expense of the imagination. During Cowley's years in France with the exiled Royalist party there appeared Scudéry's *Alaric* (1654) with its influential preface advocating a non-Biblical subject drawn from true Christian history. Four years earlier, the exchange between Davenant and Hobbes prefacing *Gondibert* laid stress on realism at the expense of machinery, fables, and fantasy.[13] The greater zeal for truth in Cowley's preface, as compared with his poem and notes (probably composed earlier), may reflect his tendency to change with his age. In the poem itself he is far from proscribing "machinery," but his treatment of it is so cool, so detached, so manifestly lacking in awe, that it already represents a step toward realism.

There are ulterior difficulties. The preface patronizes the poems of Quarles and Heywood[14] as misguided efforts to write sacred poetry, but the imputed reasons for their failures are not altogether clear. Cowley has been speaking of the books of the Bible:

> Yet, though they be in themselves so proper to be made use of for this purpose; None but a good Artist will know how to do it: neither must we think to cut and polish Diamonds with so little pains and skill as we do Marble. For if any man design to compose a Sacred Poem, by only turning a story of

13. Thus Davenant, for example: "Though the elder poets, which were then the sacred priests, fed the world with supernatural tales, and so compounded the religion of pleasure and mystery, two ingredients which never failed to work upon the people, whilst for the eternity of their chiefs, more refined by education, they surely intended no such vain provision; yet a Christian poet, whose religion little needs the aids of invention, hath less occasion to imitate such fables as meanly illustrate a probable Heaven by the fashion and dignity of courts, and make a resemblance of Hell out of the dreams of frighted women, by which they continue and increase the melancholy mistake of the people." Preface to *Gondibert,* reprinted in Spingarn, *Critical Essays of the Seventeenth Century,* 2, 5. See also Hobbes' "Answer to Davenant" in the same volume, especially pp. 61–62.

14. Cowley was referring to Thomas Heywood's *Hierarchy of the Blessed Angels,* published in 1635.

> the Scripture, like Mr. Quarles's, or some other godly matter, like Mr. Heywood of Angels, into Rhyme; He is so far from elevating of Poesie, that he only abases Divinity. In brief, he who can write a prophane Poem well, may write a Divine one better; but he who can do that but ill, will do this much worse.[15]

Quarles is guilty of having turned Scriptural stories into rhyme with too bald a simplicity. What should he have done? Evidently he should have mastered first the skills of his *métier,* the skills one can learn from profane poetry. Among other things, presumably Quarles should have imitated the classics. Cowley himself imitated them on every page and employed all the epic conventions; his notes are stuffed with allusions to Virgil and other antique poets, allusions intended to justify his own poetic procedures. But in the same preface he refers to "those mad Stories of the Gods and Heroes" which "seem in themselves so ridiculous," and numbers himself as one of those "who deride their Folly, and are weary'd with their Impertinences." [16] Thus Cowley's whole relation to antique poetry constitutes a second crucial and symptomatic confusion. He refers in his poem to a revolt of giants against Baal and is obliged to annotate this mysterious mythology by appeal to comparative mythology:

> For Baal is no other than Jupiter. *Baalsemen Jupiter Olympius.* But I like not in an Hebrew Story to use the European Names of Gods.[17]

Elsewhere the poem alludes to Fates and the note must turn about in the contrary direction:

> The Fates; that is, according to the Christian Poetical manner of speaking, the Angels, to whom the Government of this world is committed.[18]

If the notes to Gabriel's descent contain a reference to Revelation and to Aquinas, they contain as well three references to Virgil, two to Homer, others to Ovid, Servius, Pliny, Strabo, to "the

15. *Poems,* p. 14.
16. *Poems,* p. 13.
17. Book III, note 45.
18. Book II, note 60.

Rabbies," and to certain unnamed "magical Books." To the Christian poem which may well have contributed to the descent (Sylvester's Fracastoro), there is no reference at all. How Christian should a Christian epic be? Quarles must have seemed an amateur indeed.

The third of Cowley's confusions we have already encountered in Marino and Hojeda; [19] perhaps it can be found less strikingly in Tasso as well. This is the confusion exemplified by these lines of Gabriel:

> The things thou saw'est are full of truth and light . . .
> Ev'n now old Time is harnessing the years
> To go in order thus; hence empty fears . . .

The problem lies in the dream of which Gabriel is speaking; truthful it may have been, but scarcely orderly and scarcely filled with light, scarcely calculated to banish all fears. However the poet lays emphasis on the virtuous successors of David, however he rejoices in conclusion at Mary's conception of Jesus, he cannot conceal the patternless violence and suffering of the history he chooses to retail. He wanted to assert a pattern, and assert light and victory and joy, because he thought they were demanded by the genre and exemplified by the *Aeneid*. But he failed to make comprehensible poetically the "Sacred Calm" he meant to inspire. I fear that he inspires rather secular indifference. Perhaps we may thank the *Davideis* most cordially for having fulfilled its author's valedictory hope:

> Sure I am, that there is nothing yet in our Language (nor perhaps in any) that is in any degree answerable to the Idea that I conceive of it. And I shall be ambitious of no other fruit from this weak and imperfect attempt of mine, but the opening of a way to the courage and industry of some other persons, who may be better able to perform it throughly and successfully.[20]

The report has survived that Cowley, with Shakespeare and Spenser, were Milton's favorites among the English poets.[21]

19. See above, chapter 8, pp. 237–8, 251.
20. *Poems,* p. 14.
21. This report appears in Bishop Newton's edition of *Paradise Lost* (1749) and is there ascribed to hearsay conversations of the long-lived third Mrs. Mil-

ii.

The convention of the celestial messenger is here concluded with the majestic descent of Raphael to Adam in Book Five of *Paradise Lost.* There is a propriety in this, since Milton concludes so very much more; the clangor of his high style sounds the closing of an immense door within the temple of history. His poem is the more moving because it seems almost to glimpse at instants its own momentous finality.

Milton's earlier poems contains fragmentary rehearsals of Raphael's descent: in the Attendant Spirit's soliloquy that opens *Comus:*—

> Swift as the Sparkle of a glancing Star,
> I shoot from Heav'n to give him safe convoy . . .
> [80–81][22]

in the flight of Fama concluding the *Quintum Novembris,*[23] and in the charming stanza of the *Nativity Ode* which pictures Peace descending to comfort Nature:

> But he her fears to cease,
> Sent down the meek-eyd Peace,
>   She crown'd with Olive green, came softly sliding
> Down through the turning sphear
> His ready Harbinger,
>   With Turtle wing the amorous clouds dividing,
> And waving wide her mirtle wand,
> She strikes a universall Peace through Sea and Land.
> [45–52]

ton. It is quoted in *The Works of John Milton,* ed. F. A. Patterson, et al., *18* (New York, 1931–38), 390. All quotations from Milton's prose will be taken from this Columbia edition, hereafter referred to as C.E.

22. The text of all verse quotations from Milton is from *The Poetical Works of John Milton,* ed. Helen Darbishire, Oxford Standard Authors (1958).

23. Lines 204–19. Milton may have remembered one line in this passage:

> Nec mora, iam pennis cedentes remigat auras . . .

when he wrote of Raphael:

> then with quick Fan
> Winnows the buxom Air.

An archaic meaning of *buxom* was equivalent to *cedentes.* A. W. Verity compares the latter phrase to a line in Fairfax's Tasso: "With nimble fan the yielding air she rent" (18.49). The Italian original is not so close.

The outlines for projected tragedies in the Cambridge manuscript also contain at least two scenes involving the descent of an angel,[24] reflecting perhaps the influence of the Italian *sacre rappresentazioni* which commonly contained angelic epiphanies.[25] Milton alludes to the descent convention moreover in Book Three of *Paradise Lost;* when Satan feigns therein an appearance to deceive Uriel, he makes himself up to resemble the messenger we have encountered so frequently:

> And now a stripling Cherube he appeers,
> Not of the prime, yet such as in his face
> Youth smil'd Celestial, and to every Limb
> Sutable grace diffus'd, so well he feignd;
> Under a Coronet his flowing haire
> In curles on either cheek plaid, wings he wore
> Of many a colourd plume sprinkl'd with Gold,
> His habit fit for speed succinct, and held
> Before his decent steps a Silver wand.
> [III.636–44]

Milton's own messenger is to be less carefully described, but will possess a maturity and presence beyond the reach of the conventional, Tasso-esque "stripling." Is there a faint touch of scornful pride in the bedecking of Satan in these worn lineaments of literary tradition?

Satan's pretty disguise misleads Uriel only for an hour; he is driven from paradise, and on the morrow Eve is quickly restored from the painful dream he has authored. Adam and Eve proceed to pray and to work, and so engaged attract the eye of God:

> Them thus imploid beheld
> With pittie Heav'ns high King, and to him calld
> *Raphael,* the sociable Spirit, that deignd

24. The fourth draft of *Adam Unparadiz'd* opens: "The angel Gabriel, either descending or entring, shewing since this globe was created, his frequency as much on earth, as in heavn, describes Paradise." C.E., *18,* 231.

In the notes for *Sodom Burning:* "In the last scene to the king & nobles when the firce thunders begin aloft the Angel appeares all girt with flames which he saith are the flames of true love & tells the K. who falls down with terror his just suffering . . ." Ibid., 234.

25. George R. Kernodle, *From Art to Theatre* (Chicago, 1944), p. 66.

To travel with *Tobias,* and secur'd
His marriage with the seav'ntimes-wedded Maid.
Raphael, said hee, thou hear'st what stirr on Earth
Satan from Hell scap't through the darksom Gulf
Hath raisd in Paradise, and how disturbd
This night the human pair, how he designes
In them at once to ruin all mankind.
Go therefore, half this day as friend with friend
Converse with *Adam,* in what Bowre or shade
Thou find'st him from the heat of Noon retir'd,
To respit his day-labour with repast,
Or with repose; and such discourse bring on,
As may advise him of his happie state,
Happiness in his power left free to will,
Left to his own free Will, his Will though free,
Yet mutable; whence warne him to beware
He swerve not too secure: tell him withall
His danger, and from whom, what enemie
Late fall'n himself from Heav'n is plotting now
The fall of others from like state of bliss;
By violence, no, for that shall be withstood,
But by deceit and lies; this let him know,
Least wilfully transgressing he pretend
Surprisal, unadmonisht, unforewarnd.
So spake th'Eternal Father, and fulfilld
All Justice: nor delaid the winged Saint
After his charge receivd; but from among
Thousand Celestial Ardors, where he stood
Vaild with his gorgeous wings, up springing light
Flew through the midst of Heav'n; th' angelic Quires
On each hand parting, to his speed gave way
Through all th'Empyreal road; till at the Gate
Of Heav'n arriv'd, the gate self-op'nd wide
On gold'n Hinges turning, as by work
Divine the sovran Architect had fram'd.
From hence, no cloud, or, to obstruct his sight,
Starr interpos'd, however small he sees,
Not unconform to other shining Globes,

Earth and the Gard'n of God, with Cedars crownd
Above all Hills. As when by night the Glass
Of *Galileo,* less assur'd, observes
Imagind Lands and Regions in the Moon:
Or Pilot from amidst the *Cyclades*
Delos or *Samos* first appeering kenns
A cloudy spot. Down thither prone in flight
He speeds, and through the vast Ethereal Skie
Sailes between worlds and worlds, with steddie wing
Now on the polar windes, then with quick Fann
Winnows the buxom Air; till within soare
Of Towring Eagles, to all the Fowles he seems
A *Phoenix,* gaz'd by all, as that sole Bird
When to enshrine his reliques in the Suns
Bright Temple, to *Aegyptian Theb's* he flies.
At once on th' Eastern cliff of Paradise
He lights, and to his proper shape returns
A Seraph wingd; six wings he wore, to shade
His lineaments Divine; the pair that clad
Each shoulder broad, came mantling ore his brest
With regal Ornament; the middle pair
Girt like a Starrie Zone his waste, and round
Skirted his loines and thighes with downie Gold
And colours dipt in Heav'n; the third his feet
Shaddowd from either heele with featherd maile
Skie-tinctur'd grain. Like *Maia*'s son he stood,
And shook his Plumes, that Heav'nly fragrance filld
The circuit wide. Strait knew him all the Bands
Of Angels under watch; and to his state,
And to his message high in honour rise;
For on som message high they guessd him bound.
Thir glittering Tents he passd, and now is come
Into the blissful field, through Groves of Myrrhe,
And flouring Odours, Cassia, Nard, and Balme;
A Wilderness of sweets; for Nature here
Wantond as in her prime, and paid at will
Her Virgin Fancies, pouring forth more sweet,
Wilde above Rule or Art; enormous bliss.

Him through the spicie Forrest onward com
Adam discernd, as in the dore he sat
Of his coole Bowre . . .

The verse of *Paradise Lost,* and pre-eminently such a passage as this, manifests as spacious and grandiose an imagination as we are privileged to know. If, as I have suggested, a perpetual expansiveness is the habit of the epic sensibility, then Milton was supremely endowed for epic. His most typical arrangements of space do not contain the crowded complexity typical of Virgil—are not, as it were, so busy, but they compose an immensity which shrinks the cosmos of Virgil by comparison. This immensity is effected here partly by the play of perspective and the stress on seeing, by the inconspicuous tininess of earth to Raphael's sight, and his loftiness from the vantage of towering eagles. The immensity is also effected by a certain careless disposal of the astral spheres, here not arranged according to the Ptolemaic system, nor catalogued in order as they are by Dante or Tasso. The earth is

Not unconform to other shining Globes . . .

The randomness of Milton's heaven, the lack of tidy symmetry, somehow extends further its limits. We know as readers that his heaven *is* orderly in the fundamental respects, but when he writes

Down thither prone in flight
He speeds, and through the vast Ethereal Skie
Sailes between worlds and worlds . . .

or when he writes earlier of Satan's descent

Down right into the Worlds first Region throws
His flight precipitant, and windes with ease
Through the pure marble Air his oblique way
Amongst innumerable Starrs . . .
[III.562–65]

Milton's cosmos expands to a greater, more intractable vastness, wild like paradise "above Rule or Art."

The immensity of the poem moreover is not simply physical; that vastness is complemented by the learning which has wearied some readers and to others has wrongly seemed matter in itself for praise. No praise is due to pedantry, and pedantry there is occasionally in *Paradise Lost.* But on the whole it is confined to a few *loci molesti;* the wonder is that so much breadth of knowledge is saved from pedantry, so much history introduced with the natural ease of genius, so many allusions brought together without any yoking by violence. The grim, categorical, and narrow version of human history in Books Eleven and Twelve is supplemented by scattered allusions in the rest of the poem to a fuller, more various history—like the allusions above to Galileo and the pilot of the Cyclades.

If we consider only the Judaic-Christian elements in these eighty lines, their range is impressive: the original myth from Genesis; Isaiah's vision of the six-winged seraphim; [26] the homely and charming story of Tobit; echoes of the pseudo-Dionysius' angelology; [27] the late Latin poem *De Ave Phoenice* ascribed to Lactantius; the theology of Augustine, among others; the Christian epic of the Renaissance, and particularly Tasso. All of these elements appear without strain in this episode of classical derivation, because they seem to have co-existed harmoniously in Milton's sensibility with the fruit of his classical education. Lesser poets avoided the comparison with Mercury at all costs because they were too self-conscious and uncertain of their Christian Humanism. But Milton's sensibility was at peace with itself, and the uncomfortable divisions of his predecessors did not touch him. "Like Maia's son he stood," he writes of Raphael, just as he puts the Graces in Eden, and we read on untroubled. If the superb description of the angel's wings (277–85) imitates Isaiah (with a glance at Ezekiel 1, in the treatment of the second pair), the eccentricity and Asiatic remoteness of the Old Testament have been suppressed. The uppermost wings do not, as in Isaiah, cover Raphael's face, but come "mantling ore his brest with regal Ornament." In describing the angel's wings, Milton describes more than wings; he endows his creature with a grace and energy and

26. "Above it stood the seraphims: each one had six wings; with twain he covered his face, and with twain he covered his feet, and with twain he did fly." Isaiah 6:2.

27. The word *Ardors* in line 249 refers to the seraphim, the highest of the nine angelic orders, associated by the pseudo-Dionysius and later angelologists with a fervent and burning love of God.

poise and beauty beyond the concern of the prophet—qualities reminiscent rather of antique and high Renaissance sculpture. His speculative intellect may not have remained as serene, but his *intuitions* of antiquity and of Hebraic culture were so spontaneously fine that he achieved for once that miraculous fusion denied to the culture of England or of Europe as a whole.

The style of *Paradise Lost* is a product of analogous fusion. Intervolved, hypotactic, and compressed as it generally is, the style is still more flexible than it looks at first acquaintance, and while one critic may praise its classical simplicity, another speaks of its "verbal cleverness, grotesqueness and obscurity," its "primitive . . . zest." [28] Both kinds of style, as well as others, can be found in the poem. Their diversity springs not only from Milton's acute sense of decorum but from the several conceptions of language which had once lain in incipient conflict within his mind.

The first of these was the rhetorical conception Milton learned as a boy at Saint Paul's and from his tutor Thomas Young. The training in classics given at a Renaissance school was based upon the idea, descended from Isocrates and Cicero, that the perspicuous and accomplished use of language fosters the dignity, wisdom, and even the moral elevation of men. If, as I suggested in Chapter Two, the use of language always involves an implicit confrontation with the magical or demonic powers in words, then Humanist rhetoric took a middle position toward them. By stressing clarity and precision, and by systematically cataloguing tropes, rhetoric tethered the demonic elements with firm bonds while still not altogether paralyzing them. Language, according to this position, is a creature of the human mind which remains its docile but immensely productive servant.[29] The rhetoricians lived by the faith that language employed with discipline and study was an instrument for attaining truth, and the younger

28. F. T. Prince, *The Italian Element in Milton's Verse* (Oxford, 1954), p. 129 n. B. Rajan, in his *Paradise Lost and the Seventeenth Century Reader* (London, 1947), is a recent critic who lays particular stress on the classicism of Milton's style.

29. "Io ho per firmo, che le lingue d'ogni paese . . . siano d'un medesmo valore, & da' mortali ad un fine con un giuditio formate; che io non vorrei che voi ne parlaste come di cosa dalla natura prodotta; essendo fatte, & regolate dallo artifitio delle persone & beneplacito loro." Sperone Speroni, "Dialogo delle Lingue," in *Dialoghi* (Venice, 1596), pp. 122–23.

Milton bears witness in a score of passages to his participation in that faith.[30]

But he was also influenced by divergent conceptions of language less compatible with that faith than he realized. On the one hand, certain passages of his prose reflect sympathy with that current of Puritanism which distrusted all rhetoric or ornamentation, a current which professed to find Scripture bare of tropes and which sought to quell the demonic elements with a strait jacket of stylistic "purity." [31] Thus Milton in an early pamphlet refers to the "sober, plain, and unaffected stile of the Scriptures," and ridicules the prelates who seek refuge in church tradition from Scripture's accusing clarity:

> They feare the plain field of the Scriptures . . . they seek the dark, the bushie, the tangled Forrest, they would imbosk . . .[32]

As he was forced to pentrate the tangled forest of controversy, forced to recognize the abuses of language by which his opponents (to his thinking) muddied truth, he became increasingly aware of the insidious deceptiveness of language, and lost a little of his rhetorical faith. In passage after passage of his prose, and even of his sonnets, he thunders against those perverse and barbarous manipulators of words who prostitute language for unworthy

30. One might cite the *Areopagitica* virtually passim in illustration, as well as large parts of the Seventh Prolusion and *Of Education*. Consider for example Milton's remark after sketching his proposed study of the trivium: "From hence, and not till now, will be the right season of forming them to be able writers and composers in every excellent matter, when they shall be thus fraught with an universal insight into things." C.E., *4*, 286.

31. Haller cites the following passage as typical: "Whereas men in their writings affect the praise of flowing eloquence and loftiness of phrase, the holy Ghost . . . hath used great simplicities and wonderful plainness, applying himselfe to the capacities of the most unlearned . . . and under the vaile of simple and plaine speech, there shineth such divine wisdome and glorious majestie, that all the human writings in the world though never so adorned with the flowers of eloquence, and sharpe conceits of wit and learning cannot so deeply pearce the heart of man." John Downame, *Christian Warfare*, pp. 339–40, quoted by William Haller, *The Rise of Puritanism* (New York, 1957), p. 130. This Puritan attitude toward language resembles in certain respects the attitude of scientific rationalists like Hobbes and Sprat, although the two attitudes are based on very different presuppositions.

32. C.E., *3*, 35.

ends.[33] The preface to his *Art of Logic* warns with disillusion that art may blunt as well as sharpen nature "when it is employed too anxiously and too subtly, and especially where it is unnecessary." [34]

This conservative conception was at variance with still a third, which Milton entertained in his hopes of becoming a Christian poet-priest. This conception led him to a truer understanding of Old Testament language, with its dense orchestration of imagery, its poetic abandon, its visionary fire, not more restrained, as some Puritans thought, but less restrained than classical poetry. The implicit theory of Hebrew prophecy was inspirationalist; it denied study and rational control; it regarded the poet as a man possessed or driven by God to speak things his rational will resisted; it released the demonic powers within the word and made of it a searing, blazing, uncontrollable thing, an antisocial explosive. Milton played with that conception when in *The Reason of Church Government* he spoke of his intention to write a great sacred poem; he quoted Jeremiah:

> His word was in my heart as a burning fire shut up in my bones.

and he alluded to the calling of Isaiah when he prayed to

> that Eternal Spirit who can enrich with all utterance and knowledge, and sends out his seraphim with the hallowed fire of his altar, to touch and purify the lips of whom he pleases . . .[35]

He was moved by the same ideal when he pictured the sacred poet "soaring in the high region of his fancies with his garland and singing robes about him." [36] Other passages in the same tract make clear that he was far from rejecting many of his Humanist-rhetorical beliefs, but the phrases I have quoted show him radically modifying or extending them.

33. C.E., *3*, 34; *5*, 5; *14*, 5; etc. Compare Sonnets XI, XII, XV, and "On the new forcers of Conscience."

34. C.E., *11*, 3.

35. C. E., *3*, 241. The quotation from Jeremiah appears at *3*, 231.

36. C.E., *3*, 235. Milton echoes the conventional classical expression of a comparable, but less "sincere," inspirationalist attitude in the opening of his *Elegia Quinta*.

All of these conceptions—the rhetorical, the Puritan, the inspirational—contributed to the style of *Paradise Lost* and were there harmonized. Of these the first is the most commonly recognized. The debt of Milton's style to classical Latin has become a truism, but the truism is meaningless if it fails to distinguish the effect of *Latin* poetry from the effect of *latinate* poetry *in English.* Milton enriched many English words by restoring to them their Latin meanings (like his use of *enormous,* in line 297 of Raphael's descent, to mean "exceeding the rule"), but in thus roughening his language he did not imitate Virgil. Virgil allowed his language a certain shadowiness when he chose, but never so much as to dim its continuous clarity. Virgil's language is seldom so *thick* as Milton's. Moreover the deliberate rearranging of normal English word order may *remind* you of Latin, but it creates an effect quite unlike Latin. English does not commonly permit the rearrangement Milton attempted, so that he arrived at something very unlike the Virgilian style. By adopting Tasso's theory of *asprezza* or "roughness" as a means to stylistic "magnificence," Milton moved away from the correctness which a later generation would associate with Virgil. His liberties with language in *Paradise Lost* are actually far greater than those authorized by antique precedent or by his education. He did not surrender rational control to inspirational abandon, but he allowed the demons in his language at least as much room as he allowed to those in his *dramatis personae.*

He had not, for all this, lost his conservative distrust of language, which had rather been deepening with the years. It affects both that style Milton accommodated to heaven and the other he accommodated to hell. In heaven it is reflected in the abstract and colorless speeches of God and the decorous choral hymns of the angels which aim at stark simplicity. Milton's own style in describing heaven (but not Raphael's style in describing the war) virtually eschews similes and his language, if elevated, is markedly less dense than elsewhere. Comparison is out of place in heaven, and even when poetry is descriptive, as in lines 247–56 of Raphael's descent, the visual brilliance is simply reported without ambiguity or metaphor or ulterior significance. We see few physical things in heaven, but those we see—such as the gate which opens to

Raphael, or the angelic crowns strewn on the sea of jasper before God's throne (III.349 ff)—are shining and pure-colored and incapable of similitude to earthly copies. The style Milton used to describe heaven might well have pleased John Calvin.

In hell the distrust of rhetoric is reflected in just the opposite way. For the speeches of Satan and the other devils are brilliant textbook models of illogic, demagoguery, wrenched syllogisms, false conclusions, sleight-of-phrase, malicious abuse of words. The impressive description of Beelzebub at the Great Consult:

> . . . with grave
> Aspect he rose, and in his rising seemd
> A Pillar of State; deep on his Front engraven
> Deliberation sat and publick care;
> And Princely counsel in his face yet shone . . .
> [II.300–04]

is a misleading portrait of the ideal Ciceronian orator-statesman which anticipates the pose of Satan at the climax of his temptation of Eve, like "som Orator renound in Athens or free Rome" (IX.670–71). Both deceptive poses are successful.

If the style which describes heaven is "pure," that which decribes hell is murkily accommodated to the darkness visible. We make out the dim, grey, physical forms through a fog of jagged syntax, deceptive similes, confusions of physical and abstract,[37] straight-faced but withering irony. In heaven Milton would have us see face to face the truth that makes us free, but in hell darkly the confusion which enslaves us. This is why the syntax of Satan's opening speech resists parsing, and the first statement about Death (II.666–70) is no statement at all but a noun followed by conditional clauses trailing off to leave the sentence incomplete. This is why Satan and Belial begin to pun during the war, "scoffing in ambiguous words." It is this style which leads Prince to speak of "cleverness, grotesqueness, and obscurity" in *Paradise Lost*.

Milton's third style, that which is accommodated to earth, represents something of a mean between his celestial and infernal manners. Terrestrial vision after the fall is obscured by the:

37. See Maynard Mack, introduction to *Milton* volume of English Masterpieces (Englewood Cliffs, New Jersey, 1961).

sideral blast,
Vapour, and Mist, and Exhalation hot,
Corrupt and Pestilent . . . [X.693–95]

and a pall of infernal confusion hovers correspondingly about the worried syntax of Adam's soliloquy:

O miserable of happie! is this the end
Of this new glorious World, and mee so late
The Glory of that Glory, who now becom
Accurst of blessed, hide me from the face
Of God, whom to behold was then my highth
Of happiness: yet well, if here would end
The miserie, I deserv'd it . . . [X.720–26]

All of Adam's posterity will be pursued by that "Ev'ning Mist," curling up in the poem's closing lines, which

Ris'n from a River ore the marish glides,
And gathers ground fast at the Labourers heel
Homeward returning. [XII.630–32]

Human vision after the fall is dimmed; the mist will darken "the glass of Galileo" when it,

less assur'd, observes
Imagind Lands and Regions in the Moon . . .

and so the pilot's sight is blurred when he

from amidst the Cyclades
Delos or Samos first appeering kenns
A cloudy spot.

The pilot's uncertainty is imitated by the uncertain grammar, which leaves the reader peering to make out the construction. *Spot* might be considered as an appositive after *Delos* and *Samos,* taken as objects of *kenns,* but one could also consider *spot* the object, and "Delos or Samos first appeering" a parenthetical absolute phrase.

Such clouded vision is the effect of the fall. But even before it, the appearances of this world are capable of misleading, and the style is a little less transparent than in heaven. Raphael's own vision, to be sure, is faultless:

From hence, no cloud, or, to obstruct his sight,
Starr interpos'd, however small he sees,
Not unconform to other shining Globes,
Earth and the Gard'n of God, with Cedars crownd
Above all Hills.

The detail of the cedars convinces us that he really does see the garden. But the syntax puts a strain on the act of vision, as soon as Raphael passes the gate of heaven, by confusing us momentarily with the absolute construction, "no cloud or . . . starr interpos'd," and by separating the adjective *small* so far from the nouns it modifies, *Earth* and *Gard'n*. But this strain is slight in comparison to the logical ambiguity surrounding the phoenix. Does Raphael literally take the form of this bird?

till within soare
Of Towring Eagles, to all the Fowles he seems
A Phoenix, gaz'd by all, as that sole Bird
When to enshrine his reliques in the Suns
Bright Temple, to Aegyptian Theb's he flies.

If one stopped reading here, there would be no difficulty: Raphael is not flying to Thebes; he is carrying no relics; one could only read this passage as a simile in which the angel is tenor and the bird vehicle. But Milton continues:

At once on th'Eastern cliff of Paradise
He lights, and to his proper shape returns
A Seraph wingd . . .

If Raphael returns to his proper shape then he *has* assumed literally the form of a phoenix, however lacking its burden and destination. Or has his flight simply deceived the "Fowles" who take him mistakenly for a superior bird? The text seems rather to support the former reading, and it appears that we must accustom ourselves to a phoenix both within and without the simile. Milton in any case has been less than ingenuous with his readers, and the more one reads him, the more disingenuous he appears.[38]

38. Compare the following passage in Book Four, where Satan as tiger seems to stray into a simile while still remaining outside it:

Down he alights among the sportful Herd
Of those fourfooted kindes, himself now one,

Why introduce a phoenix here at all, figurative or real? That too is unclear, but we remember at least the purpose of the angel's descent:

> By violence, no, for that shall be withstood,
> But by deceit and lies; this let him know . . .

This world is vulnerable to deceit, and Milton subtly underscores the passage from heaven to earth by heightening the demonic insidiousness of his language. The fallen reader's imperfect reason must strain to make out relations as the pilot strains with his physical eyes, as Galileo strains with his telescope, as the fowls gaze with mistaken recognition on the angel, as Adam and Eve will fail to strain and so blur all our vision.

Thus if Milton enriched the classical style with unorthodox and audacious liberties, he also passed judgment in a sense upon those liberties, and in his most "exalted" scenes attempted to dispense with them. This latter procedure he carried even further in *Paradise Regained,* where the poetic treatment of Christ is comparably bare, and only the temptations make lovely but intermittent demands upon the senses.

iii.

Paradise Lost is the only epic to incorporate the celestial descent into a larger, and indeed a comprehensive pattern of imagery, a pattern which includes the poem's two major events—the falls of Satan and of Adam. Milton interweaves those events into a fabric of multitudinous references to height and depth, rising and falling, which appear on virtually every page and bind every incident of the narrative into a closer unity. Sometimes witty, sometimes

---

> Now other, as thir shape servd best his end
> Neerer to view his prey . . .
> . . about them round
> A Lion now he stalkes with fierie glare,
> Then as a Tiger, who by chance hath spi'd
> In some Purlieu two gentle Fawnes at play,
> Strait couches close, then rising changes oft
> His couchant watch . . .
> (IV.396–99, 401–06)

ironic, sometimes simple and transparent, appearing now in an epithet, a phrase, a simile as well as in the sweeping lines of the action, the subtle workings of this pattern turn incessantly a moral or metaphysical mirror upon objective events, and conversely translate moral events into spatial terms.

Milton seems to have regarded this pattern—it might be called vertical imagery—as one of two patterns basic to his poem. The other is the ubiquitous imagery of light and dark. He couples them—and thereby associates his own creative act with the dramatic action—at the close of his first invocation:

What in mee is dark
Illumin, what is low raise and support . . .
[I.22–23]

He couples them again in describing Satan during the temptation of Eve:

Hope elevates, and joy
Bright'ns his Crest . . .
[IX.633–34]

And he seems to balance them in constructing Books Two and Three. Book Three is saturated with light imagery as Book Two is with vertical imagery. The hymn to light which opens Book Three is balanced by the opening of Book Two:

High on a Throne of Royal State . . .
Satan exalted sat, by merit rais'd
To that bad eminence; and from despair
Thus high uplifted beyond hope, aspires
Beyond thus high, insatiat to persue
Vain Warr with Heav'n . . . [II.1, 5–9]

Book Two ends with the punning verb *hies* as Book Three ends with the punning *lights*. In the rest of the poem the two patterns are mingled indiscriminately as they are in the first book, but the vertical imagery is perhaps the denser throughout.

Underlying this imagery is a paradox which had become a Biblical commonplace. Its most familiar forms are the prophecies of the second Isaiah:

> Every valley shall be exalted, and every mountain and hill shall be made low.[39]

and of Christ:

> Whosoever shall exalt himself shall be abased; and he that shall humble himself shall be exalted.[40]

But it takes many other forms: in the command to Ezekiel:

> Exalt him that is low, and abase him that is high.[41]

in Mary's hymn of gratitude to God:

> He hath put down the mighty from their seats, and exalted them of low degree.[42]

in the admonition of Peter:

> Humble yourselves therefore under the mighty hand of God, that he may exalt you in due time.[43]

and in many other passages.[44] The paradox appears in the poetry of men as different as Vaughan ("O let me climbe when I lye down") and Du Bartas,[45] and it recurs in the prose of the paradox-loving Donne.[46] But it found its most sophisticated expression—and the most relevant to Milton—in Saint Augustine:

> There is, therefore, something in humility which, strangely enough, exalts the heart, and something in pride which de-

39. Isaiah 40:4.
40. Matthew 23:12. Compare Luke 14:11; 18:14.
41. Ezekiel 21:26.
42. Luke 1:52.
43. I Peter 5:5–6.
44. Job 24:24. Ezekiel 31:10–18. Micah 7:8. Matthew 11:23. James 1:9–10. Ephesians 4:9–10. Philippians 2:5–10.
45. *La Premiere Sepmaine,* Premier Jour, 557–74; 669–70. The line from Vaughan is from "The Morning Watch." Compare Milton's line from the verses "At a vacation exercise": "Yet being above them, he shall be below them" (l. 80).
46. See *Devotions Upon Emergent Occasions,* Meditation #21: "I am readier to fall to the earth, now I am up, than I was when I lay in bed . . . Even rising is the way to ruin!" "Now I am up, I am ready to sink lower than before." See also Sermon XV, Folio of 1640, preached at Whitehall, March 8, 1622.

> bases it. This seems, indeed, to be contradictory, that loftiness should debase and lowliness exalt. But pious humility enables us to submit to what is above us; and nothing is more exalted above us than God; and therefore humility, by making us subject to God, exalts us. But pride, being a defect of nature, by the very act of refusing subjection and revolting from Him who is supreme, falls to a low condition; and then comes to pass what is written: "Thou castedst them down when they lifted up themselves." For he does not say "when they had been lifted up" as if first they were exalted, and then afterwards cast down; but "when they lifted up themselves" even then they were cast down—that is to say, the very lifting up was already a fall. And therefore it is that humility is specially recommended to the city of God as it sojourns in this world, and is specially exhibited in the city of God, and in the person of Christ its King; while the contrary vice of pride, according to the testimony of the sacred writings, specially rules his adversary the devil.[47]

Paradise Lost plays continually with the paradoxical duality of lowness—the lowness of humility and of moral degradation or despair—and with the duality of height—of spiritual eminence or exaltation and of pride. It plays also with the paradoxes of rising and falling, the abasement that exalts and the pride that abases. When Adam and Eve fall prostrate to the ground, confessing their sin with tears in humiliation meek, their prayers rise successfully to heaven. When the Son offers to descend to a mortal body, he is correspondingly elevated:

> because in thee
> Love hath abounded more than Glory abounds,
> Therefore thy Humiliation shall exalt
> With thee thy Manhood also to this Throne . . .
> [III.311–14]

But when Satan's ambition leads him to rebel, he enters a state of perpetual pride and thus continuous, progressive degradation. The bitterest ironies in hell are reserved for the devils' attempts

47. *City of God,* Book XIV, chapter 13.

to deny their fall, to build up their downcast pride and by so doing unwittingly to deepen their abasement. Here they are cheering themselves up:

> hee his wonted pride
> Soon recollecting, with *high* words, that bore
> Semblance of worth not substance, gently *rais'd*
> Thir fainted courage, and dispelld thir fears.
> Then strait commands that at the warlike sound
> Of Trumpets loud and Clarions be *upreard*
> His mighty Standard; that proud honour claimd
> Azazel as his right, a Cherube *tall:*
> Who forthwith from the glittering Staff unfurld
> Th'Imperial Ensign, which full *high* advanc't
> Shon like a Meteor streaming to the Wind . . .
> At which the universal Host *upsent*
> A shout that tore Hells Concave . . .
> All in a moment through the gloom were seen
> Ten thousand Banners *rise* into the Air
> With Orient Colours waving: with them *rose*
> A forrest huge of Spears . . .
> Anon they move
> In perfet Phalanx to the Dorian mood
> Of Flutes and soft Recorders; such as *rais'd*
> To *highth* of noblest temper Hero's old
> Arming to Battel . . . [I.527–53]

When earlier Satan cries:

> . . . in this abject posture have ye sworn
> To adore the Conqueror? . . .
> Awake, arise, or be for ever fall'n.
> [I.322–23, 330]

his irony is swallowed in a greater irony. Each of the speakers at the Great Consult is really concerned with regaining his former height by various means: Moloch by armed invasions; Belial, whose "thoughts were low," by appeasement; Mammon, by attempting to "raise Magnificence;—and what can Heav'n shew more?"; Beelzebub, by corrupting man that the devils may "Joy upraise" in God's disturbance. This venture, says Beelzebub, "from the lowest deep will once more lift us up" (II.392–93). And Satan as he volunteers is one whom

> now transcendent glory rais'd
> Above his fellows, with Monarchal pride
> Conscious of highest worth . . .
> [II.427–29]

The consult disbands with its leaders "rais'd by false presumptuous hope," some of them to celebrate past deeds in song but others to retire to a hill, "in thoughts more elevate," there to reason high of fate and freedom. The symbolic answer to all this is the metamorphosis in Book Ten:

> They felt themselves now changing; down thir arms,
> Down fell both Spear and Shield, down they as fast,
> And the dire hiss renewd, and the dire form
> Catchd by Contagion, like in punishment,
> As in thir crime. [X.541–45]

The descent of Raphael typifies that celestial condescension which is opposed to demonic aspiration. It is a minor instance of the solicitous compassion for man whose major instance is Christ's sacrificial redemption. The episode's opening words:

> Them thus imploid beheld
> With pittie Heav'ns high King . . .

implicitly express the paradox of divine generosity. The epithet *high* is not perfunctory; it makes the necessary quiet contrast with *pittie,* God's affective descent to earth which precedes the angel's literal descent. Raphael is chosen in turn for that gracious mansuetude toward men which he will display again toward Tobias. That he deigns now to descend to extended conversation with Adam implies as well the height of man upon the scale of creation. When after the fall Michael descends to Paradise, Adam immediately remarks the severer aspect of his mien:

> yet not terrible,
> That I should fear, nor sociably mild,

As Raphael, that I should much confide,
But solemn and sublime . . . [XI.223–36]

The fallen Adam will not be worthy then to receive the angel in "his shape Celestial" but "as Man clad to meet Man." Raphael's prelapsarian sociable mildness betokens both heavenly charity and human dignity.

That this height of dignity is threatened we are reminded by God's references to

what enemie
Late fall'n himself from Heav'n is plotting now
The fall of others from like state of bliss . . .

But for the moment the threat is muted; man remains the felicitous enjoyer of God's garden, "with Cedars crownd above all hills," for whose welfare celestial emissaries post with zealous speed.

Down thither prone in flight
He speeds . . .

The adverb is stressed by its position. Raphael's magnanimity is further underscored by the revelation of his eminence in the angelic hierarchy. He is one to whom the lesser angels pay homage warranted both by his rank and his errand:

Strait knew him all the Bands
Of Angels under watch; and to his state,
And to his message high in honour rise;
For on som message high they guessed him bound.

Adam too will pay homage, although not such as to compromise his own rank:

Mean while our Primitive great Sire, to meet
His god-like Guest, walks forth, without more train
Accompanied then with his own compleat
Perfections; in himself was all his state . . .
Neerer his presence Adam though not awd,
Yet with submiss approach and reverence meek,

As to a superior Nature, bowing low,
Thus said . . . [V.350–53, 358–61]

Both the rising of the angels and the bowing of Adam demonstrate the true and cheerful humility which, for Milton, remained consonant with self-respect and freedom.

The height of Adam's dignity before the fall is balanced by his abasement afterwards: first after Eve's sin when he "the Garland wreath'd for Eve down dropd" (X.892–93); then in the false humiliation of pride-concealing despair, when

On the ground
Outstretcht he lay, on the cold ground, and oft
Curs'd his Creation . . . [X.850–52]

and later in the true humiliation of repentance, when husband and wife

Repairing where he judg'd them prostrate fell
Before him reverent . . . [X.1099–100]

Despite the mercy earned by that act, they must leave Paradise, and the closing lines show them led "down the Cliff . . . to the subjected Plaine" of suffering and death. This to be sure is not the ultimate conclusion; that will come only when

New Heav'n and Earth shall to the Ages rise,
Or down from Heav'n descend. [X.647–48]

That is the conclusion the poem glimpses hopefully, but it remains in the distance. The true curve of the poem's major action follows the fallen couple down into the valley of humiliation.

In thus ending with a downward movement, *Paradise Lost* reverses the visionary ascent with which Milton almost habitually concluded his earlier poems. The youthful optimism of his Christian Humanism is reflected in the soaring visions of redemption which conclude *On Time, At a Solemn Musick, Epitaph on the Marchioness of Winchester, On the Death of the Bishop of Winchester, Manso, Damon's Epitaph, Lycidas,* and *Comus.* The same optimism informs the visionary conclusion of his first published prose work, *Of Reformation in England.* We can contrast that period of hope with the pessimism of twenty years later by noticing the downward movement with which *The Ready and Easy*

Way concludes. The final words of that tract warn against the "precipice of destruction" to which the "deluge" of Royalist "epidemic madness would hurry us, through the general defection of a misguided and abused multitude." [48] At the time these words were written, *Paradise Lost* was already well begun. The descent with which the epic concludes has none of the tract's desperate alarm, but their common movement downward is significant. In both works the poet struggles—as indeed he does in all the later works—to reconcile the high potentialities of man with his fallen perversity. The vertical imagery in *Paradise Lost* registers the progress of that noble and fearful struggle within a great man's moral imagination.

iv.

The richness of Milton's similes is unique in epic poetry. The finest of them are marvels of compression, and their relationship to their respective tenors seems almost inexhaustible. They form thus a sharp contrast with the similes of the *Iliad* which, as we have seen, tend to provide relief from the narrative rather than commentary upon it. Virgil's similes do comment, in broad and generally moral terms, but they do not imitate the tenor in specific point after point; no ingenuity or wit has gone into their making. Milton's similes are immensely ingenious; they are little Chinese boxes of meaning. His conception of the simile may have been influenced less by the classical epics than by the theory and practice of George Chapman's translations. Chapman believed in the detailed correspondence between Homer's similes and their tenors, and tried to demonstrate his belief with desparate ingenuity in his translation as well as his notes.[49]

Certain of Milton's literary and historical allusions are in themselves incipient similes, like the Tobias allusion which precedes Raphael's descent:

> Them thus imploid beheld
> With pittie Heav'ns high King, and to him calld
> Raphael, the sociable Spirit, that deignd

48. C.E., *6*, 149.

49. See for example Chapman's *Iliad,* 2.72 ff., and his commentary on this passage.

To travel with Tobias, and secur'd
His marriage with the seav'ntimes-wedded Maid.

Milton is implicitly comparing the two descents. The ostensible point of comparison is the sociability of Raphael discussed above, that quality by which he deigns "half this day as friend to friend" to converse with Adam just as he will deign to travel with Tobias. This is the ostensible point in common, but here as in most Miltonic similes, the ostensible point is not the most important. The purpose of Raphael's visit is to warn Adam against Satan, and we remember that in the Tobias story Raphael succeeds in bilking Satan. If we had forgotten it, an earlier allusion would have reminded us:

So entertaind those odorous sweets the Fiend
Who came thir bane, though with them better pleas'd
Then Asmodeus with the fishie fume,
That drove him though enamourd, from the Spouse
Of Tobits Son, and with a vengeance sent
From Media post to Aegypt, there fast bound.
[IV.166–71]

Asmodeus or Satan has sexual designs upon Sara, the spouse of Tobias, just as Satan designs to seduce Eve. Raphael appears in Tobit as the protector of a marriage ("secur'd his marriage with the seav'ntimes-wedded Maid."), the role which he is about to play here. When God considers Adam and Eve "thus imploid . . . with pittie," they stand as patterns of a perfect marriage. They have first manifiested their conjugal harmony in the morning hymn, and now their cooperative labor involves a second kind of wedding:

they led the Vine
To wed her Elm; she spous'd about him twines
Her mariageable arms, and with her brings
Her dowr th'adopted Clusters, to adorn
His barren leaves. Them thus imploid . . .
[V.215–19]

They deserve pity because they exemplify marriage threatened by the devil. Raphael's solicitude in *Tobit* for the uniquely human institution also graces the domestic scenes in Adam's bower. But this spouse he cannot protect.

The phoenix simile—since it *is* at least partly a simile—remains more difficult to elucidate because the history of the phoenix legend is immensely complex, and because Milton helps less to focus his meaning by qualifying particulars. The meaning of such an image really has an open end, and no one can know precisely at what point to delimit it; we cannot even be absolutely sure how much comparative mythology Milton knew.[50] The texts most obviously in the background of the simile are Tasso's description of Armida (*Ger. Lib.*, 18.35), his beautiful *canzone, La Fenice,* and the simile from Vondel's descent which we noticed in the last chapter. All of these passages use the bird as an image of brilliance and beauty and éclat, qualities which Milton is at pains to confer upon his angel and which may in themselves have led him to the image. From the *Odyssey* and *Aeneid* downward, the descent convention involved a bird simile, and what more natural than to choose for *Paradise Lost* the most fabulous of birds, the unique, indeed the legendary king of birds? [51]

Behind the Renaissance allusions lie the manifold descriptions in antique prose and verse. Among the fullest of these are the poems on the phoenix by Claudian and Lactantius, if the attribution to the latter is correct. In both of these poems much is made of the excitement engendered by the bird's arrival in Egypt, so precious and sacred was it considered to be. Not only is it greeted joyfully by men, but the very birds acclaim and escort it. Claudian's poem specifically names the eagle as a member of this escort, and the same poet returns to the image elsewhere in a passage strikingly close to Milton's:

> So when by that birth in death the Phoenix renews its youth and gathers its father's ashes and carries them lovingly in its

50. I am indebted to my colleague Geoffrey Hartmann for valuable bibliographical information on the phoenix in antiquity. The most useful single study is by J. Hubaux and M. Leroy, *Le Mythe du Phénix dans les Littératures Grecque et Latine* (Liège, 1939).

51. Milton may have taken a hint from Marino who, in his *Gerusalemme Distrutta,* compared all the angels in heaven to phoenixes (Zirardini, ed., p. 493). Another extended description of the bird can be found in Du Bartas (*Premiere Sepmaine,* Cinquiesme Jour, 551–98), although Milton did not follow the common association of the phoenix with Christ found there.

> talons, winging its way, sole of its kind, from the extreme east to Nile's coasts, the eagles gather together and all the fowls from every quarter to marvel at the bird of the sun; afar its living plumage shines, itself redolent of its father's fragrant pyre.[52]

A reader familiar with such a passage as this would recognize in Milton's allusion the note of religious and joyful momentousness.

Neither the poets of antiquity—Ovid, Claudian, Lactantius—nor the prose authors—Herodotus, Pliny, Tacitus, etc.—who speak of the phoenix describe it as a celestial messenger, but this role was anciently assigned to it, or a bird like it, in the Orient and Egypt. An English scholar writes as follows of Egyptian beliefs regarding birds:

> The bird, of whatever kind, is the obvious choice for a messenger since it is essential to the whole idea of the reservoir of power that it should be unattainable by mere mortals. The traffic is both ways, the bird is the messenger from men to gods or, more exactly, the soul of the departed who traverses the boundary between the two worlds and the angel of the gods who comes from the divine numinous regions of power. In the latter case the message from the gods is the announcement of ineluctable fate, the re-appearance of some temporarily absent physical phenomenon—a star, a season, an inundation of the Nile, or it can be the declaration of a new age or phase of good or evil luck.[53]

One bird singled out particularly for the role of messenger was the *Bn.w* bird, which seems to have been a mythographic ancestor of the phoenix.

> On the whole the *Bn.w* bird is an angel, announcing stellar events or dates and, by an extension, the fate of mankind.[54]

Milton could not have known this belief in anything like its original form, but some derived version of it may conceivably have

52. Claudian, "On Stilicho's Consulship," trans. M. Platnauer, Loeb Classical Library, 2 (London and New York, 1922), 414–20.

53. R. T. Rundle Clark, "The Origin of the Phoenix," *Birmingham Historical Journal,* 2 (1949–50), 132.

54. Ibid., p. 133.

reached him. In any case the phoenix became an obvious symbol for a new age and for collective or individual renewal. Just as Vida had applied it to the resurrected Christ,[55] so Milton would use it as a great climactic symbol of Samson's regeneration.[56] It is suggestive that in his other verse reference to the phoenix, in the *Epitaphium Damonis*,[57] he represents it watching the dawn arise. And when in *Paradise Lost* God predicts the end of the fallen world, he uses language which recalls the phoenix legend:

> The World shall burn, and from her ashes spring
> New Heav'n and Earth . . . [III.334–35]

Raphael's discourse to Adam will record the end of that earlier age which was closed by the angels' revolt, as well as the beginning of the new in the majestic *allegresse* of creation. His descent is vitalized by the sense of fresh and hopeful life springing from a great cosmic renewal. Perhaps it does not strain excessively the subtlety of Milton's imagery to associate the phoenix' "reliques" with the history Raphael is charged to communicate.

The reference to these relics introduces another curious element of the legend. Most antique writers repeat that version by which the bird dies not in fire but in a ball of spices. This ball it is which the offspring bears to the temple of the sun in Heliopolis (or as Milton has it, Thebes). The offspring's plumage is itself fragrant with spices; this detail appears both in the above quotation from Claudian and with more emphasis in his poem on the phoenix.[58] It can be no coincidence that Raphael's wings also effuse fragrance:

> Like Maia's son he stood,
> And shook his Plumes, that Heav'nly fragrance filld
> The circuit wide.

55. Cranwell edition, pp. 354–55.
56. *Samson Agonistes*, 1699 ff.
57. 185 ff.
58. divino spirant altaria fumo
Et Pelusiacas productus ad usque paludes
Indus odor penetrat nares completque salubri
Tempestate viros et nectare dulcior aura
Ostia nigrantis Nili septena vaporat.

What are more curious are the subsequent references to spices in Paradise, references which Professor Bush also associates with the phoenix material:[59]

> Thir glittering Tents he passd, and now is come
> Into the blissful field, through Groves of Myrrhe,
> And flouring Odours, Cassia, Nard, and Balme;
> A Wilderness of sweets . . .

All four of the plants named here appear in Lactantius' *De Ave Phoenice,* and three of the four in Ovid.[60] The resemblance is the more interesting when it is remembered that Lactantius and Claudian situated the birth and death of the phoenix in an oriental paradise protected from all evil. In this paradise Lactantius places the spices which also flourish in Milton's Eden. A favorite site for this other paradise was Arabia Felix, whose spicy fragrance has been compared to the odors of Eden in an earlier simile:

> now gentle gales
> Fanning thir odoriferous wings dispense
> Native perfumes, and whisper whence they stole
> Those balmie spoiles. As when to them who saile
> Beyond the Cape of Hope, and now are past
> Mozambic, off at Sea North-East windes blow
> Sabean Odours from the spicie shoare
> Of Arabie the blest . . . [IV.156–63]

I am far from sure that these tantalizing parallels can be fitted into a single coherent interpretation. It is possible that we have left interpretation behind and blundered into the psychology of poetic creation. But one unpretentious conclusion is surely justified. To the instructed reader, the phoenix simile intensifies the imagery of storied remoteness and oriental lushness with which Milton saturates his Paradise. If his story is the true, original, archetypal story which later history and myth fragment and distort, the poet must nonetheless employ those distorted fragments

59. *Mythology and the Renaissance Tradition,* p. 281.
60. The fourth, *Balme* or balsam, is related to the fourth plant, cinnamon, in Ovid. The three in Ovid also appear in Du Bartas.

to reconstruct for us a living experience of the true.[61] Milton would have regarded the phoenix' paradise as such a distortion of the true, and he edges as much of it into his poem as he needs to enrich the great arch-image of the garden.

The spices contribute, quite apart from any legend, to a certain lulling heaviness in the atmosphere of Paradise, a Keatsian excess of pleasure which the ensuing lines intensify:

> A Wilderness of sweets; for Nature here
> Wantond as in her prime, and plaid at will
> Her Virgin Fancies, pouring forth more sweet,
> Wilde above Rule or Art; enormous bliss.

The scented air and tangled flowers are not calculated to permit hard work much relevance. Thus the "Sabean Odours" of the Arabia Felix simile invite the sailors to interrupt their work:

> with such delay
> Well pleas'd they slack thir course . . .
> [IV.163–64]

In Paradise as well the fragrance seems an invitation to indolence. It even suggests an incipient sexuality. Adam's account of his first sexual union with Eve will mention the same fragrance:

> fresh Gales and gentle Aires
> Whisperd it to the Woods, and from thir wings
> Flung Rose, flung Odours from the spicie Shrub,
> Disporting . . . [VIII.515–18]

and as early a poem as the *Elegia Quinta* associates odorous breezes with seductiveness.[62] Indeed that poem's great central image—of Earth inviting and yearning for the embraces of Apollo—looks forward to Nature wantoning in Paradise.[63]

61. See Isabel MacCaffrey, *Paradise Lost as "Myth"* (Cambridge, 1959). Mrs. MacCaffrey's book seems to me one of the freshest and most seminal studies of Milton in many years, and I am happy to acknowledge my indebtedness to her.

62. ll. 57–60, 67–69.

63. The coincidence may be worthy of note that in both the poems of Lactantius (l. 34) and Claudian (l. 62) as well as in the passage from Du Bartas, (l. 581), Nature is semi-personified as she is in Milton. This appears to be additional evidence that the passage following the phoenix simile was influenced by memories of the phoenix literature.

But the nature of Paradise, redolent with a slightly drowsy sexuality, is not quite the nature of the rest of Milton's earth. From its first description, Paradise is a little enervating:

> Another side, umbrageous Grots and Caves
> Of coole recess, ore which the mantling Vine
> Layes forth her purple Grape, and gently creeps
> Luxuriant; mean while murmuring waters fall
> Down the slope hills, disperst, or in a Lake,
> That to the fringed Bank with Myrtle crownd,
> Her crystal mirror holds, unite thir streams.
> The Birds thir quire apply; aires, vernal aires,
> Breathing the smell of field and grove, attune
> The trembling leaves . . . [IV.257–66]

The waters murmur; the leaves tremble; the mantling vine creeps *gently*. One understands the artistic logic of this drowsiness. The loveliest paradise of our deepest fancy is of its essence dreamy. But Milton's nature as a whole, the nature without the garden, is *not* dreamy, before the fall or after it. The nature is vital, energetic, robust, dynamic, possessed of a Baroque joy in living movement. Such is the nature of the world whose creation is described in Book Seven. The creation is the setting in movement of a dance, the dance of jocund universal praise, wherein nothing is inert or heavy and nothing seems to rest. Its poetry is a poetry of verbs. The same vital dance is evoked—with what consistency is uncertain—by Adam and Eve in their great morning hymn:

> Moon, that now meetst the orient Sun, now fli'st
> With the fixt Starrs, fixt in thir Orb that flies,
> And yee five other wandring Fires that move
> In mystic Dance not without Song, resound
> His praise, who out of Darkness calld up Light.
> Aire, and ye Elements the eldest birth
> Of Natures Womb, that in quaternion run
> Perpetual Circle, multiform, and mix
> And nourish all things, let your ceasless change
> Varie to our great Maker still new praise . . .
> [V.175–84]

Milton's language is a magnificent reservoir of heroic energy which, when he chooses, charges the world with the grandeur of God.

But Adam and Eve and the garden about them are not so charged. To man is given the life of reason and love gratified by a wilderness of sweets, but not the life of robust energy dancing in praise. Milton was concerned, perhaps too concerned, with dramatizing the *loss* of Eden; he wanted to overwhelm us with all that we might have had. And so he conceived his great arch-image to resemble the gardens of Alcinous in the *Odyssey,* the court of Alcina in Ariosto, the island of Cupid in Camoens, Armida's garden in Tasso, Spenser's Bower of Bliss. But in these other poems the garden is represented as a place where heroic activity is interrupted or forgotten. None of those poets would have considered it dignified to remain forever there where Nature wantoned so wildly. But Milton represents it as dignified.

Raphael as he alights is brimming with divine vitality; it flows from Messiah as he wages heavenly war; Satan too retains it before it gradually drains from him in the later books. But to Adam, by art or accident, Milton denies this more potent glory. Adam's life is circumscribed by the walls of his garden, and his strength is not of that mobile or questing temper which would lead him beyond.

This limitation remains with him and his posterity after his fall. The heroism required of fallen man involves less active energy than the passive strength of fortitude and patience. The heroes in Michael's foreview of history—Abel, Enoch, Noah, Christ—are men whose wills govern nothing beyond themselves. The heroic will is no longer ambitious to extend its control. Milton's sarcastic dismissal of those heroic poems which dissect "with long and tedious havoc fabl'd Knights in Battels feignd" (IX.30–31) finds reinforcement in Michael's explanation of the Israelite itinerary after leaving Egypt:

the Race elect
Safe towards Canaan from the shoar advance
Through the wilde Desert, not the readiest way,
Least entring on the Canaanite allarmd

> Warr terrifie them inexpert, and feare
> Return them back to Egypt, choosing rather
> Inglorious life with servitude; for life
> To noble and ignoble is more sweet
> Untraind in Armes, where rashness leads not on.
> [XII.214–22]

Milton betrays something like contempt for human military prowess, although he admires angelic prowess. Perhaps it is also significant that the vigor of his language flags, for whatever reason, in just these two concluding books where human history is related and heroism exemplified. In the poignant last lines of the poem, exceptionally tender for Milton, the courage of Adam and Eve is qualified by an almost childlike hesitancy which the faltering verse rhythms underscore. The quietness and pathos of the close make a pointed, self-conscious contrast with the traditional epic.

This separation of energy and human heroism seems to me one of the most distinctive qualities of *Paradise Lost.* In part it has led to the Satanist misunderstanding. Satan is unquestionably more vital than Adam, but in the end it is clear that he is less heroic—as the poem defines *heroic.* The only real question is whether such a definition, excluding the expansive, questing impulse of the ego, suppressing vital zest in favor of dogged, self-contained integrity—whether that definition is consonant with one's idea of epic heroism or even of moral elevation. The great paradox of *Paradise Lost* lies in Milton's withholding from his human characters that spacious power which ennobled his own imagination.

v.

There is no need today to stress the heterodoxy of Milton's belief in the goodness of matter, the belief which led him to the mortalist heresy and the denial of creation *ex nihilo.*[64] It is more useful

64. Milton's faith in the goodness of matter underlies not only the profusion of Paradise but also the unconventional refusal to follow Tasso, Marino, and Cowley in dressing up his angel with a temporary body. Raphael needs to make no elaborate toilette like Cowley's Gabriel because he already has a "material" body. We see him in "his proper shape." Apparently Michael must assume a feigned appearance because the fallen Adam is no longer privileged to see him as he looks in heaven.

to examine the tensions which that belief heightened within his own mind. For he attempted to straddle, both theologically and artistically, two forms of religious experience which generally tend to oppose each other. The two forms have been described thus:

> [Puritanism] was a return to the Augustinian tradition in which the relation between the individual soul and God is all that matters. This relationship has too often been taken as a purely intelligible affair to the exclusion of the senses. In this regard, Puritanism was what we might call a religion of the "ear," i.e., the *hearing* and *understanding* of the Word and of doctrine—hence the profusion of great Puritan preachers—and not a religion of the "eye," i.e., the seeing of the sensuous aspect of the world and the physical passion of Christ.[65]

Milton was typically Puritan in his neglect of the "physical passion," but he was un-Puritan when he evoked "the sensuous aspect of the world." His religion of the eye, however, did not really diminish the greater importance he laid upon the inner ear.[66] This latter emphasis becomes immediately apparent if we think of the real purpose of Raphael's descent: to expound the truth. In this respect Milton's celestial messenger represents a unique departure from the convention. For he is dispatched neither to prod nor to encourage nor to punish but to explain, almost indeed to lecture. The success or failure of his mission will lead to visible, objective consequences, but these are actually secondary; they serve only to manifest the crucial consequences which are interior. Milton welcomed the triviality in the act of eating an apple because that triviality demonstrates the primacy of interior action. For that action all the visible imagery serves mainly as metaphorical equivalent. We have already seen how easily the transference is made by such devices as the vertical imagery.

Milton's artistic withdrawal from the visible world is implicit

65. John E. Smith, "Poetry, Religion, and Philosophy," *Review of Metaphysics, 9* (1955), 260.

66. Allen is surely in the right when he refutes the aspersions of Macaulay and Eliot upon Milton's visual imagery. *Paradise Lost* makes a great and subtle appeal to the eye, as I myself have argued. When I speak of Milton's greater emphasis on the ear, I am not of course thinking of his "verbal music" or any such thing, but of his appeal to the inner ear of understanding.

in Michael's scorn for physical heroism (a scorn which several passages confirm),[67] as perhaps it is implicit in God's phrase to Raphael:

> By violence, no, for that shall be withstood,
> But by deceit and lies . . .

But the withdrawal is carried further than this. The poet's prayer must be taken seriously when he invokes the Celestial Light to shine inward

> that I may see and tell
> Of things invisible to mortal sight.
> [III.54–55]

The blind consciousness is drawn nostalgically to the beautiful sensuous world denied it, but driven back thence to the world of things invisible. Adam will allude uncategorically to the inferiority of outward things:

> For well I understand in the prime end
> Of Nature her th'inferiour, in the mind
> And inward Faculties, which most excell . . .
> [VIII.540–42]

and Raphael later assures him that Eve, rightly governed, will "to realities yield all her shows" (VIII.575). More telling than these is the impatient remark of Michael which betrays Milton's imaginative weariness:

> Much thou hast yet to see, but I perceave
> Thy mortal sight to faile; objects divine
> Must needs impaire and wearie human sense:
> Henceforth what is to com I will relate . . .
> [XII.8–11]

Henceforth almost to the very end the eye is neglected for the ear. Michael's discourse moves, the whole poem moves, as Barker tells us all of Milton's thought moves, toward the "Paradise within thee happier far," the paradise one cannot see.

If all epics are concerned with cosmic politics, *Paradise Lost* is

67. VI.817 ff.; XI.689 ff.; XII.386 ff.

pre-eminently concerned with them, but like other lesser poems of its century, it alters the traditional form of political struggle. God is impervious to violence, but to disobedience he is not so obviously impervious; his victory has to come in the long run. The struggle works itself out in those terms which have meaning for a devout, sedentary, urban public. In thus fulfilling the seventeenth-century tendency to shift the political medium from violence to morality, Milton implicitly rejected, it seems to me, part of the basis of epic itself—the balance of objective and subjective action, the balance of executive and deliberative. In the closing books of *Paradise Lost,* the books which define human heroism, the executive episodes almost disappear. This rejection need not in itself involve grounds for criticism. But it is important to see how the last of the great poems in conventional epic dress contained within itself, not accidentally but essentially, the seeds of the genre's destruction. One of these seeds was the internalization of action, the preference for things invisible. A second was the questioning of the hero's independence; a third was the detaching of heroism from the community, the City of man in this world. Both of these latter procedures need more comment.

Heroic independence in *Paradise Lost* is weakened by Milton's juggling with the theological categories of grace and merit. If we were to grant "the better fortitude of Patience and Heroic Martyrdom" as a proper notion of epic heroism, we should still want to feel that fortitude to be the painful achievement of the hero. But Milton in more than one passage suggests that this fortitude is the gift of God. It is a little anticlimactic for the reader, after following tremulously the fallen couple's gropings toward redemption in Book Ten, to hear from the Father's lips that he has decreed it—that all of this tenderly human scene, this triumph of conjugal affection and tentative moral searching, occurred only by divine fiat. One might have been tempted to alter his ideas of heroism to include Adam's contrition, did he not encounter God's own curt dismissal of it:

> He sorrows now, repents, and prayes contrite,
> My motions in him: longer then they move,
> His heart I know, how variable and vain
> Self-left. [XI.90–93]

And so the later exemplary figures in Michael's discourse lose most of their prestige from his prefatory warning:

> good with bad
> Expect to hear, supernal Grace contending
> With sinfulness of Men . . . [XI.358–60]

It is true that we need not regard Adam and the Hebrew patriarchs as necessarily elect above the rest, recipients of that "peculiar grace" which ensures salvation, although Milton very likely did so regard most of them. Even if we choose to ignore that doctrine, the remaining ambiguity of grace and merit to which Milton's language leads effectually destroys the dramatic clarity and force which epic heroism requires. The interplay at the heart of the epic between individual excellence and limitation falters because so little ground is left for excellence. The announced intent, to turn the note to tragic, risks failure because tragedy implies a standard of human greatness surviving in spite of misfortune and even corruption. Milton maintains that standard only shakily and intermittently after the disaster of the fall. And he makes clear that man can do nothing to achieve the one thing worth achieving —nothing at least beyond the act of faith:

> his [Christ's] obedience
> Imputed becomes theirs by Faith, his merits
> To save them, not thir own, though legal works.
> [XII.408–10]

This weakening of heroic prestige is abetted by the severing of the traditional bond between hero and community. It is true that the Son considered as hero is a benefactor of the widest possible community, and even Abdiel speaks in a sense for all the loyal angelic community in his defiance of Satan. But if we agree to limit heroic awe to the human sphere, then we must speak only of individual heroes, lonely men who mount the current of common perversity. Their goodness, as Milton describes them, stands over against the universal evil; no, more than this, it outweighs the evil. Adam's comment on the deluge is offensive and immoral but Milton did not so regard it:

Farr less I now lament for one whole World
Of wicked Sons destroyd, then I rejoyce
For one Man found so perfet and so just,
That God voutsafes to raise another World
From him, and all his anger to forget.
[XI.874–78]

By the standards of Milton's arrogant moral aristocracy, the damnation of the community matters less than the salvation of the few.

Although the anatomy of evil in the poem is so brilliant as to be unsurpassed in its kind, the dramatization of goodness fails. When Michael, anticipating Saint Paul, refers to charity as "the soul of all the rest" of the virtues, we can only protest that we have seen little of it in the poem. We miss it chiefly in those places where Milton asserts it to exist. When it is scrutinized, God's generosity in dispatching Raphael turns out to be not at all a true magnanimity but a petty legalistic self-righteousness. Adam must not be allowed to "pretend surprisal, unadmonisht, unforewarnd." The majesty of Raphael's descent can only be appreciated if the awkwardness of its motive remains half-forgotten.

The aristocratic doctrine which prefers the few to the many leads directly to Adam's *felix culpa* speech and God's imputed victory over Satan. The meaning of that victory is contained in Satan's lines at the outset:

If then his Providence
Out of our evil seek to bring forth good,
Our labour must be to pervert that end,
And out of good still to find means of evil . . .
[I.162–65]

Satan has perverted the good of the angelic creation by revolt; out of that evil comes the good of the human creation. Satan will pervert that too, but he still loses the poem, Milton tells us, through the good accruing from the Incarnation and Atonement. It matters not, from this viewpoint, if the great mass of souls are damned, since for the saints

the Earth
Shall all be Paradise, farr happier place
Then this of Eden. [XII.463–65]

It is possible doubtless to share Adam's joy at this outcome, but one's participation is increased if he can personally look forward to that felicity. In this respect, I fear, by the poet's own doctrine, his audience is few indeed. For the rest of us, Michael's depressing recital of our forebears' tribulations mars the perfection of God's victory. At this point *Paradise Lost,* like so many other Christian epics, falls into that ambivalence of joy and pain which plagued the genre, as it now seems, almost inevitably. Theologically its conclusion asks us to applaud, but dramatically it brings us to tears.

This conflict finds a local solution in the concluding expulsion which I have already had occasion to praise. Here for once Milton's compassion is unmixed, and all the constituent feelings—nostalgia, resolution, remorse, bewilderment, timidity, and hope—these make a peace which owes its harmony to the poet's wise pity. These last twenty-five lines go far toward saving the great uneasy poem they conclude. But the mending is the work of image, rhythm, tone, and mood, instruments of local efficacity; as soon as we free ourselves of their atmosphere to reflect on those more abstract planes which the poem also embraces, we rediscover its profound and destructive divisions.

Perhaps however in the last analysis it is pedantic to dwell too long upon those divisions. Even if one chooses, with Sir Walter Raleigh, to regard *Paradise Lost* as a monument to dead ideas, or contradictory or even offensive ideas, one need not return to it out of wonder alone for its magisterial and insidious art. Milton's enlightened reverence for the Bible permitted him to entertain the possibility that his story was something like a myth. If we too consider it as that, in the fullest sense, if we read it with the detachment we bring to the myth of the *Iliad,* then we need not follow unmoved and unedified Milton's search for a measure and definition of human existence. The work in its plenary wholeness makes a richer definition than any one of its dogmatic parts. And just as Swift betrayed his concern for mankind by railing at it,

Milton persuades us of his humanity even in his moments of passionate severity.

vi.

An outline has survived of the blank verse epic which the aging Pope planned but only began to write—the *Brutus*. One is not surprised to discover that it was to contain an angelic descent:

> The second book opens with a picture of the supreme God in all his majesty, sitting on his throne in the highest heaven. The superintending angel of the Trojans empire (the *Regnum Priami vetus*) falls down before the throne, and confesses his justice in having overturned that kingdom, for the sins of the princes, and of the people themselves. But adds, that after having chastised and humbled them, it would now be agreeable to his mercy and goodness, to raise up a new state from their ruins, and form a people who might serve him better. That, in Brutus, his Providence had a fit instrument for such a gracious design.
>
> This prostrate angel is raised by the Almighty, and permitted to attend upon Brutus in his voyage to Britain, in order to assist him in the reduction of that island.
>
> The guardian angel, in pursuance of this commission, flies from heaven to the mountain of Calpe; and from thence causes an east wind to blow, which carries the fleet out of the streights westward to the Canary islands, where he lands.[68]

We may agree with the eighteenth century editor's opinion that if Pope had finished this poem, "it would not, perhaps, have added much to his reputation." [69] The anodyne Christianity imposed upon the exhausted cult of Virgil, the extraneous and perfunctory connection between "machinery" and action betrayed in this citation are symptomatic of the whole. The outline reads very much like the argument of one of Blackmore's epics, those productions of a neoclassic Polonius, episodic, trite, wooden, and sententious in their dullness. The shortcomings of Pope's project must eventu-

68. Owen Ruffhead, *Life of Alexander Pope* (London, 1769), p. 413.
69. *Works of Alexander Pope,* ed. Warton et al., *4* (London, 1797), 370.

ally have impressed themselves upon his alert literary intelligence.

Both the plan to write a *Brutus* and its inexecution are significant, and this document which is poetically worthless can nonetheless serve as a pretext for a valedictory to the epic. For Pope lived during an Indian summer of classical prestige, when the doctrine of imitation was still very strong and the authoritative superiority of ancient literature was challenged but not discredited. It was not yet out of the question to attempt a neo-Virgilian epic, and such poems as Glover's *Leonidas* (1737) and Wilkie's *Epigoniad* (1757), and on the continent Voltaire's *Henriade* (1723) and Klopstock's *Messiad* (1748), continued desultorily to appear. But the wiser heads of the age knew that such attempts were inauspicious. The misgivings which these critics entertained were inspired in large part by just such supernatural furniture as has concerned us in this study. Dryden echoed Boileau's doubts about Christian machinery [70] and seemed not altogether convinced that his own suggested remedy (the use of guardian spirits) would serve

70. " 'Tis objected by a great French critic . . . that the machines of our Christian religion, in heroic poetry, are much more feeble to support that weight than those of heathenism. . . . Our religion (says he) is deprived of the greatest part of those machines; at least the most shining in epic poetry. Though St. Michael, in Ariosto, seeks out Discord, to send her among the Pagans, and finds her in a convent of friars, where peace should reign, which indeed is fine satire; and Satan, in Tasso, excites Solyman to an attempt by night on the Christian camp, and brings an host of devils to his assistance; yet the arch-angel, in the former example, when Discord was restive. and would not be drawn from her beloved monastery with fair words, has the whip-hand of her, drags her out with many stripes, sets her, on God's name, about her business, and makes her know the difference of strength betwixt a nuncio of Heaven, and a minister of Hell. The same angel, in the latter instance from Tasso (as if God had never another messenger belonging to the court, but was confined like Jupiter to Mercury, and Juno to Iris) when he sees his time, that is, when half of the Christians are already killed, and all the rest are in a fair way to be routed, stickles betwixt the remainders of God's host, and the race of fiends; pulls the devils backward by the tails, and drives them from the quarry; or otherwise the whole business had miscarried, and Jerusalem remain untaken. This, says Boileau, is a very unequal match for the poor devils, who are sure to come by the worst of it in the combat; for nothing is more easy, than for an Almighty Power to bring his old rebels to reason when he pleases. Consequently, what pleasure, what entertainment, can be raised from so pitiful a machine, where we see the success of the battle from the very beginning of it?" "A Discourse concerning the Original and Progress of Satire" in *Essays of John Dryden,* ed. Ker, 2 (Oxford, 1926), 31–33.

to answer them. As early as 1690 Sir William Temple expressed an opinion which was to bear repetition when he wrote:

> The religion of the Gentiles had been woven into the contexture of all the ancient poetry with a very agreeable mixture, which made the moderns affect to give that of Christianity a place also in their poems. But the true religion was not found to become fiction as well as a false had done, and all their attempts of this kind seemed rather to debase religion than to heighten poetry.[71]

David Hume, writing almost seventy years later, reduced Temple's opinion to a series of impracticable alternatives:

> It would seem . . . that if the machinery of the heathen gods be not admitted, epic poetry, at least all the marvellous part of it, must be entirely abandoned. The Christian religion, for many reasons, is unfit for the fabulous ornaments of poetry; the introduction of allegory, after the manner of Voltaire, is open to many objections; and though a mere historical poem . . . may have its beauties, it will always be inferior to the force and pathetic of tragedy, and must resign to that species of poetry the precedency which the former composition has always challenged among the productions of human genius.[72]

Bishop Hurd was still more decisive:

> The Pagan Gods and Gothic Fairies were equally out of credit, when Milton wrote. He did well therefore to supply their room with Angels and Devils. If these too should wear out of the popular creed (and they seem in a hopeful way, from the liberty some late critics have taken with them) I know not what other expedients the epic poet might have recourse to; but this I know, the pomp of verse, the energy of description, and even the finest moral paintings, would stand him in no stead. Without *admiration* (which cannot be effected but by the marvellous of celestial intervention, I mean, the agency of superior natures really existing, or by

71. "Of Poetry," in Spingarn, *3*, 99.

72. "Letter to the Critical Review concerning the *Epigoniad* of Wilkie," in *Essays Moral, Political, Literary*, ed. Green and Grose, *2* (London & New York, 1889–1898), 434–35.

> the illusion of the fancy taken to be so) no epic poem can be long-lived.[73]

Each of these writers attests to the slow awakening from that dream first dreamt by Petrarch on a Good Friday in the Vaucluse.

The Renaissance produced distinguished poetry which failed, in varying degrees and for varying reasons, of its intention to reproduce the classical epic. The eighteenth century produced almost no distinguished poetry which was so intended, and it realized with increasing clarity that the very intent was misguided. Hurd thought that the thing had become difficult since Milton, but Temple and Hume suggested that any Christian poet would find it difficult. These latter critics were closer to the truth. But with the added hindsight of two centuries we can trace today the growth of those habits of mind which dispelled even the "impure" epic temper of the Renaissance.

A study of that process, pursued to its natural limits, would require its own volume. In this one there is room only for the briefest of remarks on the contracting of the neoclassic imagination—remarks which can conveniently attach themselves to the work of Pope. His Preface to the *Iliad* and Postscript to the *Odyssey* reveal a fine, sensitive, and enthusiastic mind limited in certain respects by the confining preconceptions of its age. Thus when Pope speaks of Homer's epithets and repetitions, we encounter that Augustan insensitivity to ritualistic language which would render a whole dimension of Homer invisible. For the ritual of poetic language is inseparable from a ritualistic relation to experience. Pope writes of Homer's epithets:

> Upon the whole, it will be necessary to avoid that perpetual repetition of the same epithets which we find in Homer, and which, though it might be accommodated (as has been already shewn) to the ear of those times, is by no means so to ours.[74]

and he writes again of the repetitions:

> I hope it is not impossible to have such a regard to these, as neither to lose so known a mark of the author on the one hand, nor to offend the reader too much on the other.[75]

73. *Dialogues, 3* (London, 1765), 313.
74. *The Prose Works of Alexander Pope,* ed. Ault, *1* (Oxford, 1936), 248.
75. Ibid., p. 249.

In each of these discussions he goes on to make remarks which are sensible, given the taste of his age. But it is clear that such a taste must close its eyes to a prime element in Homer and perhaps in all epic—the sense of ceremony. Lewis has argued eloquently that ceremony is essential to epic style. The Augustans would not have understood him, but they sensed that they were lacking something, and they sometimes aimed at a "dark" sublime style which left behind the niceties of logic and grammar. Pope writes:

> The sublime style is more easily counterfeited than the natural; something that passes for it, or sounds like it, is common in all false writers.[76]

The false sublime which Pope found so ubiquitous probably owed its existence to a frustrated hankering for the true.

It is only a step from the false sublime to the mock-heroic, as Pope well knew.[77] Mock-heroic is simply the false sublime under control. It was popular because people were beginning to find the pretensions of serious epic extravagantly pompous and thus funny. Mock-heroic represents a gesture of school-boyish impudence toward the stock divinities of the lower form, a blow for independence and realism. But it also represents the uneasy casting about for standards of measurement by a society unsure of its place in the cosmos. It derives from the same play with perspective which inspired the first two voyages of Gulliver. Epic had portrayed man upon an heroic scale which made the new century uncomfortable. "You can't wonder," wrote Pope to Addison, "my thoughts are scarce consistent, when I tell you how they are distracted."

> Every hour of my life, my mind is strangely divided; this minute perhaps I am above the stars, with a thousand systems round about me, looking forward into a vast Abyss, and losing my whole comprehension in the boundless space of creation . . . the next minute I am below all trifles groveling in the very centre of nonsense . . . Good God! What an incongru-

76. "Postscript to the *Odyssey*," *Works,* ed. J. Warton, *4* (London, 1822), 423–24.

77. "The use of pompous expression for low actions or thoughts is the true sublime of *Don Quixote.* How far unfit it is for Epic Poetry, appears in its being the perfection of the Mock Epic." Ibid., p. 422.

> ous animal is man . . . What is he altogether but one mighty inconsistency! [78]

Pope was struggling for a scale by which to measure man; *The Rape of the Lock* and *The Dunciad* show him experimenting with the comedy engendered when two scales are superimposed. The example of Dryden authorized his experiments—Dryden, who planned an heroic poem and praised the epic as "the greatest work which the soul of man is capable to perform," [79] but who contented himself with translating Virgil and writing *MacFlecknoe*. Dryden was of help, but perhaps the deeper shadow over Pope's pages was that of Pascal, who had given the ambiguities of perspective their classic formulation. Pascal had written:

> L'homme ne sait à quel rang se mettre. Il est visiblement égaré, et tombé de son vrai lieu sans le pouvoir retrouver. Il le cherche partout avec inquiétude et sans succès dans des ténèbres impénétrables.[80]

and again:

> Qu'est-ce que l'homme dans la nature? Un néant à l'égard de l'infini, un tout à l'égard du néant, un milieu entre rien et tout. Infiniment éloigné de comprendre les extrêmes, la fin des choses et leur principe sont pour lui invinciblement cachés dans un secret impénétrable, également incapable de voir le néant d'où il est tiré, et l'infini où il est englouti.[81]

The profoundest passages of the *Essay on Man* reflect Pascal's paradoxes, but their fuller artistic translation is to be found in the less ambitious but richer comic poems. That very duality, noticed by recent criticism, in Pope's artistic demeanor—alternating between the stiffly formal and the pungently satirical—betokens the new hesitation between alternative postures toward the universe. The would-be author of the unwritten *Brutus* was the actual author of an impertinent "Receipt to make an Epic Poem." [82]

78. Letter to Addison, December 14, 1713.
79. *Essays of Dryden,* ed. Ker, 2, 154.
80. *Pensées et Opuscules,* ed. Brunschwicg (Paris, n. d.), p. 521.
81. Ibid., p. 350.
82. "For the Machines: Take of Deities, male and female, as many as you

The generation which followed Pope would complete the transition by producing a radically iconoclastic genre of greater endurance than the mock-heroic. The novel was born quite literally from parody, burlesque, and mock-heroic: with Cervantes in Spain, with Sorel, Scarron, and Furetière in France, with Fielding in England and the Smollett who wrote *Sir Launcelot Greaves.* All of these authors and their successors ridiculed the *faux bon* of the pompous genres, the solemnity, sublimity, hypocrisy, subservience to rules, improbability, infidelity to common experience. All of them attempted, however uncertainly, to explore the interest of the individual and interior consciousness, a focus which Milton had introduced into *Paradise Lost* only with a certain awkwardness. His treatment of Adam and Eve after the fall does not lack delicacy and insight, but it makes an uncomfortable melange with epic generality and "nobility." The true place for so intimate a study is the novel, a genre which by and large forsakes the immensity of space for the here and now, the particular, the trivial, the mincemeat of local detail with which Pope, anticipating the novelists, stuffed his satires.

It may be that the *capacity* to perpetuate authentic epic poetry was threatened in Europe as early as the introduction of Christianity, which is imperfectly compatible with heroic awe. But the *impulse* to epic weakened only when man found himself overawed by the void around him, when his assurance dwindled before an unknown and ever-expanding heaven. An epic poem, in its respect for human potentiality and domineering command of space, is a declaration, however qualified with tragedy, of metaphysical pride. "Quand je considère," wrote Pascal, ". . . le petit espace que je remplis et même que je vois, abîmé dans l'infinie immensité des espaces que j'ignore et qui m'ignorent, je m'effraie." [83] This sense

can use: Separate them into two equal parts, and keep Jupiter in the middle; Let Juno put him in a ferment, and Venus mollify him. Remember on all occasions to make use of volatile Mercury. If you have need of Devils, draw them out of Milton's Paradise, and extract your Spirits from Tasso. The use of these Machines is evident; since no Epic Poem can possibly subsist without them, the wisest way is to reserve them for your greatest necessities. When you cannot extricate your Hero by any human means, or yourself by your own wit, seek relief from Heaven, and the Gods will do your business very readily." *The Art of Sinking in Poetry,* ed. E. L. Steeves (New York, 1952), pp. 83–84.

83. *Pensées et Opuscules,* p. 427.

of lonely isolation qualified that greatness, *grandeur,* which Pascal counterpoised against human wretchedness, and it has qualified progressively modern conceptions of greatness. As man's pride has been increasingly humbled since the seventeenth century, it has taken less assertive literary form. The imagination has responded to Pascal's vertigo by producing the novel, which turns from awe to analysis, from heaven and hell to the subtly and minutely human. During the brief adventure of the Romantic movement, and notably with Goethe and the prophetic books of Blake, the old audacity flared up into short but authentic life. Throughout the nineteenth century, and particularly in France, an unflagging effort to renew the epic spirit continued,[84] but the century's end saw it still further displaced from the mainstream of serious literature, forced to risk either bombast or triviality. And the heroes of the twentieth century are hemmed in by the intractable. These developments are scarcely subject to cavil, but one prizes the more gratefully the older, arrogant testimonies to an unintimidated fancy.

84. See H. J. Hunt, *The Epic in Nineteenth Century France* (Oxford, 1941).

Appendix.

PRE-HOMERIC ANCESTORS OF THE CELESTIAL MESSENGER THEME

One of the rapidly broadening avenues of Homeric scholarship concerns the relation of Homeric Greece with older Mediterranean and Asiatic cultures. It is tantalizing to encounter a fragmentary Hittite poem from the middle of the second millenium B.C. containing details strikingly close to details in Homer's descent theme. The poem has been named the *Song of Ullikummi;* it contains four episodes which involve a celestial messenger, three of them repeating the key details. I quote the least fragmentary episode, omitting indications of scholarly conjecture and emendation:

> Kumarbi spake these words to Impaluri: "O Impaluri! To the words I speak to thee lend thine ear! Into thy hand take a stick, unto thy feet put the swift shoes! Hurry and go to the Irsirra-gods! And these words speak before the Irsirras: 'Come! Kumarbi, father of the gods, calleth ye! . . . About what matter he calleth ye, ye know not. Now come promptly!'
>
> "The Irsirras will take the child and they will carry it to the dark earth . . ."

> Impaluri . . . and took the stick in his hand, put the swift shoes on his feet . . . he went, Impaluri, and came to the Irsirra. Then spake Impaluri, to repeat the words to the Irsirra: "Come! Kumarbi, the father of the gods, calleth ye! About what matter he calleth ye, ye know not. Now hurry, come!"
>
> When the Irsirras heard these words, they made haste and hurried.[1]

The structure of this episode follows in general the structure of the Homeric descent: scene in heaven, speech in direct discourse by the superior god, preparations for the journey, the journey itself, the messenger's repetition of the speech verbatim, again in direct discourse, the ensuing action of the message's recipient. But this general resemblance might be coincidental. The striking resemblance lies in the stick and the shoes which here, as in Hermes' descents in both the *Iliad* and *Odyssey,* involve the only preparations the messenger must make. Here would seem to be firm evidence of a precise oriental ancestor of the Homeric theme.

This hypothesis, though, is not without its difficulties. The links remain unclear which connect Homer with this Hittite version of a Hurrian poem ascribed to the fifteenth century B.C. Herr Güterbock, its editor and translator, suggests that Hittite mythology and literature might have reached the Greeks through Phoenicia, and points to convincing resemblances between the action of this poem and the action of Hesiod's *Theogony.*[2] If we assume some such link existed, however, we still ought to note a discrepancy between the two episodes. In the Homeric poems, the staff and sandals are associated with Hermes, whereas in the *Song of Ullikummi* they are associated with no single figure but with the act of departure. *Any* messenger must take up his stick and put on his swift shoes. There is even a passage in the *Song* which describes the departure of the superior god Kumarbi himself, and this departure also requires the taking of a stick and donning of shoes.[3]

Such considerations cast some doubt upon the parentage of the Hittite and Homeric episodes. But they do not altogether disprove it. One might hypothesize an interim stage when these two preparatory acts came to be regarded as proper only to messengers and were

1. *Kumarbi. Mythen vom churritischen Kronos aus den hethitischen Fragmenten zusammengestellt, übersetzt und erklärt,* ed. and trans. by Hans Gustav Güterbock (Istanbul, 1946), pp. 16–17. Partly translated into English by Güterbock, "The Hittite Version of the Hurrian Kumarbi Myths: Oriental Forerunners of Hesiod" in *AJA,* 52 (1948), 123–34. See particularly pp. 126–27. Three dots in the text indicate a break in the tablet.

2. Güterbock, "Hittite Version," pp. 130–33.

3. Ibid., p. 126.

named formulaically only at a messenger's departure (not for the departure of a superior god like Kumarbi). At a later stage the stick and shoes might have been associated only with the messenger god of the Olympian Pantheon.[4] Still later, particular properties of Hermes' staff and sandals could have been invented. This hypothesis is supported by a passage in the *Odyssey* which describes Athene's preparations for descent:

> . . . She ceased and drew upon her feet those golden sandals (whose fairness no use could dim) that carried their mistress as surely and wind-swiftly over the waves as over the boundless earth. She laid hold of her guardian spear, great, heavy, and close-grained, tipped with cutting bronze. When wrath moved the goddess to act, this spear was her weapon: with it, and stayed by her pride of birth, she would daunt serried ranks of the very bravest warriors. Downward she now glided . . .[5]

It seems possible that these details of sandals and spear go back to a very ancient literary tradition which is also the source of Hermes' sandals and staff.

4. These suggestions assume that Hermes had been regarded as a messenger long before the writing of the *Iliad.* But this is not certain. Hermes in the *Iliad* is represented as a guide, and only replaces Iris as Zeus' messenger in the *Odyssey.* Miss Jacqueline Chittenden argues that the Greek word *diaktoros,* translated by Lattimore (and others) as "courier," actually meant "guide." This word is frequently applied to Hermes. See her "Diaktoros Argeiphontes," *AJA,* 52 (1948), 24.

5. *The Odyssey of Homer,* trans. Shaw (New York, 1951), p. 3.

INDEX OF NAMES AND ANONYMOUS WORKS